Study Guide

W9-ALU-356

West Federal Taxation
Individual Income Taxes

2003 Edition

William H. Hoffman, Jr.

University of Houston

James E. Smith

College of William and Mary

Eugene Willis

University of Illinois – Urbana

Prepared by

Gerald E. Whittenburg

San Diego State University

THOMSON

SOUTH-WESTERN

Australia · Canada · Mexico · Singapore · Spain · United Kingdom · United States

THOMSON

SOUTH-WESTERN

Individual Income Taxes Study Guide 2003 Edition

William H. Hoffman, Jr., James E. Smith, Eugene Willis prepared by Gerald E. Whittenburg

Editor-in-Chief:
Jack W. Calhoun

Publisher:
Melissa S. Acuña

Acquisitions Editor:
Jennifer L. Codner

Developmental Editor:
Craig Avery

Marketing Manager:
Mark Linton

Senior Production Editor:
Marci Combs

Manufacturing Coordinator:
Doug Wilke

Printer:
Globus
Minster, Ohio

Design Project Manager:
Michelle Kunkler

Cover Designer:
Paul Neff Design, Cincinnati

For more information
contact South-Western,
5191 Natorp Boulevard,
Mason, Ohio 45040.
Or you can visit our Internet site at:
http://www.swcollege.com

For permission to use material from this
text or product, contact us by
Tel (800) 730-2214
Fax (800) 730-2215
http://www.thomsonrights.com

CONTENTS

PREFACE

PREFACE

This Study Guide has been designed to be used as a supplement to the 2003 Edition of *West's Federal Taxation: Individual Income Taxes.* Its purpose is to help you master the material presented in the text.

This Study Guide contains two features to help you understand income taxes.

> *Chapter Highlights*B This section provides statements about key concepts presented in the text.

> *Tests for Self-Evaluation*B Hundreds of questions and problems are presented (with answers) so that you may evaluate how well you understand the material in the text. The answers are keyed to the page numbers in the text.

I recommend the following approach as a method to use this Study Guide effectively:

> Y   Study the textbook chapter.

> Y   Review the *Chapter Highlights* section of the Study Guide. If something is not clear to you, review the chapter in the textbook.

> Y   Mark the *Test for Self-Evaluation* and resolve your missed answers by referring to the solutions and to the textbook.

It is important that you use this Study Guide as an aid to mastering the material in the textbook, and not as a replacement for it. I suggest that you incorporate (as outlined above) the Study Guide into your regular study routine.

I would like to express my appreciation to Martha Altus for her help in preparing this edition of the Study Guide.

G.E. Whittenburg, March 2002

CHAPTER 1

An Introduction to Taxation and Understanding the Federal Tax Law

CHAPTER HIGHLIGHTS

A review of the history of the U.S. Federal tax system is helpful for the student to gain an understanding of the principles, which have shaped the development of the system. This chapter introduces the student to the structure of the U.S. Federal tax system, the major types of taxes, and the organizational aspects of administering the tax law.

KEY TERMS

Tax Rate Structure
Property Tax
Sales Tax
Excise Tax

Estate and Gift Tax
Income Tax
Tax Administration

Revenue/Economic Consideration
Social/Equity/Political
   Considerations

OUTLINE

I.   **HISTORY OF U.S. TAXATION**

    A.   There have been several income taxes in the past. The first North American income tax was enacted in 1634 in the Massachusetts Bay Colony. The first U.S. income tax was passed in1861 to help finance the Civil War. In 1894, the Supreme Court, in *Pollock v. Farmers' Loan and Trust Co.,* held that an early version of the individual income tax was unconstitutional. In response to this Supreme Court decision, a constitutional amendment was passed to authorize the individual income tax. The Sixteenth Amendment, which was ratified in 1913, gave Congress the power to impose and collect an income tax. Before the Sixteenth Amendment, the corporate income tax was held to be an excise tax, and therefore deemed to be constitutional by the Supreme Court.

    B.   Various Revenue Acts were passed between 1913 and 1939. In 1939 these Acts were codified into the Internal Revenue Code of 1939, which was later recodified in 1954 and renamed in 1986 as the *Internal Revenue Code of 1986.*

    C.   Over the years the income tax has become the major source of revenue for the Federal government. During World War II, the tax went from a select tax to a mass tax.

II.   **CRITERIA USED IN THE SELECTION OF A TAX STRUCTURE**

Adam Smith listed certain criteria with which to evaluate a particular tax or tax structure. These "canons of taxation" are *equality, convenience, certainty,*and *economy.*

III.   **THE TAX STRUCTURE**

    A.   Tax Base. The tax base is the amount to which the tax rate is applied.

    B.   Tax Rates. Tax rates are the percentage applied to the tax base.

A *progressive tax* is one in which the tax rates increase as the tax base increases. The Federal income, gift, and estate taxes and most state income taxes are progressive taxes.

A *proportional tax* is one in which the rate of tax remains constant despite the size of the tax base.

    C.   The *incidence of taxation* is the degree to which each segment of society shares the total tax burden.

IV.   **MAJOR TYPES OF TAXES**

    A.   Property taxes or *ad valorem* taxes are taxes that are based on value. The tax is usually imposed on realty or personalty. Realty taxes are a major source of revenue for local government, while personalty taxes generally have low compliance by taxpayers, except personal property taxes on items such as inventory, automobiles, boats, etc.

    B.   Transaction taxes impose a tax on transfers of property and are normally computed as a straight percentage of the value of the property involved.

Excise taxes are taxes on products such as gasoline, telephone usage, air travel, alcohol, and tobacco. Both the Federal and state governments usually impose some form of excise tax.

Sales taxes differ from excise taxes in that sales taxes are applied to many different transactions, while excise taxes are applied to one product or transaction. A use tax is designed to prevent circumvention of the sales tax, such as where a resident of a state with a sales tax buys products in another state in an attempt to avoid the sales tax. Many states allow local sales taxes by cities, counties, etc., besides the general sales tax.

    C.   Death taxes are taxes imposed on either the right to transfer property at death (estate tax) or the right to receive property from a decedent (inheritance tax).

The Federal estate tax is designed to prevent large concentrations of wealth from being kept within the same family. The unified transfer credit eliminates or reduces the estate tax liability for small estates. The Federal government does not impose an inheritance tax.

Most states levy some form of death tax. If the death tax is an inheritance tax, the rates are generally lower for close family members and get larger the more distant the heir.

D.   The Federal gift tax was enacted into law to complement the estate tax because without it, it would be possible to avoid the estate tax by making lifetime gifts and eliminating the gross estate. The Federal gift tax is determined by taking into account prior taxable gifts so that the tax rate is based on cumulative taxable gifts.

E.   In the United States, income taxes are levied by the Federal government and most state governments and are the most popular forms of tax. Income taxes are imposed on individuals, corporations, and certain estates and trusts. The tax formula for individuals is shown as follows:

> Income broadly conceived
> (Exclusions)
> Gross income
> (Certain business deductions)
> Adjusted gross income
> (Greater of itemized deductions or the standard deduction)
> (Exemptions)
> Taxable income
>
> Tax on taxable income
> (Credits and withholding)
> Tax due or refund

For individual taxpayers a standard deduction amount is available to taxpayers who do not itemize deductions.

The Federal income tax applies to corporations. The taxable income of a corporation is the difference between gross income and deductions.

Nearly all of the states impose a state income tax on individuals and corporations. Most states pattern their income tax after the Federal income tax and use an adjusted Federal taxable income figure as a base on which to apply the tax. Most states have some form of withholding procedures. The states taxing authorities work closely with the IRS and share information about audits and other changes in tax returns.

F.   Employment taxes such as the FICA (Federal Insurance Contributions Act) tax are collected by the Federal government. The FICA tax consists of the old age, survivors, and disability insurance tax and the hospital insurance tax.

FICA taxes fund the Social Security system and are levied on both the employee and the employer. Employees pay FICA tax and Medicare tax on wages they earn. See the textbook for rates and annual wage limits. The employer must match the employee's contribution. If an employee pays too much FICA tax because he or she worked two or more jobs, a credit for the excess amount may be claimed.

The FUTA tax is levied only on the employer with the purpose of providing the states with funds to administer the unemployment program. A credit is allowed for any FUTA paid to a state government.

G.   Other U.S. Taxes. Federal Customs Duties are tariffs on certain imported goods. In recent years, Customs Duties are used more to protect U.S. industries from foreign competition than to raise revenue to run the government.

There are several miscellaneous state and local taxes such as franchise taxes, occupational taxes, etc.

H.   Proposed U.S. Taxes. There are several proposed changes to the U.S. tax system. These changes include The Flat Tax, The Value Added Tax, and a national sales tax. The Flat Tax would keep the income tax with substantial changes. The other two taxes would replace the U.S. income tax with a different system of taxation altogether.

V.   TAX ADMINISTRATION

   A.   The Internal Revenue Service (IRS), which is part of the Treasury Department, has responsibility for administering the Federal tax law. The IRS uses statistical sampling techniques to select tax returns for an audit.

   B.   IRS audits are classified as "office audits" or "field audits." Office audits are restricted in scope and are conducted inthe IRS office. A field audit is comprehensive and is conducted on the premises of the taxpayer or the taxpayer's representative.

   C.   The general statute of limitations for an IRS assessment is three years from the date the return is filed, unless the return is filed early in which case the limitation period runs from the date the return is due. There is no statute of limitations if no return or a fraudulent return is filed.

   D.   The interest rate used by the federal government is adjusted quarterly. Besides interest, various penalties are applied for noncompliance. For "failure to file" a tax return a penalty of five percent per month, or fraction thereof, is charged up to a 25 percent maximum. The penalty for "failure to pay" is one-half percent per month, or fraction thereof, up to a maximum of 25 percent. If both penalties apply to the same return, the failure to file penalty is reduced by the failure to pay penalty. Penalties also apply where the underpayment is due to negligence or fraud.

VI.   UNDERSTANDING THE FEDERAL TAX LAW

   A.   Revenue Needs

   Raising revenue is a major function of taxation. However, there are several other functions of the U.S. tax law. The tax law is also used to control the economy. Attempts at stimulation or temperance of the national economy have led to many amendments to the Internal Revenue Code.

   B.   Economic Considerations

   The tax law contains many provisions to encourage investment and capital formation.

   Lowering the tax rates gives taxpayers more income to spend, and is another method used to stimulate the economy. An increase in tax rates would have the opposite effect.

   Another economic consideration of the tax law is to encourage certain activities. The favorable incentives granted research and development expenditures, the rapid amortization of pollution control facilities, and Foreign Sales Corporations (FSC) are examples of these types of provisions in the tax law. IRAs and other pension plans are examples of using the tax law to help the economic problem of capital formation.

   The encouragement of certain industries is another economic consideration of the tax law. Agriculture, for example, is an industry that has special tax benefits.

   Small businesses are generally considered good for the economy as a whole. Therefore, certain provisions of the tax law are designed to help small businesses. The S Corporation election is an example of one of the methods Congress uses to help small businesses through tax law provisions.

   C.   Social Considerations. The U.S. tax law contains many provisions intended to achieve social objectives. Examples of such social provisions are:
     1)   Nontaxability of employer-sponsored accident and health plans
     2)   Nontaxability of employer paid premiums for group-term insurance
     3)   Qualified pension and profit sharing plans
     4)   Deductions for contributions to charitable organizations
     5)   Credit for child care expenditures
     6)   Disallowance of deductions for expenditures that are against public policy (fines, penalties, etc.)

   D.   Equity Considerations

   The Federal tax law attempts to alleviate the effect of multiple taxation in several areas. Examples include the deduction for state, local, and foreign income tax and the foreign tax credit.

The wherewithal to pay concept recognizes the inequity of taxing a transaction where the taxpayer lacks the means with which to pay the tax. Sometimes the Federal tax rules, such as those applicable where a taxpayer reinvests the proceeds from an involuntary conversion (e.g., a casualty loss) in similar property, allow the taxpayer to defer recognition of gain when his or her economic situation has not changed significantly.

Mitigating the effect of the concept of an annual accounting period is an equity consideration that deals with the inequities, which arise from the arbitrary use of the annual accounting period to divide the taxpayer's life into taxable segments. The annual accounting period concept could lead to different treatment of two individuals who are, from a long-range standpoint, in the same economic position. Measures to alleviate this inequity include the carryover procedure for net operating losses, excess capital losses and excess charitable contributions, and the installment method of recognizing gain.

One major problem in recent years has been bracket creep, which was caused by inflation. Taxpayers were pushed into higher tax brackets without a real increase in income. This problem is addressed by indexing. Each year, beginning in 1989, the tax brackets and the standard deduction are indexed upward by the amount of inflation. The personal and dependency exemptions are also indexed based on inflation.

E.   Political Considerations

Special interest legislation includes tax provisions sponsored because of the instigation of influential constituents. Such legislation is inevitable in our political system and can sometimes be justified on economic, social, or utilitarian grounds.

Political expediency is responsible for the passage of tax provisions that have popular appeal such as measures that insure wealthy taxpayers pay their "fair" share of tax, the lowering of individual income tax rates, and increasing the exemption amount.

State and local influences explain the nontaxability of interest received on state and local obligations, and the extension under Federal tax law of community property tax advantages to residents of common law states.

F.   Influence of the IRS

As protector of the revenue, the IRS has a great deal of influence on shaping the tax law. In this role the IRS tries to close what it sees as loopholes in the tax law.

Many provisions of the tax law are for administrative feasibility, and exist because they simplify the work of the IRS in collecting the revenue or administering the tax law. Withholding procedures place taxpayers on a pay-as-you-go basis and so aid the IRS in the collection of revenue. Interest and penalties imposed for noncompliance with tax laws are also of considerable help to the IRS.

G.   Influences of the Courts

The Federal courts have influenced the tax law. Some court decisions have been of such consequence that Congress has incorporated them into the Internal Revenue Code. The rule that allows tax-free stock dividends is an example of a court decision being codified.

TEST FOR SELF-EVALUATION—CHAPTER 1

True or False

Indicate which of the following statements is true or false by circling the correct answer.

T	F	1.	The first U.S. Federal income tax was enacted to provide revenues for the Civil War.
T	F	2.	The Supreme Court held that the 1894 income tax law was constitutional since it was a direct tax.
T	F	3.	The Sixteenth Amendment was necessary to enact the corporate income tax of 1909.
T	F	4.	The first Internal Revenue Code was the Internal Revenue Code of 1939.
T	F	5.	The current tax law is the Internal Revenue Code of 1986, as amended.
T	F	6.	The corporate income tax provides the largest percentage of Federal tax revenues.
T	F	7.	During World War II, the income tax was converted from being a select tax to being a mass tax.
T	F	8.	The responsibility for administering the Federal tax law rests with the Treasury Department.
T	F	9.	The Internal Revenue Service openly reveals its audit selection techniques.
T	F	10.	The purpose of the gift tax is to prevent widespread avoidance of the estate tax.
T	F	11.	The amount of salary to which the old age, survivors, and disability insurance (OASDI) portion of the FICA tax is subject to an annual maximum amount.
T	F	12.	Tax rates are applied to a tax base to determine a taxpayer's liability.
T	F	13.	Tax collections from individual income taxes are the largest portion of the Federal government's budget receipts.
T	F	14.	Ad valorem taxes are taxes that are based on income derived from property.
T	F	15.	Property taxes on personalty have a high rate of compliance, while taxes on realty have a low rate of compliance.
T	F	16.	Excise taxes are levied on specific transactions or products, while sales taxes are collected on transactions involving a wide range of products.
T	F	17.	Excise taxes are sometimes used to influence social behavior.
T	F	18.	The Federal government is the only government allowed to impose excise taxes on products.
T	F	19.	The primary purpose of the estate tax is to generate revenue with which to operate the Federal government.
T	F	20.	In addition to the Federal gift tax, several states impose a state gift tax on their residents.
T	F	21.	State inheritance taxes usually tax all heirs at the same rate.
T	F	22.	The annual exclusion for Federal gift tax purposes is $47,000 per year per donee.
T	F	23.	A taxpayer can minimize his Federal gift tax liability by making several small taxable gifts rather than a single large taxable gift.

T	F	24.	All states impose some form of income tax on individuals who reside in that state.
T	F	25.	Some cities impose an income tax along with the federal and state income taxes.
T	F	26.	In recent years, tariffs have served the nation more as an instrument forcarrying out protectionist policies than for generating revenue.
T	F	27.	The interest rates applicable to underpayments and overpayments of federal income taxes used by the Internal Revenue Service are determined every quarter.
T	F	28.	The progressiveness of the U.S. Federal income tax rate structure for individuals has varied over time.
T	F	29.	Certain provisions of the U.S. income tax law are designed to help small businesses.
T	F	30.	An example of a social considerationin the tax law is the nontaxability of health plan benefits.
T	F	31.	The wherewithal to pay concept states that a taxpayer should pay the tax on all gains, even when his economic position has not changed.
T	F	32.	Many provisions of the tax law can be explained by looking at the influence of pressure groups on Congress.
T	F	33.	One role assumed by the Internal Revenue Service is that of "protector of the revenue."
T	F	34.	Some of the tax law is justified because it complicates the Internal Revenue Service's task of collecting revenue.
T	F	35.	The courts have established the rule that the relief provisions of the Code are to be broadly interpreted.
T	F	36.	Some court decisions have been of such consequence that Congress has written them into the tax laws.
T	F	37.	The tax law attempts to encourage technological progress.
T	F	38.	Economic considerations in the tax law help regulate the economy.
T	F	39.	One equity consideration of the tax law is the alleviation of multiple taxation.
T	F	40.	Carryback and carryover procedures help mitigate the effect of limiting a loss or deduction to the accounting period in which it was realized.
T	F	41.	The amounts of the standard deduction, exemptions, and tax brackets will be indexed for inflation in the future.
T	F	42.	In future years, budget deficit problems will probably influence many new tax provisions passed by Congress.
T	F	43.	For purposes of the gift tax, a special election applicable to married persons allows 75 percent of a gift made by a donor spouse to be treated as made by the nondonor spouse.

Multiple Choice

Choose the best answer for each of the following questions.

———— 1.   Which of the following is an employment tax?

   a.   The Gift Tax
   b.   FICA Tax
   c.   Customs duties
   d.   Excise taxes

———— 2.   Which of the following items will not be subject to indexing under the tax law?

   a.   The standard deduction
   b.   Personal and dependency exemptions
   c.   The child care credit
   d.   The tax brackets

———— 3.   The total FICA tax rate imposed on individual taxpayers is?

   a.   OASDI rate plus the FUTA rate
   b.   OASDI rate less the FUTA rate
   c.   OASDI rate plus the Medicare rate
   d.   OASDI rate less the Medicare rate

———— 4.   The installment method of reporting gains can be justified on the basis of:

   a.   Mitigation of the annual accounting period
   b.   Wherewithal to pay
   c.   Social consideration
   d.   Both mitigation of the annual accounting period *and* wherewithal to pay

———— 5.   Jack's gross income is $60,000 and he has business deductions of $6,000. His itemized deductions are $10,000 and he has one personal exemption. Jack's taxable income is calculated as:

   a. $60,000 − 6,000 − 10,000
   b. $60,000 − 6,000 − 10,000 − exemption
   c. $60,000 − 6,000 − 10,000 + exemption
   d. $60,000 − 6,000 − exemption

———— 6.   Jeanne earned wages of $120,000. The total amount of FICA tax due from Jeanne and her employer is:

   a.   [(OASDI rate × annual maximum) + (Medicare rate × $120,000)]
   b.   [(OASDI rate × annual maximum) + (Medicare rate × $120,000)] × 2
   c.   [(OASDI rate + Medicare rate) × annual maximum] × 2
   d.   [(OASDI rate + Medicare rate) × $120,000] × 2

———— 7.   The total FUTA tax payable by their employer before any state credits is calculated as:

   a.   FUTA wages × FUTA rate
   b.   (FUTA wages × FUTA rate) × 2
   c.   (FUTA wages × FUTA rate) × 50%
   d.   FUTA wages × (FUTA rate − FICA rate)

_____ 8.   Byron files his tax return 45 days late. Along with the return he remits a check for $6,000, which is the balance of the tax owed. Disregarding interest, what is Byron's penalty for failure to file?

     a. $–0–
     b. $60
     c. $540
     d. $600

_____ 9.   The value added tax is:

     a.   used by several European Union countries.
     b.   a form of income tax on corporations.
     c.   a tax on consumption.
     d.   Both used by several European Union countries *and* a tax on consumption.

_____ 10.   John received $140,000 when the state condemned his house for a new freeway. The house cost John $84,000. John immediately purchased a new home for $140,000. From this sale John should report a taxable gain of:

     a. $–0–
     b. $56,000
     c. $140,000
     d. $84,000

_____ 11.   If the quarterly rate charged by the IRS for taxpayer assessments (underpayments) is 8%, then the rate paid for tax refunds (overpayments) is:

     a.   6%
     b.   7%
     c.   8%
     d.   9%

_____ 12.   Vicky filed her 19X3 individual tax return on January 15, 19X4. The return was properly signed and filed. The statute of limitations for Vicky's 19X3 return expires on:

     a.   January 15, 19X7
     b.   April 15, 19X7
     c.   January 15, 19X0
     d.   April 15, 19X0

_____ 13.   Mike had two jobs during the current year. He earned $60,000 from his first employer and $40,000 from his second employer. All of the wages were subject to the FICA tax. When Mike files his tax return his credit for excess (non-Medicare) FICA is calculated how?

     a.   [($60,000 + $40,000) × OASDI rate]
     b.   [($60,000 + $40,000) × OASDI rate] – (personal exemption amount)
     c.   [($60,000 + $40,000) × OASDI rate] – (annual maximum × OASDI rate)
     d.   [($60,000 + $40,000) × OASDI rate] – (annual maximum × FUTA rate)

_____ 14.   Which of the following is not an economic consideration of the tax law?

     a.   Encouragement of small business
     b.   Encouragement of certain industries
     c.   The wherewithal to pay concept
     d.   Encouragement of certain activities

_____ 15. The net operating loss provision of the tax law is an example of:

    a. An economic consideration
    b. A social consideration
    c. A political consideration
    d. An equity consideration

_____ 16. Which of the following is not a social consideration in the tax law?

    a. Qualified pension and profit-sharing plan
    b. Expensing soil and water conservation costs
    c. Child care credit
    d. A speeding ticket paid by a truck driver is nondeductible

_____ 17. Which of the following is the best example of a tax law provision designed to aid in controlling the economy?

    a. Depreciation deduction
    b. Child care credit
    c. Personal exemption
    d. Net operating loss carryover

_____ 18. Smith Corporation pays $2,000 per month rent on a building to Mary Smith, its sole shareholder. The fair market value of the rent determined at "arm's length" would be $900 per month. Smith Corporation will be allowed a monthly rental deduction of:

    a. $–0–
    b. $900
    c. $1,000
    d. $2,000

_____ 19. A father rents property to his daughter for $10,000 a year. If the IRS wants to examine this transaction it will be interested in:

    a. The tax benefit rule
    b. Installment sales rules
    c. The arm's length concept
    d. Public policy limitations

_____ 20. Several years ago, Fran entered into an agreement to rent a building to Meg for 20 years. During the first year of the lease, Meg made $60,000 in capital improvements to the building. This year the lease is terminated and Fran takes possession of the building. The fair market value of the capital improvements in the year of termination is $75,000. In the year of the termination of the lease, Fran must recognize taxable gain of?

    a. $–0–
    b. $15,000
    c. $60,000
    d. $75,000

_____ 21. On a tax return that is filed 45 days late, Christy pays $33,000 in additional taxes. Of this amount $10,000 is attributable to Christy's negligence. What is Christy's negligence penalty?

    a. $–0–
    b. $500
    c. $2,000
    d. $6,600

_____ 22.   When a tax base is $20,000, the tax liability is $6,000 and when the tax base is $200,000, the tax liability is $60,000. This tax rate structure is:

    a.   Progressive
    b.   Regressive
    c.   Proportional
    d.   Parallel

_____ 23.   When a tax base is $20,000, the tax liability is $6,000 and when the tax base is $200,000, the tax liability is $80,000. This tax rate structure is:

    a.   Progressive
    b.   Regressive
    c.   Proportional
    d.   Parallel

_____ 24.   For 1913 individual tax returns filed on March 1, 1914, the maximum marginal tax rate was?

    a.   6%
    b.   10%
    c.   12%
    d.   15%

_____ 25.   The pay-as-you-go system of withholding used by the United States Government was passed into law in?

    a.   1913
    b.   1925
    c.   1943
    d.   1954

_____ 26.   A(n) _____ tax is an ad valorem tax (usually at the same rate as the sales tax) on the utilization, consumption, or storage of tangible property.

    a.   Excise
    b.   Severance
    c.   Luxury
    d.   Use

_____ 27.   Which of the following states does not impose an income tax on individuals?

    a.   Virginia
    b.   Nevada
    c.   Vermont
    d.   Alabama

SOLUTIONS TO CHAPTER 1 QUESTIONS

True or False

1.	T	The U.S. income tax was for the Civil War. [Early Periods, p. 1–2]
2.	F	The income tax was unconstitutional because it was not apportioned. [Early Periods, p. 1–2]
3.	F	The 1909 corporate income tax was held to be constitutional. [Early Periods, p. 1–2]
4.	T	The first Code was the 1939 Code. [Revenue Acts, p. 1–3]
5.	T	The current tax law is the Internal Revenue Code of 1986. [Revenue Acts, p. 1–3]
6.	F	The individual income tax provides the largest percent. [Historical Trends, p. 1–3]
7.	T	The income tax went from a select tax to a mass tax in WWII. [Historical Trends, p. 1–3]
8.	T	The Treasury Department administers the income tax. [Internal Revenue Service, p. 1–19]
9.	F	The IRS does not disclose its audit selection techniques. [The Audit Process, p. 1–19]
10.	T	Preventing the avoidance of the estate tax is the purpose of the gift tax. [The Federal Gift Tax, p. 1–13]
11.	T	Salary for OASDI tax is subject to an annual maximum. [FICA Taxes, p. 1–16]
12.	T	Tax rates are applied to the tax base. [Tax Rates, p. 1–5]
13.	T	Individuals income taxes are the largest portion of the budget receipts. [Historical Trends, p. 1–3]
14.	F	Ad valorem taxes are based on the value of the property. [Property Taxes, p. 1–6]
15.	F	The tax on realty has a high compliance rate. [Ad Valorem Taxes on Realty, p. 1–6]
16.	T	Excise taxes are on specific transaction and sales taxes are general. [General Sales Taxes, p. 1–10]
17.	T	Excises are used to influence behavior. [Federal Excise Taxes, p. 1–8]
18.	F	State and local governments can also impose excise taxes. [State Excise Taxes, p. 1–9]
19.	F	The estate tax is intended to prevent concentrations of wealth. [The Federal Estate Tax, p. 1–11]
20.	T	Several States impose a gift tax. [State Gift Taxes, p. 1–14]
21.	F	Inheritance taxes generally are imposed on distant heirs at a higher rate. [State Death Taxes, p. 1–12]
22.	F	The exclusion is $10,000 in 2001 ($11,000 in 2002) per year. [The Federal Gift Tax, p. 1–13]
23.	F	The gift tax is based on the taxpayer's cumulative taxable gifts. [The Federal Gift Tax, p. 1–13]
24.	F	Several states do not have a state income tax. [State Income Taxes, p. 1–15]
25.	T	Some cities impose an income tax. [Local Income Taxes, p. 1–16]
26.	T	Recently, Tariffs have served to carry out protectionist policies. [Federal Customs Duties, p. 1–17]
27.	T	Interest rates are determined quarterly. [Interest and Penalties, p. 1–22]
28.	T	The progressiveness of tax rates has varied over time. [Incidence of Taxation, p. 1–6]
29.	T	Certain tax law provisions are to help small business. [Encouragement of Small Business, p. 1–26]
30.	T	Nontaxability of health plans is a social consideration. [Social Considerations, p. 1–26]

31. F The wherewithal to pay concept recognizes that under some circumstances, even though a gain has been realized by the taxpayer, the taxpayer's economic position may not have changed. [The Wherewithal to Pay Concept, p. 1–28]

32. T Pressure groups influence the tax law. [Political Expediency Situations, p. 1–30]

33. T Protector of the Revenue is one role of the IRS. [The IRS as Protector of the Revenue, p. 1–31]

34. F Some of the law is justified because it simplifies the work of the IRS. [Administrative Feasibility, p. 1–31]

35. F The relief provisions are narrowly interpreted. [Judicial Concepts Relating to Tax, p. 1–32]

36. T Some Court decisions are codified. [Judicial Influence on Statutory Provisions, p. 1–33]

37. T Technological progress is encouraged by the tax law. [Encouragement of Certain Activities, p. 1–25]

38. T The tax law helps regulate the economy. [Control of the Economy, p. 1–25]

39. T The tax law helps alleviate multiple taxation. [Alleviating the Effect of Multiple Taxation, p. 1–27]

40. T Accounting periods are mitigated by carrybacks and carryovers. [Mitigating the Effect of the Annual Accounting Period Concept, p. 1–28]

41. T The standard deduction, exemptions, and tax brackets are indexed for inflation. [Coping with Inflation, p. 1–29]

42. T Budget deficits influence many tax provisions. [Encouragement of Certain Activities, p. 1–25]

43. F The gift is split 50–50. [The Federal Gift Tax, p. 1–13]

Multiple Choice

1. b FICA is an employment tax. [Employment Taxes, p. 1–16]

2. c The child care credit is not indexed. [Coping with Inflation, p. 1–29]

3. c The OASDI rate plus Medicate rate is the total rate. [FICA taxes, p. 1–16]

4. d The installment method mitigates the annual accounting period. [Mitigating the Effect of The Annual Accounting Period Concept, p. 1–28]

5. b $60,000 – 6,000 – 10,000 – exemption. [Federal Income taxes, p. 1–14]

6. b [(OASDI rate × annual maximum) + (Medicare rate × $120,000)] × 2. [FICA Taxes, p. 1–16]

7. a FUTA wages × FUTA rate. [FUTA Taxes, p. 1–17]

8. c 5% per month or fraction thereof, or 10% × $6,000 = $600, less failure to pay penalty of .5% per month or fraction thereof, (1% × $6,000 = $60), which equals $540. [Interest and Penalties, p. 1–22]

9. d The VAT is a consumption tax used bey several European countries. [Value Added Tax, p. 1–18]

10. a The gain is not taxable. [The Wherewithal to Pay Concept, p. 1–28]

11. b The underpayment rate is 2% higher than the overpayment rate. [Interest and Penalties, p. 1–22]

12. b The statute of limitations is 3 years from due date of the return. [Statute of Limitations, p. 1–21]

13. b [($60,000 + $40,000) × OASDI rate] – (annual maximum × OASDI rate). [FICA Taxes, p. 1–16]

14. c Wherewithal to pay is an equity consideration. [Equity Considerations, p. 1–27]

15. d NOLs are an equity consideration. [Mitigating the Effect of the Annual Accounting Period Concept, p. 1–28]

16. b Soil and Water conservation expensing is an economic consideration. [Encouragement of Certain Industries, p. 1–26]

17. a The depreciation deduction aids in controlling the economy. [Control of the Economy, p. 1–25]

18. b The amount is what would be paid to an unrelated third party. [Judicial Concepts Relating to Tax, p. 1–32]

19. c Rentals between related parties a judged by the *arms length* concept. [Judicial Concepts Relating to Tax, p. 1–32]

20. a The improvements are not income. [Judicial Influence on Statutory Provisions, p. 1–33]

21. c $2,000 = 20% × $10,000 [Interest and Penalties, p. 1–22]

22. c When the tax rate stays the same the tax is proportional. [Tax Rates, p. 1–5]

23. a When the tax rate increases the tax is progressive. [Tax Rates, p. 1–5]

24. a The 1913 maximum marginal tax rate was 6%. [Early periods, p. 1–2]

25. c The pay-as-you-go system was passed in 1943. [Historical Trends, p. 1–3]

26. d A use tax is an Ad Valorem tax. [General Sales Taxes, p. 1–10]

27. b Nevada does not have a state income tax. [State Income Taxes, p. 1–15]

CHAPTER 2

Working With the Tax Law

CHAPTER HIGHLIGHTS

Familiarity with the statutory, administrative, and judicial sources of the tax law is essential in learning to work with tax legislation. This chapter considers the sources of the tax law, the application of research techniques to tax problems, and the effective use of tax planning procedures.

KEY TERMS

Administrative Sources
Judicial Sources
Statutory Sources
Court of Appeals

Court of Federal Claims
District Court
Regulations
Revenue Ruling

Supreme Court
Tax Court
Tax Research
Tax Planning

OUTLINE

I.   **TAX SOURCES**

    A.   Statutory Sources of the Tax Law. The Internal Revenue Code of 1939 was the first codification of all Federal tax provisions into a logical sequence. The 1939 Code was recodified into the 1954 Code, which was renamed the Internal Revenue Code of 1986. New tax laws are integrated into the 1986 Code.

       For a tax bill to become law, it must be passed by both houses of Congress and signed by the President. Tax legislation is first considered in the House by the Ways and Means Committee. Legislation, once approved by the House of Representatives, is then considered by the Senate Finance Committee, and finally by the entire Senate. When the House and Senate cannot agree on the tax bill, the differences are worked out by the Joint Conference Committee.

       The Code is arranged by Subtitles, Chapters, Subchapters, Parts, and Sections. However, to identify any part of the Code, it is only necessary to know the Section number because these numbers are not repeated. The normal progression for a citation is Section, Subsection, Paragraph, and Subparagraph.

       Tax Treaties are negotiated with most foreign countries. If a treaty comes in conflict with the Code, the most recent item will take precedence. A taxpayer must disclose (subject to penalties for non-disclosure) on a tax return if a treaty overrides a provision of the tax law.

    B.   Administrative Sources of Tax Law. There are numerous administrative sources of Federal tax law. These can be grouped as Treasury Department Regulations, Revenue Rulings and Procedures, and other pronouncements. All are issued by the U.S. Treasury Department or one of its instrumentalities such as the Internal Revenue Service or a District Director.

       Treasury Department Regulations are the Internal Revenue Service's official interpretation of the Code. They are arranged in Code section sequence with a prefix to designate the type of Regulation.

       Revenue Rulings and Procedures are official pronouncements of the National Office of the IRS. They do not, however, carry the same legal force as Regulations. Revenue Rulings are usually concerned with a restrictive problem or area, while Revenue Procedures are concerned with internal management practices of the IRS. Both Revenue Rulings and Procedures are published weekly by the U.S. government in the *Internal Revenue Bulletin*. Every six months the weekly bulletins are published in a bound volume entitled the *Cumulative Bulletin*.

       Individual Letter Rulings are issued by the National Office of the IRS in response to a taxpayer's request and describe how the IRS will treat a proposed transaction. Individual Letter Rulings are available for public inspection after identifying details are removed.

       Determination Letters are rulings that generally deal with completed transactions, and are issued by District Directors, instead of the National Office of the IRS.

       The IRS also makes the following administrative communications:

       Treasury Decisions (TDs) are issued by the Treasury Department to promulgate new Regulations, amend or change existing Regulations, or to announce the government's position on selected court decisions.

       Technical Advice Memoranda, released by the National Office of the IRS, are private rulings initiated by the IRS during its audit activities.

       Other pronouncements (e.g., Announcements and Notices) allow the IRS to communicate necessary information to taxpayers.

    C.   Judicial Sources of the Tax Law. After a taxpayer has exhausted the remedies available with the IRS, a dispute can be taken to the Federal courts. The dispute is first heard by a trial court (the court of original jurisdiction) with any appeal taken to the appropriate appellate court. A description of the various courts is as follows:

District Courts. *The Federal District Courts are organized into geographical regions, and will hear cases involving any Federal matter, both tax and nontax issues. Taxpayers cannot choose a particular District Court, but must use the one having jurisdiction over the case. Each District Court has only one judge and it is the only court in which the taxpayer may have a jury trial.*

U.S. Claims Court. *The U.S. Claims Court has sixteen judges and meets in Washington, D.C. The purpose of this court is to hear any case involving a monetary claim against the Federal government.*

U.S. Tax Court. *The U.S. Tax Court is a national court with nineteen judges. However, only one judge hears a case unless it is unusual. The Tax Court hears only cases involving tax matters. The Tax Court will follow decisions of the Court of Appeals in the jurisdiction in which the case is being heard. The Tax Court is the only court in which the taxpayer need not pay the deficiency before taking the dispute to court. Before 1943, the Tax Court was called the Board of Tax Appeals (BTA).*

Small Claims Division of U.S. Tax Court. *The small claims division of the U.S. Tax Court will hear matters involving amounts up to $50,000. The decisions of the small claims division are final and cannot be appealed.*

U.S. Court of Appeals. *There are eleven numbered Court of Appeals plus one for the District of Columbia, and one for the Federal District. Each Court of Appeals has jurisdiction in a specific geographical region of the country, except the Federal District, which hears cases only from the U.S. Claims Court.*

U.S. Supreme Court. *The Supreme Court, a nine-judge panel, has final say in all tax matters. Appeal to the Supreme Court is by Writ of Certiorari, and acceptance is not automatic.*

Court decisions are reported in a variety of publications. Decisions of the District Court, U.S. Claims Court, Court of Appeals, and Supreme Court that deal with tax matters are reported in both the CCH *U.S. Tax Cases* (USTC) and the RIA (formerly P-H) *American Federal Tax Reports* (AFTR) series. All District Court decisions are published by West Publishing Company in their *Federal Supplement Series* (currently F.Supp. 2d.). All decisions of the U.S. Claims Court beginning October 1982 are published in the *Claims Court Reporter* (Cl.Ct.), by West Publishing Company. All decisions of the Courts of Appeals and U.S. Claims Court decisions are currently published by West in a reporter designated as the *Federal Third Series* (F.3d). Supreme Court decisions are published by West in its *Supreme Court Reporter* (S.Ct.), by the U.S. Government Printing Office in the *United States Supreme Court Reports* (U.S.), and by the Lawyer's Cooperative Publishing Company in its *United States Reports, Lawyer's Edition* (L.Ed.).

The Tax Court issues two kinds of decisions, Regular and Memorandum. Generally, Regular decisions deal with a new or unusual point of law, while Memorandum decisions deal with an established point of law. The Regular decisions of the Tax Court are published by the U.S. Government Printing Office (GPO) in a series designated *Tax Court of the United States Reports* (T.C.). Memorandum decisions are published by CCH in *Tax Court Memorandum Decisions* (TCM) and by RIA in *T.C. Memorandum Decisions*.

Citations of a court decision generally consist of two parts: (1) the name of the case and the abbreviated title of the report volume and (2) the number or page of the report that contains the text of the decision. After each citation, a parenthetical reference identifies the court rendering the decision and the year the decision was reached.

If the IRS loses at the trial court level and does not appeal the decision this does not indicate that the IRS agrees with the result or that it will not litigate similar situations in the future.

II. **WORKING WITH THE TAX LAW—TAX RESEARCH**
A. Identifying and Refining the Problem. The first step in tax research is to identify and define the problem. All facts having a bearing on the problem must be gathered since any omission could have

a substantial impact on the conclusion reached. Once a problem has been identified, it should be refined. New facts may lead to a faster problem solving or lead to the discovery of new problem areas.

B. Locating the Appropriate Tax Law Sources. The second step in tax research involves locating the appropriate sources of tax law. Most tax research begins with the index volume of a tax service. A tax service is a comprehensive set of books on Internal Revenue law. The major tax services are arranged by Code section number or topic. When using any tax service one should always check for current developments. Besides the tax services there are many tax periodicals that are indexed in CCH's *Federal Tax Articles*.

C. Assessing the Validity of the Tax Law Sources. The third step in tax research, once a source of tax information has been located, is to assess the source in relation to the problem at hand. Some of the characteristics of sources that need to be assessed would include conflicting Code provisions, the relative importance of Treasury Regulations, Revenue Rulings, and court decisions.

The language of the Code can be extremely difficult to comprehend, with extremely long sentences and many cross references between interrelated provisions. Also, occasional conflicts between old and new Code provisions arise. For these and other reasons, great care should be exercised when interpreting the Code.

The Treasury Regulations are not the law, but have the force and effect of law if they are reasonable interpretations of the Code. The burden of proof rests with the taxpayer to show that a Regulation is wrong. Certain "legislative regulations" are virtually impossible to overturn.

Revenue Rulings carry less weight than the Regulations, but are important reflections of the IRS's position on certain tax matters.

The validity of a court decision depends on the level of the court, the residence of the taxpayer, and the status of the decision.

D. Arriving at the Solution or at Alternative Solutions. The fourth step of the tax research process is arriving at a solution based on the information gathered. Often a clear-cut answer is impossible to obtain, and a guarded judgment is the best solution that can be given.

E. Communicate Tax Research. Once a conclusion has been reached, it is necessary to communicate the findings to the client. This is normally done by preparing a memo that explains the findings and how the conclusions were reached.

The contents of a Tax Memo are as follows:
1. A clear statement of the issue(s).
2. A short review of the factual pattern.
3. A review of the tax law.
4. Any assumptions.
5. The solution recommended and the logic supporting the conclusion.
6. References consulted while doing the research.

After the memo is prepared, a letter based on the memo is written and sent to the client.

The tax practitioner should follow-up, where necessary, on the solution reached during the research process. Developments could occur that might alter the conclusion reached at the end of the research project.

F. Follow up. The tax researcher should follow up on the solution (where appropriate) in light of any new developments.

III. **WORKING WITH THE TAX LAW—TAX PLANNING**
A. Nontax Considerations. In tax planning, it is necessary to take into account many nontax considerations. What may produce the best tax result may not be an acceptable alternative to the taxpayer. Generally, tax planning involves producing the smallest tax within the nontax and legal constraints. Tax considerations should not impair the exercise of sound business judgment by the taxpayer.

B.   Tax Avoidance and Tax Evasion. There is a difference between tax avoidance and tax evasion. Tax avoidance is merely minimization through legal means, while evasion is illegal tax planning.

C.   Follow-up Procedures. A change in the tax law could alter a conclusion. Additional research may be necessary to test any solution in light of current developments.

D.   Electronic Tax Research. Computer tax research is part of the day-to-day tax practice for many tax professionals. The computer data bases provide the tax practitioner instant access to the entire legal database. The four major CD-ROM tax research databases are WESTLAW, RIA, CCH, and Kleinrock's. These databases are searched by using a system of key words. The document(s) that meet the search criteria are then displayed on the computer screen for the tax researcher.

LEXIS/NEXIS, WESTLAW, RIA, and CCH provide online tax research services. These services are very up-to-date and are expensive because of their real time ability. The Internet (World Wide Web) provides many sites with tax information.

There are also many web sites that provide the tax research with useful and timely tax information. Among the sites are those maintained by the Internal Revenue Service, law schools, commercial tax publishers, large CPA firms, and other professional organizations. Many of these sites are offered for free to the public. See the textbook for site addresses.

TEST FOR SELF-EVALUATION—CHAPTER 2

True or False

Indicate which of the following statements is true or false by circling the correct answer.

T F 1. Both Revenue Rulings and Revenue Procedures are published weekly by the U.S. Government in the *Internal Revenue Bulletin.*

T F 2. There is only one U.S. Court of Federal Claims and it meets most often in Washington, D.C.

T F 3. The U.S. Claims Court has seven judges and the Tax Court has nineteen judges.

T F 4. Regulation Section 1.61 refers to Internal Revenue Code Section 61.

T F 5. Appeal to the Supreme Court is by Writ of Certiorari.

T F 6. Revenue Ruling 2001–48 relates to Section 48 of the Internal Revenue Code.

T F 7. In general, a U.S. Tax Court Regular decision deals with a new or unusual point of law.

T F 8. The Internal Revenue Service usually acquiesces or nonacquiesces to all regular Tax Court decisions.

T F 9. To go to the Tax Court, a taxpayer must pay the tax and sue for a refund.

T F 10. A jury trial may be obtained in the Tax Court.

T F 11. *Bradford v. Comm.*, 56–1 USTC Para. 9552 (CA-6, 1956) is an example of a citation from Commerce Clearing House's *United States Tax Cases.*

T F 12. RIA publishes Revenue Rulings in its *American Federal Tax Reports* (AFTR).

T F 13. The United States Tax Court is one of the federal trial courts that is a court of original jurisdiction.

T F 14. When confronted with a particularly troublesome problem, the taxpayer may always obtain an Individual Letter Ruling.

T F 15. *Morris Alexander v. Comm.*, 61 T.C. 278 is an example of a citation from Commerce Clearing House's *Tax Court of the United States Reports.*

T F 16. Temporary Regulations are also issued as Proposed Regulations and automatically expire within three years after the date of issuance.

T F 17. In a challenge by the IRS, the burden of proof is on the taxpayer to show that a Regulation is wrong.

T F 18. Tax avoidance is illegal tax planning while tax evasion is legal tax planning.

T F 19. A case is appealed from the U.S. Claims Court to the Court of Appeals for the Federal Circuit and then to the Supreme Court.

T F 20. *John Doe*, T.C. Memo 2002–32 is the thirty-second Tax Court Memorandum decision of 2002.

T F 21. The Tax Court follows the decisions of the Court of Appeals for the appropriate jurisdiction of the case being heard.

T F 22. The District Courts hear cases involving both tax and nontax litigation.

T   F   23.   The appellate courts are the Supreme Court, Courts of Appeals, and the U.S. Claims Court.

T   F   24.   The *Cumulative Bulletins* contain the IRBs for a semiannual period.

T   F   25.   The prefix "1" designates an income tax Regulation when referring to a Treasury Department Regulation.

T   F   26.   Tax legislation originates in the House of Representatives' Ways and Means Committee.

T   F   27.   Technical Advice Memoranda are not available for public inspection.

T   F   28.   A taxpayer must pay any tax deficiency assessed by the IRS and then sue for a refund in the U.S. Claims Court.

T   F   29.   The phrase *Cert. Granted* indicates that the Supreme Court will hear the tax case.

T   F   30.   For a taxpayer residing in California, a decision of the Ninth Circuit Court of Appeals has more precedence than one rendered by the Eleventh Circuit Court of Appeals.

T   F   31.   If a taxpayer loses in the Tax Court Small Claims Division, he or she may not appeal to the regular U.S. Tax Court.

T   F   32.   Since Letter Rulings apply to only one taxpayer, the IRS is not required to make Letter Rulings public.

T   F   33.   *Technical Advice Memoranda* (TAMs) are only issued on proposed transactions while Letter Rulings are only issued on completed transactions.

T   F   34.   Under the doctrine of *stare decisis*, each case (except in the Small Claims Division) has precedential value for future cases with the same set of controlling facts.

T   F   35.   Tax forms and publications can be downloaded from the IRS site on the Internet.

T   F   36.   Many large accounting firms (e.g., Ernst & Young) maintain home pages on the World Wide Web.

Multiple Choice

Choose the best answer for each of the following questions.

_____   1.   Appeal from the Tax Court is to the:

   a.   Court of Appeals
   b.   District Court
   c.   U.S. Claims Court
   d.   Supreme Court

_____   2.   If taxpayers choose not to pay a tax deficiency, then they must petition which court?

   a.   District Court
   b.   U.S. Claims Court
   c.   Tax Court
   d.   Court of Appeals

_____ 3. Which of the following court(s) would have jurisdiction if a taxpayer paid a tax deficiency and sued for a refund (instead of petitioning the court)?

    a.   Tax Court
    b.   District Court and U.S. Claims Court
    c.   Tax Court and District Court
    d.   U.S. Claims Court

_____ 4. A decision of which of the following courts could not be found in CCH's *U.S. Tax Cases*?

    a.   District Court
    b.   Court of Appeals
    c.   Supreme Court
    d.   Tax Court

_____ 5. Which of the following does not publish a tax service?

    a.   Commerce Clearing House
    b.   Matthew Bender
    c.   Research Institute of America
    d.   Government Printing Office

_____ 6. The *Federal Tax Articles* index is a three-volume service published by:

    a.   Government Printing Office
    b.   BNA
    c.   Commerce Clearing House
    d.   Matthew Bender, Inc.

_____ 7. Tax evasion is:

    a.   Legally minimizing taxes
    b.   Illegally minimizing taxes
    c.   The same as tax avoidance
    d.   None of the above

_____ 8. In *Walter H. Johnson,* 34 TCM 1056, 34 stands for:

    a.   The year of decision
    b.   The page number
    c.   The volume number
    d.   The paragraph number

_____ 9. Decisions by which court is published by West Publishing Company in its *Federal Supplement Series* (currently F.Supp. 2d.)?

    a.   District Court
    b.   Tax Court
    c.   U.S. Claims Court
    d.   Court of Appeals

_____ 10. The largest subdivision of material in the Internal Revenue Code is the:

    a.   Subtitle
    b.   Chapter
    c.   Part
    d.   Subchapter

_____ 11.   The annual maximum dollar amount that is within the jurisdiction of the Small Claims Division
of the United States Tax Court is:

    a. $5,000
    b. $10,000
    c. $25,000
    d. $50,000

_____ 12.   Which of the following Federal courts has limited geographical jurisdiction within the United
States?

    a.   Supreme Court
    b.   District Court
    c.   U.S. Claims Court
    d.   United States Tax Court

_____ 13.   The United States Tax Court:

    a.   Has nineteen judges
    b.   Will hear any Federal case
    c.   Is an appeals court
    d.   Has jurisdiction over the District Courts

_____ 14.   The *Standard Federal Tax Reporter* is published by:

    a.   BNA
    b.   Commerce Clearing House
    c.   Research Institute of America
    d.   Bureau of National Affairs

_____ 15.   According to the text, the primary purpose of effective tax planning is:

    a.   Eradicating the tax entirely
    b.   Deferring the receipt of income
    c.   Converting ordinary income into capital gain
    d.   None of the above

_____ 16.   What is the name of the free IRS online tax newsletter?

    a.   The Digital Daily
    b.   Tax Week
    c.   Taxes Today
    d.   Tax Alert

_____ 17.   At the completion of the tax research process the results are generally set forth in which of the
following ways?

    a.   A phone call to the client
    b.   A note to the IRS
    c.   Preparing a tax research memo
    d.   Adding the results to the LEXIS database

_____ 18.   Which of the following is not a tax periodical?

    a.   *The Journal of Taxation*
    b.   *TAXES—The Tax Magazine*
    c.   *The American Tax Journal*
    d.   *Estate Planning*

_____ 19. Which of the following is a primary source of tax law?

    a. Tax treaties
    b. Legal journals
    c. Tax magazines
    d. Tax textbooks

_____ 20. In Letter Ruling 200215087, the 087 refers to the:

    a. Year of the Letter Ruling
    b. Issue of the Bulletin in which the Letter Ruling appears
    c. Day of the year the Letter Ruling was issued
    d. The number of the Letter Ruling issued during the week

_____ 21. According to the textbook, which of the following trial court decisions is sometimes believed to have the "highest" authority in a tax matter?

    a. Tax Court Memorandum decisions
    b. Tax Court Regular decisions
    c. Tax Court Small Claims decisions
    d. Tax Court Annotation decisions

_____ 22. What statement is true of a Temporary Regulation?

    a. It is issued simultaneously as a Revenue Ruling
    b. It may be cited as precedent
    c. It automatically expires after one year from the date of issuance
    d. It is issued simultaneously as a Revenue Procedure

_____ 23. Which of the following has the lowest tax validity?

    a. Letter Ruling
    b. Regulation
    c. Revenue Ruling
    d. Revenue Procedure

_____ 24. Which of the following courts has the lowest tax validity?

    a. Supreme Court
    b. Court of Appeals for the 9th Circuit
    c. Tax Court
    d. Court of Appeals for the Federal Circuit

_____ 25. Which of the following is a secondary source of tax law?

    a. Revenue Ruling
    b. Internal Revenue Code
    c. Tax treaty
    d. An article on partnership tax in the _Tax Adviser_

_____ 26. Which of the following would be considered "authority" for purposes of the accuracy-related penalty under Section 6662?

    a. Legal opinion of an attorney who is a tax specialist
    b. _Harvard Law Review_ article
    c. IRS Letter Ruling
    d. A tax article in the _Journal of Taxation_

_____ 27. In general, when a provision of a tax treaty comes in conflict with a provision of the Internal Revenue Code, which has precedence?

    a. The Treaty provision
    b. The Code provision
    c. The provision that was passed earliest
    d. The provision that was passed latest

_____ 28. In which of the following states would a taxpayer appeal a decision of a U.S. District Court to the Ninth Court of Appeals?

    a. Florida
    b. Wyoming
    c. North Dakota
    d. Nevada

_____ 29. In which of the following court reporters could be found a decision of the Small Case division of the United States Tax Court?

    a. TCM
    b. USTC
    c. T.C.
    d. Tax Court Small Case divisions are not published

_____ 30. A tax research memo should *not* contain which of the following elements?

    a. a clear statement of the issue(s)
    b. a review of the tax law sources
    c. any assumptions made
    d. reference to taxpayers not directly involved

_____ 31. At the end of a tax research project, which of the following is usually sent to the taxpayer by the tax practitioner?

    a. a client letter
    b. a copy of the tax research memo
    c. copies of the tax research material found by the researcher
    d. nothing is sent, a phone call is made to the taxpayer

_____ 32. Which of the following does not have an online tax research service?

    a. WESTLAW
    b. LEXIS/NEXIS
    c. RIA
    d. IRS

_____ 33. Which of the following is not available from the IRS online newsletter site?

    a. Tax forms
    b. Instructions for tax forms
    c. News releases
    d. Tax Court cases

_____ 34. The _____ has 19 judges (not counting Special and Senior judges).

    a. Tax Court
    b. District Court
    c. U.S. Court of Federal Claims
    d. U.S. Supreme Court

_____ 35. A jury trial is available in which court?

    a. Tax Court
    b. District Court
    c. U.S. Court of Federal Claims
    d. U.S. Supreme Court

_____ 36. The _____ is a general trial court.

    a. Tax Court
    b. District Court
    c. U.S. Court of Federal Claims
    d. U.S. Supreme Court

_____ 37. The _____ hears only tax cases.

    a. Tax Court
    b. District Court
    c. U.S. Court of Federal Claims
    d. U.S. Supreme Court

_____ 38. Appeal is to the U.S. Court of Appeals for the Federal Circuit is from which court?

    a. Tax Court
    b. District Court
    c. U.S. Court of Federal Claims
    d. U.S. Supreme Court

_____ 39. The _____ hears mostly criminal and civil cases.

    a. Tax Court
    b. District Court
    c. U.S. Court of Federal Claims
    d. U.S. Supreme Court

_____ 40. A taxpayer does not have to pay a tax deficiency before going to trial in this court?

    a. Tax Court
    b. District Court
    c. U.S. Court of Federal Claims
    d. U.S. Supreme Court

SOLUTIONS TO CHAPTER 2 QUESTIONS

True or False

1.   T   Revenue Rulings and Procedures are published in the IRB. [Revenue Ruling and Procedures, p. 2–9]

2.   T   The only Court of Federal Claims meets often in Washington D.C. [Trial Courts, p. 2–15]

3.   F   The U.S. Claims Court has sixteen judges. [Trial Courts, p. 2–15]

4.   T   Reg. Section 1.16 refers to Section 61. [Treasury Department Regulations, p. 2–8]

5.   T   A writ of Certiorari is how to appeal to the Supreme Court. [Appellate Courts, p. 2–16]

6.   F   It is the 48th Revenue Ruling of 2001. [Revenue Ruling and Procedures, p. 2–9]

7.   T   A Tax Court Regular decision deals with a new or unusual point of law. [Judicial Citations—The U.S. Tax Court, p. 2–20]

8.   F   IRS acquiesces or nonacquiesces to decisions it loses. [Judicial Citations—The U.S. Tax Court, p. 2–20)

9.   F   The taxpayer generally does not have to pay the tax in order for the Tax Court to have jurisdiction. [Trial Courts, p. 2–15]

10.   F   A jury trial is available only in the District Courts. [Trial Courts, p. 2–15]

11.   T   This is a citation from CCH's *United States Tax Cases*. [Judicial Citations—The U.S. District Court, Court of Federal Claims, and Court of Appeals, p. 2–21]

12.   F   Court decisions are published in the AFTR. [Judicial Citations—The U.S. District Court, Court of Federal Claims, and Court of Appeals, p. 2–21]

13.   T   The Tax Court is one of the federal trial courts that is a court of original jurisdiction. [Trial Courts, p. 2–15]

14.   F   There are many issues on which the IRS will not rule. [Letter Rulings, p. 2–11]

15.   F   *Tax Court of the United States Reports* is published by the U.S. Government. [Judicial Citations—The U.S. Tax Court, p. 2–20]

16.   T   Temporary Regulations are also issued as Proposed Regulations and they expire within three years. [Treasury Department Regulations, p. 2–8]

17.   T   The burden of proof is on the taxpayer to show that a Regulation is wrong. [Assessing the Validity of a Treasury Regulation, p. 2–28]

18.   F   Tax planning (avoidance) is legal while tax evasion is illegal. [Tax Avoidance and Tax Evasion, p. 2–34]

19.   T   Cases are appealed from the U.S. Claims Court to the Court of Appeals for the Federal Circuit and then to the Supreme Court. [The Judicial Process in General, p. 2–14]

20.   T   This case is the thirty-second Tax Court Memorandum decision of 2002. [Judicial Citations—The U.S. Tax Court, p. 2–20]

21.   T   The Tax Court follows the decisions of the appropriate Court of Appeals. [Appellate Courts, p. 2–16]

22.   T   The District Courts try cases involving both tax and nontax litigation. [Trial Courts, p. 2–15]

23.   F   The U.S. Claims Court is a court of original jurisdiction. [The Judicial Process in General, p. 2–14]

24.   T   The *Cumulative Bulletins* contain the IRBs for a semiannual period. [Revenue Rulings and Revenue Procedures, p. 2–9]

25.   T   The prefix A1" designates an income tax Regulation. [Treasury Department Regulations, p. 2–8]

26.   T   Tax legislation originates in the House Ways and Means Committee. [The Legislative Process, p. 2–4]

27.   F   They must be made available to the public. [Other Administrative Pronouncements, p. 2–12]

28.   T   A taxpayer must pay any tax deficiency and then sue for a refund in the U.S. Claims Court. [Appellate Courts, p. 2–16]

29.   T   *Cert. Granted* indicates that the Supreme Court will hear the tax case. [Appellate Courts, p. 2–16]

30.   T   For a taxpayer residing in California, a decision of the Ninth Circuit Court of Appeals has more precedence. [Appellate Courts, p. 2–16]

31.   T   Losses in the Tax Court Small Claims Division, may not be appealed to the regular U.S. Tax Court. [The Judicial Process in General, p. 2–14]

32.   F   Letter Rulings are public information. [Letter Rulings, p. 2–11]

33.   F   TAMs are on completed transactions, while Letter Rulings are on proposed transactions. [Other Administrative Pronouncements, p. 2–14]

34.   T   Under the doctrine of *stare decisis,* each case (except in the Small Claims Division) has precedential value for future cases. [The Judicial Process in General, p. 2–13]

35.   T   Tax forms and publications are available from the IRS site on the Internet. [The Internet, p. 2–38]

36.   T   Many large accounting firms maintain home pages on the World Wide Web. [The Internet, p. 2–38]

Multiple Choice

1.   a   Appeal is to the Court of Appeals. [Trial Courts, p. 2–15]

2.   c   If taxpayers do not to pay a tax deficiency, then they must petition the Tax Court. [Trial Courts, p. 2–15]

3.   b   If taxpayers pay a tax deficiency, then they must sue for a refund in the District Court or U. S. Claims Court. [Trial Courts, p. 2–15]

4.   d   Tax Court decisions cannot be found in the USTC. [Judicial Citations, p. 2–21]

5.   d   The Government Printing Office does not publish a tax service. [Locating the Appropriate Tax Law Sources, p. 2–25]

6.   c   The *Federal Tax Articles* index is a three-volume service published by CCH. [Tax Periodicals, p. 2–26]

7.   b   Tax evasion is illegally minimizing taxes. [Tax Avoidance and Tax Evasion, p. 2–34]

8.   c   In *Walter H. Johnson,* 34 TCM 1056, 34 stands for the volume number. [Judicial Citations—The U.S. Tax Court, p. 2–20]

9.   a   Decisions by the District Court are published in the Federal Supplement Series. [Judicial Citations—The U.S. District Court, Court of Federal Claims, and Court of Appeals, p. 2–21]

10.   a   The largest subdivision of material in the Code is the Subtitle. [Arrangement of the Code, p. 2–6]

11.   d   The annual maximum dollar amount that is within the jurisdiction of the Small Claims Division of the United States Tax Court is $50,000. [The Judicial Process in General, p. 2–14]

12.   b   The District Court has limited geographical jurisdiction within the United States. [Trial Courts, p. 2–15]

13.   a   The Tax Court has nineteen judges. [Trial Courts, p. 2–15]

14. b   The *Standard Federal Tax Reporter* is published by Commerce Clearing House. [Locating the Appropriate Tax Law Sources, p. 2–25]

15. d   According to the text, the primary purpose of effective tax planning is legal tax minimization. [Tax Avoidance and Tax Evasion, p. 2–34]

16. b   The IRS online newsletter is called the Digital Daily. [The Internet, p. 2–38]

17. c   At the completion of the tax research process the results are generally set forth in a tax memo. [Communicating Tax Research, p. 2–31]

18. c   The American tax journal is not a tax periodical. [Tax Periodicals, p. 2–26]

19. a   Tax Treaties are a primary source of tax law. [Assessing the Validity of Other Sources, p. 2–30]

20. d   In Letter Ruling 8515087, the 087 refers to the number of the Letter Ruling issued during the week. [Letter Rulings, p. 2–11]

21. b   Tax Court regular decisions have the highest authority. [Assessing the Validity of Judicial Sources of the Tax Law, p. 2–29]

22. b   A Temporary Regulation may be cited as precedent. [Treasury Department Regulations, p. 2–8]

23. a   A Letter Ruling has the lowest validity. [Exhibit 2–1, p. 2–9]

24. c   The Tax Court has the lowest validity of the courts listed. [Assessing the Validity of Judicial Sources of the Tax Law, p. 2–29]

25. d   Tax journals are secondary sources. [Assessing the Validity of Other Sources, p. 2–30]

26. c   A Letter rulings is authority for Section 6662 purposes. [Assessing the Validity of Other Sources, p. 2–30]

27. d   When a provision of a tax treaty comes in conflict with a provision of the Internal Revenue Code, the provision that was passed latest has precedence. [Effect of Treaties, p. 2–7]

28. d   Arizona is in the Ninth Circuit. [Appellate Courts, p. 2–16]

29. d   Small Case decisions are not published. [Trial Courts p. 2–15]

30. d   A tax research memo should contain a clear statement of the issue(s), a review of the tax law sources, any assumptions made, but should not contain a reference to other taxpayers not directly involved. [Communicating Tax Research, p. 2–31]

31. a   At the end of a tax research project, a client letter is usually sent to the taxpayer. [Communicating Tax research, p. 2–31]

32. d   The IRS does not have online tax research service available. [Online Systems, p. 2–37]

33. b   Tax Court cases are not available on the IRS Digital Daily. [The Internet, p. 2–38]

34. a   The Tax Court has 19 judges. [Trial Courts, p. 2–15]

35. b   A jury trial is available in the District Court. [Trial Courts, p. 2–15]

36. b   The District Court is a General Trail Court. [Trial Courts, p. 2–15]

37. a   The Tax Court hears only tax cases. [Trial Courts, p. 2–15]

38. c   The U.S. Court of Federal Claims appeals are to the Federal Circuit. [Trial Courts, p. 2–15]

39. b   The District Court hears mostly criminal and civil cases. [Trial Courts, p. 2–15]

40. a   A taxpayers does not pay a deficiency before going to the Tax Court. [Trial Courts, p. 2–15]

CHAPTER 3

Tax Determination; Personal and Dependency Exemptions; An Overview of Property Transactions

CHAPTER HIGHLIGHTS

This chapter continues to develop the components of the individual income tax formula. To determine a taxpayer's Federal tax liability, an amount known as taxable income must be computed. Taxable income includes all realized income less deductions specifically provided in the tax law. The standard deduction and personal exemption are available for most taxpayers. An overview of property transactions is helpful at this point, although the subject will be covered in greater detail in later chapters.

KEY TERMS

Adjusted Basis	Exemptions	Kiddie Tax
Adjusted Gross Income	Filing Requirements	Standard Deduction
Capital Gains and Losses	Filing Status	Tax Determination

OUTLINE

I.   **THE TAX FORMULA**
     A.   Components of the Tax Formula. Taxable income is calculated based on the following formula:

Income (broadly conceived)	$xxxx
Less: Exclusions	xxxx
Gross Income	xxxx
Less: Deductions for AGI	xxxx
Adjusted Gross Income (AGI)	$xxxx
Less: the greater of Itemized Deductions, or the Standard Deduction	xxxx
Exemptions	xxxx
Taxable Income	$xxxx

The tax formula can be broken down as follows.
1) Income includes all taxable and nontaxable income of the taxpayer.
2) Exclusions are items of income that Congress has chosen to exclude from the tax base due to various social, economic, equity, and other considerations.
3) Gross income is defined in the Code as "all income from whatever source derived," but does not include unrealized gains.
4) Deductions for adjusted gross income include ordinary and necessary expenses incurred in a trade or business, alimony paid, and deductible IRA contributions, among others.
5) Adjusted gross income (AGI) is an important subtotal that serves as a basis for calculating limitations on certain itemized deductions.
6) Itemized deductions are expenses, personal in nature, for which Congress has specifically allowed a deduction. Taxpayers are allowed to use a standard deduction in lieu of itemizing deductions. The base standard deduction amounts are shown below.

Filing Status	2001	2002
Single	$4,550	$4,700
Married, filing jointly	$7,600	$7,850
Surviving spouse	$7,600	$7,850
Head of Household	$6,650	$6,900
Married, filing separately	$3,800	$3,925

For 2002, blind and aged (65 years old) taxpayers are given additional standard deduction amounts of either $1,150 or $900, depending on their filing status.
     B.   Individuals Not Eligible for the Standard Deduction. Certain taxpayers are not allowed to use the standard deduction. These taxpayers are:
     1) a married taxpayer filing a separate return when either spouse itemizes deductions;
     2) a nonresident alien; and
     3) an individual with a short tax year, resulting from a change in the annual accounting period
     C.   Special Limitations for Individuals Who Can be Claimed as Dependents. The calculation of taxable income for an individual who can be claimed as a dependent is subject to special provisions. Dependents cannot claim a personal exemption for themselves on their own tax returns. Also, a

dependent's standard deduction is limited to the greater of $750 (for 2002) or the individual's earned income for the year plus $250. However, if the individual's standard deduction based on earned income exceeds the normal standard deduction amount, then the standard deduction is limited to the normal amount shown in the text.

II. **PERSONAL AND DEPENDENCY EXEMPTIONS**

A. Personal Exemptions. The law provides for a personal exemption for the taxpayer and an additional exemption for the spouse if a joint return is filed. The determination of marital status is made at the end of the taxable year. If spouses enter a legal separation agreement before the end of the taxable year, they are considered unmarried at the end of the taxable year. For 2002, the exemption amount is $3,000.

B. Dependency Exemptions. For an individual to qualify as a dependent, five tests must be met. These tests are:

1) support
2) relationship or member of the household
3) gross income
4) joint return
5) citizenship or residency

For the *support test* to be met, over one-half of the dependent's "support" must be furnished by the taxpayer. The term "support" generally includes expenditures for food, shelter, clothing, medical care, and education.

The *relationship* test requires that the dependent be a relative as specified in the Code or an individual who has a principal place of residence in the taxpayer's household for the entire year.

The dependent's *gross income* must be less than $3,000 (the 2002 exemption amount) unless the dependent is the taxpayer's child under the age of 19, or the taxpayer's child who is a full-time student under the age of 24.

If the dependent is married, the supporting taxpayer is not permitted a dependency exemption if the person being supported files a *joint return* with his or her spouse, unless neither the dependent nor the dependent's spouse is required to file a return.

A dependent must be a *U.S. citizen* or a resident of the U.S. or a country that is contiguous to the U.S.

Multiple Support Agreements. Under a multiple support agreement, one member of a group of taxpayers who together furnish over one-half of the support of a dependent can claim a dependency exemption even when no one person provides more than 50 percent of the support. Any person who contributed more than 10 percent of the support is entitled to claim the exemption if each person in the group who contributed more than 10 percent files a written consent.

Divorced Parents. For divorced parents, the Code has established rules to help settle disputes as to who is eligible to claim the children as dependents. For divorce decrees after 1984, the parent with custody is allowed to claim the exemption except where the parents agree in writing that the noncustodial parent can claim the exemption (providing the other conditions for dependency are met).

Exemptions Phase-out. The personal and dependency exemptions are phased out when adjusted gross income reaches a certain level. The exemptions are phased out at the rate of 2 percent for each $2,500 ($1,250 for married filing separately), or fraction thereof, of adjusted gross income above the threshold amount. The threshold amount varies based on the taxpayer's filing status. The 2002 amounts are as follows:

Filing Status	Threshold
Married-joint/Surviving Spouse	$206,000
Head of Household	$171,650
Single	$137,300
Married-separate	$103,000

Child Tax Credit. In addition to a dependency exemption, a child of a taxpayer may be allowed tax credit. For 2002, the credit is $600 for each child under the age of 17. The credit is phased out as family income increases from $110,000 to $122,000. Taxpayers filing joint returns lose $50 credit for every $1,000, or portion thereof, of AGI over $110,000 (over $75,000 for other taxpayers).

III.   **TAX DETERMINATION**
   A   Tax Table Method. Most taxpayers compute their tax using a Tax Table. Taxpayers who cannot use the tax tables include estates and trusts, individuals filing a short period return, and individuals with taxable income larger than the maximum amounts in the tables.
   B.   Tax Rate Schedules. All other taxpayers use the Tax Rate Schedules (X, Y, & Z). For 2002, a taxpayer's income may be subject to tax at rates of 10 percent, 15 percent, 27 percent, 30 percent, 35 percent, and 38.6 percent.
   C.   Computation of Net Taxes Payable or Refund Due. The pay-as-you-go feature of the Federal income tax system requires payments of all or part of a taxpayer's tax liability during the year. These prepayments (along with certain credits discussed in Chapter 13) are applied against the tax from the Tax Table or Tax Rate Schedule to determine if the taxpayer will get a refund or pay additional tax.
   D.   Unearned Income of Children Under Age 14 Taxed at Parents' Rate. The "unearned income" of minor children is taxed at their parent's marginal rate. The provision applies to any child if the child:
   1)   has not reached age 14 by the close of the tax year,
   2)   has at least one living parent, and
   3)   has net unearned income for the tax year.

   In 2002, net unearned income is unearned income less $750 and less the greater of a $750 standard deduction or the amount of allowable itemized deductions directly connected with the production of the unearned income.

   For a child under age 14, the parents may elect to report the child's unearned income on the parent's tax return if the following conditions are met:
   1)   gross income is from dividends and interest only
   2)   gross income is over $700 and less than $7,000
   3)   no estimated tax has been paid by the child
   4)   there is no backup withholding on the child

IV.   **FILING CONSIDERATIONS**
   A.   Filing Requirements. An individual taxpayer must file a tax return if certain minimum amounts of gross income have been received (see text for the current dollar amounts).

   A self-employed individual with net earnings from self-employment of $400 or more must file a tax return whatever the dollar amount of gross income.

   Special filing requirements apply to individuals who can be claimed as dependents on another taxpayer's return. See table in text.

   Individual taxpayers file either a Form 1040 (long form), Form 1040A (short form), or 1040EZ (certain single taxpayers).

B. Filing Status. There are five different statuses under which a taxpayer can file. These are single, married filing jointly, married filing separately, head of household, and qualifying widow(er). The tax liability will vary with the filing status. The filing statuses are:

Single (Schedule X). Taxpayers, who are unmarried on December 31, are single unless they qualify as head of household.

Married (Schedule Y–1 or Y–2). Taxpayers who are married on December 31, are married and must use married filing jointly or married filing separately tax rates.

Head of Household (Schedule Z). Taxpayers may file as head of household if the following conditions are met:
1) they are unmarried on December 31,
2) they provide over one-half the cost of a household, and
3) they have a dependent relative as defined in the Code living in the household (certain unmarried relatives such as a child need not qualify as a dependent and a dependent parent of the taxpayer need not live in the taxpayer's home).

Surviving Spouse (Schedule Y). A taxpayer who maintains a household for a dependent child may file as a surviving spouse (joint return rates apply) for the two years immediately following the death of one spouse.

V. **GAINS AND LOSSES FROM PROPERTY TRANSACTIONS—IN GENERAL**
   A. The sale or other disposition of property may result in gain or loss. Realized gain or loss is the *amount realized less the adjusted basis of the property*. In general, the adjusted basis is the cost of the property plus capital additions, less depreciation (if any). The calculation is as follows:

Amount realized from sale	$xxxxx
Adjusted basis	−xxxxx
Realized gain or loss	$xxxxx

   B. All realized gains are recognized for tax purposes unless some provision of the tax law provides otherwise. Realized losses may or may not be recognized as a deduction for tax purposes. Losses on personal use property are generally not recognized.

VI. **GAINS AND LOSSES FROM PROPERTY TRANSACTIONS—CAPITAL GAINS**
   A. Definition of a Capital Asset. The Code defines a capital asset as property owned by the taxpayer other than items such as inventory, accounts receivable, depreciable property, or real estate used in a business.

The principal capital assets held by individuals for personal (nonbusiness) use include automobiles, a personal residence, and assets held for investment (such as stocks, bonds, and land).

For 2002, capital gains are taxed at the following maximum rates:

Short-term Gains (held for 12 months or less)	38.6%
Long-term Gains (held over 12 months)	10.0% or 20.0%

Collectibles (e.g., art, gems, metals, etc.) held over 12 months are taxed at a maximum of 28 percent and certain real estate recapture is taxed at 25 percent. Further, if a taxpayer has long-term gain and his or her regular tax bracket for the year is 15 percent, the 20 percent capital gains rate is reduced to 10 percent (8 percent for assets held over 5 years).

   B. Computation of Net Capital Gains and Losses. Gains and losses from capital assets must be classified as long-term or short-term. After such classification, long-term and short-term gains and losses are netted against one another. If an excess loss results, it is shifted to the category with the highest tax rate.

C. Capital Loss Limitations. Capital losses are first offset against capital gains. For individuals, net capital losses are deductible against other income up to a maximum of $3,000 per year. Any loss more than $3,000 annually carries forward for an unlimited period.

TEST FOR SELF-EVALUATION—CHAPTER 3

True or False

Indicate which of the following statements is true or false by circling the correct answer.

T	F	1.	For divorce decrees after 1984, the mother is always eligible to claim the dependency exemption for any child of divorced parents.
T	F	2.	The standard deduction amount for single taxpayers is larger than that for head of household.
T	F	3.	Itemized deductions are deductible even if they do not exceed the standard deduction amount.
T	F	4.	If married individuals file separate returns and one spouse itemizes, both must itemize.
T	F	5.	For 2002, the personal and dependency exemption amount is $3,000.
T	F	6.	Taxpayers are allowed additional standard deduction amounts for old age and blindness.
T	F	7.	If taxpayers are married at the end of the taxable year, they are considered married for the entire year.
T	F	8.	The additional standard deduction amount for old age or blindness can apply to a dependent of the taxpayer who is not the taxpayer's spouse.
T	F	9.	For the support test to be met, a taxpayer must furnish over one-half of the support of the dependent.
T	F	10.	Amounts received by a taxpayer, but not spent, are not considered in determining whether or not the support test for the dependency exemption has been met.
T	F	11.	An adopted child qualifies as the taxpayer's child for purposes of determining an exemption allowance.
T	F	12.	For 2002, all individuals whose gross income is $3,000 or more cannot be a dependent of another taxpayer.
T	F	13.	If an individual is married and files a joint return with her spouse, she generally cannot qualify as a dependent of another taxpayer.
T	F	14.	A person who lives in Mexico or Canada could qualify as a dependent of a taxpayer.
T	F	15.	To qualify for a multiple support agreement, a group of taxpayers must supply over 50 percent of the support of an individual.
T	F	16.	In order for a taxpayer's dependent parents to qualify him or her for head of household filing status, the parents must live in the taxpayer's home.
T	F	17.	All realized gains are recognized for tax purposes unless some specific provision of the tax law provides otherwise.
T	F	18.	For individual taxpayers, net long-term capital losses carry forward for five years and carry back for three years.
T	F	19.	For 2002, net (long-term) capital gains from the sale of corporate stock by individual taxpayers are taxed at a maximum rate of 20 percent.

| T | F | 20. | Capital assets must be held for over 12 months in order for realized gains to be considered long-term capital gains. |

| T | F | 21. | In 2002, parents may elect to include their 10-year-old child's interest income of $9,250 on their tax return to prevent the child from having to file a tax return. |

| T | F | 22. | For the tax year 2002, the additional standard deduction amount for a blind single taxpayer is $900. |

| T | F | 23. | A nonresident alien taxpayer is allowed a standard deduction of $4,700 (in 2002) if he or she is single. |

| T | F | 24. | In 2002, when filing his or her own tax return, a dependent's basic standard deduction is limited to the greater of $750 or the individual's earned income plus $250 income for the year. |

| T | F | 25. | A father-in-law and a mother-in-law meet the relationship test for claiming a dependency exemption. |

Multiple Choice

Choose the best answer for each of the following questions.

_____ 1. For 2002, the standard deduction amount for a single taxpayer is:

    a. $–0–
    b. $3,925
    c. $4,700
    d. $7,850

_____ 2. Gail, a single taxpayer with no dependents, has adjusted gross income of $20,000. She has itemized deductions of $7,500. What is Gail's taxable income?

    a. $20,000 minus $7,500
    b. $20,000 minus $7,500 minus 1 exemption
    c. $20,000 minus 1 exemption
    d. $20,000 minus $7,500 minus the single standard deduction

_____ 3. Jimmy is 10-years-old and during 2002 has interest earnings of $1,900 from a savings account at a local bank. If Jimmy is claimed as a dependent on his parent's tax return, what is Jimmy's "net unearned income?"

    a. $–0–
    b. $1,900
    c. $1,500
    d. $400

_____ 4. For 2002, the maximum tax rate applicable to capital gains on collectibles of individual taxpayers is:

    a.   38.6%
    b.   33%
    c.   28%
    d.   20%

_____ 5.   A head of household taxpayer uses which of the following tax rate schedules?

        a.   Schedule X
        b.   Schedule Y
        c.   Schedule Z
        d.   Schedule G

_____ 6.   A taxpayer's child who is under 19 or who is a full-time student under 24 does not have to meet which of the following dependency tests?

        a.   Support test
        b.   Relationship test
        c.   Joint return test
        d.   Gross income test

_____ 7.   Walter is a divorced individual. He has a dependent son, age six, who is in the custody of his ex-wife. In addition, Walter supports his dependent mother who does not live in Walter's home. Walter's filing status would be:

        a.   Head of household
        b.   Married filing jointly
        c.   Married filing separately
        d.   Single

_____ 8.   Which of the following is subtracted from the original basis to obtain the adjusted basis of an asset?

        a.   Capital improvements
        b.   The gain realized
        c.   The gain recognized
        d.   Depreciation

_____ 9.   During the current year, Tim sells his truck for $8,000 (adjusted basis of $7,000) and Exxon stock for $20,000 (adjusted basis of $10,000). What is Tim's recognized gain?

        a. $11,000
        b. $10,000
        c. $8,000
        d. $1,000

_____ 10.   Dee is 66-years-old and files as a single taxpayer. For 2002 her standard deduction amount is:

        a. $4,700
        b. $5,800
        c. $5,600
        d. $7,800

_____ 11.   Which of the following is a capital asset?

        a.   Inventory
        b.   Accounts receivable
        c.   Stock held as an investment by an individual taxpayer
        d.   Real estate used in a business

_____ 12. The maximum deduction for capital losses against an individual taxpayer's ordinary income in 2002 is:

    a. $6,000
    b. $5,000
    c. $4,000
    d. $3,000

_____ 13. Which of the following is not a deduction for adjusted gross income?

    a.   Deductible IRA contributions
    b.   Trade or business expenses
    c.   Alimony
    d.   Medical expenses

_____ 14. For individual taxpayers, unused capital losses can be carried forward:

    a.   3 years
    b.   4 years
    c.   5 years
    d.   unlimited

_____ 15. Trudy had a long-term capital gain of $8,000 and a short-term capital loss of $2,000. What is the net amount included in income for Trudy?

    a. $8,000
    b. $6,000
    c. $5,000
    d. $–0–

_____ 16. Mike owns machinery, with an adjusted basis of $50,000, for use in his car-washing business. In addition, Mike owns his personal residence and furniture, which together cost him $100,000. The capital assets amount to:

    a. $–0–
    b. $50,000
    c. $100,000
    d. $150,000

_____ 17. The highest individual tax rate in the United States for 2002 is:

    a.   15.0%
    b.   36.4%
    c.   38.6%
    d.   28.0%

_____ 18. In 2002, for single taxpayers, the 30 percent tax bracket starts at taxable income levels over:

    a. $14,625
    b. $27,950
    c. $67,700
    d. $36,690

_____ 19. Mr. and Mrs. Gold, both age 48, file a joint tax return for 2002. They provide all the support for their son who is 20-years-old and has no income. Their daughter, age 22, is a full-time student at a local college. She had $5,300 of income and provided 60 percent of her own support. How many exemptions should Mr. and Mrs. Gold claim on their 2002 joint tax return?

    a.   2
    b.   3
    c.   4
    d.   5

_____ 20.   Felix, age 20, is a full-time student at Big State University (BSU) and is claimed as a dependent on his parents' tax return. During the summer, Felix earned $1,800 from a part-time job. His only other income was $1,200 interest on his savings account. What is Felix's taxable income?

    a. $1,800
    b. $950
    c. $3,000
    d. $1,200

_____ 21.   Hank, a widower, maintains a home in which he and his unmarried 17-year-old daughter reside. His daughter does not qualify as Hank's dependent. Hank's wife died in 1998. What is Hank's filing status for 2002?

    a.   Head of household
    b.   Surviving spouse
    c.   Married filing jointly
    d.   Single

_____ 22.   For 2002, Kyle's adjusted gross income is $96,000, and his taxable income is $80,000. Kyle is single. Using the tax rate schedules (not the tax tables), what is Kyle's income tax liability before any credits for 2002?

    a. $14,625.00 plus 27%($80,000 minus $27,950)
    b. $14,625.00 plus 27%($80,000 minus $67,700)
    c. $14,625.00 plus 30%($80,000 minus $67,000)
    d. $3,892.50 plus 30%($80,000 minus $67,000)

_____ 23.   For 2002, exemptions are phased out as adjusted gross income exceeds specified amounts. For taxpayers who are married filing jointly, the phase-out starts at?

    a. $206,000
    b. $171,650
    c. $137,300
    d. $103,000

_____ 24.   Fred is retired and lives with his son Andy. Fred's total support is provided as follows:

Son Andy	$4,000
Son Bob	$2,000
Daughter Cathy	$1,000
Social Security	$4,300

Which of Fred's children can file a multiple support agreement and claim Fred as a dependent?

    a.   Andy, Bob, or Cathy
    b.   Andy or Cathy
    c.   Andy or Bob
    d.   Bob or Cathy

_____ 25. Sam is 67-years-old and files a joint tax return with his wife, Zelda, who is 66-years-old. They have the following income and expense items for the current year:

Salary	$20,000
Interest income	$ 5,000
Alimony from ex-wife	$15,000
Gift from Uncle George	$12,000

Using the above information what is Sam and Zelda's *gross income* for the year?

    a. $52,000
    b. $25,000
    c. $35,000
    d. $40,000

_____ 26. Sara had the following items of income and expenses during the current year:

Salary	$32,000
Interest	$ 2,000
STCG	$ 2,000
LTCL	$ 2,500
Itemized deductions	$ 7,300

Sara also paid $625 in state income tax during the year. What is Sara's *adjusted gross income* for the year?

    a. $32,000
    b. $34,000
    c. $33,500
    d. $36,000

_____ 27. Carrie earned a salary of $70,000 in 2002. She sold common stock she had owned for eight months for a $2,000 loss and she sold her jet ski for a loss of $1,800. Carrie also sold a painting for a gain of $8,000. The painting was acquired in 1980. What is Carrie's AGI for 2002?

    a. $76,000
    b. $78,000
    c. $74,200
    d. $70,000

_____ 28. In 2002, Jan is in the 15 percent tax bracket and has the following capital gains for the year:

Red Corporation stock (held 24 months)	$2,000
Blue Corporation stock (held 8 months)	$1,000

What is Jan's tax on these transactions?

    a. $400
    b. $450
    c. $600
    d. $350

_____ 29. In 2002, Bruce is in the 30 percent tax bracket and has the following capital transactions for the year:

Gold Corporation stock (held 7 months)	$2,000
Green Corporation stock (held 10 months)	$6,000
Coin Collection (held 5 years)	$5,000
Land (held 3 years)	$8,000

What is the tax on these transactions?

- a. $1,800
- b. $2,600
- c. $1,880
- d. $2,790

_____ 30. John and Marsha file a joint tax return. They have three dependent children. Able, age 13, and Bea, age 17, live at home. Charles, age 21, is a college student at Football State University (FSU), where he lives in the dormitory. If their AGI is $95,000, what is John and Marsha Child credit for 2002?

- a. $600
- b. $1,200
- c. $1,800
- d. $2,400

_____ 31. Alimony received, for an individual taxpayer would

- a. never be included in gross income
- b. always be included in gross income
- c. sometimes be included (in whole or part) in gross income
- d. be treated as a tax credit

_____ 32. Dividends received, for an individual taxpayer would

- a. never be included in gross income
- b. always be included in gross income
- c. sometimes be included (in whole or part) in gross income
- d. be treated as a tax credit

_____ 33. Child support payments received, for an individual taxpayer would

- a. never be included in gross income
- b. always be included in gross income
- c. sometimes be included (in whole or part) in gross income
- d. be treated as a tax credit

_____ 34. Embezzled funds, by an individual taxpayer would

- a. never be included in gross income
- b. always be included in gross income
- c. sometimes be included (in whole or part) in gross income
- d. be treated as a tax credit

_____ 35. Social Security benefits received, for an individual taxpayer would

- a. never be included in gross income
- b. always be included in gross income
- c. sometimes be included (in whole or part) in gross income
- d. be treated as a tax credit

_____ 36.   Welfare payments received, for an individual taxpayer would

      a.   never be included in gross income
      b.   always be included in gross income
      c.   sometimes be included (in whole or part) in gross income
      d.   be treated as a tax credit

_____ 37.   Pension payments received, for an individual taxpayer would

      a.   never be included in gross income
      b.   always be included in gross income
      c.   sometimes be included (in whole or part) in gross income
      d.   be treated as a tax credit

_____ 38.   Jury duty payments received, for an individual taxpayer would

      a.   never be included in gross income
      b.   always be included in gross income
      c.   sometimes be included (in whole or part) in gross income
      d.   be treated as a tax credit

_____ 39.   Inheritances received, for an individual taxpayer would

      a.   never be included in gross income
      b.   always be included in gross income
      c.   sometimes be included (in whole or part) in gross income
      d.   be treated as a tax credit

_____ 40.   Severance pay received, for an individual taxpayer would

      a.   never be included in gross income
      b.   always be included in gross income
      c.   sometimes be included (in whole or part) in gross income
      d.   be treated as a tax credit

_____ 41.   Employer provided meals and lodging, for an individual taxpayer would

      a.   never be included in gross income
      b.   always be included in gross income
      c.   sometimes be included (in whole or part) in gross income
      d.   be treated as a tax credit

_____ 42.   Military pay received, for an individual taxpayer would

      a.   never be included in gross income
      b.   always be included in gross income
      c.   sometimes be included (in whole or part) in gross income
      d.   be treated as a tax credit

Problems

1.   In each of the independent cases below, indicate the total number of exemptions for the taxpayer, T. Assume any test not mentioned has been met.

    a.   T is age 70, his wife is age 64, and they file a joint return.

    b.   T is age 73, blind, and has adjusted gross income of $10,000. His wife is 66 and they file a joint return.

c. T is age 66 and his wife is age 34. During the year, Mrs. T gave birth to a son.

d. T is unmarried and supports her 10-year-old sister who does not live with her. The sister had income of $3,865 from interest on a savings account.

e. T and his wife, W, have a foster child who lived with them the entire year. They provide over one-half the support of the foster child.

f. T and his wife furnish all the support of F, T's father. F is 80-years-old and blind. T and W file a joint return claiming F as a dependent.

2. Cathy is a secretary, and for 2002 her salary was $38,630. Cathy is single, lives in an apartment and cannot itemize deductions. During the year, her employer withheld $5,300 of Federal income taxes from her salary. River Bank paid Cathy $750 of interest on her savings account. Determine the following amounts for Cathy for 2002.

Adjusted Gross Income	_____
Standard Deduction	_____
Exemption	_____
Taxable Income	_____
Tax Liability	_____
Withholding	_____
Tax Due or (Refund)	_____

SOLUTIONS TO CHAPTER 3 QUESTIONS

True or False

1.   F   Exemptions are generally based on which parent has custody. [Dependency Exemptions, p. 3–11]

2.   T   The standard deduction amount for head of household is more than that for single taxpayers. [Standard Deduction, p. 3–6]

3.   F   If itemized deductions do not exceed the standard deduction, the taxpayer will compute taxable income using the standard deduction amount. [Standard Deduction, p. 3–6]

4.   T   If married individuals file separate returns and one spouse itemizes, then both must itemize. [Individuals Not Eligible for the Standard Deduction, p. 3–9]

5.   T   For 2002, the exemption amount is $3,000. [Personal and Dependency Exemptions, p. 3–10]

6.   T   Taxpayers are allowed additional standard deduction amounts for old age and blindness. [Standard Deduction, p. 3–6]

7.   T   If taxpayers are married at the end of the taxable year, they are married for the year. [Rates for Single Taxpayers, p. 3–26]

8.   F   The additional standard deduction for old age or blindness applies only to the taxpayer's spouse. [Standard Deduction, p. 3–6]

9.   T   To meet the support test, a taxpayer must provide over one-half of the support of the dependent. [Support Test, p. 3–11]

10.   T   Amounts received by a taxpayer, but not spent, are not considered in determining if the support test has been met. [Support Test, p. 3–13]

11.   T   An adopted child qualifies as the taxpayer's child for an exemption allowance. [Relationship or Member-of-the-Household Test, p. 3–14]

12.   F   Certain children of the taxpayer do not have to meet the gross income test. [Gross Income Test, p. 3–14]

13.   T   If an individual is married and files a joint return, generally, cannot qualify as a dependent. [Joint Return Test, p. 3–14]

14.   T   A resident of Mexico or Canada could qualify as a dependent of a taxpayer. [Citizenship or Residency Test, p. 3–14]

15.   T   Under a multiple support agreement, a group of taxpayers must supply over 50 percent of the support of an individual. [Support Test, p. 3–11]

16.   F   Dependent parents do not have to live in the taxpayer's home. [Rates for Heads of Households, p. 3–28]

17.   T   Realized gains are recognized for tax purposes unless some specific provision provides otherwise. [Gains and Losses from Property Transactions—In General, p. 3–27]

18.   F   Net capital losses of individual taxpayers carry forward indefinitely. [Treatment of Net Capital Loss, p. 3–31]

19.   T   For 2002, net (long-term) capital gains from the sale of corporate stock by individual taxpayers are taxed at a maximum rate of 20 percent. [Taxation of Net Capital Gain, p. 3–30]

20.   T   Capital assets must be held for over 12 months in order for gains to be long-term capital gains. [Taxation of Net Capital Gain, p. 3–30]

21.　F　The child's gross income must be less than $7,500. (2002) [Tax Determination, p. 3–20]

22.　F　The amount is $1,100. (2002) [Standard Deduction, p. 3–6]

23.　F　Nonresident aliens are not allowed any standard deduction. [Individuals Not Eligible for the Standard Deduction, p. 3–9]

24.　T　In 2002, when filing a tax return, a dependent's basic standard deduction is limited to the greater of $750 or their earned income plus $250. [Special Limitations for Individuals Who Can be Claimed as Dependents, p. 3–9]

25.　T　A father-in-law and a mother-in-law meet the relationship test for a dependency exemption. [Relationship or Member-of-the-Household Test, p. 3–13]

Multiple Choice

1.　c　The 2002 standard deduction for a single taxpayer is $4,700. [Standard Deduction, p. 3–6]

2.　c　$20,000 minus $7,500 minus 1 exemption [Application of the Tax Formula, p. 3–8]

3.　d　$1,900 – $750 – $750 = $400 (2002) [Tax Determination, p. 3–20]

4.　c　The maximum rate on collectibles capital gain is 28 percent. [Taxation of Net Capital Gain, p. 3–30]

5.　c　Head of Household uses Schedule Z. [Appendix A, p. A–2]

6.　d　A taxpayer's child who is under 19 or who is a full-time student under 24 does not have to meet the gross income test. [Gross Income Test, p. 3–14]

7.　a　The taxpayer would be Head of Household. [Rates for Heads of Household, p. 3–28]

8.　d　Depreciation is subtracted from the original basis to obtain the adjusted basis of an asset. [Gains and Losses from Property Transactions—In General, p. 3–29]

9.　a　The gain is $11,000 ($1,000 on the truck and $10,000 on the stock). [Gains and Losses from Property Transactions—In General, p. 3–29]

10.　d　$4,700 + 1,100 = $5,800 (2002) [Standard Deduction, p. 3–8]

11.　c　Stock held as an investment is a capital asset. [Gains and Losses from Property Transactions—Capital Gains and Losses, p. 3–30)

12.　d　The maximum deduction for capital losses against an individual taxpayer's ordinary income in 2002 is $3,000. [Treatment of Net Capital Loss, p. 3–31]

13.　d　Medical expenses are not a deduction for AGI. [Deductions for Adjusted Gross Income, p. 3–5]

14.　d　There is no time limit on the carryforward period. [Treatment of Net Capital Loss, p. 3–31]

15.　b　$8,000 – $2,000 = $6,000. [Determination of Net Capital Gain, p. 3–31]

16.　c　$100,000, the business machinery is not a capital asset. [Definition of a Capital Asset, p. 3–30]

17.　c　38.6 percent is the highest individual bracket for 2002. [Introduction, p. 3–2]

18.　c　For single taxpayers the 30 percent bracket starts at $67,700 in 2002. [Tax Table Method, p. 3–17]

19.　b　The daughter does not meet the support test. [Support Test, p. 3–11]

20.　b　($1,800 + $1,200) – ($1,800 + $250) (max standard deduction) = $950 [Special Limitations for Individuals Who Can be Claimed as Dependents, p. 3–9]

21.　a　A taxpayer's child does not have to be a dependent to use head of household rates. [Rates for Heads of Household, p. 3–28]

22. c $14,625.00 plus 30% ($80,000 minus $67,700) (2002) [Tax Rate Schedule Method, p. 3–17]

23. a   In 2002, the exemption phase out for married filing jointly starts at $206,000. [Phase-Out of Exemptions, p. 3–15]

24. c   Daughter Cathy does not supply at least 10 percent of the total support, therefore, she is not eligible to claim the exemption. [Dependency Exemptions, p. 3–11]

25. d $20,000 + $5,000 + $15,000 = $40,000 [Gross Income, p. 3–3]

26. c $32,000 + $2,000 − $500 = $33,500 [Gross Income, p. 3–3]

27. a $70,000 + $8,000 − $2,000 = $76,000. The jet ski is not deductible. [Gains and Losses From Property—In General p. 3–29]

28. d $(10\% \times \$2,000) + (15\% \times \$1,000) = \$350$ [Taxation of Net Capital Gain, p. 3–30]

29. c $(20\% \times \$8,000) + (28\% \times (\$2,000 − \$6,000 + \$5,000)) = \$1,880$ [Determination of Net Capital Gain, p. 3–30]

30. a   ($500 × 1) Only Able counts for the child credit, Bea and Charles are too old. [Child Tax Credit, p. 3–16]

31. b   Alimony is included. [Gross Income, p. 3–3]

32. b   Dividends are included. [Gross Income, p. 3–3]

33. a   Child support payments are not included. [Gross Income, p. 3–3]

34. b   Embezzled funds are included. [Gross Income, p. 3–3]

35. c   Social Security benefits are sometimes included. [Gross Income, p. 3–3]

36. a   Welfare payments are not included. [Gross Income, p. 3–3]

37. b   Pensions are included. [Gross Income, p. 3–3]

38. b   Jury duty payments are included. [Gross Income, p. 3–3]

39. a   Inheritances are not included. [Gross Income, p. 3–3]

40. b   Severance pay is included. [Gross Income, p. 3–3]

41. c   Meals and lodging are sometimes included. [Gross Income, p. 3–3]

42. c   Military pay is sometimes not included. [Gross Income, p. 3–3]

Problems

1. a.   2; 2 personal [Personal and Dependency Exemptions, p. 3–10]

    b.   2; 2 personal [Personal and Dependency Exemptions, p. 3–10]

    c.   3; 2 personal, 1 dependency [Personal and Dependency Exemptions, p. 3–10]

    d.   1; 1 personal, sister fails the gross income test [Personal and Dependency Exemptions, p. 3–10]

    e.   3; 2 personal, 1 dependency [Personal and Dependency Exemptions, p. 3–10]

    f.   3; 2 personal, 1 dependency [Personal and Dependency Exemptions, p. 3–10]

2.   AGI: ($38,630 + $750) $39,380
        Standard Deduction: −$ 4,700
        Exemption: −$ 3,000

        Taxable Income: $31,680

        Tax Liability: ($3,892.50 + 27%($31,680 − $27,950)) $ 4,899

        Withholding: −$ 5,300

        Refund: $ 401

        (2002) [Application of the Tax Formula, p. 3–9]

CHAPTER 4

Gross Income:
Concepts and Inclusions

CHAPTER HIGHLIGHTS

The calculation of gross income is the first computation needed in the formula for taxable income. This chapter defines gross income and describes certain sources of gross income. The effect of the cash and accrual methods of accounting on the calculation of gross income is also discussed.

KEY TERMS

Alimony/Child Support	Community Property	Prizes/Awards
Annuities	Gross Income	Social Security Benefits
Cash/Accrual	Group Term Life Insurance	Year of Inclusion

OUTLINE

I. **GROSS INCOME—What Is It?**

   A. Section 61(a) of the tax law defines gross income as "all income from whatever source derived." However, this definition is rather broad so the courts have established the principle that for income to be recognized for tax purposes, it must be realized. Therefore, increases in value (economic income) would not be taxed as income until the property is sold or exchanged.

   B. Although financial accounting and tax accounting measurement concepts are frequently parallel, they have different purposes. The primary goal of financial accounting is to provide useful information to management, shareholders, creditors, and other interested parties, while the goal of tax accounting is the equitable collection of revenue.

   C. Gross income is not limited to cash received. Income can be realized as money, property, or services received by the taxpayer.

   D. Under the "recovery of capital doctrine" the proceeds from the sale or disposition of property are reduced by the basis of the property sold to determine gross income. This is to ensure that income is not taxed until the capital initially invested is recovered.

II. **YEAR OF INCLUSION**

   A. As a rule, taxpayers are required to use a calendar year to report income. However, taxpayers who keep adequate books and records (and meet certain other tests) may use a fiscal year.

   B. The three major methods of accounting used in computing taxable income are the cash method, the accrual method, and the hybrid method.

   The cash method of accounting is used by most individuals and many small businesses. Under the cash method, property or services are included in the taxpayer's gross income in the "year of actual or constructive receipt."

   The accrual method of accounting is used by many corporations. Under this method, income is recognized "in the year it is earned," no matter when it is collected. Income is considered earned when (1) all events have occurred which fix the right to receive such income and (2) the amount of the income can be determined with reasonable accuracy.

   The hybrid method is a combination of cash and accrual accounting concepts.

   C. Exceptions applicable to the cash method include the following:

   1) The "doctrine of constructive receipt" limits an individual's ability to shift income arbitrarily to a later taxable year. If a taxpayer is entitled to receive income and the income is made available to him, it must be included in gross income.

   2) Income set apart or made available is not constructively received if it is subject to substantial restrictions. For example, the increase in cash surrender value on ordinary life insurance is not taxed as the policy increases in value.

   3) When a lender makes a loan with an original issue discount, the accrued interest must be reported each year, despite the taxpayer's accounting method. Interest on long-term bonds issued at a discount must also be accrued.

   4) Interest on U.S. Series E or EE Savings Bonds is usually deferred until the bonds mature; however, a taxpayer may make an election to use the accrual method which requires that the annual increase in the bond's redemption value be included in gross income. By making the accrual election, the taxpayer prevents the bunching of income in a future year.

   5) No income is realized when money is borrowed. Receipt of funds under an obligation to repay is not a taxable event.

   D. Exceptions to the accrual method include the following:

   1) "Prepaid income" is generally taxed in the year of receipt. Many court cases have been brought against the IRS by taxpayers arguing that the proper matching of revenue and expenses requires that income be recognized only when it is earned (e.g., the accrual method). The IRS has modified its position in several areas.

2)   Generally, a taxpayer can elect to defer "advance payments for goods" if the taxpayer's method of accounting for the sale is the same for tax and financial reporting purposes.

3)   A taxpayer can defer "advance payments for services" to be performed by the end of the tax year following the year of receipt. Such "services" do not include prepaid interest, amounts received under guarantee or warranty contracts, or prepaid rent.

III.   INCOME SOURCES

A.   Income from personal services must be included in the gross income of the person who "performs the services." A mere assignment of income will not shift the tax liability.

B.   Income from property (e.g., interest, dividends, rent) must be included in the gross income of the "owner of the property."

When property is sold with accrued interest, part of the selling price is treated as interest and taxed to the seller in the year of sale. Under IRS rules, interest accrues daily.

Dividends, unlike interest, do not accrue on a daily basis. Dividends are normally taxed to the taxpayer who is entitled to receive them (i.e., the holder of the stock on the corporation's record date).

C.   Income received by a taxpayer's agent is considered received by the taxpayer, thus a cash basis taxpayer must recognize income at the time it is received by his or her agent.

D.   A partner in a partnership or a shareholder in an S Corporation must "include his or her share of income" from these entities on his or her individual tax return. The income must be included in the partner's or shareholder's return for the year with or within which the entity's tax year ends. Beneficiaries of estates and trusts are generally taxed on income earned by the estate or trust that is actually distributed or required to be distributed to them. Any excess income is taxed to the estate or trust.

E.   In nine states—Louisiana, Texas, New Mexico, Arizona, California, Washington, Idaho, Nevada, and Wisconsin—marital rights to the ownership of property are controlled by community property laws. Income from personal services (e.g., salaries and wages) is treated as earned equally by both spouses. Income from community property is taxable as community income, one-half to each spouse. Income from separate property is taxable to the person who owns the property, except in Texas, Louisiana, Wisconsin, and Idaho, where the income from separate property is community income.

F.   Under Section 66, spouses living apart in community property states will be taxed only on their separate earnings from personal services if certain conditions occur. These conditions are:
1)   The individuals live apart for the entire year.
2)   They do not file a joint return with each other.
3)   No portion of the income is transferred between the individuals.

IV.   ITEMS SPECIFICALLY INCLUDED IN GROSS INCOME

A.   For divorces after 1984, alimony is cash payments meeting the following three conditions:
1)   The decree does not specify the cash payments are not alimony.
2)   The payor and payee are not members of the same household.
3)   There is no liability for payments after the death of the payee.

If the payment meets the definition of alimony, the amount is deductible by the payor and included in the gross income of the payee.

If the divorce decree is executed after 1986, special recapture rules apply if the payments exceed $15,000 in the first or second year. In the third year, the payor must include the excess alimony payments for the first and second years in gross income and the payee is allowed a deduction for the excess alimony payments. The recaptured amount is computed as follows:

$$R = D + E$$

$$D = B - (C + \$15{,}000)$$

$$E = A - [(B - D + C)/2 + \$15{,}000]$$

Where,

R = amount of recapture in Year 3.

D = recapture from Year 2.

E = recapture from Year 1.

A, B, C are the alimony payments in Years 1, 2, and 3, respectively.

For post-1984 decrees, if cash payments would be reduced by a "contingency related to a child," then the amount of the potential reduction in the payments is considered child support. The amount of the payment, which is considered child support under this provision, is not deductible by the payor or income to the payee.

Under post-1984 rules, transfers of appreciated property to a former spouse under a divorce decree are not taxable events.

B. Imputed Interest on Below-Market Loans. If a taxpayer makes a "below-market interest rate" loan to a related party, there can be imputed interest. The imputed interest is income to the lender and deductible to the borrower. The rate of imputed interest is the rate the Federal government pays on new borrowing, compounded semiannually. This rate is adjusted monthly and published by the IRS. These rules apply to the following types of loans:
1) Gift loans
2) Compensation-related loans
3) Corporation-shareholder loans
4) Tax avoidance loans

The below-market rules do not normally apply to gift loans between individuals where the total loans between the related parties are $10,000 or less, unless income producing property is purchased. On loans between individuals of $100,000 or less, the imputed interest cannot be greater than the net investment income earned by the borrower in that year, unless there is evidence of tax avoidance. Interest is not imputed on loans of $100,000 or less if the borrower's net investment income is $1,000 or less, unless there is evidence of tax avoidance.

C. Income From Annuities. Amounts received, as annuity payments are included in gross income subject to the following rules:

For collections on or after the annuity starting date, the recipient may exclude part of the payment that represents a recovery of his or her investment. The formula is as follows:

$$\text{Percent Excluded} = \frac{\text{Investment in the contract}}{\text{Total expected return}}$$

The exclusion ratio applies until the annuitant has recovered his or her investment in the contract. Once the investment is recovered, all subsequent payments are fully taxable. If the annuitant dies before recovering his or her investment, the unrecovered cost is deductible in the year the payments cease.

D. Prizes and Awards. Under Section 74, the fair market value of "prizes and awards" (other than qualified scholarships) is included in gross income. If the award is for recognition of religious, charitable, scientific, educational, artistic, literary, or civic achievement, the recipient transfers the prize to a qualified governmental unit or nonprofit organization, the recipient is selected with no action on his or her part, and if no substantial future services are required, then the award may be excluded from gross income. Certain employee achievement awards can be excluded from gross income. The maximum amount of such an employee award is $400 ($1,600 for qualified plan awards).

E. Group Term Life Insurance. There is an exclusion for premiums on up to $50,000 of group term life insurance provided to employees. An amount, based on a Uniform Premium table supplied by the Internal Revenue Service, must be included in the employee's gross income for each $1,000 of coverage more than $50,000. If the group term insurance plan discriminates in favor of certain key employees, the Section 79 exclusion does not apply and special rules apply in determining the amount to be included in the employee's gross income.

F. Unemployment Compensation. All unemployment compensation benefits are included in gross income.

G. Social Security Benefits. Part of a taxpayer's Social Security benefits may be included in gross income. The amount included is the lesser of the amount calculated under two different formulas.

The first set of base amounts is as follows:
1) $32,000 for married taxpayers filing jointly
2) $0 for married taxpayers who did not live apart for the entire year but filed separate returns
3) $25,000 for all other taxpayers

The second set of base amounts is as follows:
1) $44,000 for married taxpayers filing jointly
2) $0 for married taxpayers who did not live apart for the entire year but filed separate returns
3) $34,000 for all other taxpayers

If modified adjusted gross income (MAGI) plus one-half of Social Security benefits exceeds the first set of base amounts, but not the second set, the taxable amount of Social Security benefits is the lesser of the following:

$$.50(\text{Social Security benefits})$$
$$.50[\text{MAGI} + .50(\text{Social Security benefits}) - \text{base amount}]$$

If MAGI plus one-half of Social Security benefits exceeds the second set of base amounts, the taxable amount of Social Security benefits is the lesser of the following:

$$.85(\text{Social Security benefits}), \text{ or}$$
Sum of:

$$.85[\text{MAGI} + .50(\text{Social Security benefits}) - \text{base amount}]$$
lesser of:

Amount included by the first formula, or
$4,500 ($6,000 for married filing jointly)

TEST FOR SELF-EVALUATION—CHAPTER 4

True or False

Indicate which of the following statements is true or false by circling the correct answer.

T   F   1. The general definition of gross income is found in Section 61(a) of the Internal Revenue Code.

T   F   2. The term "income" is used in the Code but is not separately defined.

T   F   3. Economic income is the sum of the taxpayer's change in net worth and the actual consumption of goods and services during the tax period.

T   F   4. An accountant's concept of income is based on the recognition principle.

T   F   5. For any individual taxpayer, financial income and taxable income are always the same amount.

T   F   6. For post-1984 divorce decrees, payments must be made in cash to qualify as deductible alimony.

T   F   7. Under the *recovery of capital doctrine*, sellers can reduce their gross receipts (selling price) by the adjusted basis of the property sold.

T   F   8. Corporate taxpayers must always use the cash method of accounting.

T   F   9. A cash basis taxpayer defers income recognition on an account receivable until it is collected.

T   F   10. The benefits of the group term life insurance premium exclusion are not available to proprietors and partners.

T   F   11. The interest on U.S. "Series EE" savings bonds must always be reported using the cash method of accounting.

T   F   12. Prepaid income received is not always income in the year payment is received.

T   F   13. Taxable income from personal services can be shifted to other taxpayers such as family members.

T   F   14. In all community property states (Texas, California, etc.), income derived from separate property is separate income.

T   F   15. On the sale of stock, dividends are generally taxed to the person who is entitled to receive the dividends.

T   F   16. Income from property must be included in the gross income of the owner of the property.

T   F   17. If a taxpayer is entitled to receive income, which is made available to him, he cannot "turn his back" on it and refuse the income.

T   F   18. Most individual taxpayers use the cash method of accounting.

T   F   19. The recovery of capital doctrine means that the amount received from a sale of property is reduced by the adjusted basis in arriving at the taxable gain on the property sold.

T   F   20. There is a maximum amount of Social Security benefits that must be included in the taxable income of an individual taxpayer.

T   F   21.   The premiums on the first $50,000 worth of nondiscriminatory group term life insurance provided to an employee can generally be excluded from gross income.

T   F   22.   If the interest charged on a loan is less than the Federal rate, the imputed interest is the difference between the amount that would have been charged at the Federal rate and the amount actually charged.

T   F   23.   If a group term life insurance plan discriminates in favor of key employees, the key employees must include in gross income the lesser of the actual premiums paid by the employer or the amount calculated from the Uniform Premiums table.

T   F   24.   A cash basis taxpayer must recognize income when a check is received, even if the check is received after banking hours.

T   F   25.   A taxpayer includes funds received from an agent (such as an auctioneer) in the year the funds are received from the agent, not in the year the agent collected the funds.

Multiple Choice

Choose the best answer for each of the following questions.

_____ 1.   A bank deposits $500 in interest in a savings account on December 31, Year 1. The depositor withdraws $2,000 on January 3, Year 2. How much income must be recognized for Year 1?

   a. $2,000
   b. $500
   c. $1,500
   d. $2,500

_____ 2.   On December 1 of the current year, Drew receives $9,000 for three months rent (December, January, and February) of an office building. Drew is an accrual basis taxpayer. How much income must be recognized in the current year?

   a. $–0–
   b. $3,000
   c. $6,000
   d. $9,000

_____ 3.   Chris is a 30-year-old single taxpayer. He has one dependent child living with him. During the current year, Chris received all of the following items:

Salary	$45,000
Child support	$ 6,000
Alimony	$ 9,000
Unemployment compensation	$ 4,000
Interest on U.S. Treasury bonds	$ 400
Lotto Winnings (Net)	$ 600

Of the above amounts, how much must Chris include in his gross income for the current year?

   a. $45,000
   b. $39,000
   c. $34,600
   d. $38,000

_____ 4.   Dan and his wife live in Texas. During the year, Dan earned a salary of $50,000 and his wife earned a salary of $40,000. If they file separate income tax returns, Dan would report how much income?

   a. $–0–
   b. $50,000
   c. $45,000
   d. $40,000

_____ 5.   Which of the following is not a community property state?

   a.   Texas
   b.   Georgia
   c.   California
   d.   Arizona
   e.   Washington

_____ 6.   Dave, a calendar year taxpayer, owns 30 percent of Wirra Corporation, an S Corporation. Wirra Corporation had taxable income of $100,000. During the year the corporation made distributions of $20,000. Dave's dividend income from other corporations was $25,000. What is Dave's taxable income from the corporations?

   a. $25,000
   b. $45,000
   c. $55,000
   d. $125,000

_____ 7.   Jill, a single taxpayer, received $10,000 in Social Security benefits. Her adjusted gross income was $31,000 and she had no tax-free interest income. How much of the Social Security benefits should Jill include in her income?

   a. $–0–
   b. $5,000
   c. $10,000
   d. $7,500

_____ 8.   Jill, a single taxpayer, received $10,000 in Social Security benefits. Her adjusted gross income was $70,000 and she had no tax-free interest income. How much of the Social Security benefits should Jill include in her income?

   a. $–0–
   b. $5,000
   c. $8,500
   d. $10,000

_____ 9.   Judy has savings bonds (Series EE), which increased in redemption value by $600 during the current year. In addition, Judy has $1,000 in interest on her savings account at Big Town Savings & Loan. If Judy has not made any elections and she is a cash basis taxpayer, she should report taxable interest income of:

   a. $–0–
   b. $600
   c. $1,000
   d. $1,600

_____ 10. A lawyer drafts a will for a dentist in exchange for dental work. The dentist would normally have charged $400 for this work. Since the attorney normally charges $300 for drafting a will, he paid the dentist $100 in cash. Based on this transaction, how much should the dentist include in his gross income?

   a. $–0–
   b. $100
   c. $300
   d. $400

_____ 11.   Erin, a cash basis calendar year taxpayer, received the following from her employer during the current year:

Salary	$50,000
Bonus	$ 6,000
Travel advance ($1,800 of which was used for business travel)	$ 2,000
Rental value of company car used for vacation (Erin paid for the gasoline)	$ 700

What is Erin's gross income from the above Items?

   a. $56,000
   b. $56,700
   c. $56,200
   d. $56,900

_____ 12.   Lisa owned stock in Nulabor Corporation, which originally cost $100,000. She sold the stock for $75,000 plus 10 percent of Nulabor's income in the year of sale plus 10% of five additional years of income. The value of the future income cannot be determined in the year of sale. In the first year, Lisa received payments of $84,000 from the purchaser. What is Lisa's taxable gain in the first year?

   a. $–0–
   b. $9,000
   c. $25,000
   d. $16,000

_____ 13.   In November Year 1, John entered into a contract to deliver goods to a customer in March Year 2 for $12,000. John uses the *accrual method* of accounting for both financial and tax purposes. He collected $8,000 in Year 1 and the balance in Year 2. John did not have the goods in stock on December 31, Year 1. The cost of the goods to him is $9,000. How much net income must John report in Year 1?

   a. $–0–
   b. $1,000
   c. $5,000
   d. $8,000

_____ 14.   Sky Corporation sells service contracts for 12 and 24 month periods. In September Year 1, the company sold $8,000 of the 12-month contracts and $10,000 of the 24-month contracts. If the company services each customer each month (October, November, and December Year 1), how much income should be reported for Year 1 if Sky Corporation follows Rev.Proc. 71–21?

   a. $2,000
   b. $6,000
   c. $8,000
   d. $12,000

_____ 15.   Vicki owns 25 percent of K&A Partnership. The partnership had net income of $200,000. During the year, Vicki withdrew $35,000 from the partnership. What is Vicki's reported share of net income from K&A?

a. $–0–
b. $35,000
c. $50,000
d. $200,000

_____ 16.   On July 15, the Board of Directors of Goolwa Corporation declared a $1 per share dividend payable July 30 to shareholders of record on July 25. As of July 15, Norman owned 1,000 shares. On July 16, he sold 700 shares to Sam for the fair market value, and he gave 300 shares to his son. How much dividend income must Norman report?

a. $–0–
b. $300
c. $700
d. $1,000

_____ 17.   Dave, an employee of Purple, Inc., is covered by a group term life insurance policy that has a face amount of $60,000. The company pays all the policy premiums which amount to $500 per year. According to Reg. Section 1.79–3, the cost of a policy for a man Dave's age is 43 cents per $1,000 per month. How much income should Dave report on his tax return?

a. $–0–
b. $51.60
c. $500.00
d. $309.60

_____ 18.   Robert is divorced in the current year. He makes cash payments to his ex-wife of $1,000 per month. When their son, who is in the wife's custody, turns 18-years-old, the payments are reduced to $600 per month. How much can Robert deduct as alimony each month?

a. $–0–
b. $400
c. $600
d. $1,000

_____ 19.   Nicky goes on the T.V. game show, Wheel-of-a-Deal. She wins cash of $15,000 and a new car with a fair market value of $20,000. How much income must Nicky report from these winnings?

a. $–0–
b. $15,000
c. $20,000
d. $35,000

_____ 20.   In the current year Dave receives stock from his employer worth $25,000. The stock cannot be sold by Dave for seven years. Dave estimates that the stock will be worth $60,000 after the seven years. In the current year how much income must Dave recognize?

a. $–0–
b. $25,000
c. $35,000
d. $60,000

_____ 21.   Hank retired last year after investing $100,000 in an annuity, which pays $12,000 per year. Hank had a life expectancy of ten years at the annuity starting date. What is Hank's income for the current year, assuming Hank receives $12,000 during the current year?

a. $–0–
b. $2,000
c. $10,000
d. $12,000

_____ 22.   Larry, a cash basis taxpayer, paid $42,000 for an 18-month certificate-of-deposit with a maturity value of $50,000. The effective interest rate on the certificate was 12 percent. If Larry bought the certificate on June 30 of the current year, how much interest income should he report?

       a. $2,520
       b. $3,000
       c. $5,040
       d. $6,000

_____ 23.   Under a current year's divorce decree, Oliver has to pay his ex-wife alimony. The cash payments are as follows:

Year 1	$32,000
Year 2	$25,000
Year 3	$ –0–

What is Oliver's alimony deduction for Year 1?

       a. $–0–
       b. $32,000
       c. $22,000
       d. $12,000

_____ 24.   Under a current year's divorce decree, Oliver has to pay his ex-wife alimony. The cash payments are as follows:

Year 1	$32,000
Year 2	$25,000
Year 3	$ –0–

What is Oliver's alimony deduction for Year 3?

       a. $–0–
       b. $10,000
       c. $19,500
       d. $9,500

_____ 25.   Under a current year's divorce decree, Vance transfers appreciated property to his ex-wife. The property has a fair market value of $150,000 and an adjusted basis to Vance of $60,000. From the transaction, Vance should report a taxable gain of:

       a. $–0–
       b. $60,000
       c. $90,000
       d. $150,000

_____ 26.   Under a current year's divorce decree, Vance transfers appreciated property to his ex-wife. The property has a fair market value of $150,000 and an adjusted basis to Vance of $60,000. If Vance's wife were to sell the property three years later for $160,000, how much gain should she report?

       a. $–0–
       b. $90,000
       c. $100,000
       d. $10,000

_____ 27.   Assume during the first six months of the current year the Federal imputed interest rate is nine percent and during the second six months, it is ten percent. On January 1, a father gives his son an interest-free loan of $50,000. The son has $5,000 of investment income for the year. For the current year, what is the interest income that the father must recognize, and what amount of interest expense is the son treated as incurring?

     a. $–0–
     b. $4,863
     c. $4,750
     d. $5,000

_____ 28.   Assume during the first six months of the current year the Federal imputed interest rate is nine percent and during the second six months, it is ten percent. On January 1, a father gives his son an interest-free loan of $50,000. The son has $5,000 of investment income for the year. How much of a "gift" has the father made to his son?

     a. $–0–
     b. $4,863
     c. $4,750
     d. $5,000

_____ 29.   Kathy, a cash basis taxpayer, gave away Green, Inc. bonds with a face amount of $10,000 to her son Bill. The bonds have a stated annual interest rate of nine percent. The gift was made on February 10, Year 1 and interest was paid to Bill on December 31, Year 1. How much interest income must Kathy recognize in Year 1?

     a. $–0–
     b. $101
     c. $799
     d. $900

_____ 30.   Mabel owned the following stock on January 1, Year 1:

	Basis	FMV
Red Corp.	$200	$220
Yellow Corp.	$175	$170

During the year, Mabel sold the Red stock for $215 and the Yellow stock for $180. Mabel's income under the *economic* concept of income is:

     a. $–0–
     b. $5
     c. $20
     d. $35

_____ 31.   On June 30, Year 1, Wendy purchased for $7,500 a 30-month, $10,000 certificate of deposit from Shakie Bank & Trust. The yield to maturity on the certificate was 12 percent, interest compounded semiannually. What is Wendy's interest income for the six months ended on December 31, Year 1?

     a. $–0–
     b. $600
     c. $500
     d. $450

_____ 32.   Gold Corporation purchased a group term life insurance plan that covered only management and officers of the company. Mr. Gold received $250,000 of life insurance under this plan. The cost to Gold Corporation for the premiums of Mr. Gold's insurance was $3,100. The Uniform Premium amount for each $1,000 of insurance for a man Gold's age is $9 annually. Mr. Gold must include in gross income:

   a. $–0–
   b. $2,250
   c. $2,575
   d. $3,100

_____ 33.   Peg owns a life insurance policy with a face amount of $100,000. On January 1, Year 1, the policy had a cash surrender value of $15,000 and on December 31, Year 1 the cash surrender value was $16,500. During the year, Peg paid premiums on the policy of $2,500. What amount of income must Peg report from this insurance policy for Year 1?

   a. $–0–
   b. $1,000
   c. $1,500
   d. $2,500

_____ 34.   Devona, age 54, purchased and annuity for $100,000 under which she is to receive $600 per month for life. Her life expectancy is 29.5 years at the annuity starting date. Thus, her expected return is $600 × 12 × 29.5 = $212,400 and the annual exclusion amount is $3,390 [($100,000/$212,400 × $7,200)]. If Devona dies after four years, how much is the deduction (if any) from the annuity on her final return?

   a. $–0–
   b. $13,560
   c. $86,440
   d. $212,400

_____ 35.   Bill, age 57, receives an annuity distribution of $600 per month for life from a qualified retirement plan. His investment in the contract is $139,500. How much of each payment is excluded from Bill's income using the Simplified Method of Annuity Distributions from Qualified Plans?

   a. $–0–
   b. $150
   c. $450
   d. $600

SOLUTIONS TO CHAPTER 4 QUESTIONS

True or False

1. T The definition of gross income is found in Section 61. [Definition, p. 4–3]

2. T "Income" is not separately defined. [Definition, p. 4–3]

3. T Economic income is the taxpayer's change in net worth and the actual consumption of goods and services. [Economic and Accounting Concepts, p. 4–3]

4. F The accountant's concept is based on the realization principle. [Economic and Accounting Concepts, p. 4–3]

5. F Financial income concepts may differ from those used in determining taxable income. [Comparison of the Accounting and Tax Concept of Income, p. 4–5]

6. T Payments must be made in cash to qualify as deductible alimony after 1984. [Post-1984 Agreements and Decrees, p. 4–21]

7. T Sellers, under the *recovery of capital doctrine*, reduce their gross receipts by the basis of the property sold. [Recovery of Capital Doctrine, p. 4–6]

8. F Most corporations use the accrual method. [Accounting Methods, p. 4–8]

9. T Cash basis taxpayers defer income recognition on accounts receivable until collected. [Accounting Methods, p. 4–8]

10. T The group term life insurance premium exclusion is not available to proprietors and partners. [Group Term Life Insurance, p. 4–33]

11. F Taxpayers may elect the accrual method. [Series E and Series EE Bonds, p. 4–12]

12. T In some cases an accrual basis taxpayer may be able to defer recognition of the income under Rev. Proc. 71–21. [Deferral of Advance Payments for Goods, p. 4–14]

13. F The assignment of income does not shift the tax liability. [Personal Services, p. 4–14]

14. F In Texas, Louisiana, Wisconsin, and Idaho income derived from separate property is community income. [Income in Community Property States, p. 4–18]

15. T Dividends are generally taxed to the person entitled to receive the dividends. [Dividends, p. 4–16]

16. T Income from property must be included in the income of the owner. [Income from Property, p. 4–15]

17. T If a taxpayer is entitled to income, he cannot "turn his back" on it and refuse the income. [Constructive Receipt, p. 4–10]

18. T Most individual taxpayers use the cash method. [Accounting Methods, p. 4–8]

19. T The recovery of capital doctrine means that the amount received from a sale is reduced by the adjusted basis in arriving at the taxable gain. [Recovery of Capital Doctrine, p. 4–6]

20. T There is a maximum amount of Social Security benefits that must be included in taxable income. See text for the percentage. [Social Security Benefits, p. 4–34]

21. T The premiums on the first $50,000 worth of group term life insurance provided to an employee is excluded from gross income. [Group Term Life Insurance, p. 4–33]

22. T If the interest on a loan is less than the Federal rate, the imputed interest is the difference between the Federal rate and the amount actually charged. [Imputed Interest on Below-Market Loans, p. 4–24]

23. F   The *greater* of the actual premiums paid by the employer or the amount calculated from the Uniform Premiums table must be included in the employee's gross income. [Group Term Life Insurance, p. 4–33]

24. T   A cash basis taxpayer must recognize income when a check is received. [Cash Receipts Method, p. 4–8]

25. F   It is taxable in the year collected by the agent. [Income received by an Agent, p. 4–17]

Multiple Choice

1. b   Only the interest is income. [Cash Receipt Method, p. 4–8]

2. d   The entire $9,000 is taxable when received. [Deferral of Advanced Payments for Services, p. 4–14]

3. b $25,000 + $9,000 + $4,000 + $400 + $600 = $39,000 [Multiple Sections throughout Chapter]

4. c   50% ($50,000 + $40,000) = $45,000. [Income in Community Property States, p. 4–18]

5. b   Georgia is not a community property state. [Income in Community Property States, p. 4–18]

6. c   30% ($100,000) + $25,000 = $55,000. [Income From Partnerships, S Corporations, Trusts, and Estates, p. 4–17]

7. b $5,000 = Lesser of: (1) 50% × $10,000 = $5,000, or (2) 50% × [$31,000 + 50%($10,000) − $25,000] = $5,500. [Social Security Benefits, p. 4–35]

8. c $8,500 = Lesser of: (1) 85%($10,000) = $8,500, or (2) Sum of: 85% [$70,000 + 50%($10,000) − $34,000] = $34,850, plus lesser of: (a) $5,000, amount from first formula (see question No. 7), or (b) $4,500 [Social Security Benefits, p. 4–34]

9. c   The Series Bond interest is not taxable. [Series E and Series EE Bonds, p. 4–12]

10. d $300 + 100 = $400. [Form of Receipt, p. 4–6]

11. d $50,000 + $6,000 + $200 + $700 = $56,900 [Multiple Sections throughout Chapter]

12. a   The $84,000 is a recovery of capital. [Recovery of Capital Doctrine, p. 4–6]

13. a   The income is reported in Year 2. [Deferral of Advance Payments for Goods, p. 4–14]

14. d   3/12 ($8,000) + $10,000 = $12,000. [Deferral of Advance Payments for Services, p. 4–14]

15. c   25% ($200,000) = $50,000. [Income from partnerships, S Corporations, Trusts, and Estates, p. 4–17]

16. b   Norman is taxed on the dividends related to 300 shares because the gift was made after the declaration date. He is not taxed on the shares sold. [Dividends, p. 4–16]

17. b $.43 × [($60,000 − 50,000)/ $1,000] × 12 months = $51.60. [Group Term Life Insurance, p. 4–33]

18. c   The contingent amount is "disguised child support." [Child Support, p. 4–23]

19. d   All the winnings are income. [Prizes and Awards, p. 4–32]

20. a   The stock is restricted property [Exceptions Applicable to Cash Basis Taxpayers, p. 4–10]

21. b $100,000/($12,000 × 10 years) × $12,000 = $10,000 excluded

         $12,000 − 10,000 = $2,000 included. [Income From Annuities, p. 4–28]

22. a   (.12 × $42,000) × 1/2 year = $2,520. [Exceptions Applicable to Cash Basis Taxpayers, p. 4–10]

23. b   First year alimony is deductible. [Post-1984 Agreements and Decrees, p. 4–21]

24. c D = $25,000 − ($0 + 15,000) = $10,000,

E = $32,000 − [($25,000 − 10,000 + 0)/2 + $15,000] = $9,500,

R = $10,000 + 9,500 = $19,500. [Front-Loading, p. 4–22]

25. a Transfers subject to a divorce decree are not taxable. [Alimony and Separate Maintenance Payments, p. 4–20]

26. c $160,000 − $60,000 = $100,000. [Alimony and Separate Maintenance Payments, p. 4–20]

27. b $4,863 = $2,250 (9% × $50,000 × 1/2 year for January 1 to June 30) + $2,613 (10% × $52,250 × 1/2 year for July 1 to Dec. 31) [Imputed Interest on Below-Market Loans, p. 4–24]

28. b The imputed interest is a gift for tax purposes. [Imputed Interest on Below-Market Loans, p. 4–24]

29. b 9% × $10,000 × (41 days/365 days) = $101. [Income from Property, p. 4–15]

30. b Economic income is the change in the FMV of the taxpayer's assets. ($215 − $220) + ($180 − $170) = $5 [Economic and Accounting Concepts, p. 4–3]

31. d Wendy must use the current interest method, $7,500 × .12 × (6/12) = $450. [Original Issue Discount, p. 4–12]

32. d The plan is discriminatory, therefore the greater of the actual premiums paid or the Uniform Premium amount is included in income. [Group Term Life Insurance, p. 4–33]

33. a The increase in value is not taxed because of "substantial restrictions" on the life insurance policy. [Exceptions Applicable to Cash Basis Taxpayers, p. 4–10]

34. c $100,000 − (4 × $3,390) = $86,440. [Income from Annuities, p. 4–28]

35. c $139,500 / 310 months = $450. [Simplified Method for Annuity Distributions from Qualified Retirement Plans, p. 4–30]

CHAPTER 5

Gross Income: Exclusions

CHAPTER HIGHLIGHTS

This chapter focuses on those items, which are specifically excluded from gross income by Congress. Exclusions are not deductions, they are items that are by definition not income. Deductions are items that are subtracted from income.

KEY TERMS

Exclusions

Gift & Inheritances

Life Insurance

Scholarships

Health Insurance

Employee Fringe Benefits

Foreign Earned Income

Tax Benefit Rule

OUTLINE

I. **EXCLUSIONS FROM GROSS INCOME**

Generally, everything received by a taxpayer is income unless a "specific statutory exclusion" can be found. Congress has chosen to exclude certain items from gross income for various social, economic, and equity purposes.

II. **GIFTS AND INHERITANCES**
   A. In General. The value of property received by gift or inheritance is excluded from gross income under Section 102. A gift is "a voluntary transfer of property by one taxpayer to another without any valuable consideration or compensation therefrom." The payment must be made "out of affection, respect, admiration, charity, or like impulses."

   Gifts made in a business setting often represent compensation for past, present, or future services and are not gifts. In most cases, transfers from employers to employees may not be treated as gifts.
   B. Gifts to Employees. Cash or property received by an employee cannot be excluded from the employee's income unless it fits into one of the statutory provisions.
   C. Employee Death Benefits. In certain circumstances employer payments (death benefits) to a deceased employee's surviving spouse, children, or other beneficiaries can be excluded from income by the recipient. However, if the deceased employee had any claim to the payments the IRS will consider the payments as income to the recipient

III. **LIFE INSURANCE PROCEEDS**
   A. In General. The proceeds of life insurance are excluded from the income of the beneficiary of the policy.
   B. Accelerated Death Benefits. If an insured is terminally or chronically ill, then he or she may take advanced payments or assign the policy to a qualified third party and not be taxed on the proceeds. Taxpayers who are not terminally or chronically ill are taxed on any gain from accelerated life insurance death benefits.
   C. Transfers for Valuable Consideration. If a life insurance policy is transferred for valuable consideration or is an amount due from the decedent, the net proceeds of the policy will be included in income. The net proceeds will not be included if the policy is transferred to the following:
      1) a partner of the insured
      2) a partnership in which the insured is a partner
      3) a corporation in which the insured is an officer or a shareholder
      4) a transferee whose basis in the policy is determined by reference to the transferor's basis

   The first three exceptions facilitate the use of life insurance to fund buy-sell agreements.

IV. **SCHOLARSHIPS**
   A. In General. For tax purposes a scholarship is defined as "an amount paid or allowed to, or for the benefit of, an individual...to aid such individual in the pursuit of study or research." The recipient must be a candidate for a degree at an educational institution. Scholarship grants for tuition and related expenses are excluded from income under Section 117 of the Code. Other scholarship amounts received (e.g., room and board) are included in the taxable income of the recipient.
   B. Timing Issues. The amount eligible for exclusion may not be known at the time a scholarship is received. In this case, the transaction is held open until the educationexpenses are paid.
   C. Disguised Compensation. Employer-sponsored scholarships made available solely to the children of key employees are generally includible in the incomeof the parent-employee.
   D. Qualified Tuition Reduction Plans. Employees of nonprofit education institutions are allowed to exclude a tuition waiver from gross income. Generally, the exclusion is limited to undergraduate tuition waivers.

V. **COMPENSATION FOR INJURIES AND SICKNESS**
   A. Damages. A person who suffers harm caused by another is often paid damages. Generally, the reimbursement for loss of income is taxed in the same manner as the income being replaced by the damages. If the damages represent a recovery of a previously deducted expense, income may arise under the tax benefit rule. Payments for personal injury are specifically excluded from the gross income of the person receiving the payment.

   Punitive damages arising from a claim of physical injury or physical sickness are excluded from gross income, while all other punitive damages are fully taxable.

   B. Workers' Compensation. Payments received by a taxpayer from workers' compensation and benefits from accident and health insurance policies purchased by the taxpayer are specifically excluded from gross income under Section 104.
   C. Accident and Health Insurance Benefits. The income tax treatment of accident and health insurance benefits depends on whether the policy providing the benefits was purchased by the taxpayer or the taxpayer's employer. Benefits under policies purchased by the taxpayer are excludible; see below for employer plan rules.

VI. **EMPLOYER-SPONSORED ACCIDENT AND HEALTH PLANS**

   Premiums paid on "employer sponsored" accident and health plans are excluded from the income of the employee and are deductible by the employer. When the employee collects the insurance benefits, such benefits are considered taxable income with the following exceptions:
   1) Payments received for the medical care of the employee, spouse, and dependents are excluded except to the extent the payments are reimbursements for medical expenses which were deducted in the previous year or the payments are reimbursements of expenses that do not meet the test for deduction as a medical expense under the Code.
   2) Payments for the permanent loss or the loss of the use of a member or function of the body or the permanent disfigurement of the employee, spouse, or dependent are also excluded.
   A. Medical Reimbursement Plans. Amounts received under employer medical reimbursement plans are excluded from gross income unless the plan discriminates in favor of certain groups of employees (e.g., management level). Benefits, which are paid only to a particular group of employees, must be included in income.
   B. Long-Term Care Benefits. Generally long-term care insurance is treated the same as accident and health insurance. Thus, premiums paid by an employer are not income to an employee. The maximum exclusion for benefits is the greater of $210 per day (in 2002) or actual cost of the care.

VII. **MEALS AND LODGING**
   A. Furnished for the Convenience of the Employer. The value of meals and lodging provided to an employee, the employee's spouse, and the employee's dependents is excluded from gross income if certain conditions are met. To qualify for the exclusion, meals must be furnished by the employer on the business premises of the employer and be for the convenience of the employer. In addition to these tests, lodging must be a condition of employment for an employee to be able to exclude it.
   B. Other Housing Exclusions. Under certain conditions, an employee of an educational institution can exclude the value of campus housing provided by the employer. Generally, the employee does not recognize income if he or she makes annual rent payments equal to or greater than 5 percent of the value of the facility; however, if the rent payments are less than 5% of the value of the facility, the difference must be included in gross income. A "minister of the gospel" can exclude the rental value of a home furnished as compensation. Military personnel are allowed exclusions under various circumstances.

VIII. **OTHER EMPLOYEE FRINGE BENEFITS**
   A. Specific Benefits. Certain employee benefits are excluded from the gross income of an employee by special provisions in the tax law. These are:
   1) The value of child care services paid by an employer, enabling the employee to work, limited to the lesser of $5,000 annually ($2,250 if married, filing separately), or the taxpayer's earned

income. For married taxpayers, the earned income of the spouse with the lesser amount of earned income is used for the limitation.

    2)   The value of gymnasium and athletic facilities.

    3)   Qualified employer provided educational assistance, limited to $5,250 annual amount.

    4)   Adoption Assistance Tax Provisions.

B.   Cafeteria Plans. A cafeteria plan is an employee plan that offers an employee a choice between cash and some other form of compensation (i.e., a benefit). If a plan meets the requirements under the tax law, then the employee can choose between nontaxable benefits (e.g., health insurance) or taxable income in the form of a cash payment.

C.   Flexible Spending Plans. Under these plans, an employee accepts lower cash compensation in return for the employer agreeing to pay certain costs the employer (e.g., dental expenses) can pay without the employee recognizing gross income.

D.   General Classes of Excluded Benefits. The tax law establishes four broad classes of nontaxable employee benefits. These benefits are:

    1)   No-additional cost services (e.g., an employee of an airline can fly for free if the seat would otherwise be empty).

    2)   Qualified employee discounts. In the case of services, employees do not have to report as income employee discounts up to 20 percent. In the case of property, employees do not have to report as income employee discounts provided the discount does not exceed the employer's gross profit margin. The exclusion is not available for real property.

    3)   Working condition fringes. Employees can exclude those items from gross income that would be deductible if the employees had paid them. In addition, certain nondeductible items such as free parking do not have to be included as income.

    4)   *De minimis* fringes. Small benefits, such as using the company copy machine, do not have to be reported as income.

    5)   Qualified transportation fringe benefits.

    6)   Qualified moving expense reimbursements.

E.   Taxable Fringe Benefits. Employee fringe benefits that do not qualify for specific exclusions must be recognized as gross income equal to the fair market value of the benefit(s).

IX.   FOREIGN EARNED INCOME

A U.S. citizen is generally subject to U.S. tax on total worldwide income. However, qualified U.S. citizens working abroad can exclude earned income up to a certain amount, see text for annual amount limitatioon. In addition, an exclusion is allowed for a reasonable amount of housing costs in the foreign country in excess of a base amount. The base amount of "housing allowance" is 16 percent of the pay for a GS-14 (Step 1) Federal employee.

To qualify for the exclusion the taxpayer must either be a resident of the foreign country, or present in the country for 330 days during any 12 consecutive months.

The taxpayer may include the foreign income in gross income and elect to claim a credit for foreign taxes paid as an alternative to the credit.

X.   INTEREST ON CERTAIN STATE AND LOCAL GOVERNMENT OBLIGATIONS

Taxpayers can exclude interest on the "obligations of state and local governments" from their gross income. However, the interest on certain types of state and local government bonds is taxable.

XI.   DIVIDENDS

A.   In General. A dividend payment to a shareholder with respect to the ownership of stock is normally included in income to the extent of the corporation's earnings and profits. Distributions in excess of earnings and profits are a nontaxable recovery of capital to the extent of the taxpayer's basis in the corporation's stock and any distributions in excess of basis are taxed as capital gains.

The following items are not considered regular dividends for tax purposes:
1)   payments received on savings and loan association deposits,
2)   patronage dividends from cooperatives,
3)   mutual life insurance dividends, and
4)   capital gain distributions from mutual funds.

B.   Stock Dividends. Generally, no income is recognized on the receipt of stock dividends on stock.

XII.   EDUCATIONAL SAVINGS BONDS

A.   For certain savings bonds issued after 1989, an exclusion is available with respect to bonds redeemed to provide funding for higher education. Taxpayers may exclude interest on Series EE savings bonds that are redeemed to pay for qualified higher education expenses. To qualify, the following requirements must be met:
1)   the bonds must be issued after December 31, 1989, and
2)   the bonds must be issued to an individual who is at least 24 years old at the time of issuance.

B.   Once modified adjusted gross income exceeds certain amounts, the exclusion begins to be phased out, see text for annual amount thresholds. Thus, the exclusion is phased out entirely when modified adjusted gross income reaches certain levels. See text for the exclusion calculation.

XIII.   QUALIFIED STATE TUITION PROGRAMS

Several states have plans to allow parents to prepay tuition for the child's future college education. Under a qualified state tuition program, the amounts contributed must be used for qualified higher education expenses. Amounts spent on higher education in excess of the prepaid amount are income to the student (not the parent).

If the child does not attend college, the excess refunded to the parents is income to the parents.

XIV.   TAX BENEFIT RULE

Under the tax benefit rule if a taxpayer obtains a deduction for an item in one tax year and in a later year recovers a portion of the prior deduction, the recovery is included in taxable income in the year it is received. Examples of items subject to this rule include bad debts, prior taxes, and delinquency amounts.

The recovery of a deduction, which did not yield a tax benefit in a prior year, is not included in gross income under the tax benefit rule.

XV.   INCOME FROM DISCHARGE OF INDEBTEDNESS

The transfer of appreciated property in satisfaction of a debt is treated first as a sale of the property and then as payment of the debt. Any gain on the sale of the property must be recognized as income.

Under the Bankruptcy Act, the discharge of indebtedness is not recognized as income to the taxpayer whose debt is forgiven. The realized gain from the discharge of the debt is applied against the taxpayer's basis in the assets, effectively deferring the gain until the assets are sold.

TEST FOR SELF-EVALUATION—CHAPTER 5

True or False

Indicate which of the following statements is true or false by circling the correct answer.

T F 1. Public assistance payments (welfare) are generally taxable.

T F 2. Gifts in a business setting are always excluded from gross income.

T F 3. In a flexible spending plan, the employee accepts lower cash wages in return for the employer agreeing to pay certain costs of the employee.

T F 4. Life insurance proceeds are always excluded from the gross income of the recipient.

T F 5. The interest element received by a beneficiary on life insurance proceeds taken in installments is excluded from income.

T F 6. A transfer of appreciated property in satisfaction of a debt is a realizable event for income tax purposes.

T F 7. The maximum exclusion for employee child care fringe benefits is $5,000 per year or the earned income of the spouse who has the lesser amount of earned income.

T F 8. Under the tax benefit rule, if a taxpayer obtains a deduction in one year and later recovers a portion of the prior deduction, the recovery produces taxable income.

T F 9. There are limits on the use of tax-exempt bonds to finance private business activities.

T F 10. A United States citizen is generally subject to U.S. tax on his total (world-wide) income regardless of the geographic origin of the income.

T F 11. To be excluded from gross income, meals furnished by an employer to an employee must be on the business premises and be for the convenience of the employer.

T F 12. Workers' compensation benefits are included in the gross income of the taxpayer receiving the benefits.

T F 13. The foreign earned income exclusion is subject to an annual maximum amount, plus a limited exclusion for foreign housing costs.

T F 14. To qualify for the foreign earned income exclusion, the taxpayer must be a bona fide resident of either the foreign country or present in the country for 250 days during any 12 consecutive months.

T F 15. Dividends on a mutual life insurance policy are taxable to the owner of the policy only if the policy has a cash surrender value of $5,000 or more.

T F 16. "Cafeteria" plans allow employees to choose nontaxable benefits rather than cash compensation and have the benefits remain nontaxable to the employee.

T F 17. Ministers can exclude from gross income the rental value of a home furnished as compensation or a rental allowance used to provide a home.

T F 18. Professor Gomez's son is enrolled as an undergraduate at the nonprofit university where he teaches. The university waived the tuition of $6,000 for the son. Professor Gomez must include the $6,000 in his income because his son went to school for free.

T   F   19.   Scholarship income used for expenses of room and board is treated as earned income for purposes of calculating the standard deduction for one who is claimed as a dependent of another taxpayer.

T   F   20.   If the amount of a scholarship eligible for exclusion is not known at year-end the transaction is held open until the education expenses are paid.

T   F   21.   Generally, punitive damages are not taxed to the recipient because they represent a penalty to the person causing the damages.

T   F   22.   Generally, if an employee has an option of taking cash instead of employer-provided housing then the amount is taxable.

T   F   23.   Employer-paid parking for company officers qualifies as a working condition fringe benefit and would not be income to the officers.

T   F   24.   The annuity rules are used to apportion an installment payment of life insurance proceeds between the principal and interest on earnings from reinvestment of the life insurance proceeds.

T   F   25.   Under a cafeteria plan, an employee is permitted to choose between cash and nontaxable benefits (e.g., child care).

T   F   26.   Leslie is a graduate research assistant. She receives $4,000 for working 400 hours during the semester. In addition, she receives a $5,000 tuition waiver from the university. The $5,000 is excluded from Leslie's income.

T   F   27.   Long-term care benefits received by a taxpayer are excluded to the greater of actual costs or $195 per day.

T   F   28.   Qualified employer reimbursed adoption expenses are phased out as adjusted gross income increases from $150,000 to $190,000.

Multiple Choice

Choose the best answer for each of the following questions.

_____ 1.   Andrew, a single taxpayer, received $1,100 in dividends on his Texaco, Inc. stock and $600 on BHP, Inc. stock (an Australian Corporation). Assuming Andrew is a cash basis, calendar year taxpayer, what amount would be included in his gross income?

    a. $–0–
    b. $1,100
    c. $1,700
    d. $1,600

_____ 2.   Bess received gifts of $9,000 in cash and an automobile with a fair market value of $2,000 (cost $12,000). Assuming Bess is a cash basis, calendar year taxpayer, what amount would be included in her gross income?

    a. $–0–
    b. $2,000
    c. $9,000
    d. $11,000

_____ 3.   Conrad Corporation sues Amber Corporation and recovers $500,000 in lost income damages and $300,000 in punitive damages for loss of income. Assuming Conrad is a cash basis, calendar year taxpayer, what amount would be included in its gross income?

     a. $–0–
     b. $300,000
     c. $500,000
     d. $800,000

_____ 4.   In the current year, Doris recovered $12,000 of $18,000 that was deducted for tax purposes two years ago. Assuming Doris is a cash basis, calendar year taxpayer, what amount would be included in her current year gross income?

     a. $–0–
     b. $12,000
     c. $18,000
     d. $6,000

_____ 5.   On the death of his father, Edgar received $50,000 (cash value of the policy is $24,000) as the beneficiary of his father's life insurance policy. Assuming Edgar is a cash basis, calendar year taxpayer, what amount would be included in his gross income?

     a. $–0–
     b. $150,000
     c. $24,000
     d. $126,000

_____ 6.   Fay inherited several AT&T bonds. The bonds had a fair market value of $70,000 at the date of death. After receiving the bonds, she was also paid $2,000 in interest. Assuming Fay is a cash basis, calendar year taxpayer, what amount would be included in her gross income?

     a. $–0–
     b. $72,000
     c. $70,000
     d. $2,000

_____ 7.   As the result of an accident on the job Garth is disabled. Under workers' compensation insurance, he received $7,200. Assuming Garth is a cash basis, calendar year taxpayer, what amount would be included in his gross income?

     a. $–0–
     b. $2,000
     c. $7,200
     d.   Some other amount

_____ 8.   Pat (a single taxpayer) received the following income:

Salary	$30,000
Dividends from G.M. stock	$ 1,000
Interest on City of Houston bonds	$ 2,000
Life insurance proceeds	$10,000
Dividends on Mexican stock	$ 1,600

What is Pat's gross income?

    a. $42,600
    b. $31,000
    c. $32,600
    d. $30,000

_____ 9.   Sam paid $20,000 into a qualified (Section 529) state tuition program for his son, Bill. When Bill went to college the plan balance was $35,000 due to earnings in the plan. During the year, $7,000 was used for the son's college tuition. How much must Bill include in income from utilizing the plan?

    a. $-0-
    b. $3,000
    c. $4,000
    d. $7,000

_____ 10.   Jill works for a hospital that provides employees free meals in a lunchroom. During the year, the value of the meals received by Jill is $2,300. If Jill had eaten all the meals available at the hospital, she would have eaten $4,800 worth of meals. The reason the hospital provides the meals is so that employees will be available for emergencies. How much will Jill have to include in her income from the free meals?

    a. $-0-
    b. $2,300
    c. $4,800
    d. $2,500

_____ 11.   In the current year Armadillo Airlines covers an employee with a qualified dental plan at a cost of $200. In addition, its employees are allowed to fly for free on a standby basis, and this same employee takes free flights valued at $3,000. The employee is also provided with free parking at the airport worth $400 per year. Of these amounts, how much must the employee include in his gross income for the current year?

    a. $-0-
    b. $200
    c. $3,200
    d. $3,600

_____ 12.   Chris had adjusted gross income of $5,000 after deducting a bad debt of $2,000. Her itemized deductions and personal exemptions were $6,600. The next year, much to her surprise, Chris collected the bad debt. How much must she include in income for the year of recovery?

    a. $-0-
    b. $200
    c. $400
    d. $1,000

_____ 13.   Janis owed Friendly Bank and Trust $50,000 on an unsecured note. She paid off the note with stock worth $50,000 (basis of $40,000). How much gain must Janis recognize on the transfer of the stock to the bank?

    a. $-0-
    b. $10,000
    c. $40,000
    d. $50,000

_____ 14.   Mike is an employee of Mega Corporation. As an employee, Mike received the following fringe benefits.

Benefit	Value
Free use of company gym	$200
10% discount on $250 TV (employer's standard gross profit margin, 25%)	$ 25
Free company parking	$400
Personal use of copy machine	$ 8

If the plan does not discriminate, what amount of these fringe benefits must Mike report as income on his tax return?

    a. $–0–
    b. $1,233
    c. $600
    d. $400

_____ 15.   During the current year Alfred sustained a serious injury while on the job. As a result of his injury, Alfred received the following amounts during the same year:

Workers' compensation payments	$2,400
Reimbursement from employer's accident and health plan formedical expenses paid by Alfred	$1,800
Damages for personal injuries	$8,000

How much of the above amounts should Alfred include in his gross income for the current year?

    a. $12,200
    b. $8,000
    c. $1,800
    d. $–0–

_____ 16.   Lyle and Maria are married and live in Palm Springs. They receive the following distributions from securities during the year:

Lyle:	ATT, cash dividends	$200
	City of Las Vegas Bonds, interest	$500
Maria:	Southwest Airlines, cash dividends	$ 50
	Bank of Canada, cash dividends	$300
	Citibank, stock dividend on com. stock	$ 75

Lyle and Maria file a joint return. Of the above items, what amount must be included in ordinary income for the year after any exclusions?

    a. $250
    b. $700
    c. $550
    d. $625

_____ 17.   Phyllis, a cash basis, calendar year taxpayer, works for the Very Big Corporation of America. Her salary is $75,000 per year. Also, she received the following fringe benefits from Very Big during the current year:

Free parking (provided to all employees)	$480
Personal use of Xerox machine	$ 30
Personal long distance calls	$ 70
Personal letters typed	$100
Membership in a local health club	$600
Personal use of firm's hunting lodge	$125

What amount of these fringe benefits must be included in Phyllis's gross income?

a. $–0–
b. $600
c. $725
d. $825

_____ 18. Kurt received the following interest payments during the year:

Interest on municipal bonds	$700
Interest on Series HH savings bonds	$500
Increase in value of Series EE savings bonds	$400
Interest on last years federal income tax refund	$200
Interest on contract settlement from dispute two years ago	$500

If Kurt is a cash basis taxpayer and has made no special elections, what should he include in gross income from the above amounts?

a. $–0–
b. $1,200
c. $1,700
d. $700

_____ 19. Mary is employed as the manager of an apartment complex. Her employer gave her the option of two compensation schemes:

(1) Cash salary of $40,000 per year, or
(2) Cash salary of $32,000 per year plus a free apartment worth $7,000 per year

If Mary selects option two, what amount should she include in gross income?

a. $40,000
b. $32,000
c. $33,000
d. $39,000

_____ 20. John, who was 58 at the time of his death on July 1, received $1,000 of interest on municipal bonds. John's wife Emma, age 57, received a $300 television set as a "gift" for opening a long-term savings account at a bank. On John's death, Emma received life insurance proceeds of $60,000 under a group policy paid for by John's employer. Emma did not remarry and she is the executor of John's estate.

How much taxable interest was received by John and Emma?

a. $–0–
b. $300
c. $1,000
d. $1,300

_____ 21.   John, who was 58 at the time of his death on July 1, received $1,000 of interest on municipal bonds. John's wife Emma, age 57, received a $300 television set in as a "gift" for opening a long-term savings account at a bank. On John's death, Emma received life insurance proceeds of $60,000 under a group policy paid for by John's employer. Emma did not remarry and she is the executor of John's estate. How much of the group-term life insurance proceeds should be excluded from taxable income?

    a. $–0–
    b. $5,000
    c. $50,000
    d. $60,000

_____ 22.   In the current year, Claire's proceeds from the redemption of qualified educational savings bonds during the taxable year were $10,000 (principal of $6,000 and interest of $4,000). Her qualified higher education expenses were $8,000. How much of the interest is excludible (before any phase-out)?

    a. $–0–
    b. $4,000
    c. $3,200
    d. $1,771

_____ 23.   In the current year, Claire's proceeds from the redemption of qualified educational savings bonds during the taxable year were $10,000 (principal of $6,000 and interest of $4,000). Her qualified higher education expenses were $8,000. Assume Claire's modified adjusted gross income is $55,000 and she files as a single taxpayer. How much interest is excludible after the phase-out?

    a. $–0–
    b. $3,200
    c. $1,259
    d. $1,941

_____ 24.   Andy, age 20, is a full-time student at Small State University and is studying for his bachelor's degree. During the current year, he received the following cash payments:

Scholarship:		
Books and tuition	$5,000	
Meals and lodging	$2,000	$7,000
Interest income		$ 600
Cash support from a rich uncle		$2,000
Loan from financial aid office		$4,000

What is Andy's adjusted gross income?

    a. $–0–
    b. $2,600
    c. $7,600
    d. $11,600

_____ 25.   Pete purchased an insurance policy on his life with his son as the beneficiary. Pete paid $28,000 in premiums. The policy had a cash surrender value of $34,000 when Pete died and his son collected the face amount of $150,000. How much income must the son report as beneficiary of the policy?

a. $–0–
b. $28,000
c. $34,000
d. $150,000

_____ 26. Paula was required to pay $200 of nondeductible interest and $100 of nondeductible penalties because her tax return was filed late. Her tax return was late because her CPA was overworked and did not get a chance to finish the return. The CPA reimbursed Paula $300 for the interest and penalties due the IRS. How much of the reimbursement is income to Paula?

a. $–0–
b. $100
c. $200
d. $300

_____ 27. Jude was reimbursed by his employer-sponsored health insurance plan for the following medical expenses:

Doctor visits	$2,000
Hospital stay for son's illness	$5,000
Cost of hair transplant	$3,000
Prescription drugs	$2,000

How much income (if any) must Jude report from these reimbursements?

a. $–0–
b. $2,000
c. $3,000
d. $12,000

_____ 28. Silver Corporation's management is allowed to purchase goods from the company for a 20 percent discount and all other employees are allowed a ten percent discount. The employer's usual gross profit margin is 25 percent. Bill, president of the company, purchased from Silver Corporation goods for $1,600 when the price charged to customers was $2,000. How much income must Bill report from the purchase of the goods?

a. $–0–
b. $400
c. $1,600
d. $200

_____ 29. Big Private University (BPU) allows the children of employees to attend for a special tuition rate that is 30 percent of the regular tuition. Joel is an employee of BPU and his child attends the school on a full-time basis (paying the special tuition rate). Regular tuition at BPU is $10,000 per year. How much does Joel have to include in income from the tuition reduction?

a. $–0–
b. $3,000
c. $7,000
d. $10,000

_____ 30. Lance qualifies for the foreign earned income credit. He was present in Ecuador for 344 days in the current year. Lance's salary for the year was $110,000. Assuming a 365-day year, how is Lance's earned income exclusion calculated?

a.   (344 days/365 days) × $110,000
b.   (344 days/365 days)/365 days × annual maximum
c.   [(365 days − 344 days)/365 days] × annual maximum
d.   (365 days/344 days) × $110,000

_____ 31.   Edna owns and operates a profitable onion farm. Determine Edna's gross income from the following receipts for the current year:

Gain on sale of Texas bonds	$1,000
Interest on U.S. bonds	$ 600
Interest on State tax refund	$ 200
Interest on Texas bonds	$ 800
Patronage dividend from Onion Growers Coop	$3,000

The patronage dividend was received in April of the current year for amounts paid and deducted on Edna's (schedule F) for the previous year.

a. $1,800
b. $1,600
c. $4,800
d. $5,600

_____ 32.   Betty owned a $100,000 term life insurance (total premiums paid of $10,000) policy when she was diagnosed as having a terminal illness. She sold the policy for $75,000 to Bass Benefits, Inc., a company that is qualified by the state of Texas to purchase such policies. How much income must Betty recognize on the date of the policy?

a. $–0–
b. $10,000
c. $65,000
d. $75,000

_____ 33.   Betty owned a $100,000 term life insurance (total premiums paid of $10,000) policy when she was diagnosed as having a terminal illness. She sold the policy for $75,000 to Bass Benefits, Inc., a company that is qualified by the state of Texas to purchase such policies. How much must Bass Benefits recognize upon Betty's death if Bass pays an additional $7,000 in premiums?

a. $–0–
b. $75,000
c. $100,000
d. $18,000

_____ 34.   Employer services equal to 30% of the customer price provided to an individual employee are

a.   included in gross income
b.   partially included from gross income
c.   excluded from gross income
d.   deducted from taxable income

_____ 35.   AICPA dues paid by an employer for an individual employee are

a.   included in gross income
b.   partially included from gross income
c.   excluded from gross income
d.   deducted from taxable income

_____ 36.   Qualified parking with a value of $250 per month paid for an individual employee is

       a.   included in gross income
       b.   partially included from gross income
       c.   excluded from gross income
       d.   deducted from taxable income

_____ 37.   An employer provided bus pass worth $50 per month for an individual employee is

       a.   included in gross income
       b.   partially included from gross income
       c.   excluded from gross income
       d.   deducted from taxable income

_____ 38.   Occasional use of an employer's Xerox machine for personal copies by an individual employee is

       a.   included in gross income
       b.   partially included from gross income
       c.   excluded from gross income
       d.   deducted from taxable income

_____ 39.   For an individual employee, a medical reimbursement that is available only to officers of the company is

       a.   included in gross income
       b.   partially included from gross income
       c.   excluded from gross income
       d.   deducted from taxable income

SOLUTIONS TO CHAPTER 5 QUESTIONS

True or False

1. F Welfare is not generally taxable. [Items Specifically Excluded from Gross Income, p. 5–2]

2. F Gifts in a business setting may be included in gross income. [General, p. 5–4]

3. T In a flexible spending plan, the employee accepts lower wages in return for the employer agreeing to pay certain employee costs. [Flexible Spending Plans, p. 5–20]

4. F Proceeds may be included in gross income if the policy was transferred for valuable consideration. Transfer for Valuable Consideration, p. 5–7]

5. F The interest portion of the installment payment received is generally included in income. [Transfer for Valuable Consideration, p. 5–7]

6. T Transfer of appreciated property in satisfaction of a debt is realizable for income tax purposes. [Income from Discharge of Indebtedness, p. 5–32]

7. T The maximum exclusion for child care fringe benefits is $5,000 per year. [Specific Benefits, p. 5–18]

8. T If a taxpayer obtains a deduction in one year and later recovers a portion of the prior deduction, the recovery is taxable income. [Tax Benefit Rule, p. 5–31]

9. T Limits exist on the use of tax-exempt bonds to finance private business activities. [Interest on Certain State and Local Government Obligations, p. 5–28]

10. T United States citizens are generally subject to U.S. tax on their total income regardless of the geographic origin. [Foreign Earned Income, p. 5–25]

11. T To be excluded, meals furnished by an employer must be on the business premises and be for the convenience of the employer. [Meals and Lodging, p. 5–15]

12. F Workers' compensation is excluded from gross income. [Workers' Compensation, p. 5–12]

13. T There is an annual maximum foreign earned income and a limited exclusion for foreign housing costs. [Foreign Earned Income, p. 5–25]

14. F 330 days, not 250 days. [Foreign Earned Income, p. 5–25]

15. F These dividends are not taxable. [General Information, p. 5–29]

16. T "Cafeteria" plans allow employees to choose nontaxable benefits and have the benefits remain nontaxable to the employee. [Cafeteria Plans, p. 5–19]

17. T Ministers can exclude the rental value of a home furnished or a rental allowance used to provide a home. [Ministers of the Gospel, p. 5–18]

18. F The tuition reduction is not income to Professor Gomez. [Qualified Tuition Reduction Plans, p. 5–10]

19. T Scholarship income used for room and board is treated as earned income in calculating the standard deduction for one who is claimed as a dependent of another taxpayer. [General Information, p. 5–8]

20. T A scholarship amount eligible for exclusion is held open, until the education expenses are paid. [General Information, p. 5–9]

21. F Punitive damages are included in gross income unless they are considered compensation for physical injuries or physical sickness. [Personal Injury, p. 5–11]

22. T If an employee has an option of taking cash instead housing then the amount is taxable. [Required as a Condition of Employment, p. 5–17]

23.   T   Employer-paid parking for company officers qualifies as a working condition fringe benefit. [Working Condition Fringes, p. 5–22]

24.   T   The annuity rules are used to apportion an installment payment of life insurance proceeds between the principal and interest. [Transfers for Valuable Consideration, p. 5–7]

25.   T   An employee is permitted under a cafeteria plan to choose between cash and nontaxable benefits. [Cafeteria Plans, p. 5–19]

26.   T   Earnings and tuition waivers of a graduate research assistant are excluded. [Qualified Tuition Reduction Plans, p. 5–10]

27.   F   The daily amount is $210 in 2002. [Long-term Care Insurance Benefits, p. 5–14]

28.   T   The phase-out is from $150,000 to $190,000. [Specific Benefits, p. 5–18]

Multiple Choice

1.   c $1,100 + 600 = $1,700 [Items Specifically Excluded from Gross Income, p. 5–2]

2.   a   Gifts are excluded [Items Specifically Excluded from Gross Income, p. 5–2]

3.   d $300,000 + 500,000 = $800,000 [Personal Injury, p. 5–11]

4.   b   Amounts recovered are income. [Tax Benefit Rule, p. 5–31]

5.   a   Life insurance proceeds are generally excluded. [General Rule, p. 5–6]

6.   d   Income on gift property is included. [General, p. 5–4]

7.   a   Workers' Compensation is excluded [Workers' Compensation, p. 5–12]

8.   c $30,000 + 1,000 + 1,600 = $32,600. [Items Specifically Excluded from Gross Income, p. 5–2]

9.   b   None of the tuition is included in Bill's income. [Qualified State Tuition Programs, p. 5–30]

10.   a   The meals are not income under Section 119. [Meals and Lodging Furnished for the Convenience of the Employer, p. 5–15]

11.   a   [Various Sections throughout the Chapter]

12.   c $7,000 – 6,600 = $400 tax benefit from deduction. [Tax benefit Rule, p. 5–31]

13.   b $50,000 – 40,000 = $10,000 [Income from Discharge of Indebtedness, p. 5–32]

14.   a   All these fringes are excluded. [General Classes of Excluded Benefits, p. 5–20]

15.   d   All these amounts are excluded [Compensation for Injuries and Sickness, p. 5–11]

16.   c $200 + $50 + $300 = $550 [Interest of Certain State and Local Government Obligations, p. 5–28]

17.   c $600 + $125 = $725 [Other Employee Fringe Benefits, p. 5–18]

18.   b $500 + 200 + 500 = $1,200 [Interest of Certain State and Local Government Obligations, p. 5–28)

19.   d $32,000 + 7,000 = $39,000 [Meals and Lodging Furhished for the Convenience of the Employer, p. 5–15]

20.   b   The value of the T.V. set "gift" is interest. [Gift and Inheritances, p. 5–4]

21.   d   The proceeds are excluded. [General Rule, p. 5–6]

22.   c   ($8,000/$10,000) × $4,000 = $3,200. [Educational Savings Bonds, p. 5–29]

23.   b $55,000 less than the phase-out amount threshold. [Educational Savings Bonds, p. 5–29]

24.   b $2,000 + 600 = $2,600. [Scholarships, p. 5–8]

25.   a   Life Insurance proceeds are excluded. [General Rule, p. 5–6]

26.   a   Under the tax benefit rule, since the reimbursement is for amounts that are not deductible (personal interest and penalties), none of the reimbursements are included in income. [Tax Benefit Rule, p. 5–13]

27.   c   A hair transplant (i.e., cosmetic surgery) is not allowed as a medical deduction; therefore, the reimbursement is included in gross income. [Employer-Sponsored Accident and Health Plans, p. 5–14]

28.   b   The plan discriminated, therefore, the discount is income. [Qualified Employee Discounts, p. 5–21]

29.   a   The tuition is excluded. [Qualified Tuition Reduction Plans, p. 5–10]

30.   b   The exclusion is calculated as (344 days/365 days) × annual maximum. [Foreign Earned Income, p. 5–25]

31.   c $1,000 + $600 + $200 + $3,000 = $4,800. [Interest of Certain State and Local Government Obligations, p. 5–28]

32.   a   The sale of the policy is excluded. [Accelerated Death Benefits, p. 5–6]

33.   d $100,000 − $75,000 − $7,000 = $18,000 [Accelerated Death Benefits, p. 5–6]

34.   b   The maximum exclusion is 20%. [Qualified Employee Discounts, p. 5–21]

35.   c   The dues are excluded. [Working Condition Fringes, p. 5–22]

36.   b   There is a monthly limit on parking [Qualified Transportation Fringes, p. 5–23]

37.   c   The bus pass is under the limit and is fully excluded. [Qualified Transportation Fringes, p. 5–23]

38.   c   The is an excluded de Minimis fringe. [De Minimis Fringes, p. 5–23]

39.   a   Discriminatory plans are not allowed an exclusion. [Nondiscrimination Provisions, p. 5–24]

CHAPTER 6

Deductions and Losses: In General

CHAPTER HIGHLIGHTS

All deductions are a matter of legislative grace. For an expenditure to be deductible, it must be specifically authorized by Congress. This chapter introduces and classifies deductions *for* adjusted gross income and deductions *from* adjusted gross income. Specific provisions in the tax law which disallow or limit certain deductions are discussed in detail.

KEY TERMS

Deduction For/From AGI
§ 162 Trade or Business
   Expenses

§ 212 Production of Income
   Expenses
Hobby Losses

Vacation Home
Related Parties

OUTLINE

I. **CLASSIFICATION OF DEDUCTIONS**

Deductions of individual taxpayers fall into one of two classifications, deductions for adjusted gross income or deductions *from* adjusted gross income.

A. Deductions for Adjusted Gross Income. Section 62 specifies the expenses which are deductible for adjusted gross income. The common deductions *for* AGI include:
    1) trade or business deductions (Section 162)
    2) certain reimbursed employee business expenses
    3) losses on the sale of property other than personal use property
    4) rent and royalty expenses
    5) alimony payments (Section 215)
    6) contributions to self-employed retirement plans
    7) deductions for retirement savings (Section 219)
    8) the deduction for moving expenses
    9) penalties on premature withdrawal of funds from savings accounts
    10) interest on student loans
    11) the deduction for one-half of any self-employment tax paid

B. The more common deductions *from* AGI (itemized) include:
    1) expenses for the production or collection of income
    2) expenses for the management, conservation, or maintenance of property held for the production of income
    3) expenses for the determination, collection, or refund of any tax
    4) charitable contributions
    5) medical expenses in excess of 7.5 percent of AGI
    6) certain state and local taxes (e.g., real estate, state and local income taxes)
    7) personal casualty losses
    8) certain personal interest
    9) certain miscellaneous deductions (in excess of 2 percent of AGI).

Deductions related to the production of rent and royalty income are referred to as deductions *for* adjusted gross income.

C. Trade or business expenses are deductible *for* AGI. For any business expenditure to be deductible it must be "ordinary and necessary." An ordinary expense is one that is normal, usual, or customary in the type of business being conducted by the taxpayer. A necessary expense is one that is appropriate and helpful in furthering the taxpayer's trade or business. Certain payments such as charitable contributions, illegal bribes and kickbacks, and fines and penalties are excluded as trade or business deductions.

Reasonableness Requirement. Besides being ordinary and necessary, the Code specifies that salaries must be "reasonable." The courts have expanded this requirement to cover all business expenses.

D. Business and Nonbusiness Losses. § 165provides that losses not covered by insurance are deductible. In general, deductible losses of individual taxpayers are limited to losses in a trade or business, investment losses, and casualty losses.

E. Itemized deductions are reported on Schedule A (and various supporting schedules) of Form 1040. Deductions for AGI are reported primarily on Schedule C (trade or business income), Schedule E (rent, royalty, S corporation, and partnership income), Schedule F (farm and ranch income), and directly on page one (traditional IRAs and alimony) of Form 1040.

II. **TIMING OF EXPENSE RECOGNITION**

A. Timing of Expense Recognition. In general, the taxpayer's method of accounting (cash or accrual) will determine the period in which a deduction can be taken. There are limitations on the use of the cash method of accounting by certain taxpayers.

B.   The expenses of cash basis taxpayers must be paid in cash before they can be deducted. The issuance of a note or other promise to pay does not qualify as a cash payment. Cash basis taxpayers and accrual basis taxpayers cannot deduct capital expenditures.

C.   Accrual basis taxpayers can deduct an expense by meeting the "economic performance test." This test is met only when the service, property, or use of property giving rise to the liability is actually performed for, provided to, or used by the taxpayer.

III.   **DISALLOWANCE POSSIBILITIES**

A.   Public Policy Limitation. The Code denies a deduction for an expenditure that is against public policy. Expenses that are against public policy include bribes, kickbacks, fines, and penalties. In general, legal expenses are deductible if incurred in the taxpayer's trade or business.

The usual expenses relating to the operation of illegal business, other than those contrary to public policy, are deductible. However, under the tax law illegal drug traffickers are not allowed a deduction for the ordinary and necessary expenses incurred in their business. They are only allowed a deduction for cost of goods sold.

B.   Political Contributions and Lobbying Activities. Generally, no business deduction is allowed for political contributions. A taxpayer may deduct certain lobbying expenditures if he has a direct interest in the proposed legislation. Dues or expenses paid to an organization of individuals with a common direct interest in proposed legislation are also deductible. Expenses which are incurred to influence the public on political matters may not be deducted.

C.   Excessive Executive Compensation. Publicly traded corporations cannot deduct executive compensation over $1,000,000 annually. This rule applies to the chief executive officer and the four most highly compensated officers. The following are not subject to the $1,000,000 annual limit:
   1)   Commissions based on individual performance
   2)   Performance-based compensation based on a formula approved by the board of directors
   3)   Payments to tax-qualified retirement plans
   4)   Payments that are excludible from the employee's gross income (e.g., certain fringe benefits)

D.   Investigation expenses for determining the feasibility of entering a new business or expanding an existing business are deductible if the taxpayer is already engaged in a similar business. If the taxpayer is not engaged in a similar business, and a new business is acquired, such expenses are capitalized and may be amortized over 60 months or more. In the event the new business is not acquired, investigation expenses are usually nondeductible.

E.   Hobby Losses. Under Section 183, if a taxpayer can show that an activity was entered with the intent of making a profit, and not for personal pleasure, then any losses are fully deductible.

The hobby loss rules apply when the taxpayer cannot show that the activity was engaged in for profit. Hobby expenses are only deductible up to the amount of hobby income. The expenses are deductible in the following order:
   1)   amounts deductible under other Code sections (e.g., property taxes).
   2)   amounts deductible as if the activity is engaged in for profit, but only if those amounts do not affect the basis of property (e.g., maintenance)
   3)   amounts deductible as if the activity is engaged in for profit which affect the basis of property (e.g., depreciation)

The tax law states that if a profit is made for "three of five consecutive years" (two of seven years for activities involving horses) then the activity is presumed to be engaged in for profit, and the hobby loss rules do not apply.

If the above presumption is not met, the activity may still qualify as a business if the taxpayer can show a profit-making intent. The Regulations stipulate nine relevant factors in distinguishing between profit-seeking activities and hobbies. The relevant factors are:

1) whether the activity is conducted in a business like manner
2) the expertise of the taxpayers
3) time and effort expended
4) expectation that the assets will appreciate
5) the previous success of the taxpayer in similar activities
6) the history of income and loss from the activity
7) the relationship of profits to losses
8) the financial status of the taxpayer
9) elements of personal pleasure in the activity

F. Vacation homes have loss rules similar to the hobby loss provisions. If the home is rented for 15 days or more and is used for personal purposes for more than the greater of 14 days or 10 percent of the days actually rented, then the deductions for depreciation, maintenance, etc., will be limited to the revenue generated. If the home is rented for 15 days or more, but personal use is not more than the greater of 14 days or 10 percent of the days rented, the home is considered rental property. Finally, if the vacation home is rented for less than 15 days, all rental income is excluded and all rental expenses, other than mortgage interest and property taxes, are disallowed.

Expenses must be allocated between personal and rental days. Expenses, other than property taxes and interest, are allocated on the basis of the total days of use. The IRS and the courts disagree on the allocation of taxes and interest. According to the courts, taxes and interest are to be allocated on the basis of 365 days; however, according to the IRS, taxes and interest should be allocated in the same manner as other expenses, on the basis of total days of use.

G. Expenditures Incurred for Taxpayer's Benefit or Taxpayer's Obligation. For an expenditure to be deductible, it must be incurred for the taxpayer's "benefit or be the taxpayer's obligation." Thus, a taxpayer cannot claim a deduction for paying the expenses of another individual.

H. Disallowance of Personal Expenditures. No deduction is allowed for personal, living, or family expenses unless specifically provided in the Code. Exceptions provided in the Code include:
1) charitable expenses
2) medical expenses
3) expenses for the determination, collection, or refund of tax
4) tax advice in divorce proceedings

I. Disallowance of Deductions for Capital Expenditures. Capital expenditures related to depreciable or amortizable property are added to the basis of the property and may be written off over the life of the property. Often it is difficult to distinguish repairs and maintenance from capital expenditures. The Code defines a capital expenditure as "any amount paid out for new buildings or for permanent improvements or betterments made to increase the value of any property or estate." Other expenditures are considered repairs and maintenance.

Sometimes, taxpayers are permitted an election to capitalize certain expenditures, such as property taxes, which would otherwise be currently expensed.

Exceptions in the Code regarding the deductibility of capital expenditures include the election to expense certain mineral development costs, intangible drilling costs, qualified farm land clearing expenditures, and research expenditures.

J. Transactions Between Related Parties. The tax law places restrictions on transactions between certain related parties due to the potential for "sham" transactions and tax avoidance schemes. Losses and unpaid expenses and interest are "not deductible" if incurred between related parties. However, any disallowed loss may be used to reduce a future gain on the property.

Related parties (as defined in Section 267) are:
1) Siblings, spouses, ancestors, and lineal descendants of the taxpayer
2) A corporation owned more than 50 percent (directly or indirectly) by the taxpayer
3) Two corporations that are members of a controlled group
4) A series of other complex relationships between trusts, corporations, estates, and individual taxpayers

Under the constructive ownership rules, stock owned by certain related parties is deemed to be owned by the taxpayer for the disallowance provisions.

K.   Substantiation Requirements. To be deductible, expenses must be substantiated by the taxpayer. Travel, entertainment, and business gifts must satisfy more stringent substantiation requirements.

L.   Expenses Related to Tax-Exempt Income. No deduction is allowed for expenses (including interest expense incurred to purchase or carry tax-exempt obligations) related to the production of tax-exempt income.

TEST FOR SELF-EVALUATION—CHAPTER 6

True or False

Indicate which of the following statements is true or false by circling the correct answer.

T F 1. The courts have established the doctrine that an item is not deductible unless a specific Code provision allows the deduction.

T F 2. To be deductible under Section 162 or 212, an item must be ordinary and necessary.

T F 3. Alimony, medical expenses, and state and local taxes are deductions from adjusted gross income.

T F 4. The term "trade or business" is clearly defined by statute in the Code.

T F 5. Expenses incurred in the determination, collection, or refund of any tax are deductible under Section 212.

T F 6. To be deductible, salaries must be reasonable.

T F 7. Generally, taxable income will be computed under the method of accounting that the taxpayer regularly uses to compute income and keep his or her books.

T F 8. Generally, accrual basis taxpayers cannot take a current deduction for capital expenditures except through amortization or depreciation over the life of the asset.

T F 9. Legal expenses are never deductible as ordinary and necessary business expenses if incurred in a trade or business activity.

T F 10. In order for an accrual basis taxpayer to deduct an expense, it must pass the "economic performance test."

T F 11. Investigation expenses are always deductible by a taxpayer entering a new trade or business.

T F 12. If an activity shows a profit for three of five years (two of seven years for activities involving horses), then the Code presumes it is not a hobby.

T F 13. If a residence is rented for 15 days or more, Section 280A limits the deductions related to the home if the taxpayer used the home for personal purposes for more than the greater of 14 days or 10 percent of the days actually rented.

T F 14. A taxpayer can claim a deduction for interest he paid on his son's mortgage. (The son is not the taxpayer's dependent).

T F 15. In general, Section 262 disallows deductions for personal, living, and family expenses.

T F 16. The tax law allows a deduction for expenses incurred in producing tax-exempt income.

T F 17. Due to the voluntary nature of the tax law, upon audit the IRS bears the burden of determining the validity of the expenses deducted on the taxpayer's return.

T F 18. Section 267 disallows losses and certain deductions between related parties.

T F 19. Goodwill is amortizable over twenty seven and one-half years for tax purposes.

T F 20. Personal legal fees are generally deductible by individual taxpayers.

T F 21. Expenses associated with a taxpayer's vacation home are deductible in full.

T	F	22.	To be deductible, an expense must be incurred for the taxpayer's benefit or arise from the taxpayer's obligation.
T	F	23.	Most expenses of hobbies (to the extent of income from the hobby) are deductible from AGI subject to the 2 percent of AGI limitation.
T	F	24.	The courts have held that taxes and interest on a vacation home should be allocated over 365 days a year, while the IRS has determined that taxes and interest should be allocated based on total days of use.
T	F	25.	Gwen rented her condo in Utah for 180 days. If Gwen used the condo for 20 days of personal use, it would be classified as a "personal/rental" asset.

Multiple Choice

Choose the best answer for each of the following questions.

_____ 1. For an individual taxpayer, which of the following is not a deduction for adjusted gross income?

    a.   Alimony
    b.   State income tax
    c.   Trade or business expenses
    d.   Traditional IRA contributions

_____ 2. Section 212 addresses expenses for the production or collection of income and tax return preparation fees. Which of the following is not a Section 212 deduction?

    a.   Repair expense on a rental house
    b.   A fee paid to a CPA for preparing a tax return
    c.   Interest expense on a personal residence
    d.   Safe deposit box rental used to store stock certificates

_____ 3. Elizabeth is a physician. In her spare time she wants to become a famous stock car racer. In the current year, Elizabeth incurs the following costs:

Stock car purchases	$140,000
Entry fees	$ 5,000
Driving lessons	$ 10,000
Travel expenses to races	$ 15,000
Total	$170,000

Of the races entered by Elizabeth this year, her total earnings (race winnings) are $250. Probably, the IRS will allow Elizabeth to deduct what amount of the above expenditures (before any 2 percent limit)?

    a. $–0–
    b. $250
    c. $30,000
    d. $170,000

_____ 4. Under Section 183, if an activity is not engaged in for profit, deductions related to the activity will be limited. Which of the following is likely to be deemed a hobby by the IRS?

   a.   A CPA in private practice
   b.   A ranch owned by an executive that has shown a profit for four of the last five years
   c.   An individual borrowing money to open a gift shop
   d.   A physician who operates a photography studio at a loss for five consecutive years

_____ 5.   During the current year, Lee pays $5,000 to an attorney to obtain a divorce. Of this amount, $2,000 is for tax advice about the divorce settlement. How much, if any, of the $5,000 is deductible before considering any limitation based on AGI?

   a. $–0–
   b. $2,000
   c. $3,000
   d. $5,000

_____ 6.   David made illegal business kickbacks of $10,000 and paid fines of $8,000 during the current year. How much of the expenses can be deducted on his tax return before considering any limitation based on AGI?

   a. $–0–
   b. $8,000
   c. $10,000
   d. $18,000

_____ 7.   If a taxpayer paid $5,000 interest on a note, the proceeds of which were used to purchase Arizona State University bonds, and the bonds produced interest income of $4,000, how much of an interest deduction would be allowed?

   a. $–0–
   b. $1,000
   c. $4,000
   d. $5,000

_____ 8.   Todd owns one-third of the stock in Todd Corporation, one-third is owned by Todd's mother, and one-third by Todd's father. On January 1, 19X1, Todd loans Todd Corporation $100,000 at 9 percent interest annually. Todd Corporation is an "accrual" basis taxpayer while Todd is a cash basis taxpayer. Todd Corporation pays the current interest on December 29, 19X1. How much interest is deductible by Todd Corporation for 19X1?

   a. $–0–
   b. $4,500
   c. $9,000
   d.   None of the above

_____ 9.   Tom pays $5,000 interest on his home mortgage, and pays $3,000 on his son's mortgage. The son does not qualify as Tom's dependent. How much of an interest deduction will Tom be allowed (before considering any deduction limitations)?

   a. $–0–
   b. $3,000
   c. $5,000
   d. $8,000

_____ 10. Tammie rents her vacation home for 30 days and lives in it for 10 days during the current year. Her gross income from rent payments was $4,000 and she incurred the following expenses:

Taxes and interest	$3,000
Utilities and maintenance	$ 800
Depreciation	$4,000
Total	$7,800

Using the IRS's approach, what amount of income or loss must Tammie report from this rental (disregard any passive loss limitations)?

    a. $–0–
    b. $200 income
    c. $3,800 loss
    d. $1,850 loss

_____ 11.   Refer to the preceding problem. If Tammie uses the home for 20 days (instead of 10 days) for personal purposes, the allowable deduction that may be claimed (disregard any passive loss limitations) is:

    a. $–0–
    b. $200 income
    c. $3,800 loss
    d. $680 loss

_____ 12.   Robert owns a chain of motels in California. He flies to Arizona to investigate the possibility of buying an auto dealership. All of the expenses for the trip are deductible in the current year if:

    a.   The automobile dealership is purchased
    b.   The auto dealership is not purchased
    c.   Would never be deductible
    d.   Robert already owns an auto dealership and does not purchase the Arizona dealership

_____ 13.   During the current year, Mary purchased a lot with an old house on it for $100,000. She immediately had the house demolished at a cost of $15,000. Four months later the lot was sold for $160,000. How much gain should be recognized by Mary?

    a. $–0–
    b. $15,000
    c. $45,000
    d. $60,000

_____ 14.   Under Section 267(c), the disallowance between related parties provision, which of the following is not a related family member?

    a.   Spouse
    b.   Son or daughter
    c.   Grandchild
    d.   Uncle

_____ 15.   Which of the following expenses are not deductible under Section 212?

    a.   Trade or business expenses
    b.   Expenses for the production of income
    c.   Expenses for the determination, collection, or refund of any tax
    d.   Expenses for the management, conservation, or maintenance of property held for the production of income

_____ 16.   Pancho is in the business of importing certain illegal substances. In this business, Pancho incurs the following expenses:

Cost of goods sold	$200,000
Payoffs to customs agents	$100,000
Cost of installing false bottom in trunk of car	$ 10,000
Distribution expenses	$ 50,000
Packaging (baggies)	$ 5,000
Kickbacks to narcotics agents	$ 75,000
	$440,000

Of the total, what amount would be deductible by Pancho?

a. $–0–
b. $440,000
c. $340,000
d. $200,000

_____ 17.   During the current year Xavier, a single taxpayer, had a salary of $48,000 and incurred the following expenses:

Alimony paid	$5,000
Charitable contributions	$1,000
Interest on home mortgage	$6,000
Deductible contribution to an IRA	$2,000
Moving expense	$2,000
Real estate taxes	$1,500

What is Xavier's adjusted gross income?

a. $48,000
b. $46,000
c. $41,000
d. $39,000

_____ 18.   During the current year Xavier, a single taxpayer, had a salary of $48,000 and incurred the following expenses:

Alimony paid	$5,000
Charitable contributions	$1,000
Interest on home mortgage	$6,000
Deductible contribution to an IRA	$2,000
Moving expense	$2,000
Real estate taxes	$1,500

What is Xavier's taxable income before any exemption(s)?

a. $30,500
b. $31,600
c. $33,200
d. $33,300

_____ 19.   Gene owns his own business. He hires his 19-year-old daughter (who has just passed introductory accounting with a grade of "A") as an accountant for the summer at a rate of $35.00 per hour. Gene has an accounting clerk who has worked for him for many years and he pays her $12.00 per hour. Gene, most likely, would be allowed a deductible business expense as a result of the payments to his daughter of:

a. $12.00 per hour
b. $20.00 per hour
c. $35.00 per hour
d. $25.00 per hour

_____ 20.   Bea incurred the following expenses during the current year:

Interest on son's home mortgage	$6,000
Payment of son's property taxes	$2,000
Payment of son's state income tax	$1,000
Payment of son's gambling debts	$3,000

What amount of the above can Bea consider in calculating her itemized deductions for the current year?

- a. $–0–
- b. $1,000
- c. $3,000
- d. $8,000

_____ 21. Wendy is the 100% owner of Blue Corporation. During the year, Wendy purchased from Blue Corporation depreciable property with an adjusted basis of $50,000 for $40,000, its fair market value. Blue placed this property in service six years ago. What is the available loss that Blue Corporation can claim for the current year?

- a. $–0–
- b. $10,000 ordinary loss
- c. $10,000 capital loss
- d. $10,000 Section 1231 loss

_____ 22. Which of the following are deductible as a trade or business expense?

- a. Illegal bribes and kickbacks
- b. Charitable contributions
- c. Qualified travel expense incurred by a self-employed dentist
- d. Home mortgage interest

_____ 23. Sam is the chief operating officer (CEO) of Silver Corporation, a publicly traded corporation. Silver pays Sam $2,500,000 compensation during the current year. The compensation consists of the following payments:

Salary	$1,400,000
Individual performance commission	$1,070,000
Pension plan contribution	$ 30,000
Total	$2,500,000

From the above payments, what amount can Silver Corporation deduct on its income tax return?

- a. $2,500,000
- b. $1,000,000
- c. $2,100,000
- d. $1,100,000

_____ 24. Laurie has a brokerage account at Dean Schwab, Inc. She buys stock and bonds on margin through this account. During the current year, she incurs $10,000 in margin interest in the account. Income generated through the brokerage account was:

Taxable dividends and interest	$30,000
Municipal bond interest	$20,000

What is the amount of Laurie's deductible investment interest?

- a. $–0–
- b. $4,000
- c. $6,000
- d. $10,000

_____ 25. The stock ownership of Salmon Corporations is as follows:

Shares owned by Jane	600
Shares owned by Jane's husband	300
Shares owned by Jane's brother-in-law	350
Shares owned by Jane's aunt	400
Shares owned by Jane's brother	250
Shares owned by Jane's grandson	100
Total shares	2,000

What is Jane's constructive ownership under Section 267?

a. 30%
b. 45%
c. 62.5%
d. 65%

_____ 26. Moving expenses for an individual taxpayer are

a. Deductible for AGI
b. Deductible from AGI
c. Deductible from taxable income
d. Not deductible

_____ 27. Commuting expenses for an individual taxpayer are

a. Deductible for AGI
b. Deductible from AGI
c. Deductible from taxable income
d. Not deductible

_____ 28. Medical expenses for an individual taxpayer are

a. Deductible for AGI
b. Deductible from AGI
c. Deductible from taxable income
d. Not deductible

_____ 29. Business interest for an individual taxpayer is

a. Deductible for AGI
b. Deductible from AGI
c. Deductible from taxable income
d. Not deductible

_____ 30. Business casualty losses for an individual taxpayer are

a. Deductible for AGI
b. Deductible from AGI
c. Deductible from taxable income
d. Not deductible

_____ 31. State income tax for an individual taxpayer is

a. Deductible for AGI
b. Deductible from AGI
c. Deductible from taxable income
d. Not deductible

_____ 32.   Bad debts for an individual taxpayer are

    a.   Deductible for AGI
    b.   Deductible from AGI
    c.   Deductible from taxable income
    d.   Not deductible

_____ 33.   Personal interest for an individual taxpayer is

    a.   Deductible for AGI
    b.   Deductible from AGI
    c.   Deductible from taxable income
    d.   Not deductible

_____ 34.   Reimbursed employee expenses for an individual taxpayer are

    a.   Deductible for AGI
    b.   Deductible from AGI
    c.   Deductible from taxable income
    d.   Not deductible

_____ 35.   Rent and royalty expenses for an individual taxpayer are

    a.   Deductible for AGI
    b.   Deductible from AGI
    c.   Deductible from taxable income
    d.   Not deductible

_____ 36.   Real property tax on a home

    a.   Deductible for AGI
    b.   Deductible from AGI
    c.   Deductible from taxable income
    d.   Not deductible

SOLUTIONS TO CHAPTER 6 QUESTIONS

True or False

1.   T   The courts have held that an item is not deductible unless the Code allows the deduction. [Classification of Deductible Expenses, p. 6–2]

2.   T   Under Section 162 or Section 212, an item must be ordinary and necessary to be deductible. [Ordinary and Necessary requirement, p. 6–5]

3.   F   Alimony is a deduction for AGI. [Deductions for Adjusted Gross Income, p. 6–3]

4.   F   The term is not defined in the Code. [Trade or Business Expenses and Production of Income Expenses, p. 6–5]

5.   T   Expenses incurred in the determination, collection, or refund of any tax are deductible. [Section 212 Expenses, p. 6–4]

6.   T   Salaries must be reasonable to be deductible. [Reasonableness Requirement, p. 6–6]

7.   T   Taxable income is computed under the method of accounting that the taxpayer regularly uses to keep his or her books. [Importance of Taxpayer's Method of Accounting, p. 6–7]

8.   T   Accrual basis taxpayers cannot take a deduction for capital expendi-tures except through amortization or depreciation. [Cash Method Requirements, p. 6–9]

9.   F   Legal expenses which are incurred in connection with a trade or business are deductible. [Legal Expenses Incurred in Defense of Civil or Criminal Penalties, p. 6–12]

10.   T   For an accrual basis taxpayer to deduct an expense, it must pass the "economic performance test." [Accrual Method Requirements, p. 6–9]

11.   F   The expenses are not deductible. [Investigation of a Business, p. 6–14]

12.   T   If an activity shows a profit for three of five years, then it is presumed not to be a hobby. [Hobby Loses, p. 6–15]

13.   T   If a residence is rented for 15 days or more, the deductions related to the home are limited if the taxpay-er uses the home for more than the greater of 14 days or 10 percent of the days actually rented. [Primarily Rental Use, p. 6–19]

14.   F   The mortgage is not the taxpayer's obligation. [Expenditure Incurred for Taxpayer's Benefit or Taxpayer's Obligation, p. 6–22]

15.   T   Section 262 disallows deductions for personal, living, and family expenses. [Disallowance of personal expenditures, p. 6 24]

16.   F   Section 265 disallows a deduction for expenses incurred in producing tax-exempt income. [Expenses and Interest Relating to Tax-Exempt Income, p. 6–28]

17.   F   The burden of proof for substantiating expenses deducted is on the taxpayer. [Substantiation Requirements, p. 6–27]

18.   T   Losses and certain deductions between related parties are disallowed under Section 267. [Transactions Between Related Parties, p. 6–26]

19.   F   Goodwill is amortizable over 15 years. [Capitalization Versus Expense, p. 6–25]

20.   F   Personal legal fees, other than those related to tax advice, are not deductible. [Legal Expenses Incurred in Defense of Civil or Criminal Penalties, p. 6–12]

21. F Vacation home expenses are limited to the income generated. [Rental of Vacation Homes, p. 6–18]

22. T An expense must be incurred for the taxpayer's benefit or arise from the taxpayer's obligation to be deductible. [Expenditure Incurred for Taxpayer's Benefit or Taxpayer's Obligation, p. 6–22]

23. T Most expenses of hobbies are subject to the 2 percent of AGI limitation. [Determining the Amount of the Deduction, p. 6–16]

24. T The courts have held that taxes and interest on a vacation home should be allocated over 365 days a year, however, the IRS has determined that taxes and interest should be based days of use. [Personal/Rental Use, p. 6–20]

25. T If Gwen used the condo for 20 days of personal use, it would be classified as a "personal/rental" asset because she uses it more than 18 days (10% × 180 days). [Personal/Rental Use, p. 6–20]

Multiple Choice

1. b State income tax is an itemized deduction. [Deductions for Adjusted Gross Income, p. 6–3]

2. c Interest on a personal residence in not covered in Section 212. [Section 212 Expenses, p. 6–4]

3. b Hobby expenses are limited to hobby income. [General Rules, p. 6–15]

4. d An activity should show a profit for 2 of 5 years in order not to be a hobby. [Presumptive Rule of Section 183, p. 6–16]

5. b Only the tax advice is deductible. [Legal Expenses Incurred in Defense of Civil or Criminal Penalties, p. 6–12]

6. a Kickback and fines are not deductible. [Public Policy Limitation, p. 6–11]

7. a Tax-exempt expenses are not allowed under Section 265. [Expenses and Interest Relating to Tax-Exempt Income, p. 6–28]

8. c 9% ($100,000) = $9,000; the interest is paid. [Unpaid Expenses and Interest, p. 6–28]

9. c The son's interest is not deductible by Tom. [Expenditure Incurred for Taxpayer's Benefit or Taxpayer's Obligation, p. 6–22]

10. d Note: this is "rental" property because it is only used 10 days for personal purposes.

Gross income	$4,000
Less: rental expenses	
Taxes & interest (75%)	–$2,250
Utilities and maintenance (75%)	–$ 600
Depreciation (75%)	–$3,000
Loss	–$1,850

[Primarily Rental Use, p. 6–20]

11. a

Gross income	$4,000
Less: rental expenses	
Taxes & interest (60%)	–$1,800
Utilities and maintenance (60%)	–$ 480
Depreciation (60%) (Max $1,600)	–$1,600
Loss	$ –0–

[Personal/Rental Use, p. 6–20]

12.   d   Robert must be in the trade or business for the expenses to be deductible. [Investigation of a Business, p. 6–14]

13.   c   The basis of the house is $115,000, therefore the gain is $45,000 ($160,000 – $115,000). [Capitalization versus Expense, p. 6–25]

14.   d   All the family members listed qualify under Section 267(c). [Relationship and Constructive Owner-ship, p. 6–27]

15.   a   Trade or business expense are in Section 162, not Section 212. [Trade or Business Expenses and Production of Income expenses, p. 6–5]

16.   d $200,000. Drug dealers are allowed cost of goods sold only. [Expenses Relating to an Illegal Business, p. 6–12]

17.   d

Salary	$48,000
IRA	–$ 2,000
Moving	–$ 2,000
Alimony	–$ 5,000
AGI	$39,000

[Deductions for Adjusted Gross Income, p. 6–3]

18.   a

AGI	$39,000
Mortgage interest	–$ 6,000
Charitable contributions	–$ 1,000
Taxes	–$ 1,500
Taxable income (before exemptions)	$30,500

[Itemized Deductions, p. 6–4]

19.   a   Wage payments must be reasonable to be deductible. [Reasonableness Requirement, p. 6–6]

20.   a   The payment must be for Bea's benefit or Bea's obligation. [Expenditure Incurred for Taxpayer's Benefit or Taxpayer's Obligation, p. 6–20]

21.   a   Wendy and Blue are related parties, therefore, no deduction. [Transaction Between Related Parties, p. 6–26]

22.   c   Self-employed taxpayers can deduct travel expenses [Trade or Business and Production of Income Expenses, p. 6–5]

23.   c $1,000,000 (maximum) + $1,070,000 + $30,000 = $2,100,000. [Excessive Executive Compensation, p. 6–13]

24.   c $10,000 × ($30,000/$50,000) = $6,000. [Expenses and Interest Relating to Tax-Exempt Income, p. 6–28]

25.   c   (600 + 300 + 250 + 100) / 2,000 = 62.5% [Relationships and Constructive Ownership, p. 6–27]

26.   a   Moving expenses are deductible for AGI. [Concept Summary 6–3, p. 6–31]

27.   d   Commuting expenses are not deductible. [Concept Summary 6–3, p. 6–31]

28.   b   Medical expenses are deductible from AGI. [Concept Summary 6–3, p. 6–31]

29.   a   Business interest is deductible for AGI. [Concept Summary 6–3, p. 6–31]

30.   a   Business casualty losses are deductible for AGI. [Concept Summary 6–3, p. 6–31]

31.   b   State income taxes is deductible from AGI. [Concept Summary 6–3, p. 6–31]

32.   a   Bad Debts are deductible for AGI. [Concept Summary 6–3, p. 6–31]

33.   d   Personal interest is not deductible. [Concept Summary 6–3, p. 6–31]

34.   a   Reimbursed Employee Expenses are deductible for AGI. [Concept Summary 6–3, p. 6–31]

35.   a   Rent and royalty expenses are deductible for AGI. [Concept Summary 6–3, p. 6–31]

36.   b   Real property taxes on a home are deductible from AGI. [Concept Summary 6–3, p. 6–31]

CHAPTER 7

Deductions & Losses: Certain Business Expenses & Losses

CHAPTER HIGHLIGHTS

This chapter discusses certain business expenses and losses that are deducted from gross income to arrive at the taxpayer's adjusted gross income. Casualty losses are also discussed, although personal casualty losses are considered itemized deductions rather than deductions for adjusted gross income.

KEY TERMS

Worthless Securities
Casualty Losses

Bad Debts
Theft Losses

Net Operating Loss

OUTLINE

I. **BAD DEBTS**
    A. Specific Charge-Off Method. For tax years after 1986, all taxpayers, except for certain financial institutions, must use the specific charge-off method for deducting bad debts. The specific charge-off method allows a deduction when a specific debt becomes partially (business only) or totally worthless (business or nonbusiness).
    B. Business Versus Nonbusiness Bad Debts. Bad debts fall into one of two classifications: business bad debts or nonbusiness bad debts. Debts that arise from a taxpayer's trade or business are business bad debts while all other debts are nonbusiness bad debts. The primary difference in the tax treatment is that business bad debts are ordinary deductions while nonbusiness bad debts are treated as short-term capital losses.
    C. Loans Between Related Parties. Loans between related parties create problems in determining whether the loan was bona fide or a gift. If there is no debtor-creditor relationship established, the debt to a related party may be a gift. If the debt is not repaid, the bad debt deduction will be lost and a gift tax may be incurred.
    D. Financial Institutions. Under the tax law, qualified individuals can elect to deduct losses on deposits in qualified financial institutions as personal casualty losses in the year in which the loss can be reasonably estimated.

II. **WORTHLESS SECURITIES**
    A. Losses arising from worthless securities, such as stocks and bonds, are generally treated as capital losses deemed to have occurred on the last day of the tax year.
    B. Small Business Stock. Another exception to the capital loss rule on worthless securities is for qualified "small business" or "Section 1244 stock." Individual taxpayers are allowed ordinary loss treatment limited to $50,000 ($100,000 for a joint return) per year for losses on stock that qualifies as small business stock. Any losses over the above limits are capital losses.

III. **LOSSES OF INDIVIDUAL TAXPAYERS**
    A. Casualty Losses. An individual taxpayer may deduct losses under Section 165(c) in each of the following circumstances:
        1) the loss was incurred in a trade or business,
        2) the loss was incurred in a transaction entered into for profit, or
        3) the loss was caused by casualty or theft.

        A casualty loss is "the complete or partial destruction of property resulting from an identifiable event of a sudden, unexpected, or unusual nature." Thus, casualties would include such items as hurricanes, floods, storms, shipwrecks, fires, auto accidents, and mine cave-ins.
    B. Events that are not casualties are those due to "progressive deterioration," such as termite damage, rust, and erosion. Such events are not considered casualty losses since they are not "sudden and unexpected."
    C. Theft Losses. A theft loss includes larceny, embezzlement, and robbery. It does not include misplaced items. Theft losses are deductible in the year the loss is "discovered," not the year of theft. A partial deduction is allowed if a settlement is arrived at, which is less than the property's adjusted basis.
    D. When to Deduct Casualty Losses. Generally, casualty losses are deducted in the year of the casualty. However, if the casualty is in an area designated as a disaster area by the President of the United States, then the taxpayer may elect to treat the loss as having occurred in the previous taxable year. When a "reasonable prospect of full recovery" exists, no deduction for a casualty loss may be taken.
    E. Measuring the Amount of the Loss. In computing the amount of a casualty loss, it is necessary to divide the property into that held for personal use and that held for business use. Property held for "personal use" is subject to a $100 statutory reduction in the otherwise allowable deduction. This $100 reduction does not apply to business use property. Personal casualty losses are deductible only to the extent they exceed 10 percent of AGI after reduction by the $100 floor.

The amount of the gross casualty loss deduction, before the $100 floor amount and before the 10 percent of adjusted gross income limitation applicable to personal casualty losses, is the lesser of (1) the adjusted basis of the property, or (2) the decrease in fair market value of the property.

The only exception to this rule is the complete destruction of business property, in which case, the adjusted basis is used to measure the loss.

F. Statutory Framework. Casualty and theft losses by an individual with a trade or business are deductible for AGI. The $100 per event and ten percent of AGI limits do not apply. Investment property casualty losses are not subject to the limits. If the investment losses are rent and royalties related, the deduction is for AGI, otherwise, the deduction is from AGI.

G. Personal Casualty Gains and Losses. If a taxpayer's personal casualty gains exceed personal casualty losses, the gains and losses will be treated as capital gains and losses. If the personal casualty losses exceed the personal casualty gains, then the gains and losses are netted. In determining whether personal casualty gains exceed personal casualty losses, the casualty losses must first be reduced by the $100 statutory floor. Personal casualty losses in excess of personal casualty gains are deductible subject to the 10 percent of AGI limitation. Casualty gains and losses from business properties are not netted with personal casualty gains and losses.

IV. RESEARCH AND EXPERIMENTAL EXPENDITURES

A. Section 174 of the Code controls the tax treatment of research and experimental expenditures. A taxpayer may elect to expense all such costs in the current year. If the election is made for the first year in which the expenses are incurred, the taxpayer does not need the consent of the IRS.

B. A taxpayer may also elect to defer and amortize research and experimental expenditures over a period of not less than 60 months. If the election to expense or defer is not made, the taxpayer must capitalize such expenses.

V. NET OPERATING LOSSES

A. To remove inequities that may be caused by the requirement that annual tax returns be filed, taxpayers are allowed a deduction for net operating losses (NOL). A NOL deduction is allowed in a given period for a business related loss incurred in another period. In computing an NOL, several adjustments have to be made to reflect a true economic loss.

B. Carryback and Carryover Periods. Once the NOL is calculated, the amount can be carried back or forward. For loss years, the loss is carried "back two years and forward 20 years." Alternatively, the taxpayer may elect to carry the loss forward only.

There is a three-year carry-back for any portion of an individual's NOL resulting from a casualty or theft loss. The three-year rule also applies to presidentially declared disasters which are incurred by a small business or a taxpayer engaged in farming.

C. Computation of the NOL. Adjustments must be made to an individual's taxable loss so that it reflects only losses related to the operation of a trade or business since the NOL is intended as a relief provision only for business income and losses. All casualty and theft losses, including personal casualty and theft losses, are also allowed in computing the NOL. Examples of some items that must be added to the taxpayer's taxable income to arrive at the NOL deduction are shown below.

1) The deductions for personal and dependency exemptions.
2) The NOL carryovers and carrybacks from other years.
3) Capital losses and nonbusiness deductions are limited in determining the current year's NOL.
4) The excess of nonbusiness capital losses over nonbusiness capital gains must be added back.
5) The excess of nonbusiness deductions over the sum of nonbusiness income and net nonbusiness capital gains must be added back.
6) The excess of business capital losses over the sum of business capital gains and the excess of nonbusiness income and nonbusiness capital gains over nonbusiness deductions must be added back.
7) The add-back for net nonbusiness capital losses and excess business capital losses does not include net capital losses not included in the current year's taxable income because of any capital loss limitation.

8) The excess of business capital losses over the sum of business capital gains plus the excess of net nonbusiness capital gains and nonbusiness income over nonbusiness deductions.

An NOL is carried back for two years and carried forward for a maximum of twenty years. It is first carried to the second prior year, and then to the immediately preceding year. If the loss is not used up, it is carried forward sequentially until the used up or twenty years have passed.

Taxpayers elect to forgo the carry-back and only carry the NOL forward. This is advantageous when a taxpayer was in a low marginal tax bracket in the two prior years.

A taxpayer who does not itemize deductions adds the excess of nonbusiness deductions over nonbusiness income by substituting the standard deduction amount for itemized deductions.

D. When an NOL is carried back to a prior year, the taxable income and tax liability for the year to which the loss is being carried must be recomputed. Deductions based on the amount of adjusted gross income, other than charitable contributions, must be recomputed based on the new adjusted gross income after the NOL. Any tax credits limited by tax liability must also be recomputed based on the reduced amount of tax due.

E. Calculation of the Remaining NOL. After computing the refund claim for a carryback year, it is necessary to determine the amount of the net operating loss that is left to carry into other years. The amount of the carryover loss is the excess of the NOL over the taxable income of the year to which the loss is being applied. However, the taxable income of the year to which the loss is being applied must be recalculated with certain modifications (see the textbook).

TEST FOR SELF-EVALUATION—CHAPTER 7

True or False

Indicate which of the following statements is true or false by circling the correct answer.

T F 1. To be written off as a bad debt, accounts receivable must have been previously included in income.

T F 2. Nonfinancial institutions must use the specific charge-off method for bad debts.

T F 3. Nonbusiness bad debts are deductible in the year of partial or total worthlessness.

T F 4. Losses on Section 1224 stock in excess of the annual statutory limits receive capital loss treatment.

T F 5. Amounts spent for consumer surveys, advertising, or promotions qualify under Section 174 as research and experimental expenditures.

T F 6. In certain situations, loans between related parties may be classified as gifts.

T F 7. Worthless securities always generate an ordinary loss.

T F 8. Worthless securities are treated as having become worthless on the last day of the taxable year.

T F 9. Within certain dollar limits, individual taxpayers may recognize an ordinary loss as opposed to a capital loss on the disposition of "Section 1244 stock."

T F 10. A taxpayer's loss on property used in a trade or business is not limited to loss caused by fire, storm, shipwreck, or other casualty, or by theft.

T F 11. All casualty and theft loss deductions are subject to a $100 statutory floor.

T F 12. A loss caused by rust will be deductible as a casualty loss under Section 165.

T F 13. To be deductible, casualty damage must be to the taxpayer's property.

T F 14. Disaster area casualty losses must be deducted in the year of the casualty.

T F 15. The gross amount of a personal casualty loss is the larger of (1) the adjusted basis of the property, or (2) the decrease in fair market value.

T F 16. The general rule for NOL carrybacks and carryovers is two years back and seven years forward.

T F 17. Personal and dependency exemptions are allowed as deductions in arriving at an individual taxpayer's NOL.

T F 18. A taxpayer may elect to expense research and experimental expenditures.

T F 19. The maximum loss on Section 1244 stock that may be treated as an ordinary loss is $50,000 for a joint return.

T F 20. "Small business stock" under Section 1244 can only be common stock.

T F 21. Prior year net operating losses are subtracted from taxable income in arriving at the current year net operating loss.

T F 22. In determining the amount of an NOL remaining to be carried to another tax year, modified taxable income for a year into which an NOL is carried must be determined without the deduction for personal and dependency exemptions.

Multiple Choice

Choose the best answer for each of the following questions.

_____ 1. Simon, a calendar year taxpayer, owns stock (not Section 1244 stock) in Red Corporation (a publicly-held company). The stock was acquired on May 1st of last year. The cost of the stock was $10,000. On March 1st of the current year the stock became worthless. Simon should report (before any limitations) a:

    a. $10,000 short-term capital loss
    b. $10,000 long-term capital loss
    c. $10,000 ordinary loss
    d. No gain or loss

_____ 2. Liz owns Section 1244 stock in X Corporation with a basis of $120,000. She acquired the stock three years ago. During the current year she sells the stock for $40,000. If Liz is single, as a result of the sale of the stock, she should report (before any $3,000 annual capital loss limitation):

    a. $80,000 long-term capital loss
    b. $80,000 ordinary loss
    c. $50,000 long-term capital loss and $30,000 ordinary loss
    d. $50,000 ordinary loss and $30,000 long-term capital loss

_____ 3. For tax purposes, research and experimental expenses may not be:

    a. Capitalized
    b. Expensed in the year paid or incurred
    c. Deferred and amortized over 60 months or more
    d. Deducted as a short-term capital loss

_____ 4. Robert loaned his friend, Fred, $6,000. Fred used the money to start a business. In the current year, Fred went bankrupt and the debt became worthless. Assuming he has no other capital transactions, Robert should report (in the current year):

    a. No deduction for the loss
    b. $6,000 long-term capital loss
    c. $3,000 short-term capital loss
    d. $6,000 short-term capital loss

_____ 5. Martha had a deductible casualty loss of $10,000 in x1. Her taxable income for x1 was $55,000. In x2, Martha was reimbursed $7,000 for the casualty loss. How much income must Martha report in x2 for the reimbursement?

    a. $–0–
    b. $3,000
    c. $7,000
    d. $10,000

_____ 6. During the current year, Tim's house was robbed. His personal stereo and coin collection were taken. The stereo had a basis of $600 and a FMV of $250, while the coin collection's basis was $400 and its FMV was $500. What is Tim's theft loss deduction before the 10 percent of adjusted gross income limitation?

    a. $–0–
    b. $550
    c. $650
    d. $450

_____ 7.   Which of the following would be deductible as a personal casualty loss?

    a.   Rust on the panels of an automobile
    b.   Decrease in value of a personal residence because of the construction of a new sewer plant nearby
    c.   Moth damage to clothes
    d.   Damage to the roof of a personal residence when a tree blows over in a storm

_____ 8.   Linda had a casualty gain of $6,000 in the current year and a casualty loss of $4,000 (after deducting the $100 floor). Her adjusted gross income for the year is $25,000. Both the casualties are from long-term capital assets. Linda should report:

    a. $2,000 ordinary income
    b. $1,500 casualty loss and $6,000 ordinary income
    c. $6,000 ordinary gain and $2,000 capital loss
    d. $6,000 capital gain and $4,000 capital loss

_____ 9.   Craig had adjusted income of $70,000. During the year his personal winter home was destroyed by fire. Pertinent data with respect to the winter home is as follows:

Cost basis	$40,000
FMV before casualty	$55,000
FMV after casualty	$13,000

Craig received a $23,000 insurance settlement for the fire. What is Craig's allowable casualty loss?

    a. $–0–
    b. $16,900
    c. $10,000
    d. $9,900

_____ 10.   Yellow Corporation incurred the following expenditures in connection with the development of a new product:

Salaries	$50,000
Materials	$ 6,000
Marketing survey	$ 4,000
Sales promotion	$10,000

If the corporation elects to expense research and experimental expenditures, what amount is allowed as a deduction in the current year?

    a. $50,000
    b. $56,000
    c. $60,000
    d. $70,000

_____ 11.   John has the following tax items for the current year:

Nonbusiness capital gains	$ 5,000
Nonbusiness capital losses	$ 3,000
Dividend income	$ 6,000
Itemized deductions (no casualty losses)	$10,000

What amount would John add back to his taxable income in calculating his net operating loss for the year?

    a. $2,000
    b. $3,000
    c. $4,000
    d. $10,000

_____ 12.   Marsha is married and owns her own business. She uses the cash receipts and disbursements method for tax purposes. During the current year her income, expenses, and other items were as follows:

Gross receipts	$40,000
Cost of goods sold	$24,000
General expenses	$18,000
Uncollectible accounts receivable	$ 6,000

What is Marsha's bad debt expense deduction for tax purposes?

    a. $–0–
    b. $2,000
    c. $4,000
    d. $6,000

_____ 13.   Marsha is married and owns her own business. She uses the *accrual* method for tax purposes. During the current year her income, expenses, and other items were as follows:

Gross receipts	$40,000
Cost of goods sold	$24,000
General expenses	$18,000
Uncollectible accounts receivable	$ 6,000

What is Marsha's bad debt expense deduction for tax purposes?

    a. $–0–
    b. $2,000
    c. $4,000
    d. $6,000

_____ 14.   Larry Legal and Associates, a professional corporation, loaned $125,000 to Leonard Litigious, one of the employees. Leonard left for Brazil the next day (he left a note that said "hasta la vista, baby"). As a result of Leonard's action, the corporation will never collect on the loan. What can Larry Legal and Associates deduct?

    a. $125,000 short-term capital loss
    b. $125,000 long-term capital loss
    c. $125,000 ordinary loss
    d. $3,000 short-term capital loss

_____ 15.   During x3, Tierra Corporation incurred research and experimental expenses of $37,000. In x4, the corporation had another $50,000 of such expenditures. The Corporation began realizing benefits from the project on October 31, x4. If the corporation elects the expense method for research and experimental expenditures, what amount may be deducted in x4?

     a. $–0–
     b. $37,000
     c. $50,000
     d. $87,000

_____ 16.   Teri had the following casualties during the current year:

Personal casualty loss (after the $100 limit)	$12,000
Personal casualty gain (long-term asset)	$ 5,000

If Teri's adjusted gross income for the year is $45,000, what is her casualty loss deduction?

     a. $–0–
     b. $2,500
     c. $5,000
     d. $7,000

_____ 17.   In x5, Ted (who is in the business of lending money) loaned Nick $10,000 to go on a vacation. During x5 (before paying back any of the loan), Nick declared bankruptcy. Nick expects to be able settle his debts for $.45 on the dollar. However, during x6, Nick was only able to pay $.35 on the dollar. How much should Ted deduct on his x5 tax return?

     a. $–0–
     b. $4,500
     c. $5,500
     d. $3,500

_____ 18.   In x3, Penny purchased $10,000 worth of East-West Airline's common stock. East-West Airline has since declared bankruptcy and shut down operations. As a result of a bankruptcy judge's ruling the East-West Airline stock became worthless in x7. Penny's appropriate tax treatment for loss (before any annual limits) on the stock in x7 is:

     a. $10,000 ordinary loss
     b. $10,000 long-term loss
     c. $10,000 short-term loss
     d. $–0– loss deduction

_____ 19.   Jed, who is single, had the following items for the current year:

- Salary of $90,000
- Gain of $30,000 on the sale of Section 1244 stock acquired two years ago
- Loss of $75,000 on the sale of Section 1244 stock acquired four months ago
- Worthless stock of $7,000 acquired on April 30 of the prior year and became worthless on March 10 of the current year

What is Jed's AGI for the current year?

     a. $38,000
     b. $50,000
     c. $15,000
     d. $55,000

_____ 20.   Dale parks her car on a hill and fails to properly set the brake or curb the wheels. As a result of Dale's negligence, the car rolls down the hill, damages Bill's front porch, injures Bill (who was sitting on the porch), and damages Dale's car. Due to the accident Dale is forced to pay the following amounts:

- $1,650 for medical expenses for Bill's injuries
- $2,800 for repairs to her car

- $1,000 for repairs to Bill's porch
- $120 for a fine for traffic violation

Which of the payments, if any, qualify for casualty loss treatment to Dale (before any limitations)?

  a. $–0–
  b. $2,800
  c. $3,800
  d. $5,450

_____ 21.   Andrew, a single taxpayer, sustained an NOL of $10,000 in 2003. He had no taxable income in years before 2002. For 2002, Andrew filed a tax return with the following amounts:

Adjusted Gross Income		$16,000
Itemized Deductions:		
Charitable	$3,000	
Interest	$5,000	
Taxes	$1,500	
Total deductions		–$ 9,500
2002 Exemption		–$ 3,000
Taxable Income		$ 3,500
Tax (15%)		$ 525

_____ 22.   What is Andrew's 2002 tax after applying the NOL carryback from 2003?

  a. $–0–
  b. $263
  c. $363
  d. $563

_____ 23.   Andrew, a single taxpayer, sustained an NOL of $10,000 in 2003. He had no taxable income in years before 2002. For 2002, Andrew filed a tax return with the following amounts:

Adjusted Gross Income		$16,000
Itemized Deductions:		
Charitable	$3,000	
Interest	$5,000	
Taxes	$1,500	
Total deductions		–$ 9,500
2002 Exemption		–$ 3,000
Taxable Income		$ 3,500
Tax (15%)		$ 525

What is Andrew's NOL carryover available for 2004 and future years?

  a. $–0–
  b. $3,500
  c. $6,500
  d. $6,150

_____ 24.   John is a farmer who has a $20,000 NOL caused by a flooding casualty to his farm. The flooding was declared a qualified disaster area by the President of the U.S. How many years can John carryback his NOL?

      a.   Two-years
      b.   Three-years
      c.   Five-years
      d.   There is no carryback allowed.

Problems

1.   Tom, a married individual, had the following income and deductions for Year 1:

Income:		
Gross income from business	$71,720	
Interest on savings account	$ 600	$72,320
Deductions:		
NOL carryover from 1998	$ 300	
Business expenses	$75,000	
Net loss on rental property	$ 1,000	
Itemized deductions (no casualty loss)	$16,000	(–$92,300)
Taxable income (before exemptions)		(–$19,980)

Calculate Tom's NOL for Year 1.

2.   Tim had the following casualty losses occurring in separate events:

Asset	Adj. Basis	FMV Before	FMV After
A	$2,000	$3,000	$–0–
B	$2,000	$1,800	$–0–
C	$3,000	$2,000	–0–
D	$2,000	$3,000	$500

Assets A and B are personal assets while C and D were used in Tim's business at the time of the casualty. The assets were not covered by insurance. Determine the amount of the deductible casualty loss (disregarding the 10 percent of adjusted gross income limitation where applicable) for:

Asset A   _____
Asset B   _____
Asset C   _____
Asset D   _____

SOLUTIONS TO CHAPTER 7 QUESTIONS

True or False

1. T   Accounts receivable must have been previously included in income to be written off. [Bad Debts, p. 7–3]

2. T   Nonfinancial institutions must use the specific charge-off method. [Specific Charge-Off Method, p. 7–2]

3. F   Nonbusiness bad debts are deductible only when totally worthless. [Specific Charge-Off Method, p. 7–3]

4. T   Section 1244 losses are capital over the statutory limit. [Worthless Securities, p. 7–6]

5. F   These expenditures do not qualify. [Research and Experimental Expenditures, p. 7–16]

6. T   Loans between related parties may be classified as gifts in certain situations. [Loans Between Related Parties, p. 7–5]

7. F   Losses on worthless securities are usually treated as capital losses. [Worthless Securities, p. 7–6]

8. T   Worthless securities are treated as worthless on the last day of the taxable year. [Worthless Securities, p. 7–6]

9. T   Individual taxpayers may recognize an ordinary loss (within limits) on the disposition of Section 1244 stock. [Small Business Stock, p. 7–6]

10. T   Loss on property used in a trade or business is not limited to loss caused by fire, storm, shipwreck, or other casualty, or by theft. [Losses of Individuals, p. 7–8]

11. F   Business casualty loss deductions are not subject to the $100 floor. [Reduction for $100 and 10 Percent-of-AGI Floors, p. 7–12]

12. F   Rust is not sudden and unexpected. [Events That Are Not Casualties, p. 7–9]

13. T   Casualty damage must be to the taxpayer's property to be deductible. [Losses of Individuals, p. 7–8]

14. F   They may be deducted in the prior year. [Disaster Area Losses, p. 7–10]

15. F   The deduction is equal to the lesser of the adjusted basis of the property or the decrease in FMV of the property. [Measuring the Amount of Loss, p. 7–11]

16. F   The carryforward period is 20 years. [Carryback and carryover Periods, p. 7–19]

17. F   A deduction for personal and dependency exemptions is not allowed in arriving at the taxpayer's NOL. [Computations of the Net Operating Loss, p. 7–20]

18. T   Taxpayers may elect to expense research and experimental expenditures. [Research and Experimental Expenditures, p. 7–16]

19. F   The maximum amount of loss on Section 1244 stock that may be treated as an ordinary loss is $100,000 on a joint return. [Small Business Stock, p. 7–6]

20. F   Preferred stock is included under Section 1244. [Small Business Stock, p. 7–6]

21. F   Net operating loss carryovers and carrybacks must be added back to taxable income in arriving at the current year net operating loss. [Computation of the Net Operating Loss, p. 7–20]

22. T   In determining the amount of a NOL to be carried to another tax year, modified taxable income for a year into which an NOL is carried must be determined without the deduction for exemptions. [Calculation of the Remaining Net Operating Loss Deduction, p. 7–23]

Multiple Choice

1. b   Worthless securities become bad on the last day of the tax year, thus a long-term capital loss. [Worthless Securities, p. 7–6]

2. d   On Section 1244 stock, the first $50,000 is ordinary loss. [Small Business Stock, p. 7–6]

3. d   Research and experimental expenditures can be capitalized, expensed, or deferred, but cannot be deducted as a short-term capital loss. [Research and Experimental Expenditures, p. 7–16]

4. c   Nonbusiness bad debts are treated as short-term capital losses subject to the $3,000 limit. [Business Versus Nonbusiness Bad Debt, p. 7–4]

5. c   The reimbursement is income to the extent the casualty loss resulted in a tax benefit. [When to Deduct Casualty Losses, p. 7–10]

6. b $250 (stereo) + $400 (TV) − $100 (limit) = $550. [Measuring the Amount of Loss, p. 7–11]

7. d   Storm damage is a personal casualty. [Losses of Individuals, p. 7–8]

8. d   There is a net casualty gain, therefore, all gains and losses are capital. [Personal Casualty Gains and Losses, p. 7–14]

9. d

Fair market value before casualty	$55,000
Fair market value after casualty	−($13,000)
Decrease in fair market value	$42,000
Lesser of decrease in FMV or adjusted basis	$40,000
Insurance recovery	−($23,000)
Gross loss	$17,000
Per casualty limitation	− $ 100)
Adjusted gross income limitation	−($ 7,000)
Casualty loss deduction	$ 9,900

[Measuring the Amount of Loss, p. 7–13]

10. b $50,000 + 6,000 = $56,000. [Expense Method, p. 7–17]

11. a $2,000 = $10,000 − [$6,000 + ($5,000 − 3,000)]. [Computation of the Net Operating Loss, p. 7–20]

12. a   Since Marsha is a cash basis taxpayer the accounts receivable were never included in income, thus there is no deduction for the bad debts. [Bad Debts, p. 7–3]

13. d   If the accounts receivable are included in income under the accrual method of accounting, then the bad debt is deductible. [Bad Debts, p. 7–3]

14. c   Corporations can only have business bad debts, therefore, the $125,000 is deductible as an ordinary deduction. [Business Versus Nonbusiness Bad Debts, p. 7–4]

15. c   The whole amount is deducted in the current year. [Expense Method, p. 7–17]

16. b

Casualty loss over casualty gain	$7,000
Less 10% of AGI	($4,500)
Deduction	$2,500

[Personal Casualty Gains and Losses, p. 7–15]

17. c $.55 × $10,000 = $5,500. [Specific Charge-Off Method, p. 7–3]

18. b   This loss is a long-term capital loss. [Worthless Securities, p. 7–6]

19. a

Salary		$90,000
Section 1244 ordinary loss		–$50,000
LTCG	$30,000	
LTCL ($75,000 – $50,000)	–$25,000	
Worthless Security	–$ 7,000	
		–$ 2,000
AGI		$38,000

[Small Business Stock, p. 7–25]

20. b The medical expenses do not qualify because they are not damage to Dale's property. The damage to the porch does not qualify because it is not Dale's porch. The traffic fine does not qualify because of Section 162(f) (public policy limitations). [Measuring the Amount of Loss, p. 7–11]

21. a

Adjusted Gross Income		$16,000
Less: NOL		–($10,000)
Recomputed AGI		$ 6,000
Itemized Deductions		
Charitable	$3,000	
Interest	$5,000	
Taxes	$1,500	
Total deductions	–($9,500)	
Exemption [2002]		–($3,000)
Taxable Income		–($6,500)
Tax		$ –0–

[Computation of the Net Operating Loss, p. 7–20)

22. b

Adjusted Gross Income		$16,000
Itemized Deductions		
Charitable	$3,000	
Interest	$5,000	
Taxes	$1,500	
Total deductions	(–$9,500)	
Exemption (not allowed)	–0–	
Modified taxable income		$ 6,500
NOL		(–$10,000)
Modified taxable income		$ 6,500
NOL carry forward		(–$ 3,500)

[Computation of The Net Operating Loss, p. 7–20]

23. b NOL casualties have a three-year carryback. [Carryback and Carryover Periods, p. 7–19]

Problems

1. Taxable income (loss) for Year 1   (–$19,980)
    Add:
    NOL from prior year $ 300
    Itemized deductions $16,000
    Less: Interest income   (–$ 600) $15,400
    Net operating loss for Year 0   –($ 4,280)

    [Computation of the Net Operating Loss, p. 7–20]

2. Asset A $1,900 = Lesser of decrease in FMV ($3,000 – $0) or adjusted basis ($2,000);
                   $2,000 – 100 = $1,900.

    Asset B $1,700 = Lesser of decrease in FMV ($1,800) or adjusted basis ($2,000);
                   $1,800 – 100 = $1,700.

    Asset C $3,000 = Adjusted basis of $3,000. (Note, complete destruction of business
                   property, therefore, no $100 limitation)

    Asset D $2,000 = Lesser of decrease in FMV ($3,000 – $500) or adjusted basis ($2,000)

    [Measuring the Amount of Loss, p. 7–11]

CHAPTER 8

Depreciation, Cost Recovery, Amortization & Depletion

CHAPTER HIGHLIGHTS

The tax law provides for the recovery of the cost of assets through depreciation, cost recovery, amortization, or depletion. This chapter looks at the methods by which capitalized costs may be recovered under the Code. In addition, the types of assets that qualify for some form of capital recovery are discussed.

KEY TERMS

Depreciation	ACRS/MACRS	Listed Property
Amortization	§ 179 Election	Depletion
Realty/Personalty		

OUTLINE

I.   **ACCELERATED COST RECOVERY SYSTEM (ACRS)**
   A.   General Considerations. The accelerated cost recovery system applies to most property acquired after December 31, 1980. ACRS is designed to aid capital formation by providing a rapid write-off for capital goods. The recovery periods under ACRS are based on the classification of property into "classes." ACRS was revised by the Tax Reform Act of 1986, so that the classification of property depends on whether the property was placed in service before January 1, 1987, in which case the original ACRS rules apply, or after December 31, 1986, in which case the modified ACRS (MACRS) rules apply.
   B.   Personalty: Recovery Periods and Methods. The cost of eligible personalty (and certain realty) is recovered based on recovery classes. The recovery class lives are as follows.

   Post-1986 Acquisitions

3-year:	ADR midpoints of 4 years and less (except autos and light duty trucks), certain horses.
5-year:	ADR midpoints of more than 4 years and less than 10 years, autos, light duty trucks, R&D equipment, etc.
7-year:	Property that is not included in another class, includes office furniture, fixtures, and equipment.
10-year:	ADR midpoints of 16 years or more, but less than 20 years.
15-year:	ADR midpoints of 20 years or more, but less than 25 years.
20-year:	ADR midpoints of 25 years or more.

   The post-1986 ACRS rates are based on the 200 percent declining balance method (3, 5, 7, and 10-year classes) or 150 percent declining balance method (15- and 20-year classes), using the half-year convention in both the year of acquisition and the year of disposition, and disregarding salvage value. In certain cases, a mid-quarter convention may be required.
   C.   Realty: Recovery Periods and Methods. Pre-1987 real estate under ACRS is written off over 15, 18, or 19 years depending on the date the property was placed in service. The pre-1987 rates are based on 175 percent declining balance. Depreciation for 15-year property and certain 18-year property uses a full month convention. Eighteen-year real property placed in service after June 22, 1984, and 19-year recovery property use a mid-month convention. (See text for the various ACRS tables.)

   Post-1986 real estate is written off over 15 years (land improvements), 27.5 years for residential realty, or 31.5 years (39 years after May 12, 1993) for nonresidential realty. Residential and nonresidential realty can only use the straight-line method. Property depreciated under the 27.5-year, 31.5-year, or 39-year class uses a mid-month convention.
   D.   Straight-Line Election Under ACRS and MACRS. Instead of using the accelerated methods under ACRS, taxpayers may elect to use the straight-line method of depreciation. The pre-1987 straight-line recovery periods are as follows:

3-year property:	3, 5, or 12 years
5-year property:	5, 12, or 25 years
10-year property:	10, 25, or 35 years
15-year property:	15, 35, or 45 years
18-year property:	18, 35, or 45 years
19-year property:	19, 35, or 45 years

   The election of the straight-line method is a class-by-class election for other than real property in the 15-, 18-, or 19-year classes. For real property, the straight-line election was available on a property-by-property basis. The half-year, monthly, or mid-month conventions continue to apply when the straight-line election is made.

Depreciation under the post-1986 straight-line election is based on the property's class life using a half-year or mid-quarter convention, whichever is applicable. The straight-line method is required for real property acquired after 1986.

See the text for various tables for calculating straight-line ACRS or MACRS.

E. Election to Expense. Section 179 permits an election to expense a limited amount of the cost of certain depreciable assets used in a trade or business up to a $20,000 annual limit in 2001 and 2002. The annual limit is $25,000 in 2003 and later years. The amount expensed cannot exceed the taxable income derived from the taxpayer's trade or business. Furthermore, the amount expensed is reduced dollar-for-dollar when property placed in service exceeds $200,000 for the year.

F. Business and Personal Use of Automobiles and Other Listed Property. A taxpayer must show that listed property used for both business and personal use is used predominantly for business (greater than 50 percent) to use the statutory percentage methods under ACRS or MACRS. If the property is not used predominantly for business, the depreciable basis must be recovered using straight-line deprecation under the ADS. Recapture rules apply where the business usage of listed property depreciated under the statutory percentage method drops below the greater than 50 percent requirement.

Under the "luxury auto" rules, the deduction for depreciation expense on passenger automobiles is limited. The amount of these annual limits changes each year. See the textbook for the current year's annual limits.

These limits are imposed before the percentage reduction for personal use of the automobile. In addition, the annual limits apply to any election to expense under § 179.

G. Alternative Depreciation System (ADS). For post-1986 property the ADS must be used in calculating depreciation expense for the following:
1) the alternative minimum tax calculation
2) property used outside the U.S.
3) property leased or otherwise used by a tax-exempt entity
4) property financed by tax-exempt bonds
5) certain imported property
6) determining earnings and profits

In most cases the ADS requires the use of the straight-line method, except with regard to the alternative minimum tax calculation of depreciation on personalty which uses the 150 percent declining balance method.

Taxpayers may elect to use the 150 percent declining balance method to compute the regular tax rather than the normal 200 percent MACRS method. Thus, there will be no difference between regular and alternative minimum tax. (Note: the taxpayers must use the ADS recovery periods if this election is made).

See text for the ADS calculation.

II. AMORTIZATION

Purchased intangible property, such as goodwill, used in a trade or business or for the production of income may be amortized over 15 years under § 197.

III. DEPLETION
A. Payment for natural resources is recovered through depletion. However, intangible drilling and development costs can be handled in one of two ways. Such costs can either be (1) expensed in the year incurred, or (2) capitalized (added to the depletable basis) and written off through depletion. These costs include the cost of making property ready for drilling, erecting derricks, and drilling the well.

B.   Depletion Methods. The owner of an interest in a wasting asset is entitled to a depletion deduction. The tax law allows for two types of depletion: cost and percentage.

Cost depletion is based on the adjusted basis of the asset. The basis is divided by the estimated recoverable units of the asset to arrive at a cost per unit. This cost is multiplied by the units sold to arrive at the deduction allowed. The cost per unit may be redetermined on a prospective basis, based on revised estimates of the recoverable units.

Percentage depletion is based on a percentage specified in the Code that is applied to the gross income from the property to arrive at the amount of depletion allowed. Such depletion may not exceed 50 percent of the taxable income from the property before the depletion allowance. Special limitations apply to the use of percentage depletion for certain oil and gas wells. The cost basis of the asset must be reduced by the percentage depletion claimed although the calculation is made without reference to the basis of the asset.

If intangible drilling costs are capitalized, the basis for cost depletion is increased. If such costs are expensed, the 50 percent limit for the percentage depletion deduction will be decreased.

IV. REPORTING PROCEDURES

A.   Sole proprietors engaged in a trade or business should file a Schedule C with their Form 1040. Part I of Schedule C is used for reporting items of income. Part II is used for reporting deductions such as bad debts, depletion, and depreciation. If the business requires the use of inventories and the computation of cost of goods sold, Part II must also be completed.

B.   If depreciation is claimed, it generally should be supported on Form 4562.

TEST FOR SELF-EVALUATION—CHAPTER 8

True or False

Indicate which of the following statements is true or false by circling the correct answer.

T   F   1.   If MACRS (or depreciation) is not claimed for a particular year, the basis for the asset remains unchanged.

T   F   2.   Computers and light-duty trucks are 5-year class MACRS property.

T   F   3.   The depreciable basis of personal use property converted to business use is the lower of its adjusted basis or fair market value on the date of conversion.

T   F   4.   The alternative depreciation system must be used on all automobiles.

T   F   5.   Cost depletion is determined by dividing the fair market value of the asset by the estimated recoverable units expected.

T   F   6.   Under ACRS, the cost of an asset is recovered over a predetermined period that is generally shorter than the useful life of the asset or the period the asset is used to produce income.

T   F   7.   Assets such as land, stock, and antiques are not eligible for cost recovery.

T   F   8.   Assets that do not decline in value on a predictable basis are not depreciable under ACRS.

T   F   9.   Cellular telephones, computers (not used in a regular business), and automobiles are listed property and subject to certain limits on MACRS.

T   F   10.   Depreciation, depletion, and amortization are different words to describe the process of deducting the cost of an asset.

T   F   11.   Under MACRS, an automobile acquired and used in a business is 7-year recovery property.

T   F   12.   The cost of residential rental real estate acquired after 1986 is written off over 27.5 years under MACRS.

T   F   13.   For 2002, the maximum amount that can be expensed under § 179 is $24,000.

T   F   14.   If more than 40 percent of the nonrealty assets acquired during a year are acquired in the last quarter of the tax year, then the taxpayer must use the mid-quarter MACRS tables to calculate the cost recovery deduction for all personal property placed in service during the year.

T   F   15.   The annual limits for automobile depreciation do not apply to the election to expense under § 179.

T   F   16.   ACRS and other depreciation, amortization, and depletion are reported on Form 4562.

T   F   17.   The § 179 expense election is available for real property or for property used in the production of income.

T   F   18.   A taxpayer who leases a passenger automobile must include an *inclusion amount* in gross income.

T   F   19.   Section 197 intangible property includes goodwill, going-concern value, sports franchises, trademarks, and trade names.

T   F   20.   Generally, intangible property is amortized over a 15-year period, beginning in the month in which the property was acquired.

T   F   21.   Land can generally be depleted under the tax law.

Multiple Choice

Choose the best answer for each of the following questions.

_____ 1.   On January 4 of the current year, Byrne purchased a patent that qualifies as a § 197 intangible. The cost of the patent was $204,000. In the current year Byrne may amortize how much of the patent's cost?

         a. $–0–
         b. $204,000
         c. $13,600
         d. $10,000

_____ 2.   On January 3, 20x1, Heather purchased land for $150,000. She plans to build an apartment building on the land. The apartment will have an estimated useful life of 30 years. She does in fact build the apartment building in 20x1 for $400,000. How much of the land cost can be depleted by Heather this year?

         a. $–0–
         b. $150,000
         c. $5,000
         d. $10,000

_____ 3.   White Corporation acquired an asset (10-year property) on June 6, 20x1, for $60,000. The asset is not an automobile, but it is listed property. White used the asset 40 percent of the time for business, 50 percent of the time for the production of income, and 10 percent for the personal use of the shareholder. A § 179 election is not made, what is the cost recovery for 20x1?

         a. $2,700
         b. $3,000
         c. $5,400
         d. $6,000

_____ 4.   Black Corporation acquired an asset (10-year property) on July 20, 20x1 for $60,000. The asset is not an automobile, but it is listed property. Black used the asset 60 percent of the time for business, 30 percent of the time for the production of income, and 10 percent for the personal use of the shareholder. A § 179 election is not made, what is the cost recovery for 20x1?

         a. $2,700
         b. $3,000
         c. $5,400
         d. $6,000

_____ 5.   The Big Tex Oil Company purchases an oil lease for $1,000,000. After exploration, oil is discovered and it is estimated that 100,000 barrels of oil will be recovered from the lease. If during 20x1 Big Tex produces 15,000 barrels of oil from the lease and sells 12,000 barrels, what is the amount of cost depletion allowed to Big Tex?

    a. $–0–
    b. $120,000
    c. $150,000
    d. $1,000,000

_____ 6.   The Pit Sulfur Company has gross income of $200,000 from certain property (not oil and gas property) subject to depletion. The expenses related to that property are $140,000, and a statutory depletion rate of 22 percent is applicable. What is the amount of depletion using percentage depletion?

    a. $–0–
    b. $44,000
    c. $30,000
    d. $13,200

_____ 7.   On July 1, 2002, farmer John acquires a new tractor at a cost of $30,000. If John is married and files a joint return for 2002, what amount can John expense under § 179 and what amount is subject to regular MACRS depreciation (assuming John has adequate taxable income from his business of farming)?

    a. $0, $30,000
    b. $24,000, $30,000
    c. $30,000, $24,000
    d. $24,000, $6,000

_____ 8.   Sun Corporation acquires $200,000 worth of 3-year property and $210,000 worth of 5-year property in 20x1. If the election to expense is not made, what is Sun's MACRS deduction using the half-year convention?

    a. $108,660
    b. $101,500
    c. $81,500
    d. $97,205

_____ 9.   What is the maximum amount of qualified expense property that can be placed in service during the year without causing a reduction in the § 179 expense ceiling?

    a. $100,000
    b. $125,000
    c. $150,000
    d. $200,000

_____ 10.   Under MACRS, the cost recovery tables for real estate uses a:

    a.   half-year convention
    b.   mid-quarter convention
    c.   mid-month convention
    d.   semi-annual convention

_____ 11.   On September 1, x2, Mike *places in service* an automobile with a cost of $50,000. The car is used 90 percent for business and 10 percent for personal use. Assume the x2 luxury auto limits are:

First year	$3,060
Second year	$5,000
Third year	$2,950
Subsequent years	$1,775

What is Mike's x2 MACRS deduction?

   a. $3,060
   b. $2,754
   c. $5,000
   d. $4,500

_____ 12.   On September 1, x2, Mike *places in service* an automobile with a cost of $50,000. The car is used 90 percent for business and 10 percent for personal use. Assume the x2 luxury auto limits are:

First year	$3,060
Second year	$5,000
Third year	$2,950
Subsequent years	$1,775

Assuming the same business use percentage in x3, what is Mike's MACRS deduction in x3?

   a. $3,060
   b. $2,754
   c. $5,000
   d. $4,500

_____ 13.   Maggie acquires an apartment building on June 3, 2002, for $600,000. What is Maggie's cost recovery deduction for calculating earnings and profits during 2002 under the alternative depreciation system (ADS)?

   a. $8,124
   b. $10,769
   c. $7,993
   d. $15,000

_____ 14.   The percentage depletion rate on coal is:

   a.   22%
   b.   15%
   c.   14%
   d.   10%

_____ 15.   Daniel purchases for $400,000 an apartment building in Canada. The apartment is purchased during March of the current year. What is Daniel's depreciation deduction for the first year?

   a. $7,916
   b. $11,516
   c. $10,052
   d. $8,742

_____ 16.   Tim purchases a cellular telephone for his business automobile. Cellular telephones are listed property. The phone is used 80 percent for business calls and 20 percent for personal calls. What method of cost recovery must Tim use on the phone?

   a.   Straight-line reduced by personal use percentage
   b.   Straight-line subject to recovery limits, reduced by personal use percentage
   c.   Statutory percentage reduced by personal use percentage
   d.   Statutory percentage subject to recovery limits, reduced by personal use percentage

_____ 17.   Harry purchased a 7-year business asset (not listed property) on July 30, 20x1, at a cost of $100,000. Harry did not elect to expense under § 179 nor did he elect straight-line cost recovery. Harry sold the asset on February 11, 20x3. Assuming the MACRS percentage in 20x3 is 12.49%, what is Harry's cost recovery for 20x3?

a. $–0–
b. $12,490.00
c. $6,245.00
d. $3,122.50

_____ 18.   Karen purchased an automobile on June 15, x0, at a cost of $20,000. Assume the x0 luxury auto limits are as follows:

First year	$3,060
Second year	$5,000
Third year	$2,950
Subsequent years	$1,775

Karen used the car 75 percent for business use and 25 percent for personal use in x0. In x1, Karen used the automobile 40 percent for business and 60 percent for personal use. What is Karen's excess depreciation to be recaptured in x1?

a. $–0–
b. $795
c. $1,500
d. $2,370

_____ 19.   On February 11, x1, Ann leases and places in service a passenger automobile worth $41,500. The lease is for five years. During x1, she uses the automobile 80 percent for business and 20 percent for personal use. Assuming the IRS table amount for x1 is $202, how much must Ann include in gross income for x1?

a. $–0–
b. $202.00
c. $161.60
d. $143.00

_____ 20.   On June 1, 20x1, Gwen purchased a dental practice from George for $267,000. The purchase price was allocated $225,000 to the tangible assets of the practice and $42,000 to goodwill. What is the amount of Gwen's deduction for amortization of goodwill for 20x1?

a. $–0–
b. $1,633
c. $2,800
d. $42,000

_____ 21.   Which write-off method would be used for tax purposes for a patent?

a.   MACRS
b.   Amortization
c.   Depletion
d.   Depreciation

_____ 22.   Which write-off method would be used for tax purposes for the cost of drilling an oil well?

a.   MACRS
b.   Amortization
c.   Depletion
d.   Depreciation

_____ 23. Which write-off method would be used for tax purposes for a delivery truck?

    a. MACRS
    b. Amortization
    c. Depletion
    d. Depreciation

_____ 24. Which write-off method would be used for tax purposes for the cost of clearing land to start a coalmine?

    a. MACRS
    b. Amortization
    c. Depletion
    d. Depreciation

_____ 25. Which write-off method would be used for tax purposes for a trademark?

    a. MACRS
    b. Amortization
    c. Depletion
    d. Depreciation

_____ 26. Which write-off method would be used for tax purposes for goodwill?

    a. MACRS
    b. Amortization
    c. Depletion
    d. Depreciation

_____ 27. Which write-off method would be used for tax purposes for the cost of an apartment building?

    a. MACRS
    b. Amortization
    c. Depletion
    d. Depreciation

Problems

1. Each of the following assets was acquired in the current year. Determine the appropriate MACRS recovery class for each.

    a. A used delivery truck _____
    b. A used office building _____
    c. A new farm tractor _____
    d. A new duplex held for rental _____
    e. A used apartment building _____
    f. A new computer _____

2. On August 8, Steve acquired an apartment building (27.5-year property) as an investment. The apartment cost $500,000 and has an estimated salvage value of $100,000. Using the table in the text, give the MACRS deduction for the first four years for this apartment.

    Year 1 _____
    Year 2 _____
    Year 3 _____
    Year 4 _____

SOLUTIONS TO CHAPTER 8 QUESTIONS

True or False

1. F   The basis decreases by the amount of allowable MACRS depreciation. [Cost Recovery Allowed or Allowable, p. 8–4]

2. T   Computers and light-duty trucks are 5-year class property. [Exhibit 8–1, p. 8–6]

3. T   The lower of adjusted basis or fair market value on the date of conversion is the basis of personal property converted to business use. [Cost Recovery Basis for Personal Use Assets Converted to Business or Income-Producing Use, p. 8–4]

4. F   The regular MACRS may be used for autos meeting the more than 50 percent business use test. [Automobiles and Other Listed Property, p. 8–13]

5. F   Adjusted basis is used, not fair market value. [Cost Depletion, p. 8–21]

6. T   Under ACRS, the cost of an assets is recovered over a predetermined period that is generally shorter than the useful life or the period the asset is used. [General Considerations, p. 8–3]

7. T   Land, stock, antiques are not eligible for cost recovery. [Eligible Property Under ACRS or MACRS, p. 8–4]

8. T   Assets that do not decline in value on a predictable basis cannot use ACRS. [Eligible Property Under ACRS or MACRS, p. 8–4]

9. T   Cellular telephones, computers (not used in a regular business), and automobiles are listed property. [Business and Personal Use of Automobiles and other Listed Property, p. 8–13]

10. T   Depreciation, depletion, and amortization are different way to describe the process of deducting the cost of an asset. [Overview, p. 8–2]

11. F   Automobiles are 5-year property. [Exhibit 8–1, p. 8–6]

12. T   The cost of residential rental real estate acquired after 1986 is deducted over 27.5 years. [MACRS, p. 8–9]

13. T   The 2002 maximum amount under § 179 is $24,000. [Election to Expense Assets, p. 8–11]

14. T   A taxpayer must use the mid-quarter MACRS tables if more than 40 percent of the nonrealty assets acquired during a year are acquired in the last quarter of the tax year. [Mid-Quarter Convention, p. 8–7]

15. F   The limit does apply to any amount expensed under § 179. [Limits on Cost Recovery for Automobiles, p. 8–14]

16. T   Depreciation, amortization, and depletion are reported on Form 4562. [Reporting Procedures, p. 8–24]

17. F   The election under § 179 is not available. [Election to Expense, p. 8–11]

18. T   Taxpayers who lease a passenger automobile must report an inclusion amount in gross income. [Leased Automobiles, p. 8–16]

19. F   Sports franchises are not § 197 property. [Amortization, p. 8–19]

20. T   Intangible property is generally amortized over a 15-year period. [Amortization, p. 8–19]

21. F   Land cannot be depleted. [Depletion, p. 8–20]

Multiple Choice

1.   c $\$204,000 \div 15 = \$13,600$ [Amortization, p. 8–19]

2.   a   Land cannot be depleted. [Overview, p. 8–2]

3.   a $\$60,000 \times .05 \times (1/10 \times \frac{1}{2} \text{ year}) \times (.40 + .50) = \$2,700$. Straight-line must be used because the business usage test has not been met. [Automobiles and Other Listed Property Not Used Predominantly in Business, p. 8–15]

4.   c $\$60,000 \times .10 \times .90 = \$5,400$. MACRS can be used because the business usage test has been met. [Automobiles and Other Listed Property Used Predominantly in Business, p. 8–13]

5.   b   ($\$1,000,000/100,000$ barrels) $\times 12,000$ barrels $= \$120,000$. [Cost Depletion, p. 8–21]

6.   c   ($\$200,000 - 140,000) \times 50\% = \$30,000$ maximum [Percentage Depletion, p. 8–22]

7.   d   For 2002, the § 179 expense amount is $\$24,000$. [Election to Expense, p. 8–11]

8.   a   ($\$200,000 \times 33.33\%) + (\$210,000 \times 20\%) = \$108,660$. [Table 8–1, p. 8–32]

9.   d   The maximum § 179 ceiling amount is $\$200,000$. [Annual Limitations, p. 8–12]

10.   c   MACRS uses a mid-month convention for realty. [Realty: Recovery Periods and Methods, p. 8–8]

11.   b $\$3,060$ (x2 max) $\times 90\% = \$2,754$ [Limits on Cost Recovery for Automobiles, p. 8–14]

12.   d $\$5,000$ (x2 max) $\times 90\% = \$4,500$ [Limits on Cost Recovery for Automobiles, p. 8–14]

13.   a $\$600,000 \times 1.354\% = \$8,124$ [Table 8–10, p. 8–37]

14.   d   The percentage depletion on coal is 22%. [Exhibit 8–2, p. 8–23]

15.   a $\$400,000 \times 1.979\% = \$7,916$ [Table 8–10, p. 8–37]

16.   c   The cell phone is used more than 50% for business. [Automobiles and other Listed Property Used Predominately for Business, p. 8–13]

17.   c $\$100,000 \times 12.49\% \times 2 = \$6,245$ [Classification of Property: MACRS, p. 8–5]

18.   b

MACRS for x0 $\$3,060 \times 75\% =$	$\$2,295$
Straight-line for x0 $\$20,000 \times .10 \times 75\% =$	($-\$1,500$)
Recapture amount (x1)	$\$ \ 795$

[Change From Predominately Business Use, p. 8–16]

19.   d $\$202 \times (323 \text{ days}/365 \text{ days}) \times 80\% = \$143.00$ [Leased Automobiles, p. 8–16]

20.   b   ($\$42,000/15) \times (7/12) = \$1,633$ [Amortization, p. 8–19]

21.   b   Patents are Amortized. [Amortization, p. 8–19]

22.   c   Drilling costs are depleted. [Depletion, p. 8–20]

23.   a   Trucks are depreciated. [Exhibit 8–1, p. 8–6]

24.   c   Land clearing for a coal mine costs are depleted. [Depletion, p. 8–20]

25.   b   Trademarks are amortized. [Amortization, p. 8–19]

26.   b   Goodwill is amortized. [Amortization, p. 8–19]

27.   a   Apartments use MACRS. [MACRS, p. 8–9]

Problems

1. a.   5-year [Exhibit 8–1, p. 8–6]
    b.   39-year [MACRS, p. 8–9]
    c.   7-year [Exhibit 8–1, p. 8–6]
    d.   27.5-year [MACRS, p. 8–9]
    e.   27.5-year [MACRS, p. 8–9]
    f.   5-year [Exhibit 8–1, p. 8–6]

2.   Year 1 $500,000 × 1.364% = $6,820
     Year 2 $500,000 × 3.636% = $18,180
     Year 3 $500,000 × 3.636% = $18,180
     Year 4 $500,000 × 3.636% = $18,180

     [Table 8–9, p. 8–37]

CHAPTER 9

Deductions: Employee Expenses

CHAPTER HIGHLIGHTS

This chapter identifies and categorizes employee expenses. In certain situations, employee expenses are treated as expenses incurred in a trade or business and thus are deductions *for* adjusted gross income (AGI). Most employee business expenses are deductible *from* adjusted gross income as itemized deductions. The factors that decide whether an individual is an employee of self-employed are also discussed.

KEY TERMS

Substantiation Requirements	Transportation & Travel	Educational Expenses
Meals & Entertainment	Moving Expenses	Office-in-the Home

OUTLINE

I. **EMPLOYEE VERSUS SELF-EMPLOYED**
   A. One major problem in taxation is to determine if an employee-employee relationship exists or if an individual is self-employed. An employer-employee relationship exists when the employer has the right to specify the results and the ways and means by which the results will be obtained.
   B. A self-employed person is required to file a Schedule C and all allowable expenses incurred will be deductions for adjusted gross income. In addition, statutory employees are allowed to file a Schedule C and deduct these expenses for AGI.

II. **EMPLOYEE EXPENSES—IN GENERAL**

   Employee expenses fall into one of the following categories: Transportation, Travel, Moving, Education, Entertainment, and Miscellaneous

III. **TRANSPORTATION EXPENSES**
   A. Qualified Expenditures. A taxpayer is permitted a deduction from AGI subject to the 2 percent floor for unreimbursed, employment-related transportation expenses. An example of such expenses would include those incurred by an employee commuting to a second job from a first job. However, the cost of commuting from home to work and back is not deductible.
   B. Computation of Automobile Expenses. In computing automobile expenses a taxpayer has two choices: actual cost or an automatic mileage method. In 2002, under the automatic mileage method a taxpayer can deduct $.365 per mile for all business miles. Parking fees and tolls can be deducted in addition to the amount calculated under the automatic mileage method.

   See the text for restrictions that apply to changing from one method to another, the use of a fully-depreciated vehicle, and the use of more than one vehicle for business purposes.

IV. **TRAVEL EXPENSES**
   A. Definition of Travel Expenses. An employee may be allowed a deduction for unreimbursed travel expenses subject to the 2 percent of adjusted gross income limitation. Travel expenses include transportation costs and meals (reduced by a certain percentage) and lodging while away from home in the pursuit of a trade or business, along with reasonable laundry and incidental expenses. Entertainment expenses are not included as travel and are discussed elsewhere.
   B. Away-From-Home Requirement. To meet the away-from-home test, an employee must be away from home overnight. An overnight stay is a period substantially longer than an ordinary day's work and requires rest, sleep, or relief from the work period. To be in travel status a taxpayer must be away from his tax home for a temporary period. Generally, if a taxpayer has a work assignment of less than one year it is regarded as temporary. If the work assignment is more than one year it is regarded as indefinite.
   C. Restrictions on Travel Expenses. Expenses related to attending a convention, seminar, or similar meeting are disallowed unless the expenses are related to a trade or business of the taxpayer.

   No deduction is allowed for travel that, by itself, is deemed to be educational by the taxpayer. This rule does not apply with respect to a deduction for travel necessary to engage in an activity that gives rise to a business deduction related to education.

   Expenses incurred to attend conventions outside North America are disallowed unless the taxpayer can show that it is reasonable for the convention to be held in a foreign location as in the North American area.
   D. Combined Business and Pleasure Travel. If a trip combines both business and pleasure and is within the United States, transportation is deductible only if the trip is primarily for business. If the trip is primarily a vacation, expenses relating to business, other than transportation, are still deductible. Special rules apply for trips outside the United States.

V. MOVING EXPENSES

A. Moving expenses are deductible by employees for adjusted gross income. Reimbursements from the employer must be included in gross income. The two basic tests that must be met for moving expenses to be deductible are the distance test and the time requirement test.

B. Distance Test. The distance test requires that the tax payer's new job location be at least 50 miles farther from the taxpayer's old residence than the old residence was from the former place of employment.

C. Time Requirements. A time requirement is also necessary for an employee to qualify for the moving expense deduction. An employee must be employed full-time at the new location for 39 weeks in the twelve-month period following the move and a self-employed individual must work in the new location for 78 weeks during the next two years.

D. When Deductible. Moving expenses are deductible in the year of payment. However, if the employee is to be reimbursed for the expenses in the following year, an election can be made to deduct the expenses in that year.

E. The following categories of moving expenses are deductible:

Cost of moving household and personal effects

Traveling form former to new place of residence

Note: Meals are not deductible and mileage is at 13 cents per mile (for 2002).

VI. EDUCATION EXPENSES

A. General Requirements. An employee may deduct expenses (subject to any 2 percent limit) for education as ordinary and necessary business expenses provided such items were incurred either (1) to maintain or improve existing skills required in the present job, or (2) to meet the express requirements of the employer or the requirements imposed by law to retain the employment status. However, expenses are not deductible if they are required to meet the minimum educational standards for the taxpayer's job or if they qualify the taxpayer for a new trade or business.

B. Requirements Imposed by Law or by the Employer for Retention of Employment. Many states require that teachers take additional courses to retain their position. Such expenses would qualify as deductible since they are incurred in meeting requirements imposed by law or the employer for retention of employment.

C. Maintaining or Improving Existing Skills. The deductibility of educational expenses said to "maintain or improve existing skills" is a heavily litigated subject. The deduction is disallowed in cases where the deduction qualifies the taxpayer for a new trade or business. For example, the expenses of a business executive or accountant incurred in obtaining a law degree are specifically not deductible under this provision.

D. Classification of Specific Items. Education expenses for employees are deductible as itemized deductions on an individual's tax return.

E. Other Provisions Dealing With Education. Note, that other aspects of educational expenses (e.g., scholarships and employer reimbursement) are discussed in other chapters in the textbook.

VII. ENTERTAINMENT EXPENSES

A. Dollar Limitations. Deductions for meals and entertainment (including facilities) are limited to 50 percent of the otherwise allowable amount. This rule applies to taxes and tips relating to meals and entertainment. Cover charges, parking, and room rental fees are also subject to the 50 percent rule. Certain employees are allowed a higher percentage of meal allowance. Air transportation workers, interstate truck and bus drivers, train crews, dispatchers, and merchant marines are allowed a larger percentage (see text for amounts of their qualified meals as a deduction.

B. Classification of Expenses. Entertainment expenses can be categorized as those "direction related to" business and those "associated with" business. "Directly related to" expenses are those related to an actual business meeting or discussion. "Associated with" expenses are those that promote the general goodwill of the business; however, the entertainment must serve a specific business purpose.

C. Restrictions upon Deductibility. Business meals are deductible if the following requirements are met:
   1) the meal is directly related to or associated with the active conduct of a trade or business,
   2) the expense is not lavish or extravagant, and
   3) the taxpayer (or an employee) is present at the meal

The tax law denies any deduction for club dues except for service organizations (Lions Club, Rotary, etc.).

A deduction for the cost of a ticket for an entertainment activity is limited to the face value of the ticket. Deductions for skyboxes at sports arenas are generally disallowed except to the extent of the cost of a regular ticket.

Business gifts are limited to $25 per donee per year. Excluded from the $25 limit are gift wrapping, shipping, certain gifts costing $4 or less, and gifts used for advertising.

VIII. OTHER EMPLOYEE EXPENSES

A. Office in the Home. There is no deduction for an office in the home unless it is used exclusively and on a regular basis as the taxpayer's principal place of business or as a place of business that is used by patients, clients, or customers. If the office is used in connection with the taxpayer's business as an employee, the use of the office must also be for the convenience of the employer. The deductions for an office in the home cannot exceed gross income from the business activity reduced by all other deductible expenses attributable to the business, but not allocable to the use of the home itself (unless the item would otherwise be deductible).

The U.S. Supreme Court has ruled (in *Soliman*) that the majority of the income earning activity must take place in the home office. However, for tax years after 1998, the tax law was amended to partially overturn the *Soliman* decision. Starting in 1999, a home qualifies as a principal place of business if both the following are true:
   1) The office is used by the taxpayer to conduct administrative or management activities of a trade or business, and
   2) there is no other fixed location of the trade or business where the taxpayer conducts these activities.

B. Miscellaneous Employee Expenses. Miscellaneous employee expenses such as special clothing, union dues, and professional expenses are deductible subject to the 2 percent of AGI limitation.

C. Contributions to IRAs. Individuals are allowed a deduction for adjusted gross income of up to $3,000 ($6,000 for spousal account) in 2002 to an IRA. See Chapter 19 for the details on IRA contribution limits.

IX. CLASSIFICATION OF EMPLOYEE EXPENSES

A. Accountable Plans. Employee expenses are reimbursed under accountable plans or nonaccountable plans. For a plan to be accountable two requirements must be met. The employee must: (1) Adequately account for (substantiate) the expenses and (2) Return any excess reimbursement or allowance.

Substantiation requires the employee provide the following items to the employer:
   1) The amount of the expense
   2) The time and place of travel or entertainment (or date of gift)
   3) The business purpose of each expense
   4) he business relationship of the person entertained (or receiving the gift)

The amount of an expenditure can be substantiated by a deemed substantiation (per diem) method. By using such a method the amount of the expense is proved. The maximum amount deemed substantiated is equal to the lesser of the per diem allowance or the Federal per diem rate, which varies by area and location. When the per diem method is used, the place, date, business purpose and business relationship must still be substantiated in the normal manner.

B. Nonaccountable Plans. Under a nonaccountable plan an adequate accounting or reimbursement is not required. In such plans any reimbursement is reported in its entirety as wages to the employee's W-2. Any allowable expenses are treated in the same manner as unreimbursed expenses. Thus the employee is subject to the 50 percent limit on meals and entertainment, the 2 percent miscellaneous itemized deduction limit, etc.

C. Reporting Procedures. The reporting requirements for employee expenses depend upon whether the amount is reimbursed or unreimbursed and whether the amount is paid under an accountable plan or a nonaccountable plan.

X. **LIMITATION (2 percent) ON ITEMIZED DEDUCTIONS**

After classifying deductions as *for* or *from* AGI, it is necessary to group the itemized (deductions from AGI) deductions into two groups. The deductions in the first group are deductible in full for taxpayers who itemize while the second group of deductions are added and reduced by 2 percent of AGI.

A. Miscellaneous itemized deductions subject to the 2 percent of AGI limitation include:

All Section 212 expenses other than rent and royalty expenses
All unreimbursed employee expenses (after a 50 percent reduction, if applicable)
Professional dues and subscriptions
Union dues and work uniforms
Employment-related education expenses
Malpractice insurance premiums
Job hunting expenses
Office-in-the-home and outside sales expenses
Legal, accounting, and tax return fees
Hobby expenses
Investment expenses
Custodial fees for income-producing property or IRAs
Collection fees for interest and dividends
Appraisal fees for establishing the amount of casualty losses or charitable deductions

B. Miscellaneous itemized deductions not subject to the 2 percent of AGI limitation are:

Work-related handicapped expenses
Gambling losses to the extent of gambling winnings
Certain terminated annuity payments

TEST FOR SELF-EVALUATION—CHAPTER 9

True or False

Indicate which of the following statements is true or false by circling the correct answer.

T   F   **1.** Expenses of self-employed taxpayers are deductible for adjusted gross income as trade or business expenses.

T   F   **2.** An employer-employee relationship exists if the employer has the right to specify the result and the ways and means by which the result is to be attained.

T   F   **3.** A self-employed individual is required to file Schedule Cof Form 1040.

T   F   **4.** Unreimbursed employee travel expenses are a deduction from adjusted gross income.

T   F   **5.** All miscellaneous deductions are subject to the 2 percent of AGI limitation.

T   F   **6.** To the extent employee expenses are reimbursed under an accountable plan, they are deductions for adjusted gross income.

T   F   **7.** A taxpayer may switch to the automatic mileage method on an automobile if in prior years he had used MACRS or Section 179 expensing on that automobile.

T   F   **8.** Travel and transportation expenses are defined in the same manner for tax purposes.

T   F   **9.** Commuting expenses from home to one's place of employement are not deductible.

T   F   **10.** An employee will be allowed a deduction for the cost of commuting from a primary job to a second job.

T   F   **11.** Taxpayers must always use the automatic mileage method to determine an automobile expense deduction.

T   F   **12.** If a taxpayer has two or more vehicles in use at the same time, he or she may use the automatic mileage method.

T   F   **13.** A taxpayer cannot change to the automatic mileage method if the election to expense has been made or accelerated depreciation has previously been taken.

T   F   **14.** Unreimbursed travel expenses are an itemized deduction (subject to the 2 percent floor).

T   F   **15.** Union dues are deductible (subject to the 2 percent of adjusted gross income limitation) for tax purposes.

T   F   **16.** To be deductible in the current year, a home office must be used by a taxpayer to conduct administrative or management activities and there is no other fixed location of the trade or business where taxpayers conducts these activities.

T   F   **17.** All business gift deductions are limited to $25 per donee.

T   F   **18.** Law school expenses are always deductible.

T   F   **19.** The cost of a Bar or CPA exam review course is generally deductible.

T   F   **20.** The business mileage deduction is 36.5 cents per mile for 2002.

T   F   **21.** Expenses of moving household and personal belongings are not subject to a dollar limitation.

T   F   22.   Qualified business meals are 50 percent deductible (except for certain transportation workers who are allowed 65% in 2002).

T   F   23.   For convention travel expenses to be deductible, the convention attended must be *directly related* to the taxpayer's trade or business.

T   F   24.   Travel as a form of education is not allowed as a deduction for individual taxpayers.

T   F   25.   If an employee receives reimbursement under a nonaccountable plan, then reimbursement is reported on the employee's W-2 and any allowable expenses are deductible in the same manner as unreimbursed expenses.

Multiple Choice

Choose the best answer for each of the following questions.

_____ 1.   Which of the following educational expenses would be deductible?

     a.   Travel expenses for general knowledge
     b.   CPA review course expenses
     c.   Law school educational expenses
     d.   None of the above are deductible

_____ 2.   The substantiation requirements for business entertainment under Section 274 do not include:

     a.   The amount
     b.   Credit card receipts
     c.   The business purpose
     d.   The business relationship

_____ 3.   An employee drove her automobile 6,000 miles on business during 2002. Using the automatic mileage method ($.365 for 2002), her deduction for unreimbursed expenses (before any applicable 2 percent limit) is:

     a. $2,190 for AGI
     b. $2,190 from AGI
     c.   only deductible to the extent it is reimbursed by her employer
     d.   is not deductible

_____ 4.   Which of the following miscellaneous expenses is not subject to the 2 percent of adjusted gross income limitation?

     a.   Unreimbursed employee expenses
     b.   Outside sales expenses
     c.   Union dues
     d.   Gambling losses to extent of gambling winnings

_____ 5.   Cathy is an outside sales person. She has set aside one room in her house as a home office where she does administrative work related to her job. Cathy has no other office available to her. For the year, depreciation expense is $150 and other maintenance expenses are $250 on the home office. If Cathy's Schedule C net income (without the home office items) is $45,000, how much of these expenses are deductible by Cathy?

     a. $–0–
     b. $150
     c. $250
     d. $400

_____ 6. Toni is a self-employed consultant and while traveling spends $120 on meals and $200 on transportation and lodging. What is the amount of Toni's deduction for these expenditures?

    a. $260
    b. $320
    c. $256
    d. $280

_____ 7. Terry, an employee of an accounting firm, spent $600 on dues to professional organizations and $250 for subscriptions to professional journals. Terry's AGI is $30,000. Assuming Terry itemizes deductions, how much (after the 2 percent limit) may she deduct?

    a. $–0–
    b. $850
    c. $600
    d. $250

_____ 8. Which of the following would be an employer-employee relationship?

    a. A plumber who comes to your home to do work
    b. A CPA who prepares a tax return
    c. A physician who pays a nurse to help him in his office
    d. A gardener who takes care of individual lawns for a monthly fee

_____ 9. A self-employed CPA moves from California to Texas to establish a new practice. To qualify for a moving expense deduction, which of the following must be true?

    a. He must work for another CPA in Texas for one year
    b. He must have been in practice for three years in California
    c. He must obtain a license to practice in the state of Texas
    d. He must work full time in the new location for 78 weeks during the next two years

_____ 10. Fran is a CPA who has a small tax practice in her home in addition to working her regular job. The gross income from this practice is $5,500 for the year. Based on square footage, the portion of mortgage interest and real estate taxes allocable to the business amount to $3,000. The allocable portion of maintenance, utilities, and depreciation is $3,500. Assuming no other expenses related to the business were incurred, what amount of the maintenance, utilities, and depreciation is deductible by Fran?

    a. $–0–
    b. $3,500
    c. $2,500
    d. $500

_____ 11. Mike, a staff accountant for a CPA firm, incurred the following expenses:

Travel	$200
Transportation	$500
Dues and Subscriptions	$300

Mike gave his employer an adequate accounting and received a reimbursement under an accountable plan of $1,000 to cover these expenses. What amount is deductible from adjusted gross income?

    a. $–0–
    b. $60
    c. $300
    d. $700

_____ 12. Rachel, an employee of the Big CPA firm, spent $3,000 for business expenses (none of which are subject to the 50 percent limitation). She was reimbursed $4,000 for these expenses. *An adequate accounting was not made to her employer*. If Rachel's AGI was $50,000 for the year and her employer included $4,000 on her W-2 what amount of the employee business expenses may she deduct as an itemized deduction?

    a. $–0–
    b. $2,000
    c. $3,000
    d. $5,000

_____ 13. Uriah had travel expenses of $1,500 substantiated by credit card receipts. He has a diary that provides the business purpose and relationship for $800 of these expenses. How much will Uriah be allowed as a deduction, before considering any limitation based on adjusted gross income?

    a.   a maximum of $25 per day
    b. $700
    c. $800
    d. $1,500

_____ 14. Under the deemed substantiation method of accounting for expenses, what is the maximum amount that taxpayers are allowed as a deduction without being required to substantiate the amount of the expense?

    a.   The federal per diem amount
    b. $138 per day
    c.   All expenses up to $25 per day
    d.   The state per diem rate of the state in which they live

_____ 15. Statutory employees report income and deductions on which of the following Forms or Schedules?

    a.   Form 2106
    b.   Schedule E
    c.   Form 2106 and Schedule A
    d.   None of the above

_____ 16. Kate, a self-employed CPA, attended a two-day course on auditing. She incurred the following expenses:

Airfare	$ 500
Taxi	$ 40
Meals	$ 200
Lodging	$ 300
Laundry	$ 20
Total	$1,060

How much can Kate claim as a deduction *for* AGI?

    a. $–0–
    b. $1,060
    c. $960
    d. $1,040

_____ 17.   Jason, a professor of history at a local university, attended an investment seminar. He incurred the following expenses:

Airfare	$300
Meals	$100
Lodging	$200
Total	$600

What is Jason's miscellaneous itemized deduction (before any 2 percent limit)?

a. $–0–
b. $540
c. $580
d. $600

_____ 18.   Ted incurred the following unreimbursed expenses at his country club in connection with his employment as a salesman:

Annual dues to country club	$3,000
Business meals (directly related)	$2,000
Personal meals	$1,000
Days of business use (directly related)	60
Days of personal use	40

What is Ted's entertainment deduction _before_ any 2 percent limitation?

a. $2,000
b. $1,000
c. $4,000
d. $3,040

_____ 19.   Todd purchased his automobile in Year 1 for $15,000. It was used 80 percent for business purposes. Todd drove the car for 10,000 business miles in Year 1. What is Todd's basis in the business portion of the automobile at the beginning of Year 2?

a. $15,000
b.   ($15,000 × 80%)
c.   ($15,000 × 80%) – (10,000 miles ×Year 1 auto depreciation mileage rate)
d. $15,000 – (10,000 miles × Year 1 autodepreciation mileage rate)

_____ 20.   The foreign convention expense limitation rules would apply to a convention held in which of the following?

a.   Mexico
b.   Hawaii
c.   Alaska
d.   Venezuela

_____ 21.   Peter, a civil engineer working for Amber Company, incurs a total of $5,200 in business expenses, consisting of the following:

Transportation (no commuting)	$1,500
Meals and lodging away from home	$2,000
Dues and subscriptions	$ 750
Entertainment	$ 950
Total	$5,200

Peter received reimbursement of $3,400 from his employer under an accountable plan. His itemized deductions before any limitations would be:

a. $–0–
b. $1,500
c. $1,800
d. $5,2000

_____ 22. Reed, a traveling sales representative (a statutory employee) of Pink Company, incurs the following job related business expenses:

Transportation (no commuting	$ 4,000
Meals and lodging away from home	$ 5,000
Dues and subscriptions	$ 1,000
Entertainment	$ 2,000
Total	$12,000

Reed received no reimbursement from his employer. What amount may Reed deduct *for* adjusted gross income before any 50 percent limitation for meals and entertainment?

a. $–0–
b. $4,000
c. $8,000
d. $12,000

_____ 23. Lori Legal is a self-employed lawyer. She has to fly to Hawaii on business to see a client. Lori decides to incorporate a vacation into her trip to the islands. Round trip airfare is $600. Of the ten days out of town, Lori consulted with her client for three days. How much of the airfare can Lori deduct on her Schedule C as a business expense?

a. $–0–
b. $180
c. $540
d. $600

_____ 24. During 2002, Duke changed jobs and moved from Dallas to Phoenix. Duke had the following expenses in connection with the move:

Cost of moving household goods	$4,000
Meals	$ 300
Lodging	$ 500

Duke drove his car the 1,200 miles from Dallas to Phoenix (the 2002 moving mileage rage is $.13). What is his moving expense deduction for 2002?

a. $4,000
b. $4,300
c. $4,500
d. $4,656

_____ 25.   Chad is an employee of Haddock Corporation, a commercial real estate broker. He takes a client to dinner and incurs the following expenses (all of which can be substantiated):

Taxi	$ 25
Drinks before dinner	$ 40
Meal cost	$135
Tips	$ 35
Total	$235

If Chad is reimbursed by Haddock for $235 (under an adequate accounting plan), how much of the reimbursement is income to Chad in?

a. $–0–
b. $117.50
c. $130.00
d. $205.00

_____ 26.   Chad is an employee of Haddock Corporation, a commercial real estate broker. He takes a client to dinner and incurs the following expenses (all of which can be substantiated):

Taxi	$ 25
Drinks before dinner	$ 40
Meal cost	$135
Tips	$ 35
Total	$235

If Chad is reimbursed by Haddock for $235 (under an adequate accounting plan), what is Haddock's tax deduction?

a. $–0–
b. $117.50
c. $130.00
d. $205.00

_____ 27.   Tom is a self-employed interstate truck driver and while traveling spends $120 on meals and $200 on transportation and lodging. If the "cutback rate" for 2002 is 35%, what is the amount of Tom's deduction for these expenditures in 2002?

a. $260
b. $278
c. $320
d. $242

_____ 28.   Union dues of an employee would be treated by an individual taxpayer as a

a.   Deduction for AGI
b.   Deduction from AGI, subject to the 2 percent limit
c.   Deduction from AGI, not subject to the 2 percent limit
d.   Nondeductible item

_____ 29.   Qualified moving expenses would be treated by an individual taxpayer as a

a.   Deduction for AGI
b.   Deduction from AGI, subject to the 2 percent limit
c.   Deduction from AGI, not subject to the 2 percent limit
d.   Nondeductible item

_____ 30.   Home office expenses of an employee would be treated by an individual taxpayer as a

      a.   Deduction for AGI
      b.   Deduction from AGI, subject to the 2 percent limit
      c.   Deduction from AGI, not subject to the 2 percent limit
      d.   Nondeductible item

_____ 31.   Gambling losses (to extent of gambling winnings) would be treated by an individual taxpayer as a

      a.   Deduction for AGI
      b.   Deduction from AGI, subject to the 2 percent limit
      c.   Deduction from AGI, not subject to the 2 percent limit
      d.   Nondeductible item

_____ 32.   Education expenses of a self-employed CPA would be treated by an individual taxpayer as a

      a.   Deduction for AGI
      b.   Deduction from AGI, subject to the 2 percent limit
      c.   Deduction from AGI, not subject to the 2 percent limit
      d.   Nondeductible item

_____ 33.   Work related expenses for handicapped individuals would be treated by an individual taxpayer as a

      a.   Deduction for AGI
      b.   Deduction from AGI, subject to the 2 percent limit
      c.   Deduction from AGI, not subject to the 2 percent limit
      d.   Nondeductible item

Problems

1.   Dorothy moved from San Francisco to San Diego to obtain a better job. She paid $4,000 to have her personal and household goods moved. During the move, Dorothy incurred $125 in transportation expense, lodging expense of $150 and meal expense of $50. In selling her residence, Dorothy incurred $6,500 in selling expenses. Dorothy received no reimbursement for her moving expenses. Calculate Dorothy's moving expense deduction using the following worksheet.

Moving household goods	$_____
Transportation	$_____
Lodging	$_____
Meals	$_____
House sale expenses	$_____
Moving expense deduction	$_____

2.   Ray, a collect professor, incurred the following business-related expenses for which he was not reimbursed.

Mileage (2002 rate is $.365 per mile)	16,500 miles
Travel (includes meals of $200)	$750
Air transportation	$600

Calculate Ray's employee business expense deduction for 2002 (before any 2 percent limitation).

Mileage	$_____
Travel	$_____
Transportation	$_____
Total	$_____

3.   Chee, a scientist, accepted a position with the IRS in Washington, D.C. The assignment was designated as temporary and was for a 12-month period. Chee left his wife and children in Houston and rented an apartment in Washington during his employment. Chee's AGI for the year is $50,000. He incurred the following expenses, non of which were reimbursed by the IRS.

Airfare to and from Washington, D.C.	$ 2,000
Rent on Washington apartment	$10,000
Meals, in Washington	$ 5,000

What amount is deductible by Chee? Is the deduction for AGI or from AGI? $_____

SOLUTIONS TO CHAPTER 9 QUESTIONS

True or False

1. T Expenses of self-employed taxpayers are deductible for adjusted gross income. [Employee Versus Self-Employed, p. 9–2]

2. T An employer-employee relationship exists if the employer has the right to specify the result and the ways and means of the work. [Employee Versus Self-Employed, p. 9–2]

3. T Self-employed individuals file Schedule C of Form 1040. [Employee Versus Self-Employed, p. 9–2]

4. T Unreimbursed employee travel expenses are a deduction from AGI. [Travel Expenses, p. 9–7]

5. F Only certain deductions are subject to the 2% limitation. [Miscellaneous Itemized Deductions Not Subject to the 2% floor, p. 9–27]

6. T Reimbursed employee expenses under an accountable plan are deductions for adjusted gross income. [Accountable Plans, p. 9–24]

7. F Taxpayers may not switch to the automatic mileage method. [Computation of Automobile Expenses, p. 9–6]

8. F They are different categories of deductions. [Transportation Expenses, p. 9–4]

9. T Commuting expenses are not deductible. [Commuting Expenses, p. 9–5]

10. T Employees are allowed a deduction for the cost of commuting from a primary job to a second job. [Commuting Expenses, p. 9–5]

11. F They may use actual operating costs. [Computation of Automobile Expenses, p. 9–6]

12. F Employees with two vehicles must use actual operating costs. [Computation of Automobile Expenses, p. 9–6]

13. T Taxpayers cannot change to the automatic mileage method if the election to expense has been made or accelerated depreciation has been claimed. [Computation of Automobile Expenses, p. 9–6]

14. T Unreimbursed travel expenses are an itemized deduction (subject to the 2% floor). [Travel Expenses, p. 9–7]

15. T Union dues are deductible (subject to the 2% of AGI limitation). [from AGI. [Travel Expenses, p. 9–7]

16. T A home office must be used by a taxpayer to conduct administrative or management activities and there is no other fixed location of the trade or business. [Office in the Home, p. 9–20]

17. F Gift wrapping, mailing, etc. may exceed the $25 limit. [Business Gifts, p. 9–20]

18. F The taxpayer is being qualified for a new trade or business; therefore, the education expenses are not deductible. [Maintaining or Improving Existing Skills, p. 9–15]

19. F The taxpayer has not met the minimum standards for the job. [General Requirements, p. 9–14]

20. T The business mileage deduction is 36.5 cents per mile in 2002. [Computation of Automobile Expenses, p. 9–6]

21. T Expenses of moving household and personal belongings are not subject to a limitation. [Treatment of Moving Expenses, p. 9–12]

22.   T   Qualified business meals are only 50 percent deductible for nontransportation workers. [Cutback Adjustment, p. 9–16]

23.   T   Deductible convention travel expenses be *directly related* to the taxpayer's trade or business. [Conventions, p. 9–8]

24.   T   Travel as a form of education is not allowed as a deduction for individual taxpayers. [Education, p. 9–9]

25.   T   Reimbursements under a nonaccountable plan are reported on the employee's W-2 and any allowable expenses are deductible in the same manner as unreimbursed expenses. [Reporting Procedures, p. 9–24]

Multiple Choice

1.   d   All of these are not deductible as an educational expense. [Education Expenses, p. 9–14]

2.   b   Credit card receipts are not required under Section 274. [Substantiation, p. 9–24]

3.   b   20,000 miles × $.365 = $2,190 from AGI (2002) [Computation of Automobile Expenses, p. 9–6]

4.   d   Gambling losses are not subject to the 2% limitation. [Miscellaneous Itemized Deductions Not Subject to the 2% Floor, p. 9–27]

5.   d $150 + $250 = $400 [Office in the Home, p. 9–20]

6.   a   (50% of $120) + $200 = $260 [Cutback Adjustment, p 9–16]

7.   d $600 + 250—(2% of $30,000) = $250 [Miscellaneous Itemized Deductions Subject to the 2% Floor, p. 9–27]

8.   c   A nurse hired by a doctor is an employee. [Employee Versus Self-Employed, p. 9–2]

9.   d   Self-employed taxpayers must work 78 weeks in the new location. [Time test, p. 9–12]

10.   c $5,500—3,000 = $2,500 [Office in the Home, p. 9–20]

11.   a   All of the expenses are reimbursed. [Accountable Plans, p. 9–24]

12.   b $3,000—(2% of $50,000) = $2,000 [Reporting Procedures, p. 9–24]

13.   c   Only the substantiated amount is deductible [Substantiation, p. 9–26]

14.   a   The Federal per diem rate is deemed substantiation. [Deemed Substantiation, p. 9–24]

15.   d   Statutory employees report on Schedule C. [Employee Versus Self-Employed, p. 9–2]

16.   c $500 + 40 + (50% × $200) + 300 + 20 = $960 [Classification of Specific Items, p. 9–15]

17.   a   Investment seminar expenses are not deductible. [General Requirements, p. 9–13]

18.   b $2,000 × 50% = $1,000, only the business meals are deductible at 50%. [Cutback Adjustment p. 9–16]

19.   c   ($15,000 × 80%) − (10,000 miles × Year 1 auto depreciation mileage rate) = $10,800 [Computation of Automobile Expenses, p. 9–6]

20.   d   Venezuela is out the U.S. and North American area. [Foreign travel, p. 9–10]

21.   c $5,200—$3,400 = $1,800 [Accountable Plans, p. 9–24]

22.   d   All statutory employee expenses are deductible for AGI. [Employee Versus Self-Employed, p. 9–2]

23.   a   Nothing can be deducted because the trip was not primarily for business. Only three of ten days were spent engaged in business. [Foreign Travel, p. 9–10]

24.   d $4,000 + $500 + ($.13 × 1,200 miles) = $4,656 [Treatment of Moving Expenses, p. 9–12]

25.   a   Accountable plan reimbursements are not income. [Classification of Employee Expenses, p. 9–24]

26.   c $25 + 50% of ($40 + $135 + $35) = $130 [Cutback Adjustment, p. 9–16]

27.   b   (65% of $120) + $200 = $278 [Cutback Adjustment, p 9–16]

28.   b   Union dues are a 2% limited deduction from AGI. [Miscellaneous Itemized Deductions Subject to the 2% Floor, p. 9–27]

29.   a   Moving Expenses are a deduction for AGI. [Treatment of Moving Expenses, p. 9–12]

30.   b   Employee home office expenses are deductible from AGI subject to the 2% limit. [Miscellaneous Itemized Deductions Subject to the 2% Floor, p. 9–27]

31.   c   Gambling losses are a deduction from AGI not limited to 2%. [Miscellaneous Itemized Deductions Not Subject to the 2% Floor, p. 9–27]

32.   a   Self-Employed education expenses are a deduction for AGI. [Employee Versus Self-employed, p. 9–2]

33.   c   Handicapped work expenses are a deduction form AGI not subject to the 2% limit. [Miscellaneous Itemized Deductions Not Subject to the 2% Floor, p. 9–27]

Problems

1.

Moving household goods	$4,000
Transportation	$ 125
Lodging	$ 150
Meals	$ 0
Qualified house sale expenses	$ 0
Moving expense deduction	$4,275

[Treatment of Moving Expenses, p. 9–12]

2.

Mileage 16,500 × $.365 (2002)	$6,023
Travel (50% of $200) + $550	$ 650
Transportation	$ 600
Total	$7,273

[Various Sections Throughout the Chapter]

3. The expenses are deductible from AGI, subject to the 2 percent limit. Chee's total deduction would be as follows:

Airfare	$ 2,000
Rent	$10,000
Meals 50% of ($5,000)	$ 2,500
Total	$14,500
2% of $50,000	–$ 1,000
Deduction	$13,500

[Travel Expenses, p. 9–7]

CHAPTER 10

Deductions & Losses: Certain Itemized Deductions

CHAPTER HIGHLIGHTS

Personal expenses are generally disallowed as deductions. However, Congress has identified certain personal expenses which are allowed as itemized deductions. This chapter summarizes the provisions which allow deductions for medical expenses, state and local taxes, certain interest expense, and charitable contributions. The limitations which apply to these deductions are also discussed.

KEY TERMS

Medical Expenses	Taxes	Miscellaneous Itemized
Types of Interest	Charitable Contributions	Deductions

OUTLINE

I. **MEDICAL EXPENSES**
    A. General Requirements. Taxpayers are allowed a deduction for medical expenses (net of any reimbursement) for the care of the taxpayer, spouse, and dependents. Medical expenses are deductible only to the extent that they exceed seven and one half percent of adjusted gross income.
    B. Medical Expenses Defined. The term medical care means expenditures incurred for the "diagnosis, cure, mitigation, treatment, or prevention of disease," or for "affecting any structure or function of the body."

    Expenses to improve the taxpayer's general health are not deductible. Also, expenses for elective cosmetic surgery are not deductible.

    If a patient is placed in a nursing home for personal or family reasons, expenses are deductible only to the extent of actual medical or nursing attention received. If the patient is placed in the home primarily for medical reasons, the expenses are fully deductible.

    The expenses of keeping a dependent at a special school for the mentally or physically handicapped may be deductible as medical expenses.
    C. Capital Expenditures for Medical Purposes. Capital expenditures for medical care are deductible to the extent that the cost exceeds the increase in value of the related property. However, the cost of capital expenditures that enable a handicapped individual to live independently and productively are fully deductible subject to the seven and one half percent of adjusted gross income limitation.
    D. Medical Expenses Incurred for Spouse and Dependents. Medical expenses for dependents are deductible if they are legitimate medical expenses. The gross income test and joint return test need not be met for a dependent to qualify for the medical deduction.
    E. Transportation and Lodging Expenses for Medical Treatment. Expenditures for transportation to and from the point of treatment are deductible as medical expenses. If a taxpayer uses a personal automobile, a mileage allowance of 13 cents per mile in 2002 may be claimed as a medical expense or the taxpayer may use actual out-of-pocket costs. Qualified lodging that is part of medical care is deductible up to $50 per night per person.
    F. Amounts Paid for Medical Insurance Premiums. Medical insurance premiums are included in medical expenses subject to the seven and one-half percent limitation. A self-employed person who is not covered under a medical plan may deduct as a business expense (*for* AGI) a percentage of medical insurance premiums paid for coverage for his or her family. Any excess premiums can be claimed as a medical expense.
    G. Year of Deduction. Medical expenses are deductible in the year paid by the taxpayer.
    H. Reimbursements. If a taxpayer receives an insurance reimbursement for medical expenses deducted in a previous year, the reimbursement must be included as income in the year of receipt. The reimbursement is income only if the expense provided a tax benefit in the previous year.

    If the taxpayer used the standard deduction amount in the year the medical expenses were paid instead of itemizing deductions, any reimbursements received need not be included in gross income.
    I. Medical Savings Accounts. Taxpayers can set medical savings accounts (MSAs). These accounts are intended to be used with high-deductible health insurance. The definition of high-deductible policies for individuals and families can be found in the textbook. Contributions to these accounts are deductible (65 percent for individuals, 75 percent for families) and amounts used to pay for medical care not covered by high-deductible insurance are not subject to tax. Distributions from an MSA not used to pay for medical expenses are included in gross income and subject to a 15 percent penalty if made before age 65, death, or disability.

II. **TAXES**
- A. Deductibility as a Tax. Taxpayers are allowed a deduction for the payment of certain state and local taxes to reduce the effect of multiple taxation. The law defines a tax as an enforced contribution extracted under legislative authority. Under Section 164, the following taxes are deductible:
  1) State, local, and foreign real property taxes
  2) State and local personal property taxes
  3) State and local income taxes
  4) The environmental tax

  Federal income taxes, employee FICA taxes, estate taxes, inheritance taxes, gift taxes, general sales taxes, and excise taxes cannot be deducted under this section.
- B. Property Taxes.

  For personal property taxes to be deductible, they must be ad valorem (assessed in relation to the value of the property).

  Generally, assessments for local benefits are not deductible and are added to the adjusted basis of the property.

  Real estate taxes are apportioned between the buyer and seller on the basis of the number of days the property was held by each. This apportionment is required without regard to whether the tax is paid by the buyer or seller.
- C. State & Local Income Taxes.

  State and local taxes are deductible in the year paid by a cash basis taxpayer. Withholding and actual payments are deductible under this rule and state and local tax refunds are included in gross income, providing there was a tax benefit in the prior year.

  State and local income taxes imposed on an individual are itemized deductions even if the source of the taxable income is from a trade or business or the production of income.

III. **INTEREST**
- A. Allowed and Disallowed Items. Under the tax law, individual taxpayers are allowed a deduction (within certain limits) for the following kinds of interest:
  1) Trade or business interest
  2) Investment interest
  3) Interest on passive activities
  4) Qualified residence interest
  5) Qualified education loan interest

  Personal (consumer) interest is not deductible.

  Investment interest is deductible only to the extent of net investment income. Disallowed investment interest may be carried over and deducted in future years.

  Qualified residence interest includes acquisition indebtedness up to a maximum of $1,000,000 ($500,000, if married filing separately) on a taxpayer's first and second residences, and interest on home equity borrowing of up to $100,000 ($50,000, if married filing separately).
- B. Restrictions on Deductibility and Timing Considerations. Deductions are allowed if the debt represents a bona fide obligation for which the taxpayer is liable. A taxpayer may not deduct interest paid on behalf of another. For interest to be deductible both the debtor and creditor must intend the loan to be repaid.

  Interest must be paid to secure a deduction unless the taxpayer used the accrual method of accounting. Prepaid interest must be allocated to the tax years to which the interest payments relate.
- C. Classification of Interest Expense. Interest expense can be either a deduction for or a deduction from adjusted gross income, depending on whether the loan is for business (other than that as an employee),

investment, or personal purposes. Deductions for interest charges on personal indebtedness are reported as itemized deductions on Schedule A of Form 1040 (subject to limitations).

IV. **CHARITABLE CONTRIBUTIONS**
   A. The Code permits the deduction of contributions made to qualified charitable organizations. The deduction is justified as a social consideration in the tax law.
   B. Criteria for a Gift. To qualify as a charitable contribution, the gift must be made to a qualified organization. The major elements needed for a gift to be deductible are a donative intent, the absence of consideration, and acceptance by the donee.

   If a contribution to a college or university carries the right to purchase athletic tickets, then 80 percent of the amount of the contribution is deductible.

   Contributions of services are not allowed as a deduction. Out-of-pocket expenses incurred in the performance of donated services are allowed if there is no significant element of personal pleasure, recreation, or vacation in the donated services.
   C. Qualified charitable organizations are:
      1) States or possessions of the United States or any subdivision thereof
      2) Organizations situated in the United States operated exclusively for religious, charitable, scientific, literary, or educational purposes or for the prevention of cruelty to children or animals
      3) Veterans' organizations
      4) Fraternal organizations operating under the lodge system
      5) Certain cemeteries
   D. Time of Deduction. Charitable contributions are deductible in the year paid for both cash and accrual basis taxpayers. However, an accrual basis corporation can pledge a contribution at the end of the year and deduct it if the amount is paid within two and one-half months after the close of the tax year.
   E. Record Keeping and Valuation Requirements. No deduction is allowed for contributions of $250 or more unless the taxpayer obtains *written substantiation* of the contribution from the charitable organization. The substantiation must specify the amount of cash and a description (but not value) of any property other than cash contributed.
   F. Limitations on Charitable Contribution Deduction.

   There are limitations placed on the amount of charitable contributions. For individuals, the general AGI limitations are:
      1) 50 percent for contributions to certain public charities, all private operating foundations, and certain private nonoperating foundations.
      2) 30 percent for contributions of cash and ordinary income property to private nonoperating foundations and contributions of appreciated capital gain property to 50 percent organizations. If the value of the capital gain property is reduced by any appreciation on the property, then the 50 percent limit applies.
      3) 20 percent for contributions of long-term capital gain property to certain private nonoperating foundations. See text for calculation of limits.

   If ordinary income property is contributed, the deduction is equal to the fair market value of the property less the amount of ordinary income which would have been reported if the property were sold.

   Generally, contributions may be carried over for five years. Contributions made during the carryover years are deducted before carryover amounts are applied.

V. **MISCELLANEOUS ITEMIZED DEDUCTIONS**

Taxpayers are allowed certain miscellaneous deductions if they exceed 2 percent of AGI. Examples of such deductions are: professional dues, uniforms, tax return preparation fees, job hunting expenses, safe-deposit box fees, investment expenses, appraisals for casualty losses, donated property, etc., hobby loss expenses, and unreimbursed employee expenses

Miscellaneous deductions not subject to the 2 percent limitation include: gambling losses, certain handicapped work expenses, federal estate tax or income in respect of a decedent, and certain unrecovered annuity investments.

VI.   OVERALL LIMITATION ON CERTAIN ITEMIZED DEDUCTIONS

Itemized deductions for high income taxpayers are subject to limits when AGI exceeds certain amounts. In 2002, the applicable itemized deductions are reduced by the lesser of 3 percent of the excess of adjusted gross income over $137,300 (single taxpayers and married taxpayers filing jointly), *or* 80 percent of the itemized deductions affected by the limit (see below). This limitation applies after all other limits (e.g., the 7.5 percent medical limitation) on itemized deductions have been applied.

The limitation applies to the following itemized deductions: taxes, home mortgage interest, charitable contributions, unreimbursed employee expenses subject to 2 percent of AGI floor, and all other expenses subject to the 2 percent of AGI floor.

The following deductions are **not** subject to the itemized deductions limitation: medical expenses, investment interest, nonbusiness casualty and theft losses, and gambling losses.

TEST FOR SELF-EVALUATION—CHAPTER 10

True or False

Indicate which of the following statements is true or false by circling the correct answer.

T	F	1.	For medical expenses to be deductible, they must be for the taxpayer, spouse, or dependents.
T	F	2.	The term "medical care expenditure" would include expenses that are not related to a particular ailment.
T	F	3.	Nursing home expenditures are always deductible as medical expenses.
T	F	4.	Under certain circumstances, capital expenditures can be deducted as medical expenses.
T	F	5.	The cost of special schools for the mentally or physically handicapped may be deductible as a medical expense.
T	F	6.	For other than self-employed taxpayers, 100 percent of medical insurance premiums are subject to the seven and one half percent of adjusted gross income floor.
T	F	7.	The term "medicine and drugs" does not include toothpaste, shaving lotion, deodorants, and hand lotions.
T	F	8.	The expense of unnecessary cosmetic surgery is not deductible as a medical expense.
T	F	9.	All medicine and drugs are deductible.
T	F	10.	If a taxpayer is reimbursed for medical expenses that were paid in a previous year, he or she must always include that amount in income.
T	F	11.	All amounts paid to a government are deductible under Section 164 as a tax.
T	F	12.	The IRS defines a tax as "an enforced contribution exacted under legislative authority in the exercise of taxing power, and imposed and collected for raising revenue to be used for public or governmental purposes."
T	F	13.	State and local income taxes are deductible for Federal tax purposes.
T	F	14.	For personal property taxes to be deductible, they must be ad valorem, that is, assessed in relation to the value of the property.
T	F	15.	Real property taxes include taxes assessed for local benefits such as new streets and sidewalks.
T	F	16.	Real property taxes are apportioned between the buyer and seller on the basis of the number of days each held the property.
T	F	17.	State income taxes are always deducted on the accrual method.
T	F	18.	Personal interest is not deductible by taxpayers.
T	F	19.	Cash contributions to needy individuals are deductible charitable contributions.
T	F	20.	Property donated to a charity is generally valued at fair market value at the time of the gift.

T   F   21.   Any charitable contribution is deductible for tax purposes.

T   F   22.   Interest on a principal residence mortgage is not deductible.

T   F   23.   The investment interest expense deduction is limited to net investment income.

T   F   24.   The interest deduction is always a deduction for adjusted gross income.

T   F   25.   The estate and gift taxes are deductible for income tax purposes.

T   F   26.   Points paid by the seller on the sale of a personal residence are treated as a reduction in the sales price and are deductible to the purchaser of the house.

T   F   27.   Robert drives 625 miles to obtain medical care for himself and his family. Assuming the 2002 medical mileage rate is $.13 per mile, his deduction (before any limits) for medical mileage is $81.25.

T   F   28.   In 2002 Mary drove 2,000 miles to and from a qualified charitable hospital where she is a volunteer worker and 1,000 miles to attend her church on Sunday. If the 2002 charitable mileage rate is $.14 per mile, Mary's charitable deduction is $420 ($.14 × 3,000 miles).

Multiple Choice

Choose the best answer for each of the following questions.

_____ 1.   Steve borrows $150,000 at 10 percent interest on January 3, year 1. The proceeds are used to purchase $100,000 worth of raw land and $50,000 worth of stock in Exxon. During year 1, the stock pays dividends of $2,500. Steve has deductible expenses on this investment property of $500 (after considering the 2 percent of adjusted gross income limitation). Assuming Steve pays interest of $15,000 (10 percent of $150,000) in year 1, how much is deductible?

     a. $2,000
     b. $12,500
     c. $2,500
     d. $15,000

_____ 2.   Mary had adjusted gross income of $30,000 and she paid the following medical expenses: $500 medical insurance, $600 dental charges, $1,000 physicians' charges, $100 prescription drugs, and $400 hospital costs. Assuming Mary itemizes deductions, what is Mary's medical expense deduction?

     a. $–0–
     b. $2,660
     c. $410
     d. $1,160

_____ 3.   During the current year, Tim paid $72 for California license plates for his automobile. California plates are sold at a fee of $30 plus $2 per hundred dollar valuation of the automobile. Assuming Tim itemizes his deductions, how much, if any, may Tim claim as a deduction for taxes?

     a. $–0–
     b. $30
     c. $42
     d. $72

_____ 4. Ted donated an art object to Goodwill Industries, a qualified charity. The art object cost Ted $2,000 five months ago and has a fair market value of $3,000 on the date of donation. What is the amount of Ted's charitable contribution deduction?

    a. $–0–
    b. $2,000
    c. $2,500
    d. $3,000

_____ 5. Assume the same situation as in Question 4, except the art object possesses a fair market value of $1,800 (not $3,000) on the date of donation. What is the amount of Ted's charitable contribution deduction?

    a. $–0–
    b. $1,800
    c. $2,000
    d. $1,600

_____ 6. Tom donated shares of Texaco stock to his church in satisfaction of last year's church pledge. Tom purchased the stock as an investment two years ago. The stock cost Tom $2,300 and possessed a fair market value of $2,700 on the date of donation. What is the amount of Tom's charitable contribution deduction?

    a. $–0–
    b. $2,300
    c. $2,700
    d. $2,500

_____ 7. Terry donated $650 of his time as a painter and paint with a cost basis to him of $200, to help fix up his church. How much can he deduct? What is the amount of Terry's charitable contribution deduction?

    a. $–0–
    b. $850
    c. $650
    d. $200

_____ 8. Tina works for the American Red Cross for free during each month of the current year. She would normally charge $400 per month for the type of work performed. What is the amount of Tina's charitable contribution deduction?

    a. $–0–
    b. $400
    c. $4,800
    d. Some other amount

_____ 9. What is the maximum amount of property contributions that a taxpayer may make to qualified organizations without being required to have *written substantiation*?

    a. $–0–
    b. $250
    c. $249
    d. $500

_____ 10. Pat is a cash basis taxpayer who had $1,000 of state income tax withheld from her salary in year 1. In addition, during year 1 she received a refund of year 0 state income taxes of $250. During year 1, Pat also made estimated state income tax payments of $600. For year 1, Pat's state income tax deduction is:

   a. $–0–
   b. $1,350
   c. $1,000
   d. $1,600

_____ 11.   Gene owns his own home which he bought several years ago. His original mortgage, which was used to buy the house, is $150,000. In the current year, he obtains a home equity loan on the house of $90,000. The interest on the original mortgage is $15,000 and on the new loan is $10,000. The fair market value of the house is $325,000. How much of this interest is deductible as "qualified residence interest?"

   a. $–0–
   b. $10,000
   c. $15,000
   d. $25,000

_____ 12.   Which of the following items will not qualify as a medical expense deduction?

   a.   Eyeglasses
   b.   Insulin
   c.   A trip to Arizona for the general improvement of the taxpayer's health
   d.   Transportation to and from a doctor's office

_____ 13.   The prepaid interest rules of Section 461(g) apply to all prepaid interest payments except which of the following?

   a.   "Points" on the purchase of a rental house
   b.   Construction loans
   c.   Bank auto loans
   d.   "Points" paid by a buyer of a personal residence

_____ 14.   Big Booster gives $1,000 to his alma mater's athletic department. The contribution entitles him to four football tickets for $50 each. How much is Big's charitable contribution deduction?

   a. $–0–
   b. $1,000
   c. $800
   d. $640

_____ 15.   Eric, who is single and has no dependents, had adjusted gross income of $80,000 in 2002, comprised of the following:

Salary	$74,000
Net investment income	$ 6,000

During 2002, uninsured art objects owned by Eric, with a basis of $50,000 and a fair market value of $70,000, sustained casualty fire damage reducing the fair market value to $60,000. Also, during 2002, Eric made the following payments:

Interest on margin account to stockbroker	$18,000
Real estate taxes on a condominium (owned by Eric's mother, in which Eric resides)	$ 3,000
State and city gasoline taxes	$ 180
Medical insurance premiums	$ 300
Unreimbursed dental expenses	$4,500
Contribution to political committee of elected public official	$ 500

Eric elected to itemize his deductions for 2002. How much can Eric claim as *taxes* in itemized deductions on his 2002 return?

    a. $0
    b. $180
    c. $3,000
    d. $3,180

_____ 16.   Eric, who is single and has no dependents, had adjusted gross income of $80,000 in 2002, comprised of the following:

Salary	$74,000
Net investment income	$ 6,000

During 2002, uninsured art objects owned by Eric, with a basis of $50,000 and a fair market value of $70,000, sustained casualty fire damage reducing the fair market value to $60,000. Also, during 2002, Eric made the following payments:

Interest on margin account to stockbroker	$18,000
Real estate taxes on a condominium (owned by Eric's mother, in which Eric resides)	$ 3,000
State and city gasoline taxes	$ 180
Medical insurance premiums	$ 300
Unreimbursed dental expenses	$ 4,500
Contribution to political committee of elected public official	$ 500

Eric elected to itemize his deductions for 2002. How much can Eric claim in his itemized deductions for *medical and dental expenses* on his 2002 return?

    a.   2,400
    b. $800
    c. $300
    d. $–0–

_____ 17.   Eric, who is single and has no dependents, had adjusted gross income of $80,000 in 2002, comprised of the following:

Salary	$74,000
Net investment income	$ 6,000

During 2002, uninsured art objects owned by Eric, with a basis of $50,000 and a fair market value of $70,000, sustained casualty fire damage reducing the fair market value to $60,000. Also, during 2002, Eric made the following payments:

Interest on margin account to stockbroker	$18,000
Real estate taxes on a condominium (owned by Eric's mother, in which Eric resides)	$ 3,000
State and city gasoline taxes	$ 180
Medical insurance premiums	$ 300
Unreimbursed dental expenses	$ 4,500
Contribution to political committee of elected public official	$ 500

Eric elected to itemize his deductions for 2002. How much can Eric claim in his itemized deductions for the casualty loss on his 2002 return?

    a. $–0–
    b. $1,900
    c. $2,000
    d. $9,900

_____ 18.   Carol, a resident of San Diego, travels with her dependent sick mother to see a specialist in San Francisco for medical treatment. The cost of the trip includes $400 ($200 each) for airfare and $450 for lodging in San Francisco for three nights. Disregarding the percentage limitation, what is Carol's medical deduction for this trip?

    a. $–0–
    b. $400
    c. $850
    d. $700

_____ 19.   Xavier would otherwise qualify as Zack's dependent except for the joint return test. Zack paid the following medical expenses: $2,000 operation for Xavier, $1,200 prescription drugs for Zack, $3,000 Zack's dentists bills, and $2,500 for Xavier's membership in health spa. Disregarding the percentage limitation, what is the total of Zack's deductible medical expenses?

    a. $8,700
    b. $6,200
    c. $5,000
    d. $4,200

_____ 20.   Saul, a self-employed individual taxpayer, paid the following amounts: $2,000 state income tax, $4,000 Federal income tax, $1,000 real estate tax on land in Ireland, $500 state sales tax, and $150 CPA license fee $150. What amount can Saul deduct as an itemized deduction for taxes on Schedule A of Form 1040?

    a. $3,500
    b. $3,000
    c. $2,000
    d. $1,000

_____ 21.   Cecil is a resident of a state that imposes a state income tax. During the year, Cecil had the following transactions in regards to his state income taxes: $6,000 taxes withheld, $1,000 last year's state income tax refund, $2,000 estimated payments, and $3,000 deficiency paid related to two years ago. If Cecil itemizes his deductions, how much may be claimed as a deduction for taxes on Schedule A?

    a. $5,000
    b. $8,000
    c. $10,000
    d. $11,000

_____ 22.   Scott sells his home to Ben for $200,000. After the sale, Ben pays the real estate taxes of $3,600 for the calendar year. For income tax purposes, the deduction is apportioned $2,100 to Scott and $1,500 to Ben. Assuming the real estate taxes are not prorated in escrow, what is Ben's basis in the residence?

    a. $200,000
    b. $201,500
    c. $202,100
    d. $198,500

_____ 23. Tina purchased a new residence in January year 1, for $150,000 and paid points of $4,500 to obtain mortgage financing. The mortgage is for 30 years. Her regular interest on the mortgage for the year was $6,500. What is the maximum amount Tina can deduct for interest on her home in year 1?

    a. $4,500
    b. $6,500
    c. $6,650
    d. $11,000

_____ 24. In 2002, Dale had the following income and deductions: $150,000 salary, $35,450 dividend income, $15,000 state income taxes, $13,000 qualified residence interest, and $14,000 charitable contributions. Assuming Dale is single, what is the net amount of itemized deductions that she may claim on her federal income tax return?

    a. $42,000 – $25,340
    b. $42,000 – 3% × ($185,450 – $68,650)
    c. $42,000 – 3% × ($185,450 – $137,300)
    d. $42,000

_____ 25. In 2002, Casper had the following income and deductions: $115,000 salary, $5,450 dividend income, $12,000 state income taxes, $13,000 qualified residence interest, and $14,000 charitable contributions. Assuming Casper is married and files a joint return, what is the net amount of itemized deductions that he may claim on his federal income tax return?

    a. $39,000
    b. $27,000
    c. $37,725
    d. $1,275

_____ 26. Doreen is a resident of California. During the year, Doreen had the following transactions in regards to her state income taxes: $4,000 state taxes withheld, $3,000 amount paid with last year's California tax return, $2,000 estimated payments (California), and $3,000 nonresident income taxes paid to the state of Arizona. If Doreen itemizes her deductions, how much may be claimed as a deduction for taxes on Schedule A?

    a. $7,000
    b. $9,000
    b. $4,000
    d. $12,000

_____ 27. Rick (a single taxpayer) establishes a qualified Medical Savings Account (MSA). His medical insurance has a deductible of $2,000. During the year, Rick contributes $2,200 to his MSA. What is Rick's MSA deduction?

    a. $–0–
    b. $1,300
    c. $2,000
    d. $2,200

_____ 28. On qualified education loans, interest is deductible for the first _____ months during which payments are required.

    a.   36
    b.   48
    c.   60
    d.   72

_____ 29.   For 2002, the maximum interest deduction on a qualified education loan is?

     a. $1,000
     b. $1,500
     c. $2,000
     d. $2,500

Problem

1.   Ted and Joyce, both employees of Orange Corporation, had the following items of income and expense for 2002:

Adjusted gross income	$31,500
Medical insurance	$ 500
Doctor bills	$ 1,000
Prescription drugs	$ 200
Hospital bills	$ 1,000
Medical insurance reimbursement	$ 1,200
State income tax	$ 950
Real estate taxes	$ 775
Qualified residence interest	$ 7,150
Personal interest	$ 625
Contribution to church (by check)	$ 450
Tax return preparation fee	$ 225
Professional dues	$ 600
Contribution of used goods to Goodwill	$ 150
Contribution carryover from 2001	$ 625

They file a joint income tax return. Calculate Ted and Joyce's itemized deductions using the worksheet below.

Medical expenses	_____
Insurance reimbursement	_____
Total	_____
Less 7.5 percent of AGI	_____
Medical Deduction	_____
Taxes	_____
Interest	_____
Contributions	_____
Miscellaneous (less 2 percent of AGI)	_____
Total Deductions	_____

SOLUTIONS TO CHAPTER 10 QUESTIONS

True or False

1.   T   Medical expenses must be for the taxpayer, spouse, or dependents to be deductible. [General Requirements, p. 10–2]

2.   T   "Medical care expenditure" includes expenses that are not related to a particular ailment. [Medical Expenses Defined, p. 10–3]

3.   F   The expenditure must be primarily for medical reasons. [Medical Expenses Defined, p. 10–3]

4.   T   Capital expenditures can be deducted as medical expenses in some situations. [Medical Expenses Defined, p. 10–3]

5.   T   Special schools for the mentally or physically handicapped may be deductible as a medical expense. [Medical Expenses Defined, p. 10–3]

6.   T   Except for self-employed taxpayers, 100 percent of medical insurance premiums are subject to the seven and one half percent of AGI floor. [Amounts Paid for Medical Insurance Premiums, p. 10–7]

7.   T   The term "medicine and drugs" does not include personal hygiene items. [Exhibit 10–1, p. 10–4]

8.   T   Unnecessary cosmetic surgery is not deductible as a medical expense. [Medical Expenses Defined, p. 10–3]

9.   F   Only prescription drugs are deductible. [Exhibit 10–1, p. 10–4]

10.   F   The reimbursement is included in income only to the extent of the tax benefit derived in the prior year. [Reimbursements, p. 10–8]

11.   F   Fees, unless incurred in a trade or business or as an investment expense, are not deductible. [Deductibility as a Tax, p. 10–11]

12.   T   A tax is "an enforced contribution exacted under legislative authority in the exercise of taxing power, and imposed and collected for raising revenue to be used for public or governmental purposes." [Deductibility as a Tax, p. 10–11]

13.   T   State and local income taxes are deductible for Federal tax purposes. [State and Local Income Taxes, p. 10–13]

14.   T   For personal property taxes to be deductible, they must be ad valorem, that is, assessed in relation to the value of the property. [Property Taxes, p. 10–11]

15.   F   Assessments usually increase the value of the property and are added to the taxpayer's basis of the property. [Assessments for Local Benefits, p. 10–12]

16.   T   Real estate taxes are apportioned between the buyer and seller on the basis of the number of days. [Property taxes, p. 10–11]

17.   F   Individuals deduct state income taxes on the cash method. [State and Local Income taxes, p. 10–13]

18.   T   Personal interest is not deductible by taxpayers. [Interest, p. 10–14]

19.   F   Contributions must be made to qualifying organizations. [Criteria for a Gift, p. 10–20]

20.   T   Donations to a charity are generally valued at fair market value. [Record-Keeping and Valuation Requirements, p. 10–22]

21.   F   There are limits based on 50 percent, 30 percent and 20 percent of AGI. [Limitations on Charitable Contribution Deduction, p. 10–23]

22.	F	Qualified interest on residence mortgages is deductible. [Qualified Residence Interest, p. 10–16
23.	T	Investment interest expense is limited to net investment income. [Investment Interest, p. 10–14]
24.	F	Interest for personal use is a deduction from AGI. [Classification of Interest Expense, p. 10–18]
25.	F	Estate and gift taxes are not deductible. [Exhibit 10–2, p. 10–11]
26.	T	Points paid on the sale of a personal residence are a reduction in the sales price and are deductible to the purchaser. [Interest Paid for Services, p. 10–17]
27.	T	625 miles × $.13 per mile = $81.25 [Transportation, Meal, and Lodging Expenses for Medical Treatment, p. 10–6]
28.	F	The deduction is $280 ($.14 per mile × 2,000 miles). The mileage to attend church is personal and therefore not deductible. [Contribution of Services, p. 10–21]

Multiple Choice

1.	a	The deduction is limited to net investment income. [Investment Interest, p. 10–14]
2.	c	($100 drugs + $560 insurance + $600 dental + $1,000 physicians + $400 hospitals) = $2,660 less $2,250 (7.5 percent of AGI) = $ 410 medical deduction [Medical Expenses Defined, p. 10–3]
3.	c	$72 – $30 = $42 [Property Taxes, p. 10–11]
4.	b	$3,000 – ($3,000 – $2,000) = $2,000 since the property contributed is ordinary income property. [Ordinary Income Property, p. 10–24]
5.	b	$1,800 – zero = $1,800. [Ordinary Income Property, p. 10–24]
6.	c	Fair market value is used provided the stock is not contributed to a private nonoperating foundation. [Capital Gain Property, p. 10–24]
7.	d	The donation of service is not deductible. [Contribution of Services, p. 10–21]
8.	a	The donation of free services is not deductible. [Contribution of Services, p. 10–21]
9.	c	The maximum amount is $250. [Record-Keeping Requirements, p. 10–22]
10.	d	$1,000 + $600 = $1,600 [State and Local Income Taxes, p. 10–13]
11.	d	All of the debt is considered qualified residence interest. [Qualified Residence Interest, p. 10–16]
12.	c	Travel for health improvement is not deducible. [Exhibit 10–1, p. 10–4]
13.	d	Points on a personal residence are not subject to the prepaid interest rules. [Interest Paid for Services, p. 10–17]
14.	d	($1,000 – $200) × 80 percent = $640 [Benefit Received Rule, p. 10–20]
15.	a	A taxpayer must own real estate to deduct any taxes on it. [Property Taxes, p. 10–11]
16.	d	$4,500 + $300 – 7.5 percent ($80,000) = $–0– [General Requirements, p. 10–2]
17.	b	$10,000 – $100 – 10 percent ($80,000) = $1,900 [Overall Limitation on Certain Itemized Deductions, p. 10–30]
18.	d	$400 (airfare) + (3 nights × $50 (per person) × 2 persons) = $700 [Transportation, Meal and Lodging Expenses for Medical Treatment, p. 10–6]
19.	b	$2,000 + $1,200 + $3,000 = $6,200 [Medical Expenses Incurred for Spouse and Dependents, p. 10–6]
20.	b	$2,000 + $1,000 = $3,000 [Taxes, p. 10–10]

21. d $6,000 + $2,000 + $3,000 = $11,000 [State and Local Income Taxes, p. 10–13]

22. c $200,000 + $2,100 = $202,100 [Apportionment of Real Property Taxes Between Seller and Purchaser, p. 10–12]

23. d $4,500 (points) + $6,500 (regular interest) = $11,000 [Interest Paid for Services, p. 10–17]

24. c $42,000 − 3% ($185,450 − $137,300) = $40,425 (2002) [Overall Limitation on Certain Itemized Deductions, p. 10–30]

25. a AGI does not exceed the phase-out limit of $137,300, therefore, there is no limit. (2002) [Overall Limitation on Certain Itemized Deductions, p. 10–30]

26. d $4,000 + $3,000 + $2,000 + $3,000 = $12,000 [State and Local Income Taxes p. 10–13]

27. b 65 percent of $2,000 = $1,300 [Medical Savings Accounts, p. 10–9]

28. c On education loans interest is deductible for the first 60 months. [Interest on Qualified Education Loans, p. 10–14]

29. d The maximum deduction on an education loans is $2,500. (2002) [Interest on Qualified Education Loans, p. 10–14]

Problem

1.

Medical expenses ($500 + $1,000 + $1,000 + $200)	$ 2,700	
Insurance reimbursement	−$ 1,200	
Total	$ 1,500	
Less 7.5 percent of AGI	−$ 2,363	
Medical Deduction		$ 0
Taxes ($950 + $775)		$ 1,725
Interest		$ 7,150
Contributions ($450 + $150 + $625)		$ 1,225
Miscellaneous [$225 + $600 − (2% of AGI)]		$ 195
Total Deductions		$10,295

[Overall Limitation on Certain Itemized Deductions, p. 10–30]

CHAPTER 11

Passive Activity Losses

CHAPTER HIGHLIGHTS

The treatment of at-risk amounts and passive losses are areas of concern for many taxpayers. The purpose of these rules is to limit the use of tax shelters to reduce a taxpayer's tax liability. The rules for application of the at-risk rules and the passive loss limitation are very complex, but must be understood in order to have a working knowledge of the U.S. income tax system.

KEY TERMS

At-Risk Limitations
Passive Activity Rules
Active Income

Portfolio Income
Passive Income

Material Participation
Active Participation

OUTLINE

I.   **THE TAX SHELTER PROBLEM**

For many years, tax shelters represented a popular way for taxpayers to avoid taxes. The ability of taxpayers to avoid or reduce tax using tax shelters has been limited by the at-risk rules and the passive loss rules. These two provisions have made the tax shelter investments of the past nearly obsolete. If they make investments in many activities, especially real estate, taxpayers must have a working knowledge of these provisions because of their impact on tax liability.

II.   **AT-RISK LIMITS**

A.   The tax laws provide an at-risk limitation on losses from business and income-producing activities. A loss deduction is limited to the amount the taxpayer has at risk. The amount at risk is generally the sum of the following:
   1)   The adjusted basis of property and amount of cash contributed to the activity,
   2)   Any amount borrowed for use in the activity for which the taxpayer has personal liability, and
   3)   The taxpayer's share of the net earnings, decreased by the taxpayer's share of losses and withdrawals from the activity.

   A taxpayer is not considered at risk with respect to borrowed amounts if either one of the following is true:
   1)   The taxpayer is not personally liable for repayment of the debt (nonrecourse loans).
   2)   The lender has an interest (other than as a creditor) in the activity (except to the extent provided by the Regulations).

   Recapture of previously allowed losses occurs to the extent the at-risk amount is reduced below zero. This occurs when the amount at risk is reduced by distributions to the taxpayer, changes in the status of debt from recourse to nonrecourse, or by any arrangement, that affects the taxpayer's risk of loss.

III. **PASSIVE LOSS LIMITS**

A.   Classification and Impact of Passive Income and Losses.

   The passive loss rules require income and losses to be classified into three categories. These categories are:
   1)   Active (wages, salaries, commissions, a trade or business in which the taxpayer is a material participant, etc.)
   2)   Portfolio (dividends, annuities, etc.)
   3)   Passive (rental income(with certain exceptions) or a trade or business in which the taxpayer is not a material participant)

   Carryover of Suspended Losses. If a passive loss is disallowed because of insufficient passive income to offset it, it becomes suspended. The at-risk limitations are applied first, as well as other provisions which influence the determination of taxable income, before a taxpayer's suspended loss under the passive loss provisions can be determined. A taxpayer's basis in the investment is reduced by deductions even if the deductions are not allowed in the current year because of the passive loss rules. Suspended losses are carried over indefinitely and are applied against future years' passive income. If the passive activity is disposed of, the suspended losses can be offset against active and portfolio income. Suspended losses for each passive activity must be determined separately on a pro rata basis.

   Passive Credits. Credits arising from passive activities can only be used against regular tax attributable to passive income. Any excess passive credits are carried over indefinitely into future years. If a taxpayer has a passive loss for a tax year, then no passive credits can be used. If the taxpayer's tax is calculated using the alternative minimum tax (see Chapter 12), then no passive credits can be used. The passive credit is lost if there is no regular tax generated when the activity is disposed of.

B.   Taxpayers Subject to the Passive Loss Rules.

The passive loss rules apply to individuals, estates, trusts, closely-held C corporations, and personal service corporations. The reason that the passive loss rules apply to personal service corporations is to prevent taxpayers from sheltering personal service income by acquiring passive activities at the corporate level. A personal service corporation is a corporation that meets the following conditions:
1)   The principal activity is the performance of personal services, and
2)   Services are substantially performed by owner-employees

There is one important exception to the above rules for corporations. A "closely-held" C corporation can deduct passive losses against active income but not portfolio income.

C.   Passive Activities Defined.

A passive activity is defined under Section 469 as:
1)   Any trade or business in which the taxpayer does not "materially participate."
2)   Any rental activity (regardless of the taxpayer's level of participation), subject to certain exceptions

Identification of an Activity. Identifying what constitutes an activity is the first step in applying the passive loss rules. Taxpayers with several businesses need to determine whether a segment of a business is a separate entity or part of a single activity. The Regulations state a taxpayer can treat one or more businesses as a single activity if those activities form an *appropriate economic unit* for measuring gain or loss. Taxpayers should carefully consider all tax factors in deciding how to group their activities. Once a taxpayer's activities have been grouped, they cannot be regrouped unless there is a material change in facts and circumstances. There are special rules for grouping rental activities (see the textbook).

Material Participation. If a taxpayer materially participates in a nonrental activity, any loss from that activity will be treated as an active loss that can offset other active income. The Code provides that material participation requires the taxpayer to be involved in the operation of the activity on a regular, continuous, and substantial basis. The Regulations provide the specific tests as follows:
1)   The individual participates in the activity for more than 500 hours during the year.
2)   The individual's participation in the activity for the year constitutes substantially all the participation in the activity of all individuals (including nonowner employees) for the year.
3)   The individual participates in the activity for more than 100 hours during the year, and the individual's participation in the activity for the year is not less than the participation of any other individual (including nonowner employees) for the year.
4)   The activity is a significant participation activity for the taxable year, and the individual's aggregate participation in all significant participation activities during the year exceeds 500 hours. A significant participation activity is one in which the individual's participation exceeds 100 hours during the year.
5)   The individual materially participated in the activity for any five taxable years (whether or not consecutive) during the ten taxable years that immediately precede the taxable year.
6)   The activity is a personal service activity and the individual materially participated in the activity for any three preceding taxable years (whether or not consecutive).
7)   Based on the facts and circumstances, the individual participates in the activity on a regular, continuous, and substantial basis during the year.

Rental Activities Defined. According to the tax law, a rental activity, subject to certain exceptions, is to be treated as a passive activity. A rental activity is defined as any activity where payments are principally for the use of tangible property.

There are six exceptions to the automatic treatment of an activity as a rental activity for purposes of the passive loss definition. These exceptions allow the activity to be excluded from automatic classification as a passive activity, but the activity is subject to the material participation test in order to avoid classification as a passive activity under the general rule. The six exceptions are as follows:

The average period of customer use for such property is seven days or less.

The average period of customer use for such property is 30 days or less, and significant personal services are provided by the owner of the property.

Extraordinary personal services are provided by the owner of the property without regard to the average period of customer use.

The rental of such property is treated as incidental to a nonrental activity of the taxpayer.

The taxpayer customarily makes the property available during defined business hours for nonexclusive use by various customers.

The property is provided for use in an activity conducted by a partnership, S corporation, or joint venture in which the taxpayer owns an interest.

D.   Interaction of the At-Risk and Passive Activity Limits.

A loss that is not allowed for a year because the taxpayer is not at risk with respect to the loss is suspended under the at-risk provision and it is not suspended under the passive loss rules. Also the taxpayer's basis is reduced by depreciation, even though the deduction is not currently useable because of the passive loss rules.

E.   Special Passive Activity Rules for Real Estate Activities.

For tax years after 1993, losses from real estate rental activities are not treated as passive losses for certain real estate owners. To qualify as a nonpassive activity treatment, a real estate professional must satisfy both of the following requirements:

1)   More than half of the personal services that the taxpayer performs in trades or businesses are performed in real property trades or businesses in which the taxpayer materially participates, and

2)   The taxpayer performs more than 750 hours in these real estate property trades or businesses as a material participant.

Real Estate Rental Activities. There is a limited exception for rental real estate activity losses. Under this special provision, up to $25,000 of losses on rental real estate activities of an individual may be deducted against active and portfolio income. This annual $25,000 deduction is reduced by 50 percent of the taxpayer's AGI in excess of $100,000. Thus, the entire deduction is phased out when AGI reaches $150,000. If a married taxpayer files separately, then the $25,000 deduction is normally reduced to zero. Adjusted gross income is calculated without regard to the IRA deduction, social security benefits, and net losses from passive activities. To qualify for the $25,000 deduction, the taxpayer must actively participate in the rental activity and own ten percent or more of all interests in the activity. The $25,000 allowance is considered only after all qualifying rental real estate losses and gains are netted against other passive income. Losses in excess of the $25,000 allowance are passive losses.

F.   Dispositions of Passive Interests.

When a taxpayer disposes of his or her entire interest in a passive activity, any disallowed suspended losses are deductible. In general, if the current and suspended losses of passive activities exceed the gain realized or if the sale results in a realized loss, the sum of the following is treated as a loss which is not from a passive activity:

1)   any loss from the activity for the tax year (including suspended losses of the activity disposed of), plus

2)   any loss realized on the disposition in excess of net income or gain for the tax year from all passive activities (without regard to the activity disposed of).

A transfer of a taxpayer's interest in a passive activity due to the taxpayer's death results in the suspended losses being allowed (to the decedent) to the extent that they exceed the amount (if any) of the stepped-up basis allowed. If a passive activity becomes an activity, suspended losses are allowed to the extent of income from the new active business.

TEST FOR SELF-EVALUATION—CHAPTER 11

True or False

Indicate which of the following statements is true or false by circling the correct answer.

T F 1. In general, the passive loss rules apply to real estate rental activities.

T F 2. All debt on property qualifies as an amount at-risk.

T F 3. In general, the deduction of passive losses against active and portfolio income is not allowed.

T F 4. The $25,000 exception for rental real estate losses applies only to corporations and partnerships.

T F 5. In general, the special $25,000 allowance for rental real estate losses is reduced by 50 percent of a taxpayer's modified AGI over $100,000.

T F 6. An investment as a limited partner is generally a passive activity for purposes of the tax law.

T F 7. Credits from passive activities can be used to offset a taxpayer's regular tax liability arising from passive income or a taxpayer's alternative minimum tax liability arising from passive income.

T F 8. Passive credits are carried back three years and then forward for ten years, and if not used in that time period they are lost forever.

T F 9. The amount at-risk is decreased each year by the taxpayer's share of income and by the taxpayer's share of losses and withdrawals from the activity.

T F 10. Recapture of previously allowed losses occurs to the extent the at-risk amount is reduced below zero.

T F 11. A taxpayer's amount at-risk is determined with respect to an activity at the end of the taxable year.

T F 12. Passive loss rules apply to individuals, estates, trusts, closely-held C corporations, and personal service corporations.

T F 13. Individual taxpayers are allowed to offset passive losses against portfolio income, but not against active income.

T F 14. In general, personal service corporations are subject to the passive loss rules.

T F 15. If a taxpayer participates in an activity for more than 300 hours during the year, then he is considered to have materially participated in that activity.

T F 16. If a taxpayer's participation in an activity for the taxable year constitutes substantially all the participation in the activity of all individuals for the year, then the taxpayer materially participates in the activity.

T F 17. If a taxpayer materially participated in an activity for any five of the ten preceding tax years, then the taxpayer materially participated in the activity for the current year.

T F 18. If the average period of customer use of rental property is seven days or less, then the activity is considered a nonrental activity subject to the material participation standards.

T   F   19.   The owner of a public golf course that sells weekly and monthly passes would automatically be subject to the passive loss rules.

T   F   20.   When a passive activity is sold in a taxable transaction, the suspended loss can be used to offset any realized gain.

T   F   21.   In general, a taxpayer can treat one or more trade or business activities or rental activities as a single activity if those activities form an appropriate economic unit for measuring gain or loss.

T   F   22.   Jennifer owns a woman's clothing store in Los Angeles and a laundromat in San Diego. For passive activity purposes, each activity *must* be treated as a separate activity.

Multiple Choice

Choose the best answer for each of the following questions.

_____ 1.   Colm invests $20,000 in a limited partnership that financed the rest of its operations by the use of nonrecourse loans. If Colm's share of the loss this year is $25,000, how much may he deduct on his tax return in the current year without regard to the limitations on the deduction of losses from passive activities?

    a. $–0–
    b. $5,000
    c. $20,000
    d. $25,000

_____ 2.   Art's AGI this year is $120,000 without deducting IRA contributions or passive losses. What is the maximum amount that Art can deduct if he has real estate losses of $18,000 from a rental house (Art actively participates in the activity)?

    a. $–0–
    b. $15,000
    c. $18,000
    d. $10,000

_____ 3.   Leonie's adjusted basis in a passive activity was $20,000 at the beginning of the year. Her loss from the activity during the year was $4,000 and she had no other passive activity income for the year. Her passive activity credits for the year were $1,000. At the end of the year her adjusted basis in the passive activity would be:

    a. $20,000
    b. $19,000
    c. $16,000
    d. $15,000

_____ 4.   In x0, Dale invested $25,000 in a limited partnership. Dale's share of the partnership's x0 loss was $5,000. For x1, Dale's share of the partnership's income is $10,000. What is Dale's amount at-risk at the end of x1?

    a. $–0–
    b. $25,000
    c. $30,000
    d. $15,000

_____ 5.   The passive loss rules are applied at the owner level for which of the following entities?

      a.   S corporations
      b.   Partnerships
      c.   C corporations
      d.   Trusts

_____ 6.   For year x1, Gray Inc., a closely-held C corporation (not a personal service corporation), has $600,000 of passive losses from rental activities, $500,000 of active business income, and $200,000 of portfolio income. How much of the passive loss may offset other income?

      a. $–0–
      b. $200,000
      c. $300,000
      d. $500,000

_____ 7.   For year x1, Gray, an individual, has $600,000 of passive losses from rental activities, $500,000 of active business income, and $200,000 of portfolio income. How much of the passive loss may offset other income?

      a. $ –0–
      b. $200,000
      c. $300,000
      d. $500,000

_____ 8.   Which of the following items is not portfolio income?

      a.   Interest on a savings account
      b.   Dividends on stock of a U.S. Corporation
      c.   Interest on U.S. Savings Bonds
      d.   Sales commissions

_____ 9.   If an activity is a personal service activity, how many prior years must an individual participate in the activity to be considered a material participant in the activity after withdrawal from the activity?

      a.   One
      b.   Two
      c.   Three
      d.   Five

_____ 10.   Rachel owns an apartment building and a gift shop in the same location. She materially participates in the gift shop business and is an active participant in the apartment rental business. The apartment building shows a $15,000 loss for the current year while the gift shop has a $25,000 profit. Assuming Rachel has no other income, she should report net income (loss) from these two ventures of?

      a.   ($15,000)
      b. $25,000
      c. $10,000
      d. $40,000

_____ 11.   Jody sold an apartment building with an adjusted basis of $200,000 for $250,000. In addition, Jody has current and suspended losses associated with that specific apartment building of $60,000. How much of the $60,000 loss can Jody use to offset ordinary and portfolio income?

      a. $–0–
      b. $10,000
      c. $50,000
      d. $60,000

_____ 12.　Fran, a physician, earned $300,000 from her medical practice in the current year. She received $55,000 in dividends and interest during the year. In addition, she incurred a loss of $60,000 from an investment in a passive activity. What is Fran's income for the current year after considering the loss from the passive investment?

　　　　a.　　$300,000
　　　　b.　　$305,000
　　　　c.　　$355,000
　　　　d.　　$295,000

_____ 13.　Which of the following would be a passive rental activity?

　　　　a.　　Ted rents "go-carts" to customers.
　　　　b.　　Ted owns a motel and rents rooms by the day to guests.
　　　　c.　　Ted rents tuxedos to customers for parties, etc.
　　　　d.　　Ted works 1,000 hours as a lawyer and spends 800 hours renting apartments he owns.

_____ 14.　Clancy spends 20 hours a week, for 50 weeks a year operating a clothing store. He also owns a restaurant in another state that is managed by a full-time employee. Which of the activities (if any) are passive activities?

　　　　a.　　The clothing store
　　　　b.　　The restaurant
　　　　c.　　Both are passive activities
　　　　d.　　Neither is a passive activity

_____ 15.　Carla dies owning a passive activity with an adjusted basis of $50,000. Its fair market value at that date was $85,000. There are suspended losses relating to the property of $10,000. What is the passive loss deduction allowed on Carla's final tax return?

　　　　a.　　$–0–
　　　　b.　　$5,000
　　　　c.　　$10,000
　　　　d.　　$15,000

_____ 16.　Last year, Clay invests $50,000 in the West Tex Oil Partnership. The $50,000 was obtained by the use of nonrecourse loans. West Tex has a loss of $70,000 applicable to Clay's interest during the year. What is Clay's amount at-risk at the beginning of this year?

　　　　a.　　$–0–
　　　　b.　　$20,000
　　　　c.　　$50,000
　　　　d.　　$70,000

_____ 17.　Iris made investments in three passive activities during the year. The income and loss from operations were as follows:

Activity 1	$60,000
Activity 2	–$40,000
Activity 3	$50,000
Net passive loss	–$50,000

What is the amount of suspended loss allocated to Activity 2?

    a. $–0–
    b. $50,000
    c. $40,000
    d. $20,000

_____ 18.   Ralph owns the following businesses and participates in each of them as follows:

Activity	Hours of Participation
A	150
B	100
C	300
D	225

In which of these activities is Ralph a material participant?

    a.   None of the activities
    b.   Activities C and D
    c.   Activities A, C, and D
    d.   Activity C only

_____ 19.   Ralph owns the following businesses and participates in each of them as follows:

Activity	Hours of Participation
A	150
B	125
C	300
D	225

In which of these activities is Ralph a material participant?

    a.   None of the activities
    b.   Activities C and D
    c.   Activities A, C, and D
    d.   All of the activities

_____ 20.   Dawn performed personal service activities as follows: 800 hours as a tax planner, 500 hours in real estate development and leasing, and 500 hours in real estate rental activities. Her income from tax planning is $48,000 and she has a loss of $22,000 from the real estate development and leasing and a loss of $20,000 from the real estate rental activities. How much of the $42,000 loss may she deduct against her tax planning income?

    a. $–0–
    b. $20,000
    c. $22,000
    d. $42,000

_____ 21.   Leon acquired an interest in a bakery four years ago. The loss from the activity is $60,000 in the current year. He has AGI of $150,000 before considering the loss from the bakery. Leon does not materially participate in the operation of the bakery. What is his AGI considering this investment?

    a. $150,000
    b. $120,000
    c. $90,000
    d. $60,000

_____ 22. Trout Corporation earned $500,000 from operations. Trout also received $36,000 in interest income on various portfolio investments. During the year, Trout paid $175,000 to acquire a 40 percent interest in a passive activity that produced a total loss of $100,000. If Trout is a personal service corporation, what is its taxable income?

    a. $536,000
    b. $496,000
    c. $436,000
    d. $460,000

_____ 23. Trout Corporation earned $500,000 from operations. Trout also received $36,000 in interest income on various portfolio investments. During the year, Trout paid $175,000 to acquire a 40 percent interest in a passive activity that produced a total loss of $100,000. If Trout is a closely-held nonpersonal service corporation, what is its taxable income?

    a. $536,000
    b. $496,000
    c. $436,000
    d. $460,000

_____ 24. Bob's adjusted basis in a passive activity is $20,000 at the beginning of the current year. His losses from the activity for the year are $8,000. What is Bob's deduction for the current year?

    a. $–0–
    b. $8,000
    c. $12,000
    d. $20,000

_____ 25. Bob's adjusted basis in a passive activity is $20,000 at the beginning of the current year. His losses from the activity for the year are $8,000. What is Bob's adjusted basis and amount at-risk at the end of the current year?

    a. $–0–
    b. $8,000
    c. $12,000
    d. $16,000

_____ 26. Bob's adjusted basis in a passive activity is $20,000 at the beginning of the current year. His losses from the activity for the year are $8,000. What is Bob's suspended passive loss that is carried into the current year?

    a. $–0–
    b. $8,000
    c. $12,000
    d. $16,000

_____ 27. Able works 600 hours this year in an activity. What is his material participation status?

    a. Materially participates under Test 1
    b. Materially participates under Test 2
    c. Materially participates under Test 3
    d. Does not materially participate

_____ 28. Betty works 210 hours this year in the activity and she is the only person working in the activity. What is her material participation status?

    a. Materially participates under Test 2
    b. Materially participates under Test 3
    c. Materially participates under Test 4
    d. Does not materially participate

_____ 29.   Charles works 140 hours this year in the activity and he hires one part-time employee who works 300 hours this year. What is his material participation status?

    a.   Materially participates under Test 1
    b.   Materially participates under Test 2
    c.   Materially participates under Test 3
    d.   Does not materially participate

_____ 30.   Debbie is a CPA. She spent four years in full-time practice many years ago. This year she works in an activity in which she prepares a small number of tax returns. What is Debbie's material participation status for the current year with respect to the tax return preparation?

    a.   Materially participates under Test 6
    b.   Materially participates under Test 5
    c.   Materially participates under Test 4
    d.   Does not materially participate

_____ 31.   Eddie, who owns 50 percent of a gas station, was a material participant from x1 to x6. He retired at the end of x6. What is Eddie's material participation status in x7 if he still is involved in the gas station?

    a.   Materially participates under Test 5
    b.   Materially participates under Test 4
    c.   Materially participates under Test 6
    d.   Does not materially participate

_____ 32.   Faye participates in three activities A, B, and C. She spends 300 hours in activity A, 250 hours in activity B, and 85 hours in activity C. What is Fay's material participation status with respect to activity B?

    a.   Materially participates under Test 4
    b.   Materially participates under Test 2
    c.   Materially participates under Test 3
    d.   Does not materially participate

SOLUTIONS TO CHAPTER 11 QUESTIONS

True or False

1.	T	Subject to certain exceptions, all rental activities are to be treated as passive activities. [Rental Activities Defined, p. 11–18]
2.	F	The debt cannot be nonrecourse debt. [At Risk Limits, p. 11–3]
3.	T	In general, the passive loss limits disallow the deduction of passive losses against active and portfolio income. [The Tax Shelter Problem, p. 11–2]
4.	F	It applies to individuals. [Real Estate Rental Activities, p. 11–23]
5.	T	The $25,000 allowance is reduced by 50% of modified AGI over $100,000. [Real Estate Rental Activities, p. 11–23]
6.	T	An investment as a limited partner is generally passive. [Limited Partners, p. 11–18]
7.	F	Passive credits can only be used against regular tax attributable to passive income. [Passive Credits, p. 11–8]
8.	F	Passive activity credits carry forward for an indefinite period until the activity is disposed of. [Carryovers of Passive Credits, p. 11–9]
9.	F	The taxpayer's share of income increases the amount at-risk. [At-Risk Limits, p. 11–3]
10.	T	Previously allowed losses must be recaptured to the extent the at-risk amount is reduced below zero. [At-Risk Limits, p. 11–3]
11.	T	A taxpayer's amount at risk is determined at the end of the taxable year. [At-Risk Limits, p. 11–3]
12.	T	Passive loss rules apply to individuals, estates, trusts, closely held C Corporations, and personal service corporations. [Taxpayers Subject to he Passive Loss Rules, p. 11–9]
13.	F	Passive losses cannot offset portfolio income or active income. [The Tax Shelter Problem, p. 11–2]
14.	T	Personal service corporations are generally subject to the passive loss rules. [Personal Service Corporations, p. 11–9]
15.	F	The test is more than 500 hours per year. [Material Participation, p. 11–13]
16.	T	If a taxpayer's participation in an activity for the taxable year constitutes substantially all the participation in the activity of individuals for the year, then the taxpayer materially participates in the activity. [Material Participation, p. 11–13]
17.	T	If a taxpayer materially participated in an activity for any five of the ten preceding ax years, then the taxpayer materially participates in the activity for the current year. [Material Participation, p. 11–13]
18.	T	Exception 1 to the general rental rule. [Rental Activities Defined, p. 11–18]
19.	F	Exception 5 to general rental rule. [Rental Activities Defined, p. 11–18]
20.	T	When a passive activity is sold in a taxable transaction, the suspended loss can be used to offset any realized gain. [Dispositions of Passive Interests, p. 11–25]
21.	T	In general, a taxpayer can treat one or more trade or business activities or rental activities as a single activity if those activities form an appropriate economic unit for measuring gain or loss. [Passive Activities Defined, p. 11–10]
22.	F	The activities may be grouped into a single entity. [Identification of an Activity, p. 11–11]

Multiple Choice

1. c   Limited to his amount at risk in the activity. [At-Risk Limits p. 11–3]

2. b $25,000 – (50% of AGI ($120,000) over $100,000) = $15,000 maximum. [Real Estate Rental Activities, p. 11–23]

3. c $20,000 – $4,000 = $16,000 [Interaction of the At-Risk and Passive Activity Limits, p. 11–21]

4. c $25,000 – 5,000 + 10,000 = $30,000 [At-Risk Limits, p. 11–3]

5. c   Passive loss rules are applied at the entity level for C corporations. [Taxpayers Subject to the Passive Loss Rules, p. 11–9]

6. d   Under an exception, closely-held corporations can offset passive losses against active income. [Closely Held C Corporations, p. 11–10]

7. a   Individuals cannot offset passive losses against portfolio income or active income. [The Tax Shelter Problem, p. 11–2]

8. d   Sales commissions are not portfolio income. [Classifications, p. 11–6]

9. c   Test 6, based on prior participation, applies. [Material Participation, p. 11–13]

10. c $25,000 – 15,000 = $10,000 [Real Estate Rental Activities, p. 11–23]

11. b $50,000 – 60,000 = ($10,000) [Real Estate Rental Activities, p. 11–23]

12. c $300,000 + $55,000 = $355,000– [General Impact, p. 11–6]

13. d   Ted did not spend more than 50 percent of his time in the rental activity. [Material Participation in a Real Property Trade of Business, p. 11–21]

14. b   There is no material participation in the restaurant. [Material Participation, p. 11–13]

15. a   The suspended loss is deductible only to the extent it exceeds the step-up in basis. [Disposition of Passive Activity at Death, p. 11–25]

16. a   There would be a $20,000 unused loss. [At-Risk Limits, p. 11–3]

17. d $50,000 × ($40,000/$100,000) = $20,000 [Carryovers of Suspended Losses, p. 11–8]

18. c   Material participation is achieved through test #4. [Material Participation, p. 11–13]

19. d   Material participation is achieved through test #4. [Material Participation, p. 11–13]

20. d   The rental activity is not passive since Dawn spends more than 50 percent of her time devoted to real estate activities and her material participation in those activities exceeds 750 hours. [Material Participation in a Real Property Trade or Business, p. 11–21]

21. a   The passive loss is not allowed. [Material Participation, p. 11–13]

22. a $500,000 + $36,000 = $536,000. [Personal Service Corporations, p. 11–9]

23. b $500,000 – (40% of $100,000) + $36,000 = $496,000. [Closely Held C Corporations, p. 11–10]

24. a   The passive loss limit applies and, therefore, nothing is deductible. [General Impact, p. 11–6]

25. c $20,000 – $8,000 = $12,000 [At-Risk Limits, p. 11–3]

26. b   The $8,000 disallowed by the passive loss rules is carried into the next year. [General Impact, p. 11–6]

27. a   Able has over 500 hours of participation (Test 1). [Material Participation, p. 11–13]

28. a   Betty is the only participant (Test 2). [Material Participation, p. 11–13]

29.   d   Charles fails to pass Test 1 or Test 2. [Material Participation, p. 11–13]

30.   a   Debbie passes Test 6 (Any 3 years of material participation in a service activity). [Material Participation, p. 11–13]

31.   a   Eddie passes Test 5 (Five prior years of material participation within the prior 10 years). [Material Participation, p. 11–13]

32.   b   Faye passes Test 4 (a total of 500 hours of aggregate participation), but does not have at least 100 hours in B. [Material Participation, p. 11–13]

CHAPTER 12

Alternative Minimum Tax

CHAPTER HIGHLIGHTS

This chapter deals with those situations where there is an alternative computation of tax liability for individuals and corporations, the alternative minimum tax. The purpose of the alternative minimum tax is to ensure taxpayers with economic income pay some tax. In general, the alternative minimum tax is a special tax on "loopholes" that keeps taxpayers from using several tax preferences in combination to avoid most of their tax liability.

KEY TERMS

AMT Adjustments	AMT Credit	AMT Tax Rate
AMT Preferences	AMT Exemption	

OUTLINE

I. **INDIVIDUAL ALTERNATIVE MINIMUM TAX**

   A. AMT Formula. The alternative minimum tax (AMT) must be paid if it produces a greater tax liability than an individual taxpayer would otherwise pay. This "extra" tax prevents certain taxpayers from completely avoiding the Federal income tax using special favorable tax provisions.

   The calculation of the AMT requires the determination of alternative minimum taxable income (AMTI). In its simple form, AMTI is calculated as:
   Taxable income
   Plus: Positive AMT adjustments
   Minus: Negative AMT adjustments
   Equals: Taxable income after AMT adjustments
   Plus: Tax preferences
   Equals: Alternative minimum taxable income

   The AMT adjustments are timing differences because of separate regular tax and AMT treatments of various items (such as depreciation). Because the adjustment can be both positive and negative, they are added or subtracted from taxable income as the case may be.

   B. AMT Formula: Other Components. The complete formula for computing the alternative minimum tax is shown below.

   The Individual AMT Formula

Regular taxable income:	
±:	Adjustments
Plus:	Tax Preferences
Equals:	Alternative minimum taxable income
Minus:	Exemption
Equals:	Alternative minimum tax base
Times:	26% or 28% alternative minimum tax rate
Equals:	Tentative minimum tax before foreign tax credit
Minus:	Alternative minimum tax foreign tax credit
Equals:	Tentative minimum tax
Minus:	Regular tax liability
Equals:	Alternative minimum tax (if positive)

   The noncorporate AMT tax rate for individuals is 26 percent of AMT base up to $175,000 and 28 percent over any AMT base over $175,000. For taxable capital gains after May 6, 1997, net (long-term) capital gains included in the AMT base are taxed at the favorable alternative tax rates for capital gains (20 percent or 10 percent) instead of the AMT statutory rates.

   The for 2002 alternative minimum tax exemption is equal to $49,000 for married taxpayers filing joint returns, $35,750 for single taxpayers and head of household, and $24,500 for married taxpayers filing separate returns. The 25 percent phase-out of the exemption begins when alternative minimum taxable income exceeds the following:

$112,500 for single taxpayers
$150,000 for married taxpayers filing jointly
$75,000 for married taxpayers filing separately

C.   AMT Adjustments. The AMT *adjustments* include:
1)   Circulation expenditures
2)   Certain depreciation on post-1986, pre-1999 real property
3)   Certain depreciation on post-1986 personal property
4)   Certain excess amortization on post-1986, pre-1999 pollution control facilities
5)   Expenditures requiring 10-year write-off for AMT
6)   Use of the completed contract method of accounting
7)   Incentive stock options
8)   Adjusted gains or losses on asset dispositions
9)   Alternative tax NOL deduction
10) Certain itemized deductions
   Casualty losses
   Gambling losses
   Charitable contributions
   Medical expenses over 10 percent of AGI
   Estate tax on income in respect of a decedent
   Qualified interest
11) The standard deduction (if a taxpayer did not itemize)
12) The personal and dependency exemptions

D.   AMT Preferences. The AMT tax *preferences* are always an addition to taxable income. Tax preferences include the following:
1)   Percentage depletion
2)   Intangible drilling costs
3)   Interest on certain private activity bonds
4)   Certain excess depreciation on pre-1987 property
5)   Certain post-1986, pre-1999 amortization on pollution control facilities
6)   Forty-two percent exclusion for certain small business stock

E.   AMT Credit. To provide equity for taxpayers when timing differences reverse in future periods, the regular tax liability may be reduced by a tax credit for prior years' minimum tax liability attributable to timing differences. The credit is not available in connection with AMT exclusions, which represent permanent differences rather than timing differences. Examples of AMT exclusions are the standard deduction, exemptions, excess percentage depletion, etc. The credit may be carried over indefinitely.

II.   **THE CORPORATE ALTERNATIVE MINIMUM TAX**
A.   Small Corporations. For tax years after 1997, the AMT does not apply to "qualified small corporations." A corporation with average annual gross receipts of less than $5 million for the prior three-year period is a qualified small corporation. A corporation can continue to qualify for this exemption if its average gross receipts for the preceding three-year period do not exceed $7.5 million.
B.   The corporate alternative minimum tax is similar to the individual AMT. The tax preferences that apply to the calculation of the alternative minimum tax for individual taxpayers also apply to corporations. However, corporations have certain adjustments, which differ from those that apply to individuals. The AMT rate for corporations is 20% instead of the individual rate of 26% or 28%.

The corporate AMT tax formula is:

Taxable income:	
Plus:	Income tax NOLs
±:	AMT adjustments
Plus:	Tax preferences
Equals:	AMTI before ATNOL
Minus:	ATNOL (limited to 90%)
Equals:	Alternative minimum taxable income (AMTI)
Minus:	Exemption
Equals:	Alternative minimum tax base
Times:	20% alternative minimum tax rate
Equals:	AMT before AMT foreign tax credit
Minus:	AMT foreign tax credit (may be limited to 90%)
Equals:	Tentative AMT
Minus:	Regular tax before credits less the regular foreign tax credit
Equals:	Alternative minimum tax

C.   AMT Adjustments. Corporate AMT adjustments include the following:
1) Certain depreciation on post-1986, pre-1999 real and personal property
2) Certain excess mining exploration costs
3) Certain long-term contract timing differences
4) Differences in gains and losses for asset dispositions
5) Post-1986, pre-1999 amortization on pollution control facilities
6) Alternative tax net operating loss
7) Adjusted current earnings (ACE) adjustment

The adjusted current earnings (ACE) adjustment is equal to 75 percent of the difference between adjusted current earnings and unadjusted AMTI.

D.   Tax Preferences. The tax preferences that apply to individuals also apply to corporations.

E.   Exemptions. The exemption amount for corporations is $40,000, reduced by 25 percent of the amount by which AMTI exceeds $150,000.

TEST FOR SELF-EVALUATION—CHAPTER 12

True or False

Indicate which of the following statements is true or false by circling the correct answer.

T	F	1.	The alternative minimum tax is beneficial to most high-income individual taxpayers.
T	F	2.	For 2002, the maximum rate for the individual alternative minimum tax is 28 percent.
T	F	3.	The AMT exemption for single taxpayers is $35,750 before any phase out.
T	F	4.	The AMT exemption is reduced 25 cents on the dollar for AMTI above specified amounts.
T	F	5.	Casualty losses are allowed in calculating alternative minimum taxable income for individuals.
T	F	6.	Tentative AMT less the regular tax liability is the AMT due.
T	F	7.	The standard deduction is allowed in computing alternative minimum taxable income (AMTI) for individual taxpayers.
T	F	8.	The alternative tax net operating loss cannot offset more than 90 percent of alternative minimum taxable income.
T	F	9.	The difference between modified ACRS depreciation and the ADS (alternative depreciation system) is an adjustment for AMT purposes, arising because of a timing difference.
T	F	10.	Intangible drilling costs in excess of 50 percent of net income from oil, gas, and geothermal properties is an AMT tax preference.
T	F	11.	For AMT purposes, the cost of certified pollution control facilities placed in service after 1986 and before 1999 must be depreciated using the ADS over the appropriate class life.
T	F	12.	Qualified housing interest is deductible in calculating the alternative minimum tax.
T	F	13.	The corporate AMT tax rate is 25 percent.
T	F	14.	The ACE adjustment may be either positive or negative.
T	F	15.	Losses from passive activities are not deductible in computing either the regular income tax or the AMT.
T	F	16.	For long-term contracts, the AMT computation requires that taxpayers use the percentage-of-completion method.
T	F	17.	For the individual AMT calculation, medical expenses are deductible to the extent they exceed 7.5 percent of AGI.
T	F	18.	In arriving at alternative minimum taxable income, alternative minimum tax adjustments may either increase or decrease taxable income.
T	F	19.	An individual's regular tax liability may be reduced by a credit for prior years' minimum tax liability attributable to timing differences.
T	F	20.	The corporate AMT exemption is $40,000 reduced by 25 percent of the excess of AMTI over $100,000.
T	F	21.	A passive loss computed for regular income tax purposes may differ from the passive loss computed for AMT purposes.

T   F   22.   High income taxpayers must reduce AMTI by the amount of any itemized deductions disallowed because of the 3 percent floor.

T   F   23.   The IRS requires that certain items (e.g., percentage depletion) that are limited for income tax purposes be refigured using a different limitation for AMT purposes.

T   F   24.   For property placed in service after 1998, the AMT adjustment for *real property* cost recovery is eliminated because the AMT recovery period is the same as for MACRS.

T   F   25.   For *personal property* placed in service in 2002, if a taxpayer elects to use the 150 percent declining-balance method for regular income tax depreciation, there are no AMT adjustments.

Multiple Choice

Choose the best answer for each of the following questions.

_____   1.   Carolyn's taxable income is $300,000. She has tax preferences of $75,000 and positive adjustments of $40,000. If she is a single taxpayer, what is Carolyn's alternative minimum taxable income?

    a. $300,000
    b. $375,000
    c. $415,000
    d. $340,000

_____   2.   Carolyn's taxable income is $300,000. She has tax preferences of $75,000 and positive adjustments of $40,000. If she is a single taxpayer, what is Carolyn's tentative minimum tax?

    a. $99,600
    b. $112,700
    c. $116,200
    d. $107,900

_____   3.   Which of the following is not allowed as a deduction in computing the alternative minimum tax?

    a.   Gambling losses (to the extent of winnings)
    b.   State income taxes
    c.   Charitable contributions
    d.   Casualty losses

_____   4.   Carol is single and has AMTI of $140,000. What is Carol's exemption amount for the AMT?

    a. $49,000
    b. $24,500
    c. $28,875
    d. $35,750

_____   5.   Carol has AMTI of $140,000. She is married and files a joint tax return. What is her AMT exemption?

    a. $26,875
    b. $22,500
    c. $33,750
    d. $45,000

_____ 6. On nonresidential real property placed in service after 1986 and before January1, 1999, the AMT depreciation (ADS) is based on a life of how many years?

    a.   27.5 years
    b.   31.5 years
    c.   35 years
    d.   40 years

_____ 7. Tom incurs mine exploration costs of $200,000 that are deducted for regular income tax purposes. What is Tom's adjustment in computing AMTI?

    a. $–0–
    b. $200,000 positive
    c. $180,000 positive
    d. $160,000 negative

_____ 8. Tom incurs mine exploration costs of $200,000 that are deducted for regular income tax purposes. What is Tom's adjustment next year, assuming no additional mine exploration costs were incurred?

    a. $–0–
    b. $20,000 negative
    c. $40,000 negative
    d. $200,000 positive

_____ 9. Amber Corporation (not an AMT small corporation) has adjusted current earnings of $400,000 and the corporation has unadjusted alternative minimum taxable income of $100,000. What is Amber Corporation's ACE (adjusted current earning) adjustment for the AMT?

    a. $–0–
    b. $300,000 positive
    c. $225,000 positive
    d. $150,000 positive

_____ 10. In Year 1, Ted incurred a net operating loss of $200,000. Ted had no AMT adjustments, but deducted tax preferences of $30,000. What is Ted's ATNOL carryover into Year 2?

    a. $30,000
    b. $170,000
    c. $200,000
    d. $230,000

_____ 11. Don, whose AGI is $70,000, incurred medical expenses of $10,000 during the year. What is Don's adjustment, if any, for the individual AMT?

    a. $–0–
    b. $1,750 negative
    c. $1,750 positive
    d. $7,000 negative

_____ 12. In the current year, Fern has modified ACRS depreciation of $30,420 on a nonresidential building placed in service last year (prior to January 1, 1999). Her AMT depreciation under ADS is $23,960. Fern's adjustment for computing AMTI is?

    a. $6,460 positive
    b. $6,460 negative
    c. $23,960 positive
    d. $30,420 negative

_____ 13.   Bob owns a rental duplex. His basis for regular tax purposes is $93,000 while the basis for AMT purposes is $95,000. Bob sells the duplex for $105,000 for an income tax gain of $12,000 and an AMT gain of $10,000. What is Bob's AMT adjustment from the sale?

        a. $–0–
        b. $2,000 positive
        c. $2,000 negative
        d. $10,000 positive
        e. $10,000 negative

_____ 14.   The alternative minimum tax ACE adjustment applies to which of the following?

        a.   Individuals
        b.   Corporations
        c.   Partnerships
        d.   The ACE adjustment applies to all of the above

_____ 15.   For regular income tax purposes, Andy had net investment income of $30,000 before deducting investment interest. He incurred investment interest of $45,000 during the year. In addition, Andy had interest income on private activity bonds of $12,000. What is Andy's investment interest deduction for AMT purposes?

        a. $–0–
        b. $12,000
        c. $30,000
        d. $42,000

_____ 16.   The AMT credit is available for which of the following differences between regular taxable income and AMTI?

        a.   Circulation expenditures
        b.   Standard deduction
        c.   Personal exemptions
        d.   Excess percentage depletion

_____ 17.   D owns mineral property that qualifies for a 15 percent depletion rate. At the beginning of Year 1 the basis of the property is $5,000. Gross income from the property during the year was $120,000. What is D's tax preference generated by the property?

        a. $–0–
        b. $5,000
        c. $13,000
        d. $18,000

_____ 18.   Beige Corporation (not a small corporation), a calendar year taxpayer, has alternative minimum taxable income (before the ACE adjustment) of $500,000 for Year 1. If Beige's adjusted current earnings (ACE) are $1,200,000. What is the amount of Beige Corporation's ACE adjustment?

        a. $–0–
        b. $525,000 positive
        c. $375,000 positive
        d. $900,000 negative

_____ 19. Beige Corporation (not a "small corporation"), a calendar year taxpayer, has alternative minimum taxable income (before the ACE adjustment) of $500,000 for Year 1. If Beige's adjusted current earnings (ACE) are $1,200,000, what is Beige Corporation's tentative minimum tax for Year 1?

    a. $–0–
    b. $205,000
    c. $215,250
    d. $240,000

_____ 20. Black Corporation (a calendar year taxpayer) had the following transactions:

Taxable income	$500,000
Interest on private activity bonds (issued in 1989)	$ 60,000
Excess percentage depletion	$150,000

Assuming Black Inc. is not a small corporation, what is Black's AMTI for?

    a. $710,000
    b. $560,000
    c. $500,000
    d. $650,000

_____ 21. Sarajane has total nonrefundable credits of $20,000, regular tax liability of $66,000, and tentative AMT of $50,000. How much of the nonrefundable credits can Sarajane claim in the current year?

    a. $–0–
    b. $16,000
    c. $20,000
    d. $4,000

_____ 22. Norm has the following items:

Adjusted Gross Income	$45,000
Medical expenses	$10,000
Other Itemized Deductions	$ 8,000
Taxable income	$27,000

Assuming that Norm is subject to the AMT this year, the adjustment required from the above is:

    a. $–0–
    b. $1,125
    c. $2,125
    d. $4,125

_____ 23. Paul had $22,000 in interest income from corporate bonds, $14,000 interest income from private activity bonds, and $7,000 from preferred stock. What is the amount of investment income Paul must report for AMT purposes?

    a. $–0–
    b. $7,000
    c. $21,000
    d. $43,000

_____ 24. Paul had $22,000 in interest income from corporate bonds, $14,000 interest income from private activity bonds, and $7,000 from preferred stock. He incurred investment interest expense of $12,000 related to the corporate bonds and $9,000 related to the private activity bonds. Paul also incurred

$6,000 interest on a home equity loan and used the proceeds to purchase the preferred stock. What amount of investment interest can Paul use in calculating his regular tax and his AMT tax?

   a. $12,000; $12,000
   b. $12,000; $27,000
   c. $18,000; $21,000
   d. $27,000; $27,000

_____ 25.   Paul had $22,000 in interest income from corporate bonds, $14,000 interest income from private activity bonds, and $7,000 from preferred stock. He incurred investment interest expense of $12,000 related to the corporate bonds and $9,000 related to the private activity bonds. Paul also incurred $6,000 interest on a home equity loan and used the proceeds to purchase the preferred stock. What is Paul's AMT adjustment for investment interest?

   a. $–0–
   b. $6,000
   c. $9,000
   d. $15,000

_____ 26.   Billy Bob had intangible drilling costs (IDC) of $90,000 for the current year. His net oil and gas income for the same period was $70,000. What is Billy Bob's tax preference for IDC?

   a. $–0–
   b. $9,000
   c. $35,500
   d. $45,500

_____ 27.   Roger, a single taxpayer, has taxable income of $110,000. He had positive AMT adjustments of $55,000, negative AMT adjustments of $10,000, and tax preferences of $59,500. What is Roger's AMTI?

   a. $–0–
   b. $155,000
   c. $165,000
   d. $214,500

_____ 28.   Bill has an AMT base of $400,000 including a net (long-term) capital gain of $30,000. The AMT tax rate applied to the net (long-term) capital gain is?

   a.   15%
   b.   20%
   c.   22%
   d.   26%

_____ 29.   Black Corporation has average annual sales for $3,500,000 for the three-year period prior to the current tax year. It has an AMT base of $120,000. What is Black's tentative AMT?

   a. $–0–
   b. $24,000
   c. $31,200
   d. $33,600

Problem

1. Tim and Mary Kelley are married taxpayers who file a joint tax return. For the 2002 tax year, the Kelley's have AGI of $70,000 (including $30,000 of investment income). They have excess percentage depletion of $60,000 and interest income on private activity bonds of $20,000. The amount of their investment interest expense for the year is $25,000, and they made charitable contributions of $5,000. If the Kelley's regular taxable income for 2002 is $12,000, determine the following amounts.

    a. What is the amount of their regular income tax? _____
    b. What is the amount of their tentative minimum tax? _____
    c. What is Kelley's total tax liability? _____

SOLUTIONS TO CHAPTER 12 QUESTIONS

True or False

1. F   The AMT ensures that high-income taxpayers pay some amount of tax. [Alternative Minimum Tax, p. 12–3]

2. T   A 26 percent rate applies to the first level of the AMT base and 28 percent thereafter. [AMT Rate Schedule, p. 12–8]

3. T   Single and heads of household both are entitled to a $33,750 exemption. [Exemption Amount, p. 12–8]

4. T   The 25-cents-on-the-dollar reduction is referred to as a *phase out*. [Exemption Amount, p. 12–8]

5. T   In addition to casualty losses, charitable contributions and some other deductions are also allowed. [Itemized Deductions, p. 12–17]

6. T   If the difference is negative, no tax is due. [AMT Formula, p. 12–7]

7. F   The standard deduction is not allowed. [Other Adjustments, p. 12–21]

8. T   The 90 percent ceiling exists for both carrybacks and carryforwards. [Alternative Tax Net Operating Loss Deductions, p. 12–16]

9. T   All personal property placed in service after 1986 may be taken into consideration in computing one net adjustment.[Depreciation of Post-1986 Personal Property, p. 12–11]

10. F   Intangible drilling costs in excess of 65 percent of net income from such properties is an AMT tax preference. [Intangible Drilling Costs, p. 12–22]

11. T   60-month amortization is allowed for regular income tax purposes [Adjustments Applicable to Individuals and Corporations, p. 12–29]

12. T   The deductions can be taken on up to two residences [Housing Interest, p. 12–19]

13. F   The rate is 20 percent. [Corporate Alternative Minimum Tax, p. 12–25]

14. T   AMTI is either increased or decreased by 75 percent of the difference between ACE and unadjusted AMTI. [Adjustments Applicable Only to Corporations, p. 12–29]

15. T   Although not deductible, the passive loss for AMT may differ from the passive loss for regular income tax purposes. [Passive Activity Losses, p. 12–15]

16. T   If a taxpayer is able to use the completed contract method for regular income tax, the adjustment is the difference between the two. [Use of Completed Contract Method of Accounting, p. 12–12]

17. F   The percent of AGI is 10 percent. [Medical Expenses, p. 12–18]

18. T   *Adjustments* may be either positive or negative; *preferences* are always positive [AMT Formula for Alternative Minimum Taxable Income, p. 12–3]

19. T   Also, the alternative minimum tax credit may be carried over indefinitely. [AMT Credit, p. 12–24]

20. F   The adjustment to the exemption is for AMTI over $150,000. [Corporate Alternative Minimum Tax, p. 12–25]

21. T   The rules for computing taxable income differ from the rules for computing AMTI. [Passive Activity Losses, p. 12–15]

22. T   Taxable income, the starting point for computing AMTI, is reduced by the amount of the disallowed deductions. [Itemized Deductions,p. 12–17]

23.   T   The percentage depletion preference is equal to the excess of the regular income tax deduction for percentage depletion over the adjusted basis of the property at the end of the taxable year. [Percentage Depletion, p. 12–21]

24.   T   This change was in the TRA of 1997.[Depreciation of Post-1986 Real Property, p.12–10]

25.   T   TRA of 1997 either reduced or eliminated the AMT adjustment for the depreciation of personal property. [Depreciation of Post-1986 Personal Property, p. 12–10]

Multiple Choice

1.   c $300,000 + $75,000 + $40,000 = $415,000 [AMT Formula: Other Components, p. 12–7]

2.   b   (26% × $175,000) + (28% × [$415,000 − $175,000]) = $112,700 [AMT Formula: Other Components, p. 12–7]

3.   b   State income taxes are not a deduction in computing AMT. [Itemized Deductions, p. 12–17]

4.   c $35,750 − 25% of ($140,000 − $112,500) = $28,875 [Exemption Amount, p. 12–8]

5.   d   The exemption for married taxpayers is $49,000. [Exemption Amount, p. 12–8]

6.   d   A 40 year AMT depreciation life applies between 1987 and 1998. [Depreciation on Post-1986 Real Property, p. 12–11]

7.   c $200,000 − ($200,000/10 years) = $180,000 [Expenditures Requiring 10-Year Write-off for AMT Purposes, p. 12–12]

8.   b $0 − ($200,000/10 years) = ($20,000) [Expenditures Requiring 10-Year Write-off for AMT Purposes, p. 12–12]

9.   c   ($400,000 − $100,000) × 75% = $225,000 [Adjustments Applicable Only to Corporations, p. 12–30]

10.   b $200,000 − $30,000 = $170,000 [Alternative Tax Net Operating Loss Deduction, p. 12–16]

11.   c   [$10,000 − 7.5%($70,000)] − [$10,000 − 10%($70,000)] = $1,750. [Medical Expenses, p. 12–18]

12.   a $30,420 − $23,960 = $6,460 positive [Depreciation of Post-1986 Real Property, p. 12–10]

13.   c $12,000 income tax gain − $10,000 AMT gain = $2,000 AMT negative adjustment. [Adjusted Gain or Loss, p. 12–14]

14.   b   The ACE adjustment only applies to corporations. [Adjustments Applicable Only to Corporations, p. 12–29]

15.   d $30,000 + $12,000 = $42,000 [Investment Interest, p. 12–20]

16.   a   The AMT credit is available for circulation expenditures. [AMT Credit, p. 12–24]

17.   c   (15% × $120,000) − $5,000 = $13,000 [Percentage Depletion, p. 12–21]

18.   b   75% × ($1,200,000 − $500,000) = $525,000 [Adjustments Applicable Only to Corporations, p. 12–25]

19.   b   ($500,000 + $525,000) × 20% = $205,000 [Corporate Alternative Minimum Tax, p. 12–25]

20.   a   AMTI: $500,000 + $60,000 + $150,000 = $710,000 [AMT Preferences, p. 12–21]

21.   b $66,000 − $50,000 = $16,000 [Regular Tax Liability, p. 12–8]

22.   b   [$10,000 − ($45,000 × 7.5%)] − [$10,000 − ($45,000 × 10%)] = $1,125 [Medical Expenses, p. 12–18]

23.   d $22,000 + $14,000 + $7,000 = $43,000 [Investment Interest, p. 12–20]

24. b

	Regular	AMT
Corporate	$12,000	$12,000
Private Activity	$ –0–	$ 9,000
Preferred St.	$ –0–	$ 6,000
Total	$12,000	$27,000

[Investment Interest, p. 12–20]

25. d $27,000 – $12,000 = $15,000 [Investment Interest, p. 12–20]

26. c $90,000 – ($90,000/10 years) – 65% of ($70,000) = $35,500 [Intangible Drilling Costs, p. 12–22]

27. e $110,000 + $55,000 – $10,000 + $59,500 = $214,500 [AMT Formula: Other Components, p. 12–7]

28. b   The rate on capital gain is 20 percent, the same as for regular tax purposes. [AMT Rate Schedule, p. 12–8]

29. a   Black qualifies for the small corporation exemption from the AMT. [Repeal of AMT for Small Corporations, p. 12–28]

Problem

1. a. $1,200 = 10% × $12,000
    b. $18,460 = 26% × ($70,000 + $60,000 + $20,000 – $25,000 – $5,000 – $49,000 (exemption))
    c. $18,460 = $1,200 regular tax + ($18,460 – $1,200 alternative minimum tax)

[Illustration of the AMT Computation, p. 12–23]

CHAPTER 13

Tax Credits and Payments Procedures

CHAPTER HIGHLIGHTS

This chapter discusses the tax credits available to taxpayers. The credits are primarily designed to get taxpayers to undertake certain activities that are deemed economically or socially desirable. Payment procedures used by taxpayers to pay income and employment taxes to the federal government are discussed.

KEY TERMS

Refundable Credits
Nonrefundable Credits

Earned Income Credit
Child Care Credit

Rehabilitation Credit
Research Credit

OUTLINE

I. **OVERVIEW AND PRIORITY OF CREDITS**

    A. Refundable versus Nonrefundable Credits. Certain credits are refundable while others are nonrefundable. Refundable credits are refunded to the taxpayer even if the amount of the credit exceeds the taxpayer's tax liability.

        The major refundable and nonrefundable credits are as follows:

            Refundable Credits:
            Taxes withheld on wages
            Earned Income Credit

            Nonrefundable Credits:
            Child and Dependent Care Credit
            Credit for the Elderly and Disabled
            Foreign Tax Credit
            Adoption Expenses Credit
            General Business Credits: Tax Rehabilitation Credit, Business Energy Credit, Work Opportunity Credit, Research Activities Credit, Low-income Housing Credit, and Welfare-to-Work Credit

    B. General Business Credit. Special rules apply to the general business credit. For any tax year, the general business credit is limited to the taxpayer's net income tax reduced by the greater of:

        The *tentative minimum tax,* or

        25 percent of the *net regular tax liability* over $25,000.

    C. Treatment of Unused General Business Credits. For tax years beginning before 1998, any unused credit must be carried back three years and forward 15 years. For tax years after 1997, there is a one year carryback and 20 year carryforward period. The unused credit carryovers are treated in a FIFO manner.

II. **SPECIFIC BUSINESS-RELATED TAX CREDIT PROVISIONS**

    A. Tax Credit for Rehabilitation Expenditures. Taxpayers are allowed a credit for rehabilitating industrial and commercial buildings and certified historic structures. Currently, the credit is 10 percent for nonresidential buildings, other than certified historic structures, originally placed in service before 1936 and 20 percent for residential and nonresidential certified historic structures. To qualify for the credit, the expenditure must exceed the greater of the adjusted basis of the property before the rehabilitation or $5,000.

        The rehabilitation credit must be recaptured if the property is disposed of prematurely or if it ceases to be qualifying property.

    B. Business Energy Credits. Most business energy credits have expired. However, two of the credits remain to encourage the conservation of natural resources and to develop alternate (to oil & gas) energy sources. These are the credits for solar energy property (10 percent) and geothermal property (10 percent).

    C. Work Opportunity Tax Credit. Taxpayers may take a credit for wages paid to certain targeted employees.

    D. Welfare-to-Work Credit. A welfare-to work credit is available to employers hiring individuals who have been long-term recipients of welfare.

    E. Research Activities Credits.

        Incremental Research Credit. To encourage research and experimentation, taxpayers are allowed a 20 percent credit for qualifying incremental expenditures. The credit only applies to qualified expenditures that exceed a base amount, determined by multiplying the average annual gross receipts of the taxpayer for the four preceding tax years by the taxpayer's "fixed base" percentage. The base amount may not be less than 50 percent of the qualified research expenses in the credit year. This credit is available through June 30, 2004.

The following expenditures do not qualify for the research credit:
1) Research conducted after the beginning of commercial production.
2) Surveys such as marketing research, testing, and routine data collection.
3) Research conducted outside the United States.
4) Research in the social sciences, arts, or humanities.

Qualified research expenditures can be expensed for tax purposes one of two ways:
1) The taxpayer can use the full credit and reduce the expense deduction by the amount of the credit, or
2) The taxpayer can use the full expense deduction and reduce the credit by 50 percent of the credit times the maximum corporate tax rate.

Basic Research Credit. Corporations (other than S Corporations) are allowed an additional 20 percent credit for basic research expenditure amounts paid to a qualified research organization, in excess of a base amount.

F. Low-Income Housing Credit. Owners of qualified low-income housing projects are allowed a credit based on the qualified basis of the property.

G. Disabled Access Credit. This credit is available for eligible access expenditures paid or incurred by an eligible small business after November 5, 1990. The credit is 50 percent of the eligible expenditures that exceed $250 but do not exceed $10,250. An eligible small business must satisfy one of the following:
1) Have gross receipts for the previous year of $1,000,000 or less, or
2) Have no more than 30 full-time employees during the previous year.

The depreciable basis of the access property is reduced by the amount of the credit.

H. Credit for Small Employer Pension Startup Costs. Small employers are entitled to a nonrefundable credit for setting up a retirement plan for its employees. The credit is 50 percent of the qualified cost to a maximum credit of $500 (i.e., maximum cost of $1,000).

I. Credit for Employer-Provided Child Care. Employers are allowed a credit for qualifying expenses incurred to provide employee child care during normal working hours. The credit is 25 percent of qualified child care expenses and 10 percent of qualified child care resource and referral services. The maximum for both the 25 percent and 10 percent credit is $150,000 per year. In addition, and deduction for qualifying expenses must be reduce by any credit taken during the year.

III. **OTHER TAX CREDITS**

A. Earned Income Credit. The earned income credit is designed to help certain low-income taxpayers. The earned income credit is determined by multiplying a maximum amount of earned income (based on the number of children the taxpayer has by the appropriate earned income credit percentage, see Table 13–2 in text). The credit is subject to phase out as the taxpayer's adjusted gross income or earned income reaches a certain level (see Table 13–2 in text) and once the taxpayer's earned income or adjusted gross income exceeds a certain amount, no credit is available. It is not necessary for taxpayers to compute the earned income credit because the IRS publishes Earned Income Credit Tables as part of the instruction package for Form 1040 and 1040A.

The earned income credit is a form of negative income tax because a taxpayer can receive a credit (refund) even if no tax is due.

B. Tax Credit for Elderly or Disabled Taxpayers. To qualify for the credit for the elderly, the taxpayer must be 65-years-old, or if under 65 must be retired with a permanent and total disability and have income from a public or private employer because of the disability. For taxpayers age 65 or older, the maximum credit is equal to 15 percent of $5,000 (single taxpayers or one spouse over 65), $7,500 (married with both spouses over 65), or $3,750 (married filing separately). The base amount is reduced by excluded social security and railroad retirement benefit payments, and one-half of adjusted gross income over certain amounts ($7,500 for single taxpayers, head of household and surviving spouses; $10,000 for married filing jointly; and $5,000 for married filing separately).

C.   Foreign Tax Credit. Individual and corporate taxpayers may claim a tax credit for foreign income tax paid on income earned and subject to tax in another country or U.S. possession. Unused foreign tax credits may be carried back two years and forward five years.

An overall limitation on the foreign tax credit is based on the following formula.

$$\frac{\text{Foreign taxable income}}{\text{Total taxable income}} \times \text{U.S. tax liability before the FTC}$$

D.   Child Tax Credit. Individual taxpayers are allowed a tax credit based on their number of children under age 17 and the credit is $500. The credit is phased out for taxpayers with AGI over certain amounts (see text for thresholds). The total credit is reduced by $50 for each $1,000 (or part thereof) of AGI over the threshold amount.

E.   Credit for Child and Dependent Care Expenses.

Taxpayers are allowed a credit for employment-related child and dependent care expenses. The credit is 30 percent of unreimbursed expenses reduced by 1 percent for every $2,000 (or fraction thereof) of AGI over $10,000, but not below 20 percent. The maximum qualifying expenses in any single year are $2,400 for one qualifying individual and $4,800 for two or more individuals. The eligible expenses are further limited to the taxpayer's earned income. For married taxpayers, the limitation applies to the spouse with the least amount of earned income. A taxpayer qualifies for the credit if he or she maintains a household for either of the following:

1)   A dependent under age 13
2)   A dependent or spouse who is physically or mentally incapacitated

Special rules allow taxpayers with spouses who are students to qualify for the credit. A spouse who is a full-time student is deemed to have earned income of $200 per month for one qualifying individual or $400 per month if there are two or more qualifying individuals in the household.

Taxpayers are not allowed to use amounts reimbursed to the taxpayer by an employer for dependent care and excluded from gross income. See Chapter 5 for this exclusion.

The taxpayer must provide the name, address, and taxpayer identification number of the provider of the child or dependent care.

F.   Education Tax Credits. There are two new credits available to help with educational expenses, the *HOPE Scholarship Credit* and the *Lifetime Learning Credit*. These nonrefundable credits are available for qualifying tuition and related expenses incurred by students pursuing undergraduate or graduate degrees or vocational training. Room, board, and book costs do not qualify.

The HOPE Credit is a maximum credit of $1,500 per year (100 percent of the first $1,000 of tuition expenses plus 50 percent of the next $1,000 of tuition) for the first two years of post-secondary education.

The Lifetime Learning Credit is a maximum of 20 percent of tuition expenses (up to $5,000 per year). The Lifetime Learning Credit is intended for individuals who are beyond the first two years of post-secondary education. Beginning in 2003, the Lifetime Credit will be available on the first $10,000 of qualifying costs each year.

The education credits are available for qualified tuition and related expenses incurred by a taxpayer, a taxpayer's spouse, or a taxpayer's dependent.

Both education credits are phased out when a taxpayer's AGI exceeds certain amount. See textbook.

G.   Credit for Certain Retirement Plan Contributions. Certain low income taxpayers may claim a credit for contributions to qualified retirement plans such as IRAs and Section 401(k) plans. The credit is 50 percent, 20 percent, or 10 percent of the qualified contributions with a maximum annual contribution of $2,000 per individual taxpayer. See text for rates and phase-out thresholds.

IV. **PAYMENT PROCEDURES**
   A. Procedures Applicable to Employers.

   Employers are required to withhold Federal income tax and the employees' share of FICA tax from employees' paychecks. The IRS publishes a list of which employees and wages require Federal income and employment tax withholding. The payment procedure involves the following three steps.
   1) Ascertain which employees and wages are covered by employment taxes and withholdings.
   2) Arrive at the amount to be paid/withheld.

   Report and pay the proper amount to the IRS on a timely basis.
   B. FICA Taxes. The FICA tax is comprised of two components: the Social Security tax and the Medicare tax. The Social security tax is 6.2 percent of wages to a maximum wage amount of $84,900 for 2002. The Medicare tax is 1.45 percent of wages with no limit. These amounts are paid by both the employee and by the employer (in other words the IRS collects each amount twice).
   C. Amounts of Income Tax Withholding. The procedure for withholding involves the following steps.
   1) Have the employee complete Form W–4.
   2) Determine the employee's payroll period.
   3) Compute the tax to be withheld using the wage-bracket table or the percentage method.

   In using the wage-bracket method, an employer simply looks up the tax to be withheld in a table provided by the IRS. The tables are available for various pay periods (weekly, biweekly, monthly, etc.) and for single and married taxpayers.

   The percentage method of calculating withholding requires the following procedures:

Step 1	Multiply the amount of one allowance (see text for appropriate amounts) by the employee's total allowances.
Step 2	Reduce the employee's wages by the amount in step one.
Step 3	Use the results in step two to compute the withholding using the proper percentage-method table (see text).

   Reporting and payment procedures require that the employer file the following forms with the IRS:
   1) Form SS–4 provides the employer with an identification number that must be used on all forms filed with the IRS and the Social Security Administration.
   2) Form W–2 is a summary of each employee's wages and the amount of federal income tax and FICA tax withheld. The Form W–2 must be furnished to the employee by January 31 of the following year.
   3) Form W–3 is a summary of withholdings for all employees and is filed with the Social Security Administration along with a copy of each Form W–2.
   4) Form 940 or 940EZ is used for the employer's annual accounting for FUTA.
   5) Form 941 must be filed quarterly summarizing employment taxes for the quarter. Any undeposited amounts must be deposited or accompany this form.

   Withholding on Pensions. Income tax withholding for pension payments is mandatory under the tax law unless the taxpayer elects to have no tax withheld.

   Backup Withholding. Certain taxpayers may be subject to "backup withholding" on interest and dividend payments. The backup withholding is designed to make sure that taxpayers report all their investment income. For example backup withholding applies if a taxpayer does not give his or her identification number to a bank so that any income can be reported on Form 1099.
   D. Procedures Applicable to Self-Employed Persons.

   Taxpayers who have income other than wages or who are self-employed may be required to make estimated tax payments (Form 1040ES). One-fourth of the required annual payment is due on April

15, June 15, and September 15 of the current year and January 15 of the following year. The required annual payment is the lesser of the following amounts:

1)   90 percent of the current year's tax.
2)   100 percent of last year's tax (the return must cover the full 12 months of the preceding tax year). For 2002, the 100 percent is increased to 112 percent if AGI on the proceeding tax year's return exceeds $150,000 ($75,000 if married filing separately).

No payment is required if the estimated tax is under $1,000. An underpayment occurs when any installment is less than 25 percent of the required annual payment.

The Self-Employment (SE) Tax. Self-employed taxpayers are required to pay a self-employment tax, which is to provide for Social Security benefits. Individuals with net earnings from self-employment of $400 or more are subject to this tax. The SE tax consists of two separate parts, the Social Security tax and the Medicare tax. Each part has a rate and a ceiling amount. For 2002 these amounts are:

	Rate	Ceiling
Social Security tax	12.4%	$84,900
Medicare tax	2.9%	No limit
Total	15.3%	

Taxpayers are allowed an income tax deduction for one-half of the self-employment tax paid and a deduction at one-half the self-employment tax rate for purposes of determining the self-employment tax. See text for formula.

The Social Security ceiling amounts are reduced by any wages the taxpayer has that are subject to the regular Social Security tax (FICA). Schedule SE is used to calculate the self-employment tax.

TEST FOR SELF-EVALUATION—CHAPTER 13

True or False

Indicate which of the following statements is true or false by circling the correct answer.

T   F   1.   In 2002, a single taxpayer has three qualifying children and earned income of $9,500. This taxpayer's earned income credit is $3,800.

T   F   2.   The basic research credit is 25 percent for basic research payments over a base amount.

T   F   3.   The rate for the low-income housing credit is set monthly by the IRS.

T   F   4.   The rehabilitation credit is intended to discourage businesses from moving out of the inner city and to preserve historic structures.

T   F   5.   For 2002, the earned income credit for a married filing jointly taxpayer with one child is the appropriate percentage of the first $7,370 of earned income, reduced by the appropriate percentage of adjusted gross income (or, if greater, earned income) over $14,520.

T   F   6.   The earned income credit is a form of negative income tax and can be refunded even if no tax is due.

T   F   7.   To be eligible for the earned income credit, an individual must maintain a household that is the principal abode of a qualifying child.

T   F   8.   The tax credit for the elderly is 20 percent of the Section 22 amount; reduced by excluded social security, railroad retirement benefits, and certain pension amounts.

T   F   9.   The maximum dependent care credit for three qualifying children is $800.

T   F   10.   Amounts spent for the care of a taxpayer's spouse may qualify for the dependent care credit.

T   F   11.   A transfer of property to a qualified basic research organization does not qualify for the 20 percent basic research credit.

T   F   12.   The maximum amount of general business credit than can be taken in one year is equal to the taxpayer's net income tax reduced by the greater of the tentative minimum tax or 25 percent of net regular tax over $25,000.

T   F   13.   If an employee has no regular payroll period, then he or she is considered to be paid on a daily basis.

T   F   14.   The wage-bracket method of withholding calculation requires more computation than the percentage method.

T   F   15.   Employers can always wait until the end of their taxable year before filing the required form for payroll withholding, and they do not have to deposit the withholding until the end of the year.

T   F   16.   The penalty for underpayment of estimated tax may be avoided by single individuals with AGI under $150,000 if they file timely quarterly payments (including amounts withheld) that are equal to or exceed the prior year's tax liability.

T   F   17.   Individuals with net earnings from self-employment of $200 or more are subject to the self-employment tax.

T   F   18.   The backup withholding rate is 31 percent.

T   F   19.   The self-employment tax is 70 percent deductible for income tax purposes.

T   F   20.   S corporations and personal service corporations (PSCs) are allowed the basic research credit.

T   F   21.   A taxpayer's only income is self-employment income of $100,000. The amount of her Medicare tax is $2,678.15.

T   F   22.   Earl has $20,000 of income from Country A, which imposes a 30 percent tax. His U.S. taxable income is $57,250 and he files single with one exemption. Assume his U.S. income tax is $19,000. Earl's maximum foreign tax credit (FTC) is calculated as [$20,000/($57,250 + exemption + $20,000)] × 19,000.

T   F   23.   Unused foreign tax credit is carried back 3 years and forward 5 years.

T   F   24.   In order to qualify for the adoption expense credit, a child must be under 18-years-old or physically or mentally incapable of self-care.

T   F   25.   The applicable percentage for the Retirement Plan Contribution Credit for a married filing jointly taxpayer with AGI of $47,500 is 10%.

T   F   26.   An employer spends $300,000 for a child care facility for its employees and claims a $75,000 Employer-Provided Child Credit (25% × $300,000). The tax basis in the child care facility must be reduced to $225,000 ($300,000 − $75,000) because of the credit.

Multiple Choice

Choose the best answer for each of the following questions.

_____ 1.   Ted and his wife, Wilma, pay $3,000 to keep their son, Ted Jr., in a day care center. Ted Jr. is five-years-old. Ted's earnings are $12,000 and Wilma's earnings are $15,000. What amount of child care credit can Ted and Wilma claim on a joint return assuming no other income or losses for the year?

    a. $–0–
    b. $480
    c. $504
    d. $900

_____ 2.   Ted and his wife, Wilma, pay $3,000 to keep their son, Ted Jr., in a day care center. Ted Jr. is five-years-old. Ted's earnings are $12,000 and Wilma's earnings are $1,500. What amount of child care credit can Ted and Wilma claim on a joint return assuming no other income or losses for the year?

    a. $–0–
    b. $315
    c. $504
    d. $420

_____ 3. Tim is 68-years-old and single. He has adjusted gross income of $5,000 and does not receive any social security benefits. What is Tim's tax credit for the elderly?

    a. $–0–
    b. $375
    c. $750
    d.   None of the above

_____ 4. Tim is 68-years-old and single. He has adjusted gross income of $13,000 and does not receive any social security benefits. What is Tim's tax credit for the elderly?

    a. $–0–
    b. $750.00
    c. $337.50
    d. $825.00

_____ 5. Teri, a single taxpayer, maintains a household for her child, who is 13-years-old. Teri's adjusted gross income is $7,000, all from salary. How much is Teri's 2002 earned income credit?

    a. $–0–
    b. $2,380
    c. $3,400
    d. $4,000

_____ 6. Gray Corporation has $110,000 worth of excess qualified incremental research expenditures. What is Gray's incremental research credit?

    a. $–0–
    b. $20,000
    c. $55,000
    d. $22,000

_____ 7. Bill and Betty have one child, Bobby, who is six-years-old. Bill's earnings are $15,000 and Betty's are $14,000. Other income includes interest on a savings account at San Diego Federal Savings and Loan of $450. They paid $2,600 to the Tiny Tot Day Care Center to keep Bobby so they could both work. What is their child care credit?

    a. $–0–
    b. $480
    c. $520
    d. $2,600

_____ 8. The basic research credit rate is:

    a.   10%
    b.   15%
    c.   20%
    d.   22%

_____ 9. Sheila spends $60,000 to rehabilitate a commercial building originally placed in service in 1910. The building is not a certified historic structure. What is Sheila's rehabilitation credit on the building?

    a. $–0–
    b. $6,000
    c. $9,000
    d. $12,000

_____ 10.   Sheila spends $60,000 to rehabilitate a commercial building originally placed in service in 1910. What is Sheila's rehabilitation credit if the building is a certified historic structure?

    a. $–0–
    b. $6,000
    c. $9,000
    d. $12,000

_____ 11.   Toni has net earnings from self-employment of $75,000. What is Toni's total self-employment tax?

    a. $11,475.00
    b. $10,597.16
    c. $5,298.58
    d.   Some other amount

_____ 12.   Which of the following taxpayers would not be subject to the penalty for the underpayment of estimated tax?

    a.   The taxpayer does not have the cash to make the payments.
    b.   The taxpayer's estimated payments this year exceed his tax liability for the prior year.
    c.   The taxpayer's CPA forgets to fill out the appropriate forms and send them to the taxpayer.
    d.   The estimated payments this year are equal to 70 percent of the current tax liability.

_____ 13.   Which of the following forms is the Employer's Annual Federal Unemployment Tax Return?

    a.   Form SS–4
    b.   W–2
    c.   940 or 940EZ
    d.   941

_____ 14.   Adrian is married and earns a salary of $2,525 per month in March 2002. If he claims a total of four exemptions, calculate Adrian's withholding using the *percentage method*.

    a. $100.00
    b. $96.00
    c. $98.70
    d. $152.50

_____ 15.   If backup withholding applies, the payor must withhold at what rate?

    a.   20%
    b.   25%
    c.   28%
    d.   31%

_____ 16.   White, an eligible small business, made $12,000 of capital improvements that qualify for the disabled access credit. What is the amount of White's credit?

    a. $–0–
    b. $5,000
    c. $6,000
    d. $5,875

_____ 17.   Yellow Corporation incurred the following research expenses: (1) $100,000 in-house expenditures and (2) $60,000 paid to Coonawarra University for contract research. What is the total of Yellow's qualified research expenditures?

    a. $–0–
    b. $60,000
    c. $139,000
    d. $160,000

_____ 18.   During 2002, Jan earned $65,000 in wages subject to FICA. Jan also had net earnings of $30,000 from an outside consulting business. Jan sold IBM stock for a gain of $4,000 during the year. What is the amount of Jan's net earnings from self-employment for purposes of determining the Social Security portion of the self-employment tax?

    a. $–0–
    b. $19,900
    c. $30,000
    d. $95,000

_____ 19.   Which of the following is a refundable credit?

    a.   Withholding
    b.   Child care credit
    c.   Foreign tax credit
    d.   Rehabilitation credit

_____ 20.   Orange Corporation's general business credit is $75,000. The net income tax for the year is $125,000 and the tentative AMT is $15,000. Assuming Orange has no other tax credits for the year, the general business credit allowed is:

    a. $15,000
    b. $75,000
    c. $100,000
    d. $110,000

_____ 21.   Green Corporation's general business credit is $75,000. The net income tax for the year is $125,000 and the tentative AMT is $70,000. Assuming Green has no other tax credits for the year, the general business credit allowed is:

    a. $70,000
    b. $55,000
    c. $75,000
    d. $110,000

_____ 22.   In 2002, Ray and Michelle pay $5,000 in adoption fees and $5,500 in legal fees to adopt a new baby. How much is their adoption expense credit?

    a. $–0–
    b. $5,000
    c. $10,000
    d. $10,500

_____ 23.   In 2001, Ray and Michelle pay $2,000 in adoption fees and $5,500 in legal fees to adopt a new baby. If Ray and Michelle's AGI is $100,000, what is the amount of their adoption expense credit?

    a. $–0–
    b. $5,000
    c. $5,500
    d. $1,875

_____ 24.   Bob and Jane have two children, ages 10 and 12. Their AGI for 2002 is $115,300. What is Bob and Jane's child tax credit?

    a. $1,000
    b. $900
    c. $300
    d. $1,200

_____ 25. Lew and Martha are married and have AGI of $70,000. The have two children, Bill and Betty. In Fall 2002, Bill started his freshman year of college and Betty was enrolled for her junior year. Bill's qualified tuition expenses were $1,700 and Betty's were $3,000 for the fall semester. Bill and Betty are dependents of Lew and Martha and both are full-time students. What is Lew and Martha's HOPE Credit for 2002?

  a. $–0–
  b. $1,350
  c. $1,500
  d. $340

_____ 26. Same as question 25. What is Lew and Martha's Lifetime Learning Credit for 2002?

  a. $–0–
  b. $1,500
  c. $600
  d. $1,350

_____ 27. John is single and has one child who is qualified for the HOPE Credit. In the Fall 2002, John pays $2,400 in tuition for his son to attend college. John's AGI for 2002 is $53,000. What is his Hope Credit for 2002?

  a. $–0–
  b. $600
  c. $900
  d. $1,500

_____ 28. Green Company established a qualified retirement plan for its 20 employees. It paid cost of $2,500 to startup this plan. What is Green's small employer pension credit for qualified startup cost.

  a. $–0–
  b. 50% × $2,500
  c. 50% × $2,500, with a maximum credit of $500.
  d. $2,500

_____ 29. Blue Company constructed a child care facility for $600,000 to used by it employees with preschool-aged children while they are at work. Blue paid $200,000 for worker to and other administrative cost the run the child care center for the year. What is Blue's employer-provided child care credit?

  a. (25% × $800,000)
  b. (25% × $600,000)
  c. (25% × $600,000) + (10% × $200,000)
  d. (25% × $600,000) + (10% × $200,000), not to exceed $150,000

_____ 30. Teddy and Abby are married and file a joint return. Abby works and she contributes $2,300 to her Section 401(k) plan. Teddy does not work. If their AGI is $32,000, what is the amount of Abby's retirement plan contribution credit?

  a. $–0–
  b. 50% × $2,300
  c. 20% × $2,300
  d. 20% × $2,000

SOLUTIONS TO CHAPTER 13 QUESTIONS

True or False

1.   T $9,500 \times 40\% = \$3,800$. The 40 percent credit applies up to a maximum earned income of \$9,540. [Earned Income Credit, p. 13–16]

2.   F   The credit is 20 percent. [Basic Research Credit, p. 13–12]

3.   T   See footnote 15; the rate is applied to a qualified basis which depends on the number of units rented to low-income tenants. [Low-Income Housing Credit, p. 13–13]

4.   T   The credit is for expenditures incurred to rehabilitate industrial and commercial buildings and certified historic structures. [Tax Credit for Rehabilitation Expenditures, p. 13–8]

5.   T   The phase-out begins at \$12,460 and ends at \$26,928. [Earned Income Credit, p. 13–16]

6.   T   The earned income credit is a form of negative income tax. [Advance Payment, p. 13–18]

7.   F   Taxpayers 25 to 64 years old do not have to have a qualifying child. [Eligibility Requirements, p. 13–17]

8.   F   The credit is 15 percent. [Tax Credit for Elderly or Disabled Taxpayers, p. 13–19]

9.   F   The maximum credit is $30\% \times \$4,800 = \$1,440$. [Calculation of the Credit, p. 13–24]

10.   T   The spouse must be physically or mentally disabled. [Eligibility, p. 13–23]

11.   T   Basic research payments are defined as amounts paid in cash to a qualified basic research organization. [Basic Research Credit, p. 13–12]

12.   T   The maximum amount of general business credit that can be taken in any one year is equal to the taxpayer's net income tax reduced by the greater of the tentative minimum tax or 25 percent of net regular tax over \$25,000. [General Business Credit, p. 13–6]

13.   T   The payroll period and the number of allowances determines the amount to be withheld for Federal income taxes. [Amount of Income Tax Withholding, p. 13–33]

14.   F   The wage-bracket method is where the amount is simply looked up using the appropriate table. [Amount of Income Tax Withholding, p. 13–33]

15.   F   Employers must deposit employment taxes at least quarterly. [Reporting and Payment Procedures, p. 13–37]

16.   T   If the AGI on the preceding year's return exceeded \$150,000, the percentage goes up to 105. [Estimated Tax for Individuals, p. 13–39]

17.   F   Individuals with net earnings from self-employment of \$400 or more are subject to the self-employment tax. [Self-Employment Tax, p. 13–40]

18.   T   Backup withholding is designed to ensure income tax is collected on interest and other payments reported on a Form 1099. [Backup Withholding, p. 13–38]

19.   F   It is 50 percent deductible. [Self-Employment Tax, p. 13–40]

20.   F   They are not allowed the credit. [Basic Research Credit, p. 13–12]

21.   T $\$100,000 \times 92.35\% = \$92,350 \times 2.9\% = \$2,678.15$ (2002) While the Social Security portion has a ceiling, the Medicare portion is unlimited. [Self Employment Tax, p. 13–40]

22.   T   The maximum FTC is $\$20,000/(57,250 + \text{exemption} + \$20,000)] \times \$19,000$ [Computation, p. 13–20]

23. F It is 2 years back and 5 years forward. [Computation, p. 13–20]

24. T A child must be under 18-years-old or physically or mentally incapable of self-care to qualify for the adoption credit. [Adoption Expenses Credit, p. 13–21]

25. T The applicable percentage is 10% for a married filing jointly taxpayers with AGI of $47,500. [Credit for Certain Retirement Plan Contributions, p. 13–26]

26. T The facility tax basis must be reduced by any Employer-Provided Child Care credit claimed. [Credit for Employer-Provided Child Care, p. 13–16]

Multiple Choice

1. c Credit from text: 21% of $2,400 (maximum) = $504 [Calculation of the Credit, p. 13–24]

2. d 28% of $1,500 = $420[Earned Income Ceiling, p. 13–23]

3. c 15% of $5,000 = $750 [Tax Credit for Elderly or Disabled Taxpayers, p. 13–19]

4. c 15% of ($5,000 − (($13,000 − 7,500)/2)) = $337.50 [Tax Credit for Elderly or Disabled Taxpayers, p. 13–19]

5. b 34% of $7,000 = $2,380 [Earned Income Credit, p. 13–16]

6. d (20% × $110,000) = $22,000 [Incremental Research Activities Credit, p. 13–11]

7. b $2,400 × 20% = $480 [Calculation of the Credit, p. 13–24]

8. c 20% [Basic Research Credit, p. 13–12]

9. b $60,000 × 10% = $6,000 [Tax Credit for Rehabilitation Expenditures, p. 13–8]

10. d $60,000 × 20% = $12,000[Tax Credit for Rehabilitation Expenditures, p. 13–8]

11. b $75,000 × 92.35% = $69,262.50 × 15.3% = $10,597.16[Self-Employment Tax, p. 13–40]

12. b No penalty is generally due for underpayment of estimated tax when the current year estimated payments exceed the previous year's tax liability. [Estimated Tax for Individuals, p. 13–39]

13. c Federal unemployment tax is generally reported on Form 940 or 940EZ. [Reporting and Payment Procedures, p. 13–37]

14. c 10% × ($2,525.00 − (4 × $250.00) − $538) = $98.70 (2002) [Amount of Income Tax Withholding, p. 13–33]

15. d 31% is the backup withholding rate. [Backup Withholding, p. 13–38]

16. b 50% × ($10,250 maximum − $250) = $5,000 [Disabled Access Credit, p. 13–14]

17. c $100,000 + (65% × $60,000) = $139,000 [Incremental Research Activities Credit, p. 13–11]

18. b $8,900 − $65,000 = $19,900 (2002) [Self-Employment Tax, p. 13–40]

19. a Excess withholding is refundable. [Refundable Versus Nonrefundable Credits, p. 13–5]

20. b $125,000 net income tax less the greater of: (1) $15,000 (tentative AMT), or (2) $25,000 (25% × ($125,000 − $25,000)) = $100,000, the maximum business credit allowed. Therefore, the allowable business credit is $75,000. [General Business Credit, p. 13–6]

21. b $125,000 net income tax less the greater of: (1) $70,000 (tentative AMT), or (2) $25,000 (25% × ($125,000 − $25,000)) = $55,000, the maximum business credit allowed. Therefore, the allowable business credit is $55,000. [General Business Credit, p. 13–6]

22. c $10,000 is the maximum credit for 2002. [Adoption Expenses Credit, p. 13–21]

23.   d $10,000 − [($10,000 × ($25,000/$40,000))] = $3,750 [Adoption Expenses Credit, p. 13–21]

24.   b $900 = ($600 × 2) − $300 ($50 for each $1,000 over $110,000) (2002) [Maximum Credit and Phase-Outs, p. 13–22]

25.   b $1,350 = (100% × $1,000) + (50% × $700) Note, Betty is not eligible for the Hope Credit because she is past two years of college. [Maximum Credit, p. 13–25]

26.   c $600 = 20% × $3,000 [Maximum Credit, p. 13–25]

27.   a $–0–, which is a $1,500 credit [(100% × $1,000) + (50% × $1,000)] less a phase out of $1,800 ($53,000 − $41,000)/$10,000 × $1,500]. [Maximum Credit, p. 13–25]

28.   c   The amount is 50% × $2,500, with a maximum credit of $500. [Credit for Small Employer Pension Plan Startup Costs, p. 13–15]

29.   d   The credit is (25% × $600,000) + (10% × $200,000), not to exceed $150,000. [Credit for Employer-Provided Child Care, p. 13–16]

30.   d   The credit is 20% × $2,000. Note the maximum contribution is $2,000 per individual. [Credit for Certain Retirement Plan Contribution, p. 13–26]

CHAPTER 14

Property Transactions: Determination of Gain or Loss and Basis Considerations

CHAPTER HIGHLIGHTS

When a taxpayer disposes of property, the following four questions must be answered: (1) Is there a *realized* gain or loss? (2) If so, is the gain or loss *recognized?*; (3) If the gain or loss is recognized, is it *ordinary or capital?*; and (4) What is the basis of any replacement property? This chapter (and the next chapter) deals with the determination of realized and recognized gain or loss and the determination of the basis of replacement property. Chapters 16 and 17 address the classification of gain or loss as either ordinary or capital.

KEY TERMS

Amount Realized	Gain or Loss Realized	Gift Basis
Adjusted Basis	Gain of Loss Realized	Disallowed Losses

OUTLINE

I. **DETERMINATION OF GAIN OR LOSS**
    A. Realized Gain or Loss.

    The realized gain or loss is the difference between the amount realized and the adjusted basis of the property.

    The term "sale or other disposition" is defined broadly in the tax law. The term includes nearly all dispositions of property such as trade-ins, casualties, condemnations, and bond retirements.

    The "amount realized" from the sale or other disposition of property is the sum of money received plus the fair market value of other property received, reduced by the costs of transferring the property. The amount realized includes any liability (including nonrecourse debt) on the property assumed by the buyer.

    The "adjusted basis" of the property disposed of is its original cost basis adjusted to the date of disposition. The adjustments consist of adding capital additions and subtracting capital recoveries. Capital additions include the cost of capital improvements and betterments made to the property and amortization of bond discounts. The major capital recoveries are depreciation, certain corporate distributions, and amortization of bond premiums.

    The basis in property must be reduced by the amount of any deductible casualty or theft loss. The basis is also reduced by any insurance proceeds received. In addition, if the insurance proceeds result in the recognition of gain, the basis must be increased by the recognized gain.
    B. Recognized Gain or Loss. Recognized gain is the amount of the realized gain that is included in the taxpayer's gross income. A recognized loss is deductible for tax purposes. As a rule, the entire gain or loss realized will be recognized unless specific relief is found in the Code.
    C. Nonrecognition of Gain or Loss.

    In certain cases, realized gain or loss is not recognized for tax purposes. Several such exceptions include nontaxable exchanges, losses on the sale, exchange, or condemnation of personal use assets, gains on the sale of a personal residences, and certain transactions between related parties.

    Losses realized on the sale, exchange, or condemnation of personal use property are not recognized for tax purposes, whereas gains realized on such property are generally fully taxable.
    D. Recovery of Capital Doctrine.

    The recovery of capital doctrine states that a taxpayer is entitled to recover the cost or other basis of property acquired and is not taxed on that amount. The cost of depreciable property is recovered through annual depreciation deductions and the basis is reduced by the amount of the depreciation taken.

    The relationship between the recovery of capital doctrine and the concepts of realized and recognized gain or loss can be summarized as follows:
    1) *A realized gain (or loss) that is never recognized results in the permanent recovery of more (or less) than the taxpayer's cost or other basis for tax purposes.*
    2) *When recognition of a realized gain (or loss) is postponed, a temporary recovery of more (or less) than the taxpayer's cost or other basis results for tax purposes.*

II. **BASIS CONSIDERATIONS**
    A. Determination of Cost Basis.

    The basis of property is generally its cost, where cost is the amount paid for the property in cash or other property. The basis of property acquired in a "bargain purchase" is its fair market value.

    The Regulations require that taxpayers must adequately identify stock that is sold. If the stock cannot be identified, the IRS will assume FIFO for determining the basis of the shares sold.

When a taxpayer acquires multiple assets in a lump-sum purchase, it is necessary to allocate the total cost among the individual assets. This allocation is based on the relative fair market value of the individual assets acquired. Special allocation rules apply when the purchase involves a business with goodwill as one of the assets purchased.

Shares of common or preferred stock received as nontaxable stock dividends must be allocated as part of the basis of the common stock owned. This allocation is done based on relative fair market value.

If a taxpayer receives nontaxable rights to purchase additional stock and the fair market value of the rights is less than 15 percent of the fair market value of the stock with respect to which they were distributed, the basis in the rights is zero unless the taxpayer elects to allocate part of the cost of the stock to the rights. If the value of the rights is 15 percent or more of the fair market value of the stock, then the rights must be allocated as part of the stock's basis using relative fair market values. The holding period of nontaxable rights received includes the holding period of the stock on which the rights were distributed. However, if the rights are exercised, the holding period of the new stock begins the day the rights are exercised.

B.   Gift Basis.

When property owned by a taxpayer is received by gift, there is no-cost basis, so a basis must be assigned to the asset. For gifts, the basis for dispositions that result in a gain is the donor's adjusted basis. However, if the property is disposed of at a loss, the basis to the donee is the lower of the donor's adjusted basis or fair market value on the date of the gift. If property is disposed of at an amount that falls between the basis for gain and the basis for loss, no gain or loss is realized. Gift property is called "dual basis" property.

An adjustment to the basis of property acquired by gift may be required for gift tax paid. For gifts before 1977, the full amount of the gift tax is added to the donor's basis up to the fair market value of the property. The following formula is used to calculate the donee's gain basis for gifts after 1976:

Post-1976 Gift Tax Adjustment

$$\text{Donee's gain basis} = \text{donor's adjusted basis} + \frac{\text{unrealized appreciation}}{\text{fair market value}} \times \text{gift tax paid}$$

The holding period of property acquired by gift begins on the date the property was acquired by the donor if the gain basis rule applies. Otherwise, if the loss basis rule (FMV) for gifts applies, the holding period starts on the date of the gift.

C.   Property Acquired from a Decedent.

The basis of property acquired from a decedent is generally its fair market value at the date of death or the alternate valuation date. The alternate valuation date is six months after the date of death and may be elected only if the value of the gross estate and estate tax liability will be reduced.

The holding period for property acquired from a decedent is always long-term.

The basis of community property at the time of death of one spouse becomes the fair market value of the entire amount of the property, not just the decedent's share.

Future Changes. The current system of adjusting the basis of inherited property to fair market value on the date of death has been changed by Congress. The new system states that an heir's basis in inherited property is a carryover basis (i.e., the heir's basis is the same as the decedent's basis). However, this new provision does not go into effect after 2009 and most tax observers feel it will have to be substantially modified before then.

D.   Disallowed Losses.

Under Section 267, realized losses from sales or exchanges of property, directly or indirectly, between certain related parties are not recognized. If property is acquired in such a transaction, the basis is the property's cost to the transferee. However, if a subsequent sale or other disposition of the property results in a realized gain, the amount of the gain is reduced by the loss that was previously disallowed. If the original sale involves a personal use asset, any gain realized in a subsequent sale is not reduced by the previously disallowed loss.

The most common related party transactions are those between family members, and those between an individual and a corporation in which the individual owns, directly or indirectly, more than 50 percent of the stock.

If a taxpayer acquires stock or securities in a "wash sale" under Section 1091, any loss on the sale of the stock replaced by the substantially identical stock or securities will be disallowed. The basis in the replacement stock or securities will be the cost plus any disallowed loss. A wash sale occurs when a taxpayer sells or exchanges stock or securities and within 30 days before or after such sale or exchange acquires substantially identical stock or securities. If the taxpayer acquires less than the number of shares sold in a wash sale, any loss must be prorated based on the number of shares acquired relative to the number of shares sold.

A recognized loss on "tax straddles," such as buy and sell orders in the same commodity, is limited to the amount by which the realized loss exceeds any unrealized gain on the offsetting position. Losses that are not recognized are treated as having occurred in the following taxable year.

E. Conversion of Property from Personal Use to Business or Income-Producing Use.

The basis for loss and depreciation for property converted from personal to business or income-producing use is the lower of the property's adjusted basis or fair market value on the date of conversion. The basis for gain is the adjusted basis on the date of conversion.

Depreciation is calculated for tax purposes using the basis for loss. The basis for gain, however, must also be adjusted for depreciation to determine the gain or loss on disposition.

F. Additional Complexities in Determining Realized Gain or Loss.

Amount realized. Calculating the amount realized on a transaction can be complex. Numerous positive and negative adjustments have to be made in arriving at the amount realized. The following are examples of such adjustments:
1) mortgage(s) assumed by purchaser,
2) seller's property taxes paid by the purchaser,
3) broker's commissions, and
4) points paid by seller.

Adjusted basis. Determining the adjusted basis of property can also be complex. There are many items that cause adjustments to the original basis of property (especially real estate). The following are examples of such adjustments:
1) depreciation,
2) recording costs,
3) title fees,
4) survey costs,
5) attorney's fees,
6) appraisal fees, and
7) capital improvements.

TEST FOR SELF-EVALUATION—CHAPTER 14

True or False

Indicate which of the following statements is true or false by circling the correct answer.

T   F   1.   A "realized gain" and a "recognized gain" are the same thing.

T   F   2.   Trade-ins are not dispositions and would not cause a gain or loss to be recognized.

T   F   3.   The amount realized from a sale or disposition of property includes property received at fair market value.

T   F   4.   The amount realized from a sale or disposition of property does not include any liability assumed by the buyer.

T   F   5.   The term, fair market value, is defined by the courts as the price at which property will change hands between a willing seller and a willing buyer when neither is compelled to sell nor buy.

T   F   6.   The amount realized is reduced by the costs to transfer the property.

T   F   7.   The adjusted basis of property is the original basis plus capital recoveries, less capital additions.

T   F   8.   Depreciation is an example of capital recovery.

T   F   9.   The tax law assumes all gains that are realized will be recognized unless otherwise stated.

T   F   10.   A realized loss from the sale or disposition of a personal use asset is not recognized for tax purposes.

T   F   11.   Under the cost recovery doctrine, a taxpayer may recover the cost of property acquired and will be taxed on that amount.

T   F   12.   The cost of depreciable property is recovered through annual depreciation deductions.

T   F   13.   The original basis of property is generally its cost, which is paid for by cash or other property.

T   F   14.   The basis of property acquired in a bargain purchase is its cost.

T   F   15.   If stock lots cannot be identified, the Regulations make a LIFO presumption.

T   F   16.   A lump sum cost is allocated based on relative fair market values of the individual assets acquired.

T   F   17.   For gifts, the basis to the donee for income tax purposes is the lesser of fair market value at the date of the gift or the donor's adjusted basis, if the gift is later sold for a loss.

T   F   18.   If stock rights are exercised, the holding period of the newly acquired stock begins with the date the rights are exercised.

T   F   19.   The basis of property converted to business use is always fair market value on the date of conversion.

T   F   20.   The wash sale provision applies to both gains and losses.

T   F   21.   A loss on the sale of stock, to which the wash sale provisions apply, will be disallowed if substantially identical stock or securities are acquired within thirty days before or after the date of the sale or exchange.

T   F   22.   Both the decedent's share and the surviving spouse's share of community property have a basis equal to the fair market value on the date of death.

Multiple Choice

Choose the best answer for each of the following questions.

_____ 1.   Three years ago, Don acquired Texaco stock at a cost of $200,000. This stock was worth $275,000 on the date of Don's death, March 1, 2002. Nine months before Don's death the stock was worth $500,000. The alternate valuation date is not used. If the securities are sold by Don's heirs, the basis for determining gain or loss is:

   a. $–0–
   b. $275,000
   c. $200,000
   d. $500,000

_____ 2.   Under the Internal Revenue Code, the holding period for property acquired from a decedent is always:

   a.   Long-term
   b.   Short-term
   c.   Determined by the date acquired by the decedent
   d.   Determined by the date of death

_____ 3.   On January 2, Todd converts his house into rental property. The basis of the house is $200,000 and its fair market value on the date of conversion is $188,000. Todd's basis for depreciation is:

   a. $–0–
   b. $188,000
   c. $200,000
   d. $12,000

_____ 4.   On January 2, Todd converts his house into rental property. The basis of the house is $200,000 and its fair market value on the date of conversion is $188,000. Todd's basis for "gain" in the event the property is later sold would be:

   a. $188,000 less any depreciation allowed or allowable
   b. $200,000 less any depreciation allowed or allowable
   c. $188,000 with no depreciation allowed
   d.   Some other amount

_____ 5.   On January 2, Todd converts his house into rental property. The basis of the house is $200,000 and its fair market value on the date of conversion is $188,000. Todd's basis for "loss" in the event the property is later sold would be:

   a. $188,000 less any depreciation allowed or allowable
   b. $200,000 less any depreciation allowed or allowable
   c. $200,000 with no depreciation allowed
   d.   Some other amount

_____ 6.   On July 1, Year 1, Ted sells 100 shares of Penola, Inc. stock (basis of $4,000) for $3,500. On July
              18, Year 1, he purchases 50 shares for $1,800. Ted's recognized loss on the sale is:

              a. $–0–
              b. $500
              c. $250
              d. $375

_____ 7.   On July 1, Year 1, Ted sells 100 shares of Penola, Inc. stock (basis of $4,000) for $3,500. On July
              18, Year 1, he purchases 50 shares for $1,800. Ted's basis in the 50 shares purchased on July 18,
              Year 1, would be:

              a. $–0–
              b. $1,800
              c. $2,300
              d. $2,050

_____ 8.   John Deaux of Lake Charles, Louisiana, sold common stock acquired two years ago to his brother,
              Don, at the current market price of $6,000. John's basis in the stock is $8,000. He should report:

              a.   Neither a gain nor a loss
              b.   A long-term capital loss of $2,000
              c.   An ordinary loss of $2,000
              d.   A short-term capital loss of $2,000

_____ 9.   John Deaux of Lake Charles, Louisiana, sold common stock acquired two years ago to his brother,
              Don, at the current market price of $6,000. John's basis in the stock is $8,000. The stock market
              recovered rapidly and later Don Deaux sold the stock to an unrelated third party for $9,000. Don's
              recognized gain would be:

              a. $–0–
              b. $3,000
              c. $1,000
              d. $2,000

_____ 10.   Tim received a gift of property with a fair market value of $8,000. The property had an adjusted
              basis to the donor of $8,500. There was no gift tax paid on the transfer. If Tim sold the property
              for $8,700, the gain or (loss) would be:

              a. $200
              b. $700
              c. $500
              d.   Some other amount

_____ 11.   Tim received a gift of property with a fair market value of $8,000. The property had an adjusted
              basis to the donor of $8,500. There was no gift tax paid on the transfer. If Tim sold the property
              for $7,500, the gain or (loss) would be:

              a. $500 gain
              b. $500 loss
              c. $1,000 loss
              d.   Some other amount

_____ 12.   Tim received a gift of property with a fair market value of $8,000. The property had an adjusted
              basis to the donor of $8,500. There was no gift tax paid on the transfer. If Tim sold the property
              for $8,200, the gain or (loss) would be:

a.   No gain or loss
b. $300 loss
c. $200 gain
d.   Some other amount

_____ 13.   Tony sells his house with a basis of $40,000 for $50,000 in cash. The buyer assumes Tony's mortgage of $60,000. The amount of gain realized on this transaction is:

a. $–0–
b. $10,000
c. $20,000
d. $70,000

_____ 14.   Tina buys an automobile from her employer for $8,000. The fair market value of the car is $12,000 and its basis to the employer is $14,000. Tina's basis in the automobile is:

a. $4,000
b. $8,000
c. $12,000
d. $14,000

_____ 15.   Andrew sold real estate to Lupe for $100,000 cash and Lupe assumed Andrew's mortgage of $225,000. Andrew paid brokers' commissions of $19,000 and points of $6,000. What is Andrew's amount realized?

a. $100,000
b. $325,000
c. $306,000
d. $300,000

_____ 16.   An asset used in a trade or business is damaged by a fire. The adjusted basis of the asset before the fire is $25,000 and the fair market value is $15,000 after the fire. No insurance proceeds are received. The amount of the casualty loss deduction is $10,000. What is the adjusted basis of the asset after the fire?

a. $–0–
b. $10,000
c. $15,000
d. $25,000

_____ 17.   Van purchases a rental house and land for $90,000 in a depressed real estate market. Appraisals place the value of the house at $70,000 and the land at $30,000 (a total of $100,000). What is Van's basis in the house?

a. $63,000
b. $70,000
c. $90,000
d. $100,000

_____ 18.   On March 1, Year 1, Ming received a gift of stock having a donor's adjusted basis of $60,000 at the date of the gift. At the date of the gift, the fair market value (FMV) of the property was $50,000. Ming sold the property for $56,000 on August 1, Year 1. If no gift tax was paid on the transfer, how much gain or loss should Ming report for Year 1?

a.   No gain or loss
b. $6,000 short-term capital gain
c. $4,000 short-term capital loss
d. $4,000 ordinary loss

_____ 19. Laura exchanged an old machine used in her business for a new machine to be used in her business. Laura is self-employed. The original cost of the old machine was $25,000 and its adjusted basis is $15,000. The FMV of the new machine is $29,000 and Laura paid additional cash of $12,000. What is the amount of *gain or loss realized* by Laura on this exchange?

    a. $–0–
    b. $2,000 gain
    c. $2,000 loss
    d. $9,000 gain

_____ 20. Edgar died this year leaving his entire estate to his son, Elmer. The executor of Edgar's estate elected to use the alternate valuation date. Edgar's estate contained stock in the Green Corporation that has a basis to Edgar of $300,000. The stock was distributed to Elmer four months after Edgar's death. The fair market value (FMV) of the stock on various dates was: (1) $425,000 (FMV on date of death), (2) $390,000 (FMV on date of distribution), and (3) $410,000 (FMV six months after death). Elmer's basis in the distributed stock is:

    a. $–0–
    b. $300,000
    c. $390,000
    d. $410,000

_____ 21. On March 1, 2002, Oscar learned that he was bequeathed 1,000 shares of Blue Corporation common stock under the will of his uncle. The uncle had paid $5,000 for the Blue stock five years ago. The fair market value of the Blue stock on March 1, 2002, the date of the uncle's death, was $8,000. Oscar sold the Blue stock for $9,000 on May 1, 2002, the date that the executor distributed the stock to him. Oscar's gain or loss on the sale of the Blue Company stock is:

    a. $–0–
    b. $1,000
    c. $3,000
    d. $4,000

_____ 22. On March 1, 2002, Oscar learned that he was bequeathed 1,000 shares of Blue Corporation common stock under the will of his uncle. The uncle had paid $5,000 for the Blue stock five years ago. The fair market value of the Blue stock on March 1, 2002, the date of the uncle's death, was $8,000. Oscar sold the Blue stock for $9,000 on May 1, 2002, the date that the executor distributed the stock to him. Oscar should treat the sale of the 1,000 shares of Blue stock as a:

    a.   Ordinary gain or loss
    b.   Section 1231 gain or loss
    c.   Short-term capital gain or loss
    d.   Long-term capital gain or loss

_____ 23. Tim owns land with an adjusted basis of $100,000 (subject to a mortgage of $50,000). On May 1 of the current year, Tim sells the land for $200,000 in cash, a note for $300,000, and property with a fair market value of $60,000. The $50,000 mortgage is assumed by the purchaser. What is the amount realized from this transaction?

    a. $500,000
    b. $550,000
    c. $560,000
    d. $610,000

_____ 24. The bank forecloses on Kay's office building. The property had been pledged as security on a nonrecourse mortgage, whose principal amount at the date of foreclosure is $600,000. The adjusted basis of the office building is $350,000 and the fair market value is $500,000. What is Kay's recognized gain or loss?

     a. $–0–
     b. $100,000
     c. $250,000
     d. $150,000

_____ 25.   Lucy owns City of San Diego bonds with a face amount of $10,000. Lucy purchased the bonds on January 1, Year 1, for $12,000. The maturity date is December 31, Year 4, (five years later). Assuming annual amortization of the bond premium is $400 and the annual interest rate on the bonds is 8 percent, what is Lucy's adjusted basis in the bonds as of the end of Year 1?

     a. $10,000
     b. $10,400
     c. $11,600
     d. $12,000

_____ 26.   Ginny was given a residence in 1975 that she still owns. At the time of the gift, the residence had an adjusted basis to the donor of $100,000 and a fair market value of $250,000. The donor paid gift tax of $15,000 on the gift. What is Ginny's basis for gain in the residence?

     a. $100,000
     b. $109,000
     c. $115,000
     d. $250,000

_____ 27.   Olga was given Black Company stock in Year 1. At the time of the gift, the stock had an adjusted basis to the donor of $100,000 and a fair market value of $250,000. The donor paid gift tax of $15,000 on the gift. What is Olga's basis for gain in the Black Company stock?

     a. $100,000
     b. $109,000
     c. $115,000
     d. $250,000

Problem

Lisa purchased a new house three years ago. The purchase price and related items (all paid by Lisa) were as follows:

Purchase price (new house)	$180,000
Title fees	$700
Recording fees	$300
Survey fees	$1,000
Appraisal fees	$250
Escrow fees	$500

Two years ago, Lisa added a new room onto the house at a cost of $27,000. She also deducted $2,000 in depreciation on her home office and other home office expenses of $3,500. Her real estate taxes on the house to date are $9,500. What is Lisa's adjusted basis in the house?

SOLUTIONS TO CHAPTER 14 QUESTIONS

True or False

1. F "Recognized" is a term used for tax purposes only and refers to the amount of realized gain that is included in gross income or the amount of realized loss that is deductible for tax purposes. [Recognized Gain or Loss, p. 14–6]

2. F Trade-ins are dispositions. [Sale or Other Disposition, p. 14–3]

3. T The amount realized also includes any money received. [Amount Realized, p. 14–3]

4. F Liabilities are included in determining the amount realized. [Amount Realized, p. 14–3]

5. T "Fair market value" is the price at which property will change hands between a willing buyer and seller when neither is compelled to buy or sell. [Amount Realized, p. 14–3]

6. T The amount realized is the net amount received directly or indirectly by the taxpayer from the disposition of property. [Amount Realized, p. 14–6]

7. F The adjusted basis is the original basis less capital recoveries, plus capital additions. [Adjusted Basis, p. 14–4]

8. T The original basis of depreciable property is reduced by the annual depreciation charges (or cost recovery allowances) [Capital Recoveries, p. 14–4]

9. T The tax law assumes that all realized gains will be recognized unless there is an exception in the law. [Recognized Gain or Loss, p. 14–6]

10. T Any gain realized from the sale or disposition of personal use assets is, however, generally fully taxable. [Sale Exchange, or condemnation of Personal Assets, p. 14–7]

11. F Taxpayers are not taxed on the recovery of the cost or other basis of property. [Doctrine Defined, p. 14–7]

12. T The basis is reduced as the cost is recovered over the period the property is held. [Doctrine Defined, p. 14–7]

13. T The basis of property is generally its cost. [Determination of Cost Basis, p. 14–8]

14. F The basis of property acquired in a bargain purchase is FMV. [Determination of Cost Basis, p. 14–8]

15. F The Regulations assume FIFO. [Identification Problems, p. 14–8]

16. T Allocation is required because some of the assets may be depreciable and others may not. [Allocation Problems, p. 14–9]

17. T The donee's basis in this case is referred to as the loss basis. [Gift Basis Rules if No Gift Tax is Paid, p. 14–12]

18. T If stock rights are exercised, the holding period for the newly acquired stock begins on the date the rights are exercised. [Allocation Problems, p. 14–9]

19. F The basis (for loss) of converted property is the lesser of the property's adjusted basis or FMV on the date of conversion. [Conversion of Property from Personal Use to Business or Income-Producing Use, p. 14–20]

20. F The wash sale provision only applies to losses. [Wash Sales, p. 14–19]

21.   T   *Substantially identical* means "the same in all important particulars." [Wash Sales, p. 14–19]

22.   T   The decedent's share flows to the surviving spouse from the estate; the survivors share is deemed to be acquired from the decedent. [Survivor's Share of Property, p. 14–17]

Multiple Choice

1.   b   The basis of property acquired from a decedent is generally the property's fair market value at the date of death. [General Rules, p. 14–14]

2.   a   The holding period is deemed to be long-term. [Holding Period of Property Acquired from a Decedent, p. 14–17]

3.   b   The basis for depreciation is the lesser of the adjusted basis or FMV on the date of conversion. [Conversion of Property from Personal Use to Business or Income-Producing Use, p. 14–20]

4.   b   The gain basis is the property's adjusted basis on the date of conversion. [Conversion of Property from Personal Use to Business or Income-Producing Use, p. 14–20]

5.   a   The basis for loss is also the basis for depreciating the converted property. [Conversion of Property from Personal Use to Business or Income-Producing Use, p. 14–20]

6.   c $3,500 − $4,000 = ($500), less 50% wash sale = ($250) loss allowed [Wash Sales, p. 14–19]

7.   d $1,800 + $250 = $2,050 [Wash Sales, p. 14–19]

8.   a   The loss disallowance provision applies to several types of related-party transactions. [Related Taxpayers, p. 14–18]

9.   c $9,000 − $6,000 = $3,000, less ($2,000) disallowed loss = $1,000 recognized gain [Related Taxpayers, p. 14–18]

10. a $8,700 − $8,500 = $200 [Gift Basis Rules if No Gift Tax Is Paid, p. 14–12]

11. b $7,500 − $8,000 = ($500) [Gift Basis Rules if No Gift Tax Is Paid, p. 14–12]

12. a   If the amount realized from sale or other disposition is between the basis for loss and the basis for gain, no gain or loss is realized. [Gift Basis Rules if No Gift Tax Is Paid, p. 14–12]

13. d $50,000 + $60,000 − $40,000 = $70,000 [Amount Realized, p. 14–3]

14. c   The basis of property acquired in a bargain purchase is the property's fair market value. [Determination of Cost Basis, p. 14–8]

15. d $100,000 + $225,000 − $19,000 − $6,000 = $300,000 [Amount Realized, p. 14–21]

16. c $25,000 − $10,000 = $15,000 [Capital Recoveries, p. 14–4]

17. a   ($70,000 / $100,000) × $90,000 = $63,000 [Allocation Problems, p. 14–9]

18. a   If the amount realized from sale or other disposition is between the basis for loss and the basis for gain, no gain or loss is realized. [Gift Basis Rules if No Gift Tax Is Paid, p. 14–12]

19. b $29,000 − ($15,000 + $12,000) = $2,000 gain realized [Sale or Other Disposition, p. 14–3]

20. c   The basis is the FMV six months after decedent's death unless the stock was distributed earlier, as in this question. [General Rules, p. 14–14]

21. b   The basis of property acquired from a decedent is generally the property's fair market value at the date of death. [General Rules, p. 14–14]

22. d   The holding period of property acquired from a decedent is deemed to be long term. [Holding Period of Property Acquired from a Decedent, p. 14–17]

23.   d $200,000 (cash) + $300,000 (note) + $60,000 (property received) + $50,000 (mortgage assumed by purchaser) = $610,000 (amount realized) [Amount Realized, p. 14–3]

24.   c $600,000 (mortgage) – $350,000 (adjusted basis) = $250,000 (realized gain) The recognized gain is also $250,000. [Recognized Gain or Loss, p. 14–6]

25.   c $12,000 (cost) – $400 (amortization) = $11,600 (basis at end of Year 1) [Capital Recoveries, p. 14–4]

26.   c $115,000 = $100,000 + $15,000. For gifts made before 1977, the full amount of the gift tax is added to he donor's basis. [Adjustment for Gift Tax, p. 14–13]

27.   b $109,000 = $100,000 + ($150,000) $250,000 × $15,000). The fair market value of the property is greater than the donor's adjusted basis, resulting in an allocation of the gift tax. [Adjustment for Gift Tax, p. 14–13]

Problem

Purchase price (new house)	$180,000
Title fees	+$700
Recording fees	+$300
Survey fees	+$1,000
Appraisal fees	+$250
Escrow fees	+$500
New room	+$27,000
Home office depreciation	–$2,000
Adjusted basis	$207,750

[Adjusted Basis, p. 14–22]

CHAPTER 15

Property Transactions: Nontaxable Exchanges

CHAPTER HIGHLIGHTS

Realized gains and losses arising from certain exchanges are not recognized for tax purposes. In general, new property is viewed as a continuation of an old investment, so the taxpayer is in the same relative economic position. The recognition of gain or loss is postponed until the property received in the exchange is disposed of in a taxable transaction. This chapter discusses several major types of transactions that receive nontaxable exchange treatment. Chapter 20 covers nontaxable contributions for partnership or corporate formation.

KEY TERMS

Boot
Like-Kind Exchanges
Involuntary Conversions

Nontaxable Exchange
Replacement Period

Section 121 Exclusion on Sale of a
    Residence
Transfers Pursuant to Divorce

OUTLINE

I. **LIKE-KIND EXCHANGES—Sec. 1031**

Under Section 1031, gain or loss on a like-kind exchange will not be recognized if property held for investment or for productive use in a trade or business is exchanged for like-kind property. This provision is mandatory rather than elective.

A. Like-Kind Property. The term like-kind is intended to be interpreted broadly. However, the following three general limitations are placed on what qualifies as like-kind property:
    1) livestock involved in an exchange must be of the same sex
    2) realty must be exchanged for realty
    3) personalty must be exchanged for personalty

    Real property includes rental buildings, office and store buildings, manufacturing plants, and land. Personalty consists primarily of machines, equipment, trucks, automobiles, furniture, and fixtures. Exchanges of real property located in the United States and foreign real property is not considered like-kind property.

    If the exchange involves a multiple asset business (e.g., a car dealership for a car dealership) the determination of whether assets qualify, as like-kind will not be made at business level, instead the underlying assets must be evaluated.

    Also, depreciable personalty used in a business must be exchanged for property within the same *general business class* or the same *product class*. Examples of general business classes are:
    1) Office furniture, fixtures, and equipment
    2) Information systems (computers and peripheral equipment)
    3) Airplanes
    4) Automobiles and taxis
    5) Buses
    6) Light general-purpose trucks
    7) Heavy general-purpose trucks

B. Exchange Requirement. To qualify for the like-kind treatment, property must be part of an exchange, not a sale and repurchase. In certain situations, taxpayers may want to avoid Section 1031 in order to receive a higher basis for depreciation purposes, to recognize a realized loss, or to recognize a gain that will receive favorable capital gain treatment or be available to offset passive activity losses.

C. Boot. On a like-kind exchange, gain realized will be recognized to the extent of boot received. However, the receipt of boot will not trigger the recognition of a realized loss. If boot is given, gain or loss is recognized only if the boot is appreciated or depreciated property.

D. Basis and Holding Period of Property Received. The basis of like-kind property received is equal to the fair market value of the like-kind property reduced by any postponed gain or increased by any postponed loss. Alternatively, the basis may be determined by the following formula.

	Adjusted basis of like-kind property surrendered
+	Adjusted basis of boot given
+	Gain recognized
–	Fair market value of boot received
–	Loss recognized
=	Basis of like-kind property received

The holding period of the property surrendered in the exchange carries over and "tacks on" to the holding period of the like-kind property received. Depreciation recapture potential also carries over to the property received.

The amount of any liability assumed by the transferee is treated as boot received by the transferor and boot given by the transferee.

II. **INVOLUNTARY CONVERSIONS—Section 1033**

A. General Scheme. Under Section 1033, a taxpayer who suffers an involuntary conversion may postpone the recognition of gain realized from the conversion if certain conditions are met. In general, gain is recognized to the extent that the amount realized is not reinvested in replacement property.

B. Involuntary Conversion Defined. An involuntary conversion is the result of destruction (complete or partial), theft, seizure, requisition, condemnation, or the sale or exchange under threat or imminence of requisition or condemnation of the taxpayer's property. Most involuntary conversions are casualties or condemnations.

C. Computing the Amount Realized. The amount realized from a condemnation of property usually includes only the amount received as compensation for the property. It does not generally include amounts designated as severance damages that usually occur when only part of the property is condemned.

D. Replacement Property. The replacement property for an involuntary conversion must be similar or related in service or use to the property involuntarily converted. To qualify, owner-investors must meet the taxpayer use test and owner-users must pass the functional use test for replacement property. Business or investment real property that is condemned is subject to the broader replacement rules for like-kind exchanges, which means that the taxpayer has more flexibility in selecting replacement property.

E. Time Limitation on Replacement. A taxpayer normally has two years after the close of the tax year in which any gain is realized to replace the property. For condemnations of trade or investment real property the taxpayer has three years instead of two.

F. Nonrecognition of Gain. If the conversion is directly into replacement property then the nonrecognition of gain is mandatory. The taxpayer's basis in the converted property carries over to the new property.

If the conversion is into money, a taxpayer may elect to postpone the gain or the gain may be recognized. If the election to postpone gain is made by the taxpayer, gain must still be recognized to the extent the amount realized exceeds the cost of replacement property. The basis of the replacement property purchased is its cost less any postponed gain. The holding period includes that of the converted property if postponement of the gain is elected.

Section 1033 does not modify the general rules for loss recognition. Therefore, losses from involuntary conversions of business or income producing property are recognized, whereas conversion losses (other than casualty losses) related to personal use assets are not recognized.

G. Involuntary Conversion of a Personal Residence. An involuntary conversion of a personal residence can have several tax treatments. In a loss situation, if the conversion is a condemnation, the loss realized is not recognized. If the conversion is a casualty, the taxpayer may recognize the loss subject to the personal casualty loss limitations. In a gain situation, if the conversion is a casualty, theft, or condemnation, the gain can be postponed under Section 1033 or excluded under Section 121.

H. Reporting Considerations. Supporting details should be included with the taxpayer's return in the year a gain is realized and in the year the property is replaced. If the property is not replaced within the time allotted, or it is replaced at a lower cost than anticipated, an amended return must be filed for the year the gain was realized.

III. **SALE OF A RESIDENCE**

Under Section 121, there are special rules for the taxation of gains on the sale of a personal residence. In general, the first $250,000 ($500,000 on a joint return) of gain realized is not recognized. Also, since a residence is a personal use asset, any realized loss is not recognized.

A. Requirements for Exclusion Treatment. In order to get the exclusion, the residence must have been owned and used by the taxpayer as a principal residence for at least two years of the five-year period ending on the date of sale. Note that the residence does not have to be the taxpayer's personal residence on the date of sale. Taxpayers are allowed this exclusion once every two years. The two-year requirement is waived if:

1) there is a change in place of employment of the taxpayer,
2) the personal residence is sold for health reasons, or
3) there are unforeseen circumstances as prescribed by the Regulations.

B. Calculation of the Amount of the Exclusion. The exclusion is available for up to $250,000 of realized gain. Realized gain is calculated in the normal manner (i.e., amount realized less adjusted basis). The amount realized (sales proceeds) is net of such items as advertising the property for sale, real estate commissions, legal fees, loan placement fees, and closing costs. Repairs and maintenance made by the seller as an aid to selling the property are not treated as selling expenses or as an adjustment to the adjusted basis of the residence.

If a married couple files a joint return, the $250,000 is increased to $500,000 if the following require-ments are met:

1) One spouse meets the at-least-two-year ownership requirement,
2) both spouses meet the at-least-two-year use requirement, and
3) neither spouse is ineligible for the exclusion because of the sale of another principal residence within the prior two years.

The basis of the new residence is the cost of the new residence since this provision is an exclusion and not a deferral of the gain.

If a taxpayer uses one of the relief provisions (e.g., an employment location change) the gain exclusion is treated on a prorated basis for the number of months the property qualified for the exclusion.

C. Principal Residence. A principal residence does not have to be a house. It can be a house trailer, houseboat, condominium, etc.

IV. **OTHER NONRECOGNITION PROVISIONS**

A. Exchange of Stock for Property—Section 1032. No gain or loss is recognized by a corporation dealing in its own stock, including treasury stock.

B. Certain Exchanges of Insurance Policies—Section 1035. Under Section 1035 of the Code, certain insurance contracts qualify for nonrecognition of gain or loss when exchanged.

C. Exchange of Stock for Stock of the Same Corporation—Section 1036. No gain or loss is recognized by a shareholder from the exchange of common stock for common stock, or preferred stock for preferred stock of the same corporation. An exchange of common stock for preferred stock is generally a taxable event.

D. Certain Reacquisitions of Real Property—Section 1038. When property sold on the installment basis is repossessed, only limited gain may be recognized and no loss is recognized.

E. Transfers of Property Between Spouses or Incident to Divorce—Section 1041. Transfers of property between spouses or former spouses incident to divorce or between spouses during marriage are nontaxable events. The basis of the property is carried over to the recipient.

F. Rollovers into Specialized Small Business Investment Companies—Section 1044. Gain on the sale of securities is not recognized if the amount realized is invested in a specialized small business invest-ment company (SSBIC). The proceeds must be reinvested within 30 days in order to qualify for nonrecognition treatment. The basis of the SSBIC stock must be reduced by the gain not recognized.

G. Rollover of Gain from Qualified Small Business Stock into another Qualified Small Business Stock—Section 1045. Realized gain from qualified small business stock held more than six months may be postponed if the taxpayers acquires other qualified small business stock within 60 days.

TEST FOR SELF-EVALUATION—CHAPTER 15

True or False

Indicate which of the following statements is true or false by circling the correct answer.

T F 1. Raw land held for investment does not qualify for a Section 1031 like-kind exchange.

T F 2. A store building could be exchanged for a delivery truck and qualify for a like-kind exchange.

T F 3. In a like-kind exchange, gain realized will be recognized to the extent boot is received.

T F 4. The Section 1031 like-kind exchange provision is elective, not mandatory.

T F 5. If a liability is assumed in a like-kind exchange, it will be treated as boot given by the party assuming the liability.

T F 6. The holding period of like-kind property received begins on the day the exchange takes place.

T F 7. The involuntary conversion provisions under Section 1033 apply to gains and not to losses.

T F 8. The Section 1033 involuntary conversion provision is always elective.

T F 9. In an involuntary conversion, realized gain is recognized to the extent that the proceeds are not reinvested in property that is similar or related in service or use.

T F 10. Section 1033 applies to condemnation payments if they are designated as severance damages.

T F 11. Owner-investors must conform to the functional use test to postpone gain under Section 1033.

T F 12. To qualify for nonrecognition of gain under Section 1033, taxpayers have two years from the date property is involuntarily converted to replace it.

T F 13. Under Section 121 a principal residence does not have to be a house.

T F 14. A loss on the sale of a personal residence is recognized as a capital loss to the taxpayer if the residence was used as a principal residence for two of the five prior years.

T F 15. The amount realized on the sale of a personal residence would include real estate commissions, but not legal fees.

T F 16. The exclusion is $500,000 for a married couple filing a joint return, if they meet certain ownership and use requirements.

T F 17. If a taxpayer and spouse each own a qualifying principal residence, they can separately qualify for the $250,000 exclusion on the sale of their own residence, even if they file a joint return.

T F 18. In order to qualify for the $250,000 exclusion on the sale of a principal residence, the taxpayer must live in the residence on the date of sale.

T   F   19.   If Section 1031 does not apply to a transaction, the end result of an exchange may be the recognition of capital gain in exchange for a lower basis in a newly acquired asset.

T   F   20.   Taxpayers should try to avoid Section 1031 treatment when the adjusted basis of the property being disposed of exceeds the fair market value.

Multiple Choice

Choose the best answer for each of the following questions.

_____ 1.   During the current year, Tim and Xavier exchange real estate investments. Tim gives up property with an adjusted basis of $250,000 (fair market value of $300,000), which is subject to a mortgage of $50,000 (assumed by Xavier). In return for this property, Tim receives property with a fair market value of $225,000 and $25,000 cash. What is Tim's realized gain?

       a. $-0-
       b. $50,000
       c. $75,000
       d. $100,000

_____ 2.   During the current year, Tim and Xavier exchange real estate investments. Tim gives up property with an adjusted basis of $250,000 (fair market value of $300,000), which is subject to a mortgage of $50,000 (assumed by Xavier). In return for this property, Tim receives property with a fair market value of $225,000 and $25,000 cash. What is Tim's recognized gain on the exchange?

       a. $-0-
       b. $50,000
       c. $75,000
       d. $100,000

_____ 3.   During the current year, Tim and Xavier exchange real estate investments. Tim gives up property with an adjusted basis of $250,000 (fair market value of $300,000), which is subject to a mortgage of $50,000 (assumed by Xavier). In return for this property, Tim receives property with a fair market value of $225,000 and $25,000 cash. What is Tim's basis in the new property?

       a. $225,000
       b. $250,000
       c. $275,000
       d. $300,000

_____ 4.   Tom's building, which has an adjusted basis of $100,000, is destroyed by fire in 20x1. During 20x1, Tom receives $250,000 of insurance proceeds for the loss. Tom invests $160,000 in a qualified replacement building. By what date must Tom make a new investment to come within the non-recognition provision of Section 1033?

       a.   December 31, 20x1
       b.   December 31, 20x2
       c.   December 31, 20x4
       d.   December 31, 20x4

_____ 5.   Tom's building, which has an adjusted basis of $100,000, is destroyed by fire in 20x1. During 20x1, Tom receives $250,000 of insurance proceeds for the loss. Tom invests $160,000 in a qualified replacement building. Assuming the replacement building is acquired within the required period, what is Tom's realized gain on the involuntary conversion?

a. $–0–
b. $90,000
c. $60,000
d. $150,000

_____ 6. Tom's building, which has an adjusted basis of $100,000, is destroyed by fire in 20x1. During 20x1, Tom receives $250,000 of insurance proceeds for the loss. Tom invests $160,000 in a qualified replacement building. Assuming the replacement building is acquired within the required period, what is Tom's recognized gain on the involuntary conversion providing Tom elects to be covered by Section 1033?

a. $–0–
b. $150,000
c. $90,000
d. $60,000

_____ 7. Teri is 60-years-old and sells her personal residence for $180,000 (adjusted basis of $50,000). Under Section 121, she would have a recognized gain of:

a. $–0–
b. $5,000
c. $130,000
d. $55,000

_____ 8. Tom is 40-years-old and sells his personal residence for $380,000 (adjusted basis of $50,000). Under Section 121, he would have a recognized gain of:

a. $–0–
b. $80,000
c. $330,000
d. $380,000

_____ 9. Which of the following exchanges would not qualify for like-kind exchange treatment under Section 1031?

a. Land held as an investment is exchanged for a rental house
b. A light-duty Ford business truck is exchanged for a light-duty Dodge business truck
c. A personal automobile is exchanged for a business automobile
d. All of the above would qualify

_____ 10. Three years ago, Ted acquired a capital asset for $10,000. The asset is worth $20,000 today. This property was exchanged for another capital asset worth $20,000 in a qualified Section 1031 exchange. Five months later, the new property was sold for $28,000. On this latest sale, Ted should report:

a. $10,000 long-term capital gain
b. $10,000 short-term capital gain
c. $18,000 long-term capital gain
d. $8,000 short-term capital gain

_____ 11. Section 1031, the like-kind exchange provision, applies to both gains and losses, and the Section 1033 involuntary conversion provision applies to:

a. Gains only
b. Losses only
c. Gains and losses
d. Capital gains only

———— 12.   Indicate which of the following would not qualify for involuntary conversion treatment under Section 1033:

a.   A personal residence burns down
b.   Inventory damaged by a flood
c.   A taxpayer sells his house because it is on a flood plain
d.   An office building is destroyed by a tornado

———— 13.   The Section 1033 involuntary conversion provision is:

a.   Always elective
b.   Never elective
c.   Mandatory for direct conversions
d.   Mandatory for conversions into money

———— 14.   Which of the following does not qualify as a selling expense under Section 121?

a.   Title transfer fees
b.   Painting a house to make it ready for sale
c.   Real estate commissions
d.   Advertising fees

———— 15.   Audrey sold her personal residence this year for $275,000. The residence was purchased ten years ago for $175,000. Expenses relating to the sale were:

Advertising for sale	$3,000
Broker commissions	$6,000
Title fees	$2,000
Painting inside of house	$3,000
Wallpaper bathrooms	$1,000
New hot tub	$7,000

The painting, wallpaper, and new hot tub expenses were incurred (and paid for) four weeks prior to the contract for sale. Audrey bought a new residence for $255,000. What is Audrey's realized gain?

a. $–0–
b. $275,000
c. $100,000
d. $82,000

———— 16.   John, who is single, sells his personal residence (adjusted basis of $150,000) for $310,000. He has lived in the residence for four years. John's selling expenses are $20,000 and three weeks prior to sale he paid a carpenter and a painter $3,000 to make repairs and paint the bathrooms. What is John's recognized gain?

a. $–0–
b. $137,000
c. $140,000
d. $290,000

———— 17.   Ray transfers stock to his ex-wife in a divorce settlement. The stock has a basis to Ray of $70,000 and a fair market value of $120,000 on the date of the transfer. From this transaction, Ray should recognize a gain of:

    a. $–0–
    b. $50,000
    c. $70,000
    d. $120,000

_____ 18. In the current year, Ron exchanged an office building, fair market value of $400,000, for cash of $100,000 plus another office building having a fair market value of $300,000. Ron's adjusted basis for the office building given up in the exchange was $230,000. How much gain should Ron recognize on his income tax return?

    a. $–0–
    b. $100,000
    c. $170,000
    d. $330,000

_____ 19. Under IRS Regulations, in order for depreciable tangible property to qualify for like-kind exchange treatment under Section 1031, the property must be:

    a.   in the same general business asset class or the same product class
    b.   held for at least five years prior to the exchange
    c.   similar in service or use
    d.   functionally similar

_____ 20. Part of a taxpayer's land (basis $50,000, FMV $90,000) is condemned to build a new state building. Another part of the land is rendered useless by the condemnation. The taxpayer receives $15,000 in *severance damages* for the condemnation. What is the taxpayer's basis in the land?

    a. $–0–
    b. $35,000
    c. $50,000
    d. $75,000

_____ 21. Naracoorte Corporation sold 2,000 ($10 par value) shares of its treasury stock for $50,000. The stock was acquired five years ago for $30,000. The stock was originally issued for $20 per share. How much is Naracoorte Corporation's recognized gain from this sale of stock?

    a. $–0–
    b. $10,000
    c. $20,000
    d. $30,000

_____ 22. Hom exchanges a rental cottage at the beach with an adjusted basis of $90,000 and a FMV of $80,000 for a rental condominium in the mountains with a FMV of $60,000 plus cash of $20,000. What (if any) is Hom's recognized gain or loss on this like-kind exchange?

    a. $–0–
    b. $10,000
    c.   ($10,000)
    d.   ($20,000)

_____ 23. Joey sells his Ford Motor Company stock for $20,000. His basis in the Ford stock was $14,000. If Joey reinvests (within 60 days) the $20,000 in specialized small business investment company (SSBIC) stock, his taxable gain on the sale would be?

    a. $–0–
    b. $6,000
    c. $4,500
    d. $3,000

_____ 24.   Bob lives in Houston and sells his personal residence on September 1, 20x0 with a realized gain of $200,000 that is excluded under Section 121. He purchased a new (second) residence on September 2, 20x0, for $275,000. Bob's employer transfers him to San Diego, in July 20x1. Bob sells the second Houston residence on July 2, 20x1, and has a realized gain of $60,000. He purchases a third residence in San Diego for $325,000. How much of the Section 121 exclusion is Bob allowed on the sale of the second residence within a two-year period?

     a. $–0–
     b. $25,000
     c. $50,000
     d. $60,000

_____ 25.   Devona sells her personal residence for a realized gain of $450,000. She has owned and lived in the residence for six years. Devona is married to Norval, who has lived in the residence since they were married one year ago. Norval sold his principal residence in order to move in with Devona on the date of their marriage. He used a $150,000 Section 121 exclusion when he sold his residence. How much is Devona's taxable gain on the sale of her principal residence if she files a joint return with Norval?

     a. $–0–
     b. $200,000
     c. $250,000
     d. $450,000

_____ 26.   In the current year, Paula sells her principle residence, which qualifies for the Section 121 exclusion. Her realized gain is $100,000. For the last nine years, she rented a room in the house to a college student. The total MACRS cost recovery Paula claimed on the room rental was $15,000. What is Paula's recognized gain on the sale of her personal residence?

     a. $–0–
     b. $15,000
     c. $85,000
     d. $100,000

SOLUTIONS TO CHAPTER 15 QUESTIONS

True or False

1. F Realty held for investment would qualify for a like-kind exchange. [Like-Kind Property, p. 15–4]

2. F Real estate cannot be exchanged for personal property. [Like-Kind Property, p. 15–4]

3. T The amount of the *recognized* gain is the lesser of the boot received or the realized gain [Boot, p. 15–6]

4. F Section 1031 is not elective. [Like-Kind Exchanges, p. 15–3]

5. T A liability assumed is treated as boot given by the assuming party. [Basis and Holding Period of Property Received, p. 15–7]

6. F The holding period of the newly acquired property begins on the date the original property was acquired. [Basis and Holding Period of Property Received, p. 15–7]

7. T This provision provides relief to the taxpayer who has suffered hardship and does not have the wherewithal to pay the tax on any gain realized from the conversion. [Involuntary Conversions, p. 15–9]

8. F For direct conversions into replacement property, Section 1033 is mandatory. [Direct Conversion, p. 15–13]

9. T Postponement of realized gain is permitted to the extent the taxpayer reinvests the amount realized from the conversion in replacement property. [Involuntary Conversions, p. 15–9]

10. F Section 1033 does not apply to amounts designated as severance damages. [Computing the Amount Realized, p. 15–10]

11. F Owner-investors must conform to the taxpayer use test. [Functional Use Test, p. 15–12]

12. F Taxpayers have until two years after the close of the tax year in which gain was realized. [Time Limitation on Replacement, p. 15–12]

13. T Houseboats, house trailers, and motor homes also can qualify. [Principal Residence, p. 15–20]

14. F Losses are not recognized on the sale of a personal residence. [Sale of a Residence, p. 15–15]

15. F Both real estate commissions and legal fees would be included. [General Provisions, p. 15–17]

16. T Either spouse may meet the at-least-two-years ownership requirement. [Effect on Married Couples, p. 15–18]

17. T The total exclusion is still $500,000. [Effect on Married Couples, p. 15–18]

18. F The taxpayer does not have to live in the residence on the date of sale. [Requirements for Exclusion Treatment, p. 15–15]

19. F There will be a higher (not lower) basis. [Like-Kind Exchanges, p. 15–23]

20. T If the property being disposed of were sold, a loss would be recognized. Under Section 1031, the loss would not be recognized. [Like-Kind Exchanges, p. 15–23]

Multiple Choice

1. b $225,000 + $25,000 + $50,000 − $250,000 = $50,000 [Boot, p. 15–6]

2. b   Lesser of gain realized, $50,000, or boot received, $75,000 [Boot, p. 15–6]

3. a $250,000 + zero + $50,000 − $75,000 = $225,000 [Basis and Holding Period of Property Received, p. 15–7]

4. c   The taxpayer normally has a two-year period after the close of the taxable year in which any gain is realized from the involuntary conversion to replace the property. [Time Limitation on Replacement, p. 15–12]

5. d $250,000 − $100,000 = $150,000 [Computing the Amount Realized, p. 15–10]

6. c $250,000 − $160,000 = $90,000 [Computing the Amount Realized, p. 15–10]

7. a   The is no gain recognized under $250,000 [Sale of a Residence, p. 15–15]

8. b $380,000 − $50,000 − $250,000 = $80,000 [Sale of a Residence, p. 15–15]

9. c   Property held for personal use does not qualify under the like-kind exchange provisions [Like-Kind Exchanges, p. 15–3]

10. c $28,000 − $10,000 = $18,000 LTCG [Basis and Holding Period of Property Received, p. 15–7]

11. a   If a loss occurs on involuntary conversion, Sec 1033 does not modify the normal rules for loss recognition. [Involuntary Conversions, p. 15–9]

12. c   An involuntary conversion results from the destruction (complete or partial), theft, seizure, requisition or condemnation, or the sale or exchange under threat or imminence of requisition or condemnation of the taxpayer's property. [Involuntary Conversion Defined, p. 15–9]

13. c   If conversion is into money and thus indirect, nonrecognition of gain may be elective. [Conversion into Money, p. 15–14]

14. b   Repairs and maintenance to aid in selling the property are treated neither as selling expenses nor as adjustments to the basis. [General Provisions, p. 15–17]

15. d $275,000 (selling price) − $11,000 (selling expenses) − $182,000 (adjusted basis) = $82,000 (gain realized) [General Provisions, p. 15–17]

16. a $290,000 (amount realized, $310,000 − $20,000) − $150,000 (adjusted basis) = $140,000 (realized gain). Since the gain is less than the $250,000 exclusion, there is no recognized gain. [General Provisions, p. 15–17]

17. a   The transfer is nontaxable. [Transfers of Property Between Spouses or Incident to Divorce, p. 15–22]

18. a   Gain is recognized to the extent of boot received. [Boot, p. 15–6]

19. a   This applies to depreciable tangible personal property of a like kind or class. [Like-Kind Property, p. 15–4]

20. b $50,000 − $15,000 = $35,000; [Computing the Amount Realized, p. 15–10]

21. a   See Section 1032. A corporation does not recognize gain or loss when it deals in its own stock. [Exchange of Stock for Property, p. 15–21]

22. a   Although there is a loss, $80,000 − $90,000 = ($10,000); losses are not recognized under Section 1031. [Like-Kind Exchanges, p. 15–3]

23. a   No gain is recognized under Section 1044. [Rollovers into Specialized Small Business Investment Companies, p. 15–22]

24. b $60,000 × (10 months/24 months) = $25,000 exclusion. [Relief Provision, p. 15–19]

25. a $450,000 − $250,000 = $200,000. Because Norval has used the exclusion within the last two years, it is not increased to $500,000 on their joint return. [Effect on Married Couples, p. 15–18]

26. b   The rental portion is not covered by Section 121. [Negative Effect of Renting or Using as a Home Office, p. 15–24]

CHAPTER 16

Property Transactions:
Capital Gains & Losses

CHAPTER HIGHLIGHTS

This chapter discusses the tax treatment of capital assets, including the special reporting requirements applicable to capital gains and losses. Historically, except for the years 1988 through 1990, long-term capital gains have received favorable tax treatment. Even in 1988 through 1990, when long-term capital gains were not granted favorable tax treatment, gains and losses from capital assets were required to be separately reported. The separate reporting of capital gains and losses is also necessary to apply certain limitations applicable to the deduction of capital losses.

KEY TERMS

Capital Assets
Sale or Exchange

Capital Gains

Capital Losses

OUTLINE

I. **GENERAL CONSIDERATIONS**
   A. Capital gain or loss reporting arises from the sale or exchange of a capital asset. Since capital gains and losses are subject to special tax treatment, they must be separated from other gains and losses. The reason for the separate reporting requirement is that taxable income may vary significantly when both ordinary and capital gains and losses are present. For example, after reducing capital losses by capital gains, any remaining capital losses of noncorporate taxpayers may be deducted only to the extent of $3,000 annually.
   B. General Scheme of Taxation. Gains and losses that are recognized must be properly classified. The following three characteristics determine proper classification:
      1) Tax status of the property (capital asset, Section 1231 asset, or ordinary asset)
      2) Manner of the property's disposition (sale, exchange, casualty, theft, or condemnation)
      3) Holding period of the property (short-term or long-term)

II. **CAPITAL ASSETS**
   A. The definition of a capital asset is a definition by exception. Section 1221 defines what is *not* a capital asset. A capital asset is all property held by the taxpayer (whether or not connected with his or her trade or business) other than:
      1) inventory or property held primarily for sale to customers in the ordinary course of business
      2) accounts and notes receivable
      3) depreciable property or real estate used in a business
      4) certain copyrights, literary, musical, or artistic compositions, letters or memoranda
      5) certain U.S. government publications

      The most common capital assets held by an individual are items such as a personal residence, automobile, or investment property (land, stock, bonds, etc.). Since losses on the sale or exchange of personal use property are not recognized, the taxpayer need only be concerned with the capital gain treatment of such property.
   B. Effect of Judicial Action. The courts have held that motive must be determined to distinguish a capital from an ordinary asset. Capital asset determination by the courts hinges on whether the asset is held for investment purposes (capital asset) or business purposes (ordinary asset).
   C. Statutory Expansions. There are several provisions in the Code that expand the definition of capital assets found in Section 1221.

      Dealers in securities must identify which securities are held for investment purposes; otherwise, the securities are presumed to be inventory. To receive capital gain treatment on a sale, securities held for investment must be identified as such on the date of acquisition. Losses are considered capital losses if at any time the securities have been identified as held for investment.

      Under Section 1237, if certain rules are met, real estate investors with limited development activity can avoid dealer status; thereby having any gain treated as capital gain rather than ordinary gain. See text for requirements and limitations.

      Lump-sum distributions of an employee's pension or profit-sharing plan are taxed in the current year. Under certain circumstances part of the gain may be taxed as a capital gain. See Chapter 19.

      Nonbusiness bad debts are always treated as short-term capital losses.

III. **SALE OR EXCHANGE**
   A. The recognition of a capital gain or loss requires a sale or exchange of a capital asset. The term "sale or exchange" is used in the Code, but is not defined. A sale usually involves the receipt of money or the assumption of liabilities for property, and an exchange involves the transfer of property for other property.

B. Worthless securities that are capital assets are deemed to have become worthless on the last day of the taxable year. Under Section 1244, losses on certain corporate stock is an ordinary deduction. See chapter 7 for details.

C. Special Rule—Retirement of Corporate Obligations. As a rule, collection of a debt does not constitute a sale or exchange, so it does not qualify for capital gain treatment for tax purposes. However, under Section 1271, the retirement of corporate and certain governmental obligations are considered to be an exchange and, therefore, usually qualify for capital gain or loss treatment.

D. Original Issue Discount. Bonds that are issued at less than maturity value may have an "original issue discount" (OID). If OID exists, it must generally be amortized over the life of the bond. As the OID is amortized, the basis of the bond to which the OID relates is increased by the amount of the amortization. Once the OID is fully amortized, the bond-holder's basis in the bond will be its face value, thus there will be no gain on the redemption of the bond by the issuer.

E. Options. The sale or exchange of an option to buy or sell property will generally produce a capital gain or loss if the property is (or would be) a capital asset in the hands of the option holder.

If an option holder fails to exercise an option, the lapse is considered a sale or exchange on the option expiration date. If the option is exercised, the amount paid for the option is added to the purchase price of the property. The grantee then has a larger basis and the grantor has a larger gain.

F. Patents. Under Section 1235, inventors are given long-term capital gain treatment on patents. To qualify for this provision, a holder must transfer all substantial rights to a patent. A holder is the creator, inventor, or anyone who purchases the patent rights from the creator, except the creator's employer and certain related parties. To constitute all "substantial rights," the patent rights must not be limited geographically or in duration.

G. Franchises, Trademarks, and Trade Names. Under Section 1253, the transfer of a franchise, trademark, or trade name is not considered a sale or exchange of a capital asset if the transferor retains any significant power, right, or continuing interest concerning the subject matter of the franchise, trademark, or trade name.

1) A noncontingent lump-sum payment is capitalized and amortized by the franchisee. The amortization is subject to Section 1245 recapture.

2) Contingent payments are ordinary income for the franchisor and an ordinary deduction for the franchisee.

This section does not apply to professional sports franchises.

H. Lease Cancellation Payments. Payments received by a lessee for cancellation of a lease are treated as capital gains if the lease is a capital asset. Generally, a lease would be a capital asset if the property is used for personal use and an ordinary asset if the property is used in a trade or business. Payments received by a lessor for lease cancellation are always ordinary income because they are deemed to be in lieu of rental payments.

IV. **HOLDING PERIODS**

A. There are two holding periods for capital gains and losses: short-term and long-term. The short-term is one-year or less and the long-term holding period is more than 12 months.

B. Special Holding Period Rules.

The holding period of property received in a nontaxable exchange includes the holding period of the asset exchanged if such property is a capital or Section 1231 asset.

The holding period of an asset received in a nontaxable transaction (e.g., a gift) where the basis carries over will generally include the holding period of the former owner. The holding period for inherited property is treated as long-term no matter how long the property is actually held. Taxpayers who acquire property in a disallowed loss transaction do not carry over the holding period or the basis.

C. Short Sales.

A short sale is a form of speculation where a taxpayer sells borrowed property (usually stock) and later repays the lender with substantially identical property. See text for operational rules.

V.   CAPITAL GAINS AND LOSSES OF NONCORPORATE TAXPAYERS

    A.   Capital Gain and Loss Netting Process.

Net long-term capital gain can be subject to a 28 percent, 25 percent, or 10 percent/20 percent maximum tax rate. The 28 percent rate applies to gains on collectibles (e.g., stamps and coins). The 25 percent rate applies to deprecation recapture on the disposition of certain Section 1250 assets. The 10 percent/20 percent rate applies to all other net long-term gains.

If the net short-term capital gain exceeds the net long-term capital loss, the amount receives no special tax treatment and is included with other ordinary income.

The ordering procedure for netting capital gains and losses is as follows.

1)   Group all gains and losses into short-term, 28 percent, 25 percent, 10 percent/20 percent, and long-term.

2)   Net the gains and losses within each group.

3)   Offset the net 28 percent and net 25 percent amounts if they are of opposite sign.

4)   Offset the result in step 3 against the 10 percent/20 percent amount is they are of the opposite sign. If the 20 percent/10 percent amount is a loss, offset it against the highest taxed gain first. After this step, the net amount is a net long-term capital gain or loss

5)   Offset the net short-term amount against the results of step 4 if they are of opposite sign. The netting rules offset net short-term capital loss against the highest taxed gain first. Consequently, if there is net short-term capital loss and a net gain from step 4, the short-term capital loss offsets first the 28 percent gain, then the 25 percent gain, and finally the 10 percent/20 percent gain components resulting from step 4.

    B.   Alternative Tax on Net Capital Gain. The alternative net capital gains tax is applied in layers. Each portion and type of the net long-term capital gain is taxed at various rates. The layers are taxed in the following order: 25 percent gain, 28 percent gain, 10 percent gain, and then 20 percent gain.

    C.   Capital Losses. For individual taxpayers, net capital losses are deductible from gross income to the extent of $3,000 per tax year. Excess losses carry forward indefinitely.

VI.   CAPITAL GAINS AND LOSSES OF CORPORATE TAXPAYERS

The treatment of capital gains and losses for corporations differs from that of individuals in the following areas.

    A.   An alternative tax rate of 35 percent is allowed in computing the tax on capital gains. Since the maximum corporate rate is 35 percent for ordinary income, there is nothing to be gained from the alternative capital gain tax rate.

    B.   Capital losses offset capital gains only. Capital losses may not be deducted against ordinary income.

    C.   There is a five-year carryover and a three-year carryback period for net capital losses. Corporate carryovers and carrybacks are always short-term, regardless of whether they start out as long-term or short-term capital losses.

TEST FOR SELF-EVALUATION—CHAPTER 16

True or False

Indicate which of the following statements is true or false by circling the correct answer.

T   F   1. Inventory or stock used in a trade or business is not a capital asset as defined in Section 1221.

T   F   2. A depreciable building used in a taxpayer's trade or business is not a capital asset.

T   F   3. Accounts and notes receivable acquired in the ordinary course of a trade or business or from the sale of inventory are not capital assets.

T   F   4. The taxpayer's use of property is important in determining whether the property is an ordinary or capital asset.

T   F   5. Dealers in securities will always have ordinary gains and losses on the sale of securities.

T   F   6. Under Section 1237, investors in real estate who engage in limited development activities may be allowed capital gain treatment.

T   F   7. Taxable lump-sum distributions from qualified pension and profit-sharing plans are generally ordinary income (subject to certain transition rules).

T   F   8. Nonbusiness bad debts are treated as long-term capital losses.

T   F   9. The term "sale or exchange" is defined in the Internal Revenue Code.

T   F   10. Losses on worthless securities that are capital assets are treated as arising from the sale or exchange of a capital asset on the last day of the taxable year.

T   F   11. The retirement of a corporate bond is considered an exchange and, therefore, is usually subject to capital gain or loss treatment.

T   F   12. If an option lapses, it is considered a sale or exchange on the last day of the taxable year.

T   F   13. If an option is exercised, the amount paid for the option is added to the basis of the property subject to the option.

T   F   14. The holder of a patent is entitled to long-term capital gain treatment if he or she transfers all substantial rights to the patent.

T   F   15. The sale of a franchise always generates long-term capital gain under Section 1253.

T   F   16. Lease cancellation payments received by a lessee are capital gains if the lease is a capital asset.

T   F   17. Lease cancellation payments received by a lessor are always long-term capital gains.

T   F   18. Unused capital losses of noncorporate taxpayers can be carried forward indefinitely.

T   F   19. Capital losses for corporate taxpayers are deductible against ordinary income, subject to the annual limitation.

T   F   20. An individual taxpayer's maximum deduction against ordinary income for a capital loss is $3,000.

T   F   21. A truck used in a taxpayer's trade or business is a capital asset.

T   F   22. The long-term holding period is more than 12 months.

T   F   23.   Generally, the holding period of property "sold short" is determined by the length of time the seller held the property used to close the short sale.

T   F   24.   Corporate capital losses carry back three years and forward five years and all carryovers are treated as short-term, despite the original nature of the loss.

T   F   25.   Contingent franchise payments are ordinary income to the franchisor and an ordinary deduction to the franchisee.

T   F   26.   A mode of operation, a widely recognized brand name, and a widely known business symbol are commonly called patents.

T   F   27.   A noncontingent franchise fee is capitalized and amortized over 15 years (subject to Section 1245 recapture if sold) by a franchisee.

T   F   28.   The alternative net capital gains tax is applied in layers. The layers are taxed in the following order: 28 percent gain, 25 percent gain, 20 percent gain, and then 10 percent gain.

Multiple Choice

Choose the best answer for each of the following questions.

_____ 1.   In 2002, Tom incurs a short-term capital loss of $5,000. Tom's gross income for 2002 (not including the loss) is $20,000. If Tom is single, his adjusted gross income for 2002 is:

    a. $20,000
    b. $19,000
    c. $18,000
    d. $17,000

_____ 2.   Assuming the same situation as in Question 1, what is Tom's short-term capital loss carryover to 2003?

    a. $1,000
    b. $2,000
    c. $3,000
    d. $4,000

_____ 3.   Tasty Taco sells franchises to independent operators. In 2001 it sold a franchise with an 8-year life to Wilson for $70,000 plus 3 percent of sales. Tasty Taco retains significant rights to control management. If Wilson's 2001 sales amounted to $100,000, Tasty Taco would include in its computation of Year 1 taxable income:

    a.   Long-term capital gain of $73,000
    b.   Long-term capital gain of $70,000, ordinary income of $3,000
    c.   Ordinary income of $73,000
    d.   Ordinary income of $70,000, long-term capital gain of $3,000

_____ 4.   Which of the following is a capital asset?

    a.   Inventory
    b.   Texaco stock owned by an investor
    c.   Accounts receivable
    d.   Land used in a trade or business

_____ 5.   Teri owns a tract of land and subdivides it for sale. She sells five lots for $10,000 each with a basis of $6,000 in each lot. Her total selling expenses are $2,000 and she meets the requirements of Section 1237. Teri should report:

     a.   Capital gain of $18,000
     b.   Capital gain of $500, ordinary income of $17,500
     c.   Capital gain of $17,500, ordinary income of $500
     d.   Ordinary income of $18,000

_____ 6.   Tim invents a machine that he patents. The patent is assigned to a manufacturer for $100,000, plus a $5 per machine royalty. In the same year, 1,000 machines are sold. Assuming Tim transferred all substantial rights and has a zero basis in the patent, he should report:

     a.   Long-term capital gain of $105,000
     b.   Long-term capital gain of $100,000, ordinary income of $5,000
     c.   Long-term capital gain of $5,000, ordinary income of $100,000
     d.   Ordinary income of $105,000

_____ 7.   To receive long-term capital gain treatment an asset acquired must be held a minimum of:

     a.   Two years or more
     b.   Nine months or more
     c.   More than twelve months
     d.   More than six months

_____ 8.   During 20x1, Todd has net long-term capital gains of $12,000 and a net short-term capital loss carryover of $8,000. On his 20x1 tax return, Todd should report:

     a. $12,000 net capital gain
     b. $9,000 net capital gain
     c. $8,000 net capital gain
     d. $4,000 net capital gain

_____ 9.   Ted, an individual, sells his personal automobile for $2,000. He purchased the automobile six years ago for $14,000. In addition, Ted has a $7,000 long-term capital gain from the sale of stock that he held as an investment. What amount should Ted report on his individual income tax return related to these transactions?

     a. $7,000 net capital gain
     b. $4,000 net capital gain
     c. $3,000 net capital loss
     d. $5,000 net capital loss

_____ 10.   Sue purchased stock on November 30, year 1 for $5,000. Due to a series of unfortunate events, Sue is notified on July 1, year 2 that the stock is totally worthless. Assuming Sue has no other capital transactions, what amount of loss should Sue report on her tax return for year 2?

     a. $5,000 long-term capital loss
     b. $5,000 short-term capital loss
     c. $3,000 long-term capital loss
     d. $3,000 short-term capital loss

_____ 11.   Earl has net long-term capital gains of $20,000 and net short-term capital losses of $8,000. What is Earl's "net long-term capital gain?"

     a. $20,000
     b. $17,000
     c. $12,000
     d. $8,000

_____ 12. In December, Tony receives a lump-sum distribution of $52,000 from a qualified pension plan. Tony contributed $12,000 to the plan and the employer contributed the rest. If Tony was a participant in the plan for a total of eight years, he should report:

   a.   Long-term capital gain of $24,000, ordinary income of $16,000
   b.   Long-term capital gain of $10,000, ordinary income of $30,000
   c.   Long-term capital gain of $40,000
   d.   Ordinary income of $40,000

_____ 13. Blue Corporation issues bonds at 95 percent of the face amount. The bonds are due in ten years. Which of the following is true?

   a.   The bonds are not issued with original issue discount
   b.   The bonds are issued with original issue discount
   c.   These bonds are capital assets to T Corporation
   d.   The bond-holders can only be individuals

_____ 14. Max buys an option on vacant land. He pays $4,000 for a three-year option to purchase land for $100,000. After six months Max sells the option for $9,000. From this transaction, Max would recognize:

   a.   Long-term capital gain of $5,000
   b.   Short-term capital gain of $5,000
   c.   Short-term capital gain of $9,000
   d.   Short-term capital gain of $109,000

_____ 15. Same as number 14, except Max fails to exercise the option after the three-year period. What is Max's recognized gain or loss?

   a.   Long-term capital gain of $4,000
   b.   Short-term capital gain of $4,000
   c.   Long-term capital loss of $4,000
   d.   Short-term capital loss of $4,000

_____ 16. Yolonda had the following items of income, gains, losses, and deductions: $30,000 salary, ($2,500) nonbusiness bad debt, $5,000 gain on stock held eight months, ($2,000) loss on stock held three years, and $12,000 home mortgage interest. What is Yolonda's AGI for the year?

   a. $30,500
   b. $32,500
   c. $33,000
   d. $37,500

_____ 17. Rose Corporation has ordinary income from operations of $60,000, net long-term capital gain of $20,000, and net short-term capital loss of $30,000. What is Rose Corporation's taxable income?

   a. $50,000
   b. $60,000
   c. $80,000
   d. $90,000

_____ 18. Quincy, a cash basis individual taxpayer, executed a sale of stock on December 29, Year 0. The sale was settled on January 4, Year 1. The stock has a basis to Quincy of $20,000 and was acquired five years ago. The stock was sold for $25,000. What is Quincy's tax result from the sale?

   a.   Long-term capital gain of $5,000 in Year 1
   b.   Short-term capital gain of $5,000 in Year 1
   c.   Long-term capital gain of $5,000 in Year 0
   d.   Short-term capital gain of $5,000 in Year 0

_____ 19.   When a taxpayer has a short sale of a capital asset it may be treated as:

    a.   Ordinary income or short-term capital gain
    b.   Capital gain or short-term capital gain
    c.   Short-term capital gain or ordinary income
    d.   Short-term capital gain only

_____ 20.   Corporations may carry unused capital losses to what other tax years?

    a.   Forward indefinitely
    b.   Back three and forward fifteen years
    c.   Back three and forward five years
    d.   Back three and forward seven years

_____ 21.   Mac buys an expensive painting, "St. Monroe," for $20,000. The painting is used to decorate Mac's office and is of *investment quality*. The painting is seven-year class property (14.29 percent in the first year). How does Mac treat the painting for tax purposes?

    a. $20,000 is deducted in the first year.
    b. $2,858 is deducted in the first year.
    c.   The cost of the painting cannot be deducted.
    d.   The Section 179 election applies to the painting.

_____ 22.   Nick, a single taxpayer, has taxable income of $75,000 including net long-term capital gain of $40,000. Assume the regular tax calculation on $35,000 is $6,200. What is Nick's total tax using the alternative tax on net long-term capital gains calculation?

    a. $14,200
    b. $6,200
    c. $15,000
    d. $8,000

_____ 23.   In the current year, Floyd had the following capital transactions: long-term gain $6,000, short-term gain $10,000, long-term loss ($8,000), and short-term loss ($13,000). Before the above capital transactions, Floyd had taxable income of $15,000. Calculate Floyd's current year taxable income or loss after the capital transactions and the capital loss carryover to the next tax year.

    a. $12,000, $2,000 long-term carryover
    b. $10,000, $–0– carryover
    c. $15,000, $5,000 long-term carryover
    d. $15,000, $2,000 long-term carryover and $3,000 short-term carryover

_____ 24.   Helen had the following capital transaction during Year 1: long-term gain $17,000, long-term loss ($7,000), short-term gain $24,000, and short-term loss ($7,000). What is Helen's net long-term and net short-term capital gain for Year 1?

    a. $10,000 Long-term gain; $17,000 Short-term gain
    b. $17,000 Long-term gain; $24,000 Short-term gain
    c. $24,000 Long-term gain; $31,000 Short-term gain
    d. $10,000 Long-term gain; $24,000 Short-term gain

_____ 25.   Bluegill Corporation has $18,400 of long-term capital loss for Year 1 and $20,000 of other taxable income. What is Bluegill's taxable income for Year 1?

    a. $–0–
    b. $1,600
    c. $17,000
    d. $20,000

_____ 26.   Same as question 25. What is Bluegill's capital loss carryover (if any)?

    a. $–0–
    b. $15,400 Short-term
    c. $15,400 Long-term
    d. $18,400 Short-term

_____ 27.   Tim is in the 31 percent regular tax bracket. He has a $10,000 gain on a coin collection that he has owned for 10 years. What is the alternative net long-term capital gains tax on the gain on the coin collection?

    a. $3,100
    b. $2,800
    c. $2,500
    d. $2,000

_____ 28.   Linda had the following capital transaction during 2002: 10 percent/20 percent gain $5,000, 28 percent loss ($8,000), and short-term gain $12,000. What is the nature and amount of Linda's net capital gains or losses for 2002?

    a. $9,000 short-term gain
    b. $12,000 short-term gain; $3,000 10 percent/20 percent loss
    c. $4,000 short-term gain; $5,000 110 percent/20 percent gain
    d. $17,000 short-term gain; $8,000 28 percent loss

_____ 29.   Cindy had the following capital transaction during 2002: 10 percent/20 percent loss ($6,000), 25 percent gain $5,000, 28 percent gain $10,000, and short-term loss ($3,000). What is the nature and amount of Cindy's net capital gains or losses for 2002?

    a. $3,000 short-term loss; $9,000 28 percent gain
    b. $12,000 25 percent gain; $6,000 10 percent/20 percent loss
    c. $1,000 28 percent gain; $5,000 25 percent gain
    d. $3,000 short-term loss; $5,000 25 percent gain; $4,000 28 percent gain

_____ 30.   Joyce had the following capital transaction during 2002: 10 percent/20 percent loss ($11,000 0, 25 percent gain $5,000 28 percent gain $10,000, and short-term loss ($3,000). What is the nature and amount of Joyce's net capital gains or losses for 2002?

    a. $3,000 short-term loss; $4,000 28 percent gain
    b. $1,000 25 percent gain
    c. $1,000 28 percent gain
    d. $3,000 short-term loss; $1,000 28 percent loss; $5,000 25 percent gain

Problem

1. Pat had the following stock transactions:

Description	Acquired	Sold	Sales Price	Basis
100 shs Blue, Inc.	8/01/01	11/05/02	$6,000	$2,500
100 shs Red, Inc.	6/11/02	10/03/02	$4,000	$4,500
100 shs Green, Inc.	3/12/02	08/22/02	$6,000	$5,200
100 shs Brown, Inc.	5/12/94	09/15/02	$8,000	$5,000
100 shs Yellow, Inc.	9/15/91	12/01/02	$6,000	$7,000

Calculate the following amounts to arrive at Pat's net amount included in or deducted from gross income for 2002.

Net short–term capital gain or loss   _____

Net long-term capital gain or loss   _____

SOLUTIONS TO CHAPTER 16 QUESTIONS

True or False

1. T   Inventory or stock used in a trade or business is specifically excluded from the definition of a capital asset. [Definition of a Capital Asset, p. 16–4]

2. T   Depreciable property or real estate used in a business is one of the items specifically excluded. [Definition of a Capital Asset, p. 16–4]

3. T   Excluding accounts and notes receivable prevents short-term assets from being given long-term treatment. [Definition of a Capital Asset, p. 16–4]

4. T   Capital asset determination often depends on whether the asset is held for investment purposes (capital asset) or business purposes (ordinary asset). [Effect of Judicial Action, p. 16–6]

5. F   Dealers may designate securities as held for investment. [Dealers in Securities, p. 16–7]

6. T   To receive capital gain treatment, however, the investor must meet specific requirements. [Real Property Subdivided for Sale, p. 16–7]

7. T   TRA of 1986 repealed a provision that allowed a portion of a lump-sum distribution to be treated as a capital gain, with certain transition rules. [Lump-Sum Distributions, p. 16–8]

8. F   Nonbusiness bad debts are treated as short-term capital losses. [Nonbusiness Bad Debts, p. 16–8]

9. F   The term is not defined in the Code. [Sale or Exchange, p. 16–9]

10. T   This last-day rule may have the effect of converting what otherwise would have been a short-term capital loss into a long-term capital loss. [Worthless Securities and Sec 1244 Stock, p. 16–9]

11. T   The transaction is treated as a sale or exchange. [Special Rule—Retirement of Corporate Obligations, p. 16–10]

12. F   It is a sale or exchange on the day it lapses. [Failure to Exercise Options, p. 16–11]

13. T   This increases the gain (or reduces the loss) to the grantor. [Exercise of Options by Grantee, p. 16–11]

14. T   The transferor/holder may receive payment in virtually any form. [Patents, p. 16–12]

15. F   Franchises usually produce ordinary income on their sale. [Franchises, Trademarks, and Trade Names, p. 16–13]

16. T   Lease cancellation payments received by a lessee are treated as an exchange. [Lease Cancellation Payments, p. 16–15]

17. F   Lease cancellation payments received by a lessor are ordinary income. [Lessor Treatment, p. 16–16]

18. T   Both short-term and long-term capital losses of noncorporate taxpayers may be carried forward indefinitely. [Carryovers, p. 16–28]

19. F   Corporations are not permitted to deduct capital losses against ordinary income. [Tax Treatment of Capital Gains and Losses of Corporate Taxpayers, p. 16–30]

20. T   Capital losses exceeding the loss deduction limits carry forward indefinitely. [Treatment of Net Capital Loss, p. 16–27]

21. F   Depreciable assets used in a trade or business are excluded from the definition of a capital asset. [Definition of a Capital Asset, p. 16–4]

22. T   The short-term holding period is one year or less. [Holding Periods for Capital Gain and Loss Netting Purposes, p. 16–21]

23. T There is an exception to this general rule if substantially identical property is held by the taxpayer. [General, p. 16–18]

24. T Corporate carryovers and carrybacks are always treated as short term, regardless of their original nature. [Tax Treatment of Capital Gains and Losses of Corporate Taxpayers, p. 16–30]

25. T It makes no difference whether the transferor retains a significant power, right, or continuing interest. [Contingent Payments, p. 16–14]

26. F They are called franchises. [Franchises, Trademarks, and Trade Names, p. 16–13]

27. T The amortization is subject to recapture under § 1245. [Noncontingent Payments, p. 16–14]

28. F The layers are taxed in the following order: 25 percent gain, 28 percent gain, 10 percent gain, and then 20 percent gain. [Alternative Tax on Net Capital Gain, p. 16–25]

Multiple Choice

1. d $20,000 – $3,000 (maximum) = $17,000 [Treatment of Net Capital Loss, p. 16–27]

2. b $5,000 – $3,000 = $2,000. [Treatment of Net Capital Loss, p. 16–27]

3. c $70,000 + 3% of (100,000) = $73,000 ordinary income [Contingent Payments, p. 16–14]

4. b Investment assets and personal use assets are the most common capital assets owned by individual taxpayers. [Definition of a Capital Asset, p. 16–4]

5. a 5 × $10,000 = $50,000 – $2,000 – (5 × $6,000) = $18,000 [Real Property Subdivided for Sale, p. 16–7]

6. a $100,000 + ($5 × 1,000 machines) = $105,000 [Patents, p. 16–12]

7. c If it is held one year or less, it is short-term [Holding Periods for Capital Gain and Loss Netting Purposes, p. 16–21]

8. d Taxpayers are allowed to carry over unused capital losses. [Carryovers, p. 16–28]

9. a The loss on the sale of the personal automobile is not deductible. [Definition of a Capital Asset, p. 16–4]

10. c If the security is a capital asset, the loss is deemed to have occurred as the result of a sale or exchange on the last day of the tax year. [Worthless Securities and Section 1244 Stock, pp. 16–9, 26]

11. c $20,000 – $8,000 = $12,000 [Holding Periods for Capital Gain and Loss Netting Purposes, p. 16–21]

12. d $52,000 – $12,000 = $40,000 ordinary income [Lump-Sum Distributions, p. 16–8]

13. b .25% × 10 Years = 2.5%, the maximum discount is exceeded. [Original Issue Discount, p. 16–10]

14. b $9,000 – $4,000 = $5,000 Short-term capital gain. [Sale of an Option, p. 16–11]

15. c The lapse of the option is considered a sale or exchange on the option expiration date. [Failure to Exercise Options, p. 16–11]

16. a $30,000 salary + $500 net capital gain ($5,000 – $2,500 – $2,000) = $30,500 Adjusted gross income [Holding Periods for Capital Gain and Loss Netting Purposes, p. 16–21]

17. b Net Short-term capital loss are not allowed for corporations. [Tax Treatment of Capital Gains and Losses of Corporate Taxpayers, p. 16–30]

18. c The date of sale is the date of execution. [Stock Sales, p. 16–35]

19. b Treatment depends on the holding period of the asset used to close the short sale. [General, p. 16–18]

20.   c   Corporate capital loss carryovers are five years and carrybacks are three years. [Tax Treatment of Capital Gains and Losses of Corporate Taxpayers, p. 16–30]

21.   c   Being of investment quality does not make the painting an investment asset nor make it depreciable. [Definition of a Capital Asset, p. 16–4]

22.   a $6,200 + $8,000 [20% of $40,000] = $14,200 [Holding Periods for Capital Gain and Loss Netting Purposes, p. 16–21]

23.   a $15,000 − $3,000 ST loss = $12,000 TI. In offsetting taxable income, the net short-term loss always goes first, then any net long-term loss. Since the net short-term capital loss is $3,000 (the maximum annual limit) all the long-term capital loss carries over. [Holding Periods for Capital Gain and Loss Netting Purposes, p. 16–21]

24.   a   Long-term capital gain: $17,000 − $7,000 = $10,000; Short-term capital gain: $24,000 − $7,000 = $17,000 [Holding Periods for Capital Gain and Loss Netting Purposes, p. 16–21]

25.   d   Corporation's cannot use capital losses against other income. [Tax Treatments of Capital Gains and Losses of Corporate Taxpayers, p. 16–30]

26.   d   All corporate capital loss carryovers are short-term. [Tax Treatments of Capital Gains and Losses of Corporate Taxpayers, p. 16–30]

27.   b   Collectibles are always taxed at a 28% rate. Collectibles are always taxed at a 28% rate. [Definition of Collectibles, p. 16–24]

28.   a   a)   Offset $5,000 of the 28% loss against the 10%/20% gain, reducing it to zero.
            b)   Offset the remaining $3,000 of the 28% loss against the $3,000 short-term gain, reducing it to $9,000. [Holding Periods for Capital Gain and Loss Netting Purposes, p. 16–21]

29.   c   a)   Offset the $6,000 10%/20% loss against the $10,000 28% gain, reducing it to $4,000.
            b)   Offset the $3,000 short-term loss against the $4,000 28% gain, reducing it to $1,000.
            c)   Since the 28% gain absorbed the short-term loss there is no offset against the 25% gain. [Holding Periods for Capital Gain and Loss Netting Purposes, p. 16–21]

30.   b   a)   Offset the $11,000 10%/20% loss against the $10,000 28% gain, reducing it to zero.
            b)   Offset the remaining $1,000 of 10%/20% loss against the $5,000 25% gain, reducing it to $4,000.
            c)   Then offset the $3,000 short-term loss against the $4,000 25% gain, reducing it to $1,000. [Holding Periods for Capital Gain and Loss Netting Purposes, p. 16–21]

Problem

1.   Net short-term capital gain:

Green, Inc.	$800
Red, Inc.	−$500
	$300

Net long-term capital gain:

Blue, Inc.	$3,500
Brown, Inc.	$3,000
Yellow, Inc.	−$1,000
	$5,600

[Holding Periods for Capital Gain and Loss Netting Purposes, p. 16–21]

CHAPTER 17

Property Transactions: Section 1231 and Recapture Provisions

CHAPTER HIGHLIGHTS

This chapter summarizes Code Section 1231 that grants favorable long-term capital gain treatment on the sale or exchange of business properties or involuntary conversions. Also discussed are the recapture provisions that provide that certain gains, which would otherwise qualify for capital gain treatment, are to be treated as ordinary income. These provisions are Sections 1245 and 1250 of the Code. Any amounts converted to ordinary income under these provisions are generally referred to as Section 1245 and Section 1250 recapture.

KEY TERMS

Section 1231 Asset
Section 1245 Recapture

Section 1250 Recapture
Holding Period

Casualty Gains

OUTLINE

I. **SECTION 1231 ASSETS**
    A. Relationship to Capital Assets. Section 1231 assets are not capital assets because they are excluded under Section 1221(2). The concept of Section 1231 assets was enacted by Congress in 1942 to ease the burden of taxation on the sale of business assets and to help the war effort.

        Section 1231 provides that a net gain on Section 1231 property is treated as a long-term capital gain, and a net loss is treated as an ordinary loss.
    B. Property Included. What is included in the definition of Section 1231 property is:
        1) Depreciable or real property used in a business or for the production of income
        2) Timber, coal, or domestic iron ore to which Section 631 applies
        3) Livestock held for draft, breeding, dairy, or sporting purposes
        4) Unharvested crops on land used in a business
        5) Certain purchased intangible assets that are eligible for amortization (e.g., patents and goodwill).

        Note that depreciable property or real estate used in a *trade* or *business* qualifies as Section 1231 property.
    C. Property Excluded. The property shown below is not Section 1231 property:
        1) Property held less than the long-term holding period (the long-term holding period is greater than one year)
        2) Property where casualty losses exceed casualty gains for the taxable year
        3) Inventory and property held primarily for sale to customers
        4) Copyrights; literary, musical, or artistic compositions; certain U.S. government publications
        5) Intangible assets such as accounts and notes receivable
    D. Special Rules for Certain Section 1231 Assets. The difference between the basis of timber and the fair market value on the first day of the year during which the timber is cut may be treated as Section 1231 gain, provided the timber is held for sale or use in a business and has been held for the required long-term holding period.

        Special holding period rules apply to the classification of gains and losses on livestock as Section 1231 gain or loss. Cattle and horses must be held for at least 24 months while other livestock must be held for at least 12 months. Poultry is excluded from Section 1231 treatment.

        Certain business and investment properties may be subject to Section 1231 treatment if the gain or loss is the result of a casualty or theft.
    E. General Procedure for Section 1231 Computation. The general procedure for calculating Section 1231 gains and losses is as follows:

        Step 1   Net all long-term casualty gains and losses from nonpersonal use property.
        1) If the casualty gains exceed the casualty losses, combine the excess with other Section 1231 gains.
        2) If the casualty losses exceed casualty gains, exclude all losses and gains from further Section 1231 computations. All casualty gains are then considered ordinary income and casualty losses are deductible for AGI if business related and from AGI (subject to the 2 percent of adjusted gross income limitation). If not, go to Step 2.

        Step 2   Net all Section 1231 gains (including any net casualty gains) and losses.
        1) If the gains exceed the losses, net Section 1231 gains are offset by nonrecaptured Section 1231 losses for the previous five years; the excess is treated as long-term capital gain. Any offset amount is ordinary income.
        2) If the losses exceed the gains, all gains are ordinary income and business losses are fully deductible. Other casualty losses (arising from income-producing property) are deductions from adjusted gross income.

II.   **SECTION 1245 RECAPTURE**

Congress enacted Section 1245 to prevent taxpayers from receiving the dual benefits of depreciation deductions that offset ordinary income and Section 1231 long-term capital gain treatment when the property is sold. Under Section 1245, gain on the disposition is treated as ordinary income to the extent of depreciation taken. Any excess gain is either Section 1231 gain or casualty gain if the property was disposed of in a casualty event. Section 1245 does not apply where the taxpayer has a realized loss on the disposition of an asset.

A.   Section 1245 Property. Section 1245 property includes all depreciable personal property, including livestock. Nonresidential buildings acquired after 1980 and before 1987 are subject to Section 1245 if accelerated cost recovery (ACRS) is used. The following special property is subject to Section 1245 treatment:

1)   Amortizable personal property such as patents, copyrights, leaseholds, and professional sports contracts;

2)   Amortization of reforestation expenditures and costs to remove handicap barriers;

3)   Amounts expensed under Section 179;

4)   Elevators and escalators acquired before January 1, 1987;

5)   Certain depreciable tangible real property;

6)   Amortization taken on pollution control facilities, railroad grading and tunnel boring equipment, on-the-job training, and child-care facilities;

7)   Agricultural and horticultural structures and petroleum storage facilities; and

8)   Nonresidential realty placed in service after 1980 and before 1987 (15-year, 18-year, or 19-year property) on which ACRS was taken.

B.   Observations on Section 1245.

1)   In most cases the gain on Section 1245 property results in ordinary income.

2)   Recapture applies no matter what method of depreciation is used.

3)   Recapture applies no matter what the holding periods is.

4)   Section 1245 does not apply to losses.

5)   Section 1245 gains may also be passive activity gains.

III. **SECTION 1250 RECAPTURE**

Section 1250 property includes depreciable real property that is not subject to Section 1245. Section 1250 is similar to Section 1245, but under Section 1250 only "additional depreciation" is subject to recapture. This additional amount is the accelerated depreciation taken in excess of straight-line depreciation that would have been allowed. Unless property is disposed of during the first year, Section 1250 does not apply to real property placed in service after 1986 because the straight-line method of depreciation is required.

A.   Computing Recapture on Nonresidential Real Property. For Section 1250 property, other than residential rental property, the following general rules apply:

1)   Post-1969 amount recaptured is depreciation taken in excess of straight-line after 1969.

2)   If property is held one year or less, all depreciation taken is recaptured.

B.   Computing Recapture on Residential Rental Housing. Recapture on residential rental housing is computed in the same manner as other Section 1250 property except that only additional depreciation attributable to periods after 1975 is recaptured in full. Depreciation prior to 1976 and after 1969 may be partially recaptured depending on the taxpayer's holding period.

C.   Section 1250 Recapture Situations. The Section 1250 recapture rules apply to the following property if accelerated depreciation was used:

1)   Residential rental real estate acquired before 1987.

2)   Nonresidential real estate acquired before 1981.

3)   Real property used outside the U.S.

4)   Certain government-financed or low-income housing.

D.   Unrecaptured Section 1250 Gain (25 Percent Real Estate Gain).

Certain gain on real estate is eligible for the 25 percent tax rate on unrecaptured Section 1250 gain. Unrecaptured gain is all or some of the Section 1231 gain that is taxed as long-term capital gain and related to the sale of depreciable real estate.

The maximum amount of 25 percent gain is the deprecation taken on real property sold at a gain. This gain is limited in several ways such as when the gain is less than the depreciation taken. See text for all the 25 percent gain limitations.

IV.   **CONSIDERATIONS COMMON TO SECTION 1245 AND SECTION 1250**
      A.   Exceptions. Recapture under Section 1245 and Section 1250 does not apply in the following situations:
          1)   For a gift of property, the recapture potential carries over to the donee.
          2)   If property is transferred by death the recapture does not carry to the heir.
          3)   For a charitable transfer, the recapture potential reduces the amount of the charitable deduction under Section 170.
          4)   For tax-free transactions in which the adjusted basis of the property carries over to the transferee, recapture potential also carries over. Section 351 tax-free incorporations fall into this category.
          5)   Gains recognized under the like-kind exchange or involuntary conversion provisions are subject to recapture as ordinary income under Sections 1245 and 1250.
      B.   Other Applications. Special rules apply in the following situations:
          1)   For installment sales, recapture gain is recognized in full in the year of sale. Furthermore, all gain is ordinary income until recapture potential is fully absorbed.
          2)   For a distribution of property subject to recapture, gain must be recognized by the distributing corporation to the extent of the recapture.

V.   **SPECIAL RECAPTURE PROVISIONS**
      A.   Special Recapture for Corporations. Corporations selling depreciable realty will be subject to an "ordinary gain adjustment."
      B.   Gain from Sale of Depreciable Property between Certain Related Parties. In a sale or exchange of depreciable property between an individual and a controlled corporation or partnership or between certain other related parties, any gain recognized is ordinary income. In this case, depreciable means subject to depreciation in the hands of the transferee. Recapture under Sections 1245 and 1250 is applied before recapture under the related party provisions.
      C.   Intangible Drilling Costs. Intangible drilling and development costs are recaptured on the sale or disposition of such property, if such costs were expensed instead of capitalized.

VI.   **REPORTING PROCEDURES**

Form 4797 is used to report noncapital gains and losses, including Section 1231 gains and losses, and Sections 1245 and 1250 gains. Form 4684, which is used for reporting casualties and thefts, should be completed first since a resulting net gain will impact the computation of Section 1231 gains and losses.

TEST FOR SELF-EVALUATION—CHAPTER 17

True or False

Indicate which of the following statements is true or false by circling the correct answer.

T   F   1. Section 1231 assets are the same as capital assets under Section 1221.

T   F   2. A contract to cut timber owned more than one year is a Section 1231 asset.

T   F   3. The primary tax advantage of a Section 1231 asset is that gains are ordinary income and losses are capital losses.

T   F   4. All livestock must be held for at least 24 months to qualify as a Section 1231 asset.

T   F   5. Inventory is not a Section 1231 asset.

T   F   6. Net gains from other than personal use property disposed of by casualty or theft are Section 1231 gains.

T   F   7. Section 1245 applies to depreciable personalty and requires that all depreciation be recaptured if the gain realized exceeds the potential recapture amount.

T   F   8. Depreciation on elevators and escalators acquired before 1987 is recaptured under Section 1245.

T   F   9. Professional baseball and football players' contracts are not Section 1245 property.

T   F   10. All depreciation on pre-1987 residential Section 1250 property is recaptured to the extent of gain on disposition.

T   F   11. Any net gain from the disposal of Section 1245 property that is not recaptured is either Section 1231 gain or casualty gain.

T   F   12. For gifts of property subject to depreciation recapture, the donor must recapture the depreciation, not the donee.

T   F   13. For a charitable transfer, the recapture potential reduces the amount of the charitable contribution deduction under Section 170.

T   F   14. Generally, if the adjusted basis in a transaction carries over to the transferee, the recapture potential also carries over.

T   F   15. In an installment sale, capital gain treatment applies first, then recapture under Section 1245 or Section 1250.

T   F   16. Intangible drilling costs that are expensed are recaptured to the extent of the lesser of the gain realized or the IDC expensed.

T   F   17. The net Section 1231 gain is offset by nonrecaptured Section 1231 losses from the previous six years.

T   F   18. All depreciation on post-1986 nonresidential rental property is recaptured.

T   F   19. A gift transaction triggers recapture under Section 1245, but not under Section 1250.

T   F   20. Chickens that are held for 12 months are Section 1231 assets.

T   F   21. For real property acquired after 1986, there usually will be no Section 1250 recapture because depreciation is limited to straight-line.

T	F	22.	Section 1245 recapture is often referred to as partial recapture, while Section 1250 recapture is referred to as full recapture.
T	F	23.	For Section 1245 recapture, it does not matter which method of depreciation is used.
T	F	24.	The Section 1245 recapture rules apply before there is any casualty gain.
T	F	25.	A taxpayer may elect to treat the cutting of timber held for sale or use in business as a sale or exchange under Section 631.
T	F	26.	The maximum tax rate on unrecaptured Section 1250 gain on real estate held over 18 months is 25 percent.

Multiple Choice

Choose the best answer for each of the following questions.

_____ 1.   On December 31 of the current year, Roberto owned the following assets:

A delivery truck used in his business	$ 20,000
A rental house	$110,000
Texaco stock	$ 25,000
Inventory used in his business	$150,000
Accounts receivable	$ 10,000
Racehorses	$ 50,000

What is the amount of Roberto's Section 1231 assets?

a. $180,000
b. $205,000
c. $130,000
d. $45,000

_____ 2.   On December 31 of the current year, Roberto owned the following assets:

A delivery truck used in his business	$ 20,000
A rental house	$110,000
Texaco stock	$ 25,000
Inventory used in his business	$150,000
Accounts receivable	$ 10,000
Racehorses	$ 50,000

What is the amount of Roberto's Section 1250 assets?

a. $–0–
b. $25,000
c. $45,000
d. $110,000

_____ 3. Mr. I.C. Ewe sold Exxon stock (owned 10 years) for a $25,000 gain in 2002. In addition, he had a loss of $10,000 on the sale of one acre of land used in his business. The land was purchased five years ago. Mr. Ewe's net gain from the sale or exchange of capital assets for 2002 will be:

    a. $–0–
    b. $5,000
    c. $10,000
    d. $25,000

_____ 4. On January 6, 2002, Isadora Xena sold Section 1245 business equipment. She had purchased this equipment for $5,000 three years ago and had claimed straight-line ACRS depreciation of $2,500 on it. If the selling price was $4,000, Ms. Xena should recognize:

    a.   Section 1231 gain of $1,500
    b.   Section 1245 gain of $1,500
    c.   Section 1231 loss of $500
    d.   Section 1245 loss of $500

_____ 5. On January 6, 2002, Isadora Xena sold Section 1245 business equipment. She had purchased this equipment for $5,000 three years ago and had claimed straight-line ACRS depreciation of $2,500 on it. If the selling price was $2,000, Ms. Xena should recognize:

    a.   Section 1245 loss of $500
    b.   Section 1231 loss of $500
    c.   Section 1245 loss of $2,000
    d.   Section 1231 loss of $2,000

_____ 6. On January 6, 2002, Isadora Xena sold Section 1245 business equipment. She had purchased this equipment for $5,000 three years ago and had claimed straight-line ACRS depreciation of $2,500 on it. If the selling price was $5,500, Ms. Xena should recognize:

    a.   Section 1245 gain of $3,000
    b.   Section 1231 gain of $3,000
    c.   Section 1245 gain of $2,500, Section 1231 gain of $500
    d.   Section 1245 gain of $500, Section 1231 gain of $2,500

_____ 7. Becky acquired residential rental property on January 1, 1986. Its current adjusted basis is $135,000. She used the accelerated method of cost recovery under ACRS. The asset is sold on January 1, 2002, for $250,000. Total cost recovery allowed during the period the asset was held by Becky was $64,000. Straight-line depreciation would have yielded a $42,000 total. What is Becky's recapture under Section 1250?

    a. $–0–
    b. $22,000
    c. $42,000
    d. $64,000

_____ 8. Black owns 100 percent of Black Corporation. In 2002, Black sells a truck (basis of $6,000) to Black Corporation for $7,500. Black Corporation will use the truck in its business. Black should report:

    a.   A capital gain of $1,500
    b.   A capital loss of $1,500
    c.   Ordinary income of $1,500
    d.   No gain or loss

_____ 9.   In the current year, Seth donates to Goodwill Industries Section 1245 property acquired three years ago. The property has a fair market value of $20,000 and an adjusted basis of $12,000. If the property is subject to $4,000 of Section 1245 recapture potential, what is Seth's charitable contribution deduction?

   a. $20,000
   b. $12,000
   c. $8,000
   d. $16,000

_____ 10.   Coyote Corporation distributes, as a dividend, property subject to recapture potential. If the recapture potential is $500 and the property's fair market value exceeds the adjusted basis by $800, Coyote Corporation should recognize:

   a. $500 ordinary income, $300 Section 1231 gain
   b. $800 ordinary income
   c. $300 ordinary income, $500 Section 1231 gain
   d.   No recognized gain or loss

_____ 11.   In 2002, Jim has a Section 1231 gain of $12,000 on property that he sold. During 1998, Jim reported a Section 1231 loss of $7,000, which has not been recaptured. Jim did not have any other Section 1231 gains or losses during the past five years. What is Jim's ordinary income for 2002 because of the above transactions?

   a. $–0–
   b. $12,000
   c. $7,000
   d. $5,000

_____ 12.   Ross acquired nonresidential realty in 1985 for $200,000. His total ACRS deductions claimed on the realty (assuming a straight-line election was not made), totaled $90,000, which gives him an adjusted basis of $110,000. In 2002, Ross sells the property for $230,000, for a gain of $120,000. Ross should report:

   a. $120,000 Section 1231 gain
   b. $120,000 ordinary income
   c. $30,000 Section 1231 gain and $90,000 ordinary income
   d. $30,000 ordinary income and $90,000 Section 1231 gain

_____ 13.   Several years ago, Herb purchased a tract of land with timber on it. The land cost $50,000 and the timber cost $100,000. On the first day of 2002, the timber was appraised at $175,000. In September 2002, the timber was cut and sold for $195,000. If Herb elects Section 1231 what is his Section 1231 gain on the sale of the timber?

   a. $–0–
   b. $20,000
   c. $75,000
   d. $95,000

_____ 14.   On January 1, 2002, Gwen sells nineteen-year nonresidential realty with accumulated depreciation of $200,000. The property was depreciated under an accelerated method. Straight-line depreciation would have been $110,000. The property was sold on January 1, 2002 with a recognized gain of $245,000. What is the depreciation recapture on this realty?

   a. $–0–
   b. $200,000
   c. $90,000
   d. $45,000

_____ 15. Purple Corporation sold equipment for $37,000 on December 31, 2002. The equipment had been purchased on January 4, 1996 for $40,000 and the equipment had an adjusted basis of $32,000 on the date of sale. From this transaction, Purple should report?

  a. No gain or loss
  b. $8,000 ordinary income
  c. $5,000 ordinary income
  d. $5,000 Section 1231 gain
  e. $3,000 Section 1231 loss

_____ 16. During 2002, Pat recognized Section 1231 gains of $15,000 and Section 1231 losses of $11,000. Pat's AGI before Section 1231 gains and losses is $50,000. After accounting for Section 1231 transaction, what is Pat's AGI?

  a. $50,000
  b. $65,000
  c. $39,000
  d. $54,000

_____ 17. Section 1231 property includes all of the following except:

  a. Stock held for investment
  b. Timber, coal, and domestic iron ore
  c. Real property used in a trade or business
  d. Livestock (other than poultry) held for breeding purposes
  e. Depreciable property used in a trade or business

_____ 18. During 2002, Sheng has a net Section 1231 gain of $50,000. Last year, Sheng had a net Section 1231 loss of $15,000. In 2002, Sheng should report:

  a. $50,000 long-term capital gain
  b. $50,000 ordinary income
  c. $15,000 ordinary income and $35,000 long-term capital gain
  d. $15,000 long-term capital gain and $35,000 ordinary gain

_____ 19. Ross owns business equipment with a $50,000 adjusted basis. He paid $90,000 for the equipment. Ross dies suddenly and his son, Sean, inherits the property. Sean sells the equipment for $67,000. What is the amount of Section 1245 recapture Sean must report as ordinary income?

  a. $–0–
  b. $17,000
  c. $23,000
  d. 40,000

_____ 20. Drew owns a truck with an adjusted basis of $12,000. The truck originally cost $30,000 and it is currently worth $18,000 as a used truck. Drew transfers the truck to Green Corporation in a tax-free Section 351 transaction in exchange for Green Corporation stock. What is the amount of gain Drew must report because of any Section 1245 recapture on this transaction?

  a. $–0–
  b. $8,000
  c. $12,000
  d. $18,000

_____ 21. In order for cattle and horse to qualify for Section 1231 treatment, they must be held for more than how many months?

    a.   6 months
    b.   12 months
    c.   15 months
    d.   24 months

_____ 22. Generally, which of the following are not subject to Section 1245 treatment?

    a.   Amortization of reforestation expenses
    b.   Property expensed under Section 179
    c.   Residential realty
    d.   Expenses for the removal of a handicapped barrier

_____ 23. Luke exchanges Section 1245 property with an adjusted basis of $1,000 for Section 1245 property with a fair market value of $8,000. The exchange qualifies as a like-kind exchange under Section 1031. Luke also receives $1,500 cash (boot). The property exchanged by Luke has Section 1245 recapture potential of $4,000. What is Luke's recognized Section 1245 gain on this exchange?

    a. $-0-
    b. $500
    c. $1,500
    d. $4,000

_____ 24. Jed sold real estate in 2002 (acquired in 1985) for an $80,000 recognized gain. Depreciation taken on the property totaled $100,000. Of the gain, $18,000 was recaptured under Section 1250. What is Jed's potential 25 percent gain amount on this sale?

    a. $-0-
    b. $18,000
    c. $62,000
    d. $80,000

_____ 25. In 2002, Martha, a single taxpayer, has $0 in ordinary taxable income. In addition, she has a net capital gain of $18,000, consisting of unrecaptured Section 1250 gain of $10,000 and adjusted net capital gain of $8,000. What is Martha's total tax liability?

    a. $4,000
    b. $4,500
    c. $3,600
    d. $5,040

_____ 26. Teddy sells Section 1245 property for $40,000, to be paid in 10 annual installments of $4,000 each, plus interest at 8 percent. Teddy has a realized gain of $12,000 from the sale of which $8,000 is attributable to depreciation taken. Teddy elects to use the installment method to report the sale. How much of Teddy's gain is ordinary income in the year of sale?

    a. $-0-
    b. $4,000
    c. $8,000
    d. $12,000

_____ 27. Teddy sells Section 1245 property for $40,000, to be paid in 10 annual installments of $4,000 each, plus interest at 8 percent. Teddy has a realized gain of $12,000 from the sale of which $8,000 is attributable to depreciation taken. Teddy elects to use the installment method to report the sale. How much Section 1231 will be recognized each year for the 10-year collection period?

    a. $–0–
    b. $400
    c. $1,200
    d. $4,000

_____ 28. Offshore Oil Co. has intangible drilling cost (IDC) of $1,000,000 on an oil property. The property has a basis to Offshore of $10,000,000 and it is sold to the Dryhole Oil Co. for $15,000,000 for a $5,000,000 realized gain. What is Offshore's Section 1254 recapture on this sale?

    a. $–0–
    b. $500,000
    c. $1,000,000
    d. $4,000,000

SOLUTIONS TO CHAPTER 17 QUESTIONS

True or False

1. F   Capital assets and Section 1231 assets are different. [Outline, p. 17–2]

2. T   A contract to cut timber qualifies under Section 1231. [Timber, p. 17–5]

3. F   Gains are capital gains and losses are ordinary. [Relationship to Capital Assets, p. 17–3]

4. F   Livestock, other than cattle and horses only, has to be held 12 months or more. [Livestock, p. 17–6]

5. T   Neither inventory nor property held primarily for sale to customers is a Section 1231 asset. [Property Excluded, p. 17–5]

6. T   Net gains from other than personal use properties disposed of by casualty or theft are Section 1231 gains. [Section 1231 Assets Disposed of by Casualty or Theft, p. 17–6]

7. T   The gain recaptured is the lower of the depreciation taken or the gain recognized. [Section 1245 Recapture, p. 17–12]

8. T   Generally, Section 1245 property includes all depreciable personal property. [Section 1245 Property, p. 17–14]

9. F   Player contracts are Section 1245 property. [Section 1245 Property, p. 17–14]

10. F   Only the excess over straight-line is recaptured. Only the excess over straight-line is recaptured. [Section 1250 Recapture, p. 17–15]

11. T   Any gain to the extent of depreciation taken is ordinary income; the excess is given 1231 or casualty gains treatment [Section 1245 Recapture, p. 17–12]

12. F   Recapture potential passes to the donee. [Gifts, p. 17–20]

13. T   The recapture potential reduces the amount of the contribution deduction. [Charitable Transfers, p. 17–20]

14. T   Nontaxable incorporations, nontaxable contributions to a partnership, and nontaxable reorganizations are examples. [Certain Nontaxable Transactions, p. 17–21]

15. F   In an installment sale, recapture gain is recognized in full in the year of sale.[Installment Sales, p. 17–22]

16. T   Intangible drilling costs expensed must be recaptured to the extent of the lesser of the gain realized or the IDC expensed. [Intangible Drilling Costs, p. 17–24]

17. F   The previous five years, not six years [Step 3: Sec 1231 Lookback Provision, p. 17–9]

18. F   There is no recapture because only straight-line depreciation can be used (unless the property is disposed of within the first year). [Computing Recapture on Residential Rental Housing, p. 17–17]

19. F   A transfer of property by gift does not cause recapture under Section 1250 or Section 1245. [Exceptions, p. 17–20]

20. F   Poultry is excluded from the definition of Section 1231 assets. [Livestock, p. 17–6]

21. T   Under 1250, when straight line depreciation is used, there is no Section 1250 recapture potential unless the property is disposed of in the first year of use. [Computing Recapture on Residential Rental Housing, p. 17–17]

22. F   Section 1245 recapture is called full recapture, while Section 1250 recapture is referred to as partial recapture. [Section 1245 Recapture, p. 17–12]

23. T The purpose of the 1245 recapture provisions is to cause gain to be treated as ordinary gain to the extent of depreciation taken. [Section 1245 Recapture, p. 17–12]

24. T Any remaining gain after subtracting Section 1245 recapture is Section 1231 gain or casualty gain. [Section 1245 Recapture, p. 17–12]

25. T If the taxpayer makes this election, the transaction qualifies under Section 1231. [Timber, p. 17–5]

26. T The maximum rate is 25 percent. [Unrecaptured Sec 1250 Gain (Real Estate 25 Percent Gain), p. 17–18]

Multiple Choice

1. a $20,000 + $110,000 + $50,000 = $180,000 [Property Included, p. 17–5]

2. d The rental house is both Section 1231 and Section 1250 property. [Section 1250 Recapture, p. 17–15]

3. d If the disposition of real property used in a business results in a net loss, Section 1231 treats the loss as an ordinary loss rather than as a capital loss. [Relationship to Capital Assets, p. 17–3]

4. b $5,000 − $2,500 = $2,500 adjusted basis. $4,000 − $2,500 = $1,500 gain realized, which is less than the depreciation recapture potential. Therefore, the realized gain is all Section 1245 gain. [Section 1245 Recapture, p. 17–12]

5. b $2,000 − $2,500 = ($500) Section 1231 loss [Section 1245 Recapture, p. 17–12]

6. c $5,500 − $2,500 = $3,000 gain realized, of which $2,500 is Section 1245 gain and $500 is Section 1231 gain. [Section 1245 Recapture, p. 17–12]

7. b $250,000 − $136,000 (basis) = $114,000 gain realized

  $64,000 − $42,000 = $22,000 Section 1250 recapture [Section 1250 Recapture p. 17–15]

8. c $7,500 − $6,000 = $1,500 ordinary income because of Section 1239. [Gain from Sale of Depreciable Property Between Certain Related Parties, p. 17–22]

9. d $20,000 − $4,000 = $16,000 [Charitable Transfers, p. 17–20]

10. a A corporation generally recognizes gain if it distributes appreciated property as a dividend. [Property Dividends, p. 17–22]

11. c The net Section 1231 gain is offset by the nonrecaptured net Section 1231 losses for the five preceding taxable years. [Step 3: Section 1231 Lookback Provision, p. 17–9]

12. c All of the depreciation claimed is recaptured for ACRS nonresidential real property depreciated under the accelerated method. [Section 1245 Property, p. 17–14]

13. c $175,000 − $100,000 = $75,000 [Timber, p. 17–5]

14. b The recapture is under Section 1245, therefore all the deprecation is recaptured as ordinary income. [Section 1245 Property, p. 17–14]

15. c $37,000 − $32,000 = $5,000 ordinary income [Section 1245 Recapture, p. 17–12]

16. d $50,000 + ($15,000 − $11,000) = $54,000. [Step 2: Section 1231 Netting, p. 17–8]

17. a Stock is not a Section 1231 asset. [Property Included, p. 17–5]

18. c Section 1231 "lookback" treats $15,000 as ordinary income, with the balance being a long-term capital gain. [Step 3: Section 1231 Lookback Provision, p. 17–9]

19. a Recapture potential disappears at the death of the owner of the property. [Death, p. 17–20]

20.   a   The is no recapture on a tax-free reorganization including a Section 351 transaction. [Certain Nontaxable Transactions, p. 17–21]

21.   d   Other livestock must be held only 12 months. [Livestock, p. 17–6]

22.   c   Generally, Section 1245 property includes all depreciable personal property, including livestock. [Section 1245 Property, p. 17–14]

23.   c   Gain ($8,000 − $1,000) is recognized to the extent of boot received ($1,500). [Like-Kind Exchanges (Section 1031) and Involuntary Conversions (Section 1033), p. 17–21]

24.   c $80,000 − $18,000 = $62,000 [Unrecaptured Section 1250 Gain (Real Estate 25% Gain), p. 17–18]

25.   a   ($10,000 × 25%) + ($8,000 × 20%) = $4,100 [Unrecaptured Section 1250 Gain (Real Estate 25% Gain), p. 17–18]

26.   c   In the year of sale, any gain realized is recognized as ordinary income to the extent of depreciation. [Installment Sales, p. 17–22]

27.   b   ($12,000 − $8,000)/10 years = $400 per year [Installment Sales, p. 17–22]

28.   c   Intangible drilling and development costs are subject to Section 1254 recapture when the property is disposed of. [Intangible Drilling Costs, p. 17–24]

CHAPTER 18

Accounting Periods and Methods

CHAPTER HIGHLIGHTS

This chapter discusses some of the options available to taxpayers in choosing accounting methods and periods. The cash, accrual, and hybrid accounting methods are covered along with the special accounting methods available for long-term construction contracts, installment sales, and inventory valuation.

KEY TERMS

Accounting Periods
Accounting Methods
Economic Performance

Installment Method
Inventories
Least Aggregate Deferral

Long-Term Contracts
Short Taxable Years
UNICAP

OUTLINE

I.   **ACCOUNTING PERIODS**

    A.   In General. Taxpayers may be entitled to use a calendar year or a fiscal year in filing a tax return. Most individual taxpayers use a calendar year. However, certain other taxpayers may be eligible to use a fiscal year ending on the last day of any month. If certain conditions are met, taxpayers may use a 52–53 week year so that their year always ends on the same day of the week.

        The tax year of a partnership is dependent on the tax year of the majority partners. If the majority partners do not have the same tax year, the tax year of the principal partners must be adopted. If the principal partners do not have the same tax year, the tax year that results in the least deferral of income must be used.

    B.   Partnerships, S Corporations, and Personal Service Corporations. Partnerships and S corporations generally must use a calendar year. However, Partnerships and S corporations can elect an otherwise impermissible tax year if any one of the following conditions are met:

        1)   A business purpose for the tax year can be demonstrated

        2)   The deferral period is not more than three months and the entity agrees to make "required tax payments"

        3)   The entity retains the same tax year it had for its fiscal year ending in 1987 and agrees to make "required tax payments"

        The required tax payments are computed by applying the highest individual tax rate plus 1 percent to an estimate of the deferral period income.

        Personal Service Corporations (PSCs) generally use the calendar year. A fiscal year may be retained or used if one of the following applies:

        1)   A business purpose can be demonstrated

        2)   The deferral period is not more than three months and a proportionate part of the annual salaries of shareholder-employees is paid to the shareholders during the deferral period

        3)   The same fiscal year is retained that was used for its fiscal year ending in 1987 and the required minimum salary payments are made

        See the text for the calculation of the required minimum salary payments for a personal service corporation (PSC).

    B.   Making the Election. The election to use a calendar or fiscal year is made by the timely filing of the initial calendar or fiscal year tax return.

    C.   Changes in the Accounting Period. To change an accounting period a taxpayer must have the consent of the IRS. The IRS will not usually grant a change unless the taxpayer can establish a substantial business purpose for the change. If the taxpayer has an NOL for the short period, the IRS may require that the loss be carried forward for six years.

    D.   Taxable Periods of Less Than One Year. A short year is a period of less than 12 months. A taxpayer may have a short year for the first tax reporting period, the final income tax return, or because of a change in the tax year. Due to the progressive tax rate structure, the short period tax must be "annualized" if the short year is due to a change in the tax year. Special calculations are required for the annualization of an individual taxpayer's taxable income.

        The tax is computed on the amount of the annualized income and then converted to a short period tax. The conversion is made using the following formula.

$$\frac{\text{\# of months in short period}}{12} \times \text{Tax on annualized income} = \text{Short period tax}$$

E. Mitigation of the Annual Accounting Period Concept. There are several provisions in the tax law designed to give taxpayers relief from the bunching of income because of arbitrary accounting periods. An example of such relief is the net operating loss carryover provision.

Under the "claim of right" doctrine an amount is includible in income on actual or constructive receipt if the taxpayer has an unrestricted claim to the amount, even if the taxpayer's right to the income is disputed. If the taxpayer is later required to repay such income, a deduction is allowed in the year of repayment, or in the case of amounts exceeding $3,000, the year in which the income was included if the tax benefit is greater.

II. **ACCOUNTING METHODS**

A. Permissible Methods. The Code requires taxpayers to report taxable income under the method of accounting regularly used by the taxpayer in keeping his or her books, provided the method is consistently employed and clearly reflects income. The tax law recognizes three methods: (1) cash receipts and disbursements, (2) accrual, and (3) hybrid (a combination of cash and accrual).

Taxpayers for whom inventories are a significant income-producing factor must use the accrual method in computing sales and cost of goods sold. Special accounting methods, which are discussed later in this chapter, are permitted for installment sales and long-term contracts.

B. Cash Receipts and Disbursements Method—Cash Basis. Under the cash method, income is recognized when the taxpayer actually or constructively receives cash and deductions are taken in the year of payment. There are exceptions to these rules for cash basis taxpayers. For example, capital expenditures and prepaid items such as interest cannot be deducted in the current period. Certain taxpayers cannot use the cash method. These include corporations other than S Corporations, partnerships with a corporate partner, and tax shelters. Farming businesses, qualified personal service corporations, and certain entities with $5,000,000 or less of average gross receipts are allowed to use the cash method.

C. Accrual Method. The accrual method of accounting requires that income be recognized when: (1) all events have occurred which fix the right to receive such income and (2) the amount can be determined with reasonable accuracy. An accrual basis taxpayer who receives prepaid income (e.g., rent) in advance must usually recognize the income on a cash basis. An expense is deductible for the year in which all events have occurred which determine the fact of liability and the amount of the liability can be determined with reasonable accuracy, and then only if "economic performance" has occurred. In the case of services or property to be provided, economic performance occurs in the year the services or property are actually provided. Certain liabilities, such as for taxes and worker's compensation, are not deductible until paid. There are several exceptions to the economic performance test such as for bad debt reserves of small banks, etc. See text for details.

D. Hybrid Method. A hybrid method involves the use of both cash and accrual accounting concepts. It is common for a taxpayer to report sales and cost of goods sold on the accrual method and other items of income and deductions on the cash method.

E. Change of Method. Taxpayers make an election to use an accounting method when they file an initial tax return and use a particular method. Taxpayers who later want to change a method of accounting must obtain the permission of the IRS.

A correction of errors such as incorrect postings, omissions of income or deductions, or an incorrect calculation of tax liability does not constitute a change in accounting method. An error may be corrected by filing an amended return.

Permission from the IRS is necessary to change an erroneous method of accounting to a correct method.

If the IRS requires a taxpayer to change accounting methods to clearly reflect income and the amount of a required positive adjustment exceeds $3,000, certain averaging techniques are available to prevent the bunching of income.

To *voluntarily* change accounting methods, the taxpayer must generally file a request for a change during the taxable year of the desired change. An adjustment due to a change in method initiated by the taxpayer is normally required to be spread over a four-year period, starting with the year of the change.

III. SPECIAL ACCOUNTING METHODS

A. Installment Method. The installment method applies to gains, but not losses. Under the installment method, gains are recognized from the sale of property when installments are collected.

The installment method may not be used for any of the following:
1) Gains on property held in the ordinary course of business
2) Depreciation recapture under Section 1245 or Section 1250
3) Gains on stocks or securities traded on an established market

Exceptions to the first item generally include the following:
1) Timeshare units
2) Residential lots
3) Any property used or produced by a farming business

As a rule, those sales that are eligible must be reported using the installment method. Conditions for electing out of the installment method are discussed later.

The recognized gain for installment sales is computed by using the following formula.

$$\frac{\text{Total gain}}{\text{Contact price}} \times \text{Collections} = \text{Recognized gain}$$

Total gain is the selling price reduced by selling expenses and the adjusted basis of the property. The selling price is the amount received by the seller, including receivables from the buyer and liabilities assumed by the buyer. Contract price is generally the amount the seller will receive, other than interest, from the buyer (selling price less the seller's liabilities assumed by the purchaser). Collections are payments received in the tax year less any interest income.

If the installment sale contract does not provide for interest of an amount at least equal to the Federal rate, then interest will be imputed at the Federal rate. The Federal rate is the rate the Federal government pays to borrow money and is published monthly by the IRS. The imputed interest reduces the selling price and as a result, increases the percentage relationship of the payment in the year of sale to the total selling price.

Sales between related parties may be subject to the special provisions of § 453(e) of the Code. This provision separates transactions regarding related parties into a "first" and "second" disposition. If the second disposition takes place within two years of the first disposition, then the gain on the first disposition may be recognized. See text for example.

The Code prohibits use of the installment method for sales of depreciable property between certain related taxpayers.

B. Disposition of Installment Obligations. If installment notes are disposed of, gain that was previously deferred must be recognized. The gain recognized is equal to the difference between the amount realized or the fair market value of the obligation and the basis of the obligation. Exceptions to this rule include transfers to controlled corporations, contributions to partnerships, and transfers due to the death of the taxpayer. Borrowing against installment notes causes recognition of the gain in most cases. Occasionally taxpayers may be required to make interest payments on amounts of taxes deferred by using the installment method. See text for rules.

C. Interest on Deferred Taxes. In some situations taxpayers may be required to pay interest on the taxes deferred in some installment sales.

D. Electing Out of the Installment Method. An election not to use the installment method is made by reporting the gain under the taxpayer's usual accounting method on a timely filed return. A cash basis taxpayer cannot realize less than the value of the property sold. This allows a cash basis taxpayer to report gain or loss as an accrual basis taxpayer.

If the taxpayer elects out of the installment method, permission from the IRS is required to revoke the election.

E.   Long-Term Contracts. Generally a taxpayer must accumulate all of the direct and indirect costs incurred under a contract. Mixed service costs must be allocated to production. For example, fringe benefit costs would be allocated as follows.

$$\frac{\text{Labor on the contract}}{\text{Total salaries and labor}} \times \text{Total cost of fringe benefits}$$

Taxpayers use one of the following two methods of accounting for long-term contracts:
1)   The completed contract method
2)   The percentage of completion method

The completed contract method can be used only on certain real estate construction contracts (see text). All other contractors must use the percentage of completion method.

Under the completed contract method revenue and expenses relating to the contract are recognized when the contract is completed. Under the percentage of completion method, a portion of the gross contract revenue, based on the ratio of the contract costs incurred for the period to the estimated total costs under the contract, is included in income each period.

IV.   **INVENTORIES**

A.   Determining Inventory Cost. The cost of inventory is the invoice price less any discounts, plus freight and other handling costs. The cost of goods manufactured must be determined using the uniform capitalization (UNICAP) rules. Inventory may be valued at the lower of cost or market except for LIFO inventories. Taxpayers using the LIFO method must value inventory at cost.

Taxpayers may use specific identification, FIFO, LIFO, or average cost methods of inventory valuation for tax purposes. A taxpayer may use any of these methods, but the method selected must be used consistently from year to year.

B.   The LIFO Election. A taxpayer may adopt LIFO by using the method in the tax return for the year of change and attaching to the tax return the proper form for the change. Once the election is made, it cannot be revoked unless the IRS gives permission. The change will usually be granted if the request is filed timely.

TEST FOR SELF-EVALUATION—CHAPTER 18

True or False

Indicate which of the following statements is true or false by circling the correct answer.

T   F   1.   If certain conditions are met, a taxpayer may adopt a 52–53 week fiscal year.

T   F   2.   For an accrual basis taxpayer to take a deduction, the "all events test" including economic performance must be met.

T   F   3.   If taxpayers do not keep adequate books and records, they are required to use a calendar tax year.

T   F   4.   The Internal Revenue Service will automatically grant requests for changes to fiscal years from calendar years.

T   F   5.   All short years must have the tax calculated on an annualized basis.

T   F   6.   The standard deduction will be allowed in calculating short-period income of an individual taxpayer.

T   F   7.   The Code requires that taxable income be computed under the method of accounting regularly used by a taxpayer in keeping books, provided the method clearly reflects income.

T   F   8.   Taxpayers who have more than one trade or business must use the same method of accounting for each trade or business.

T   F   9.   A cash basis taxpayer must include in income all amounts actually or constructively received as cash or its equivalent.

T   F   10.   Expenses for a cash basis taxpayer must usually be paid before they are allowed as a deduction for tax purposes.

T   F   11.   All cash expenses of a cash basis taxpayer are deductible when paid.

T   F   12.   An accrual basis taxpayer recognizes income when it is earned.

T   F   13.   Generally, reserves for expenses of an accrual basis taxpayer are allowed as a deduction.

T   F   14.   A hybrid accounting method uses elements of both cash and accrual methods.

T   F   15.   The correction of an error in a tax return is usually considered a change in accounting method.

T   F   16.   A taxpayer may file a request for a change in accounting method at any time during the tax year.

T   F   17.   A transfer at death causes deferred gain on installment notes to be recognized in full.

T   F   18.   Income from long-term contracts must always be recognized under the percentage of completion method.

T   F   19.   A taxpayer who has average annual gross receipts for the three prior years of $25,000,000 may use the completed contract method of accounting for long-term contracts.

T   F   20.   The installment method of reporting is not allowed for depreciation recapture under Section 1245 or Section 1250.

T	F	21.	Sales of real property must have a selling price of more than $1,000 to qualify for the installment method.
T	F	22.	Internal Revenue Service permission is required to adopt the LIFO inventory method for tax purposes.
T	F	23.	In periods of inflation, the use of the LIFO inventory method produces a lower tax liability than the use of the FIFO inventory method.
T	F	24.	Lower of cost or market inventory cannot be used for tax purposes.
T	F	25.	Direct costing is an acceptable method for calculating taxable income.
T	F	26.	The contract price in an installment sale is generally the total amount (except interest) the seller will collect from the purchaser.
T	F	27.	Partnerships, S corporations, and personal service corporations can never elect a fiscal year for tax years after 1986.
T	F	28.	The S corporation required tax payment is due by April 15th (or later as prescribed by the IRS) of each tax year.
T	F	29.	The IRS applies an objective gross receipts test to determine if an entity has a natural business year. Under this test, 25 percent of the gross receipts must be realized in the final two months of the tax year for the prior three consecutive years.
T	F	30.	Taxpayers may be required to pay interest on deferred taxes from an installment sale if outstanding obligations exceed $5,000,000 at the close of the year.
T	F	31.	§ 483 and §1274 provide that if a deferred payment contract for the sale of property with a selling price greater than $2,000 does not contain a reasonable interest rate, a reasonable rate is imputed.
T	F	32.	Taxpayers are permitted to adjust ending inventory for estimate shrinkage that has occurred between a nonyear-end date of a physical inventory and the last day of the tax year.

Multiple Choice

Choose the best answer for each of the following questions.

_____ 1. Red Corporation, a calendar year taxpayer, would like to switch to a fiscal year ending June 30, year 1. The last day that Red can file the election (Form 1128) is:

    a. July 15, year 1
    b. August 15, year 1
    c. September 15, year 1
    d. October 15, year 1

_____ 2. Gray Corporation obtained permission to change from a calendar year to a fiscal year ending March 31. For the short period (January 1 to March 31), the corporation had taxable income of $24,000. The annualized income for the three-month period would be:

    a. $96,000
    b. $6,000
    c. $48,000
    d. $–0–

_____ 3. Imputed interest will not be calculated in which of the following examples:

    a. A deferred contract on real estate
    b. If the interest rate is less than the Federal rate
    c. A deferred contract with a selling price of $2,500
    d. Installment sales of personalty

_____ 4. The California Limited Publishing Company invests $60,000 in printing 20,000 copies of a book. Twelve thousand copies were sold in the first two years of operation, and none have been sold over the last four years. Regardless, the company expects the books will sell in the future and thus it leaves the price the same ($20 per copy). How much may the taxpayer write off (expense) in the current year?

    a. s–0–
    b. $120,000
    c. $240,000
    d. $360,000

_____ 5. Tammy is a small building contractor who agrees to construct a building for $200,000. In year 1, she incurs costs of $90,000 and in year 2, costs of $70,000. An architect estimates the building is 60 percent complete in year 1 and the building is completed in year 2. If Tammy uses the *completed contract method* for year 1, she should report income of:

    a. $–0–
    b. $30,000
    c. $10,000
    d. $40,000

_____ 6. In January year 1, a husband sells stock to his wife for $100,000, its fair market value. The husband's basis in the stock was $45,000. Under terms of the sale, his wife pays $25,000 down and issues notes for the balance, payable over ten years plus interest at 10 percent. Four months later, the wife sells the stock for $105,000. If the husband elects installment sale treatment, how much gain should the husband report in year 1?

    a. $–0–
    b. $13,750
    c. $14,250
    d. $55,000

_____ 7. Tim sells a parcel of real estate (basis of $40,000) for $100,000, receiving $20,000 as a down payment and the buyer's note for the balance, payable over a period of five years at the Federal rate of interest. The first payment on the note is due next year. If Tim uses the installment method under Section 453, how much gain should be reported in the year of sale?

    a. $60,000
    b. $40,000
    c. $12,000
    d. $–0–

_____ 8. Tim sells a parcel of real estate (basis of $40,000) for $100,000, receiving $20,000 as a down payment and the buyer's note for the balance, payable over a period of five years at the Federal rate of interest. The first payment on the note is due next year. If Tim uses the installment method under Section 453, how much gain (excluding interest) should Tim report in each of the next five years?

    a. $9,600
    b. $16,000
    c. $80,000
    d. $48,000

_____ 9. Yoshi sold a ranch she owned as an investment on June 1 of the current year. Pertinent information on Yoshi's transaction is as follows:

Date of Acquisition	1984
Adjusted Basis	$ 20,000
Mortgage, assumed by buyer	$ 30,000
Cash down payment	$ 25,000
10-year note, payable to Yoshi	$100,000

The interest rate stated in the note exceeds the appropriate federal rate. The note payments are $10,000 per year and are due in annual installments. What is the contract price for the above sale?

    a. $100,000
    b. $125,000
    c. $120,000
    d. $135,000

_____ 10. Yoshi sold a ranch she owned as an investment on June 1 of the current year. Pertinent information on Yoshi's transaction is as follows:

Date of Acquisition	1984
Adjusted Basis	$ 20,000
Mortgage, assumed by buyer	$ 30,000
Cash down payment	$ 25,000
10-year note, payable to Yoshi	$100,000

The interest rate stated in the note exceeds the appropriate federal rate. The note payments are $10,000 per year and are due in annual installments. What amount of gain must be recognized in the year of sale?

    a. $–0–
    b. $10,000
    c. $15,000
    d. $35,000

_____ 11. Yoshi sold a ranch she owned as an investment on June 1 of the current year. Pertinent information on Yoshi's transaction is as follows:

Date of Acquisition	1984
Adjusted Basis	$ 20,000
Mortgage, assumed by buyer	$ 30,000
Cash down payment	$ 25,000
10-year note, payable to Yoshi	$100,000

The interest rate stated in the note exceeds the appropriate federal rate. The note payments are $10,000 per year and are due in annual installments. What amount must be recognized as income in the year the first installment payment is collected?

    a. $–0–
    b. $10,000
    c. $15,000
    d. $25,000

_____ 12. Green Corporation entered a $500,000 contract that will take two years to complete. Total costs of the project were estimated to be $450,000. Costs incurred during the first year were $315,000. If Green Corporation uses the percentage of completion method, how much revenue must be recognized in the first year of the contract?

    a. $–0–
    b. $250,000
    c. $350,000
    d. $500,000

_____ 13. The RGB Partnership is owned by R, G, and B. R owns 30 percent, G owns 30 percent, and B owns 40 percent. R and G close their tax years on September 30 while B uses the calendar year to report taxable income. The RGB Partnership's tax year must end on:

    a.   September 30
    b.   October 31
    c.   November 30
    d.   December 31
    e.   a date determined by the least aggregate deferral of income method

_____ 14. In year 1, Tom uses the lower of cost or market and FIFO inventory method. The FIFO cost of the ending inventory was $40,000 and its market value was $34,000. Therefore, the ending inventory for year 1 was $34,000. In year 2, Tom switched to the LIFO inventory method. How much income, if any, must Tom recognize for year 2?

    a. $–0–
    b. $2,000 ordinary income
    c. $2,000 long-term capital gain
    d. $2,000 long-term capital loss

_____ 15. Carol's corporation (a personal service corporation) paid her a salary of $132,000 during the fiscal year ended October 31, year 1. The corporation can continue to use its fiscal year, provided Carol receives a salary of how much during the period November 1 to December 31, year 1?

    a. $–0–
    b. $33,000
    c. $22,000
    d. $11,000

_____ 16. The ABCD Partnership is owned by A Corporation, B Corporation, C Corporation, and individual D. The partners have the following tax years.

A (30%)	September 30
B (25%)	September 30
C (25%)	June 30
D (20%)	December 31

On what date must the partnership's tax year end?

    a.   June 30
    b.   September 30
    c.   December 31
    d.   Any date the partnership chooses

_____ 17.   In year 0, Amber Corporation, an accrual basis taxpayer, sold defective merchandise that caused injury to the purchaser. Amber admitted liability in year 1 and paid the customer claim in January year 2. What year is the purchaser's tort claim deductible?

    a.   year 0
    b.   year 1
    c.   year 2
    d.   The tort is not deductible

_____ 18.   Silver Corporation, an accrual basis corporation, files its year 1 state income tax return in April year 2. When the return was filed, Silver had to pay an additional tax of $6,000. Due to an error in the original tax return, the corporation filed an amended California tax return in November year 2 and paid an additional $10,000 in tax. How much of the state taxes paid is deductible in year 1?

    a. $–0–
    b. $6,000
    c. $10,000
    d. $16,000

_____ 19.   Julie owns a small coin shop. She values her inventory using the lower of cost or market method. What is Julie's ending inventory based on the following information?

	Cost	Market
Gold coins	$10,000	$ 8,000
Silver coins	$12,000	$14,000
Rare silver dollars	$ 4,000	$ 9,000
Rare dimes	$ 2,000	$ 1,000
Total	$28,000	$32,000

    a. $25,000
    b. $28,000
    c. $31,000
    d. $32,000

_____ 20.   Kangarilla Corporation was to switch from the FIFO to the LIFO inventory method for tax purposes. In order to make this change, Kangarilla Corporation:

    a.   Must spread the adjustment over six years
    b.   Request permission from the IRS within 90 days of the change
    c.   Must have a "business purpose" for making the change
    d.   Must file a tax return using the LIFO method

_____ 21.   In year 1, Noarlunga Contractors, Inc. entered into a contract to build a building for a local university for $12,000,000. The estimated time to complete the building was two years and the estimated cost is $10,000,000. At the end of year 1, the accumulated costs on the project are $4,000,000. Noarlunga uses the percentage of completion method on the contract. Also, at the end of year 1, the chief engineer estimates the building is 50 percent complete. Noarlunga must recognize what amount of profit from this contract for year 1?

    a. $–0–
    b. $800,000
    c. $1,000,000
    d. $1,200,000

_____ 22.   Gold Corporation, an accrual basis taxpayer, sold defective merchandise that injured a customer. Gold was held liable for $100,000 in year 1. After an appeal, Gold Corporation pays the customer $75,000 in year 2. How does Gold Corporation treat this liability for tax purposes?

   a.   Nothing is deductible because economic performance has not occurred.
   b.   Gold can deduct $100,000 in year 1.
   c.   Gold can deduct $75,000 in year 2.
   d.   Gold deducts $100,000 in year 1 and then reports $25,000 as income in year 2.

_____ 23.   Sam, a cash basis taxpayer, sold land on January 3 for $5,000,000. He received $500,000 cash down payment and the buyer's 5 percent note for $4,500,000. At the time of the sale, the Federal rate was 9 percent. At what rate (if any) will interest be imputed on this installment sale?

   a.   6%
   b.   72%
   c.   82%
   d.   9%

_____ 24.   Susan, a cash basis taxpayer, sold land on January 3 for $450,000 to her son. She received $50,000 cash down payment and a $400,000 note from her son paying 5 percent interest. At the time of the sale, the Federal rate was 9 percent. At what rate (if any) will interest be imputed on this installment sale?

   a.   6%
   b.   72%
   c.   82%
   d.   9%

_____ 25.   On January 1, year 1, Joan sold land to her son for $30,000 cash and a 9 percent installment note with a face amount of $180,000. In year 1, after paying Joan $40,000 on the principal of the note, the son sold the land to an unrelated party. In year 1, the son paid Joan and additional $50,000 on the note principal. Joan's basis in the land was $70,000. Assuming the son sold the land for $400,000, what is Joan's taxable gain in year 1?

   a. $–0–
   b. $10,000
   c. $30,000
   d. $140,000

Problems

1. La Fonda Limited, a partnership, has a fiscal year ending on October 31. For the prior fiscal year ended October 31, year 1, La Fonda Limited had taxable income of $96,000. What is La Fonda's required tax payment that is due in year 2 (assuming there were no required tax payments in the prior year)?

2. Jill acquired a duplex in year 5 which she held as rental property. The original cost of the property was $80,000. During year 5, Jill spent $14,500 for capital improvements on the property. For tax year 5 and year 6, a total of $5,300 of depreciation was claimed on the property under the straight-line method. In the current year, year 7, Jill sold the property for $120,000, receiving $20,000 on March 1st as a cash down payment and the buyer's note for $100,000 at the Federal rate of interest. The note is payable at $10,000 per year for ten years, with each payment due on December 1st, beginning in year 7. Her selling expenses were $6,800. If Jill uses the Section 453 installment sale treatment on this transaction, calculate the amount of taxable gain that must be reported during year 7. Use the following worksheet.

    a.   Gross sales price   _____

         Selling expenses   _____

         Adjusted basis   _____

         Net profit   _____

    b.   Gross profit percentage   _____

    c.   Year 7 taxable gain   _____

SOLUTIONS TO CHAPTER 18 QUESTIONS

True or False

1. T   In that case, the year-end must be on the same day of the week each successive year. [In General, p. 18–3]

2. T   All events must have occurred to fix the taxpayer's right to receive the income and the amount of the income can be determined with reasonable accuracy. [All Events Test for Income, p. 18–13]

3. T   If they keep adequate books and records, they may be permitted to elect a fiscal year. [In General, p. 18–3]

4. F   The IRS will grant requests where there is a substantial business purpose for the change. [Changes in the Accounting Period, p. 18–7]

5. F   The tax for the first and last year does not have to be annualized. [Taxable Periods of Less Than One Year, p. 18–8]

6. F   The standard deduction is not allowed. [Taxable Periods of Less Than One Year, p. 18–8]

7. T   The cash receipts and disbursements method, the accrual method, and a hybrid method are recognized as generally permissible accounting methods. [Permissible Methods, 18–10]

8. F   A different method of accounting may be used for each trade or business. [Permissible Methods, p. 18–11]

9. T   Cash is constructively received if it is available to the taxpayer. [Cash Receipts and Disbursements Method—Cash Basis, p. 18–11]

10. T   For fixed assets, however, the cash basis taxpayer claims deductions through depreciation or amortization. [Cash Receipts and Disbursements Method—Cash Basis, p. 18–11]

11. F   Certain prepaid expenses must be capitalized and amortized. Certain prepaid expenses must be capitalized and amortized. [Cash Receipts and Disbursements Method—Cash Basis, p. 18–11]

12. T   This is true regardless of when the income is collected. [All Events Test for Income, p. 18–13]

13. F   Reserves are usually not allowed as a deduction. Reserves are usually not allowed as a deduction. [Reserves, p. 18–16]

14. T   The Code permits the use of a hybrid method provided the taxpayer's income is clearly reflected. [Hybrid Method, p. 18–16]

15. F   A correction of an error is not a change in accounting method. [Correction of an Error, p. 18–16]

16. T   After the initial return is filed, the taxpayer must obtain permission of the IRS to make a change in accounting method. [Change of Method, p. 18–16]

17. F   A transfer due to a taxpayer's death does not cause deferred gain to be recognized. [Disposition of Installment Obligations, p. 18–24]

18. F   In certain cases, the completed contract method may be used for long-term contracts. [Long-Term Contracts, p. 18–26]

19. F   The maximum is an average of $10,000,000. [Long-Term Contracts, p. 18–26]

20. T   The Code was amended specifically to deny the use of the installment method for depreciation recapture under Section 1245 or Section 1250. [Eligibility and Calculations, p. 18–19]

21. F   There is no minimum amount required for the selling price. [The Nonelective Aspect, p. 18–19]

22.   F   IRS permission is not needed. [The LIFO Election, p. 18–35]

23.   T   The LIFO method results in a lower ending inventory valuation and a higher cost of goods sold than does the FIFO method. [Determining Cost—Specific Identification, FIFO, and LIFO, p. 18–33]

24.   F   Lower of cost or market can be used for tax purposes except where the LIFO method is used. [Lower of Cost or Market, p. 18–32]

25.   F   Direct costing is not allowed for valuing inventories. [Inventories, p. 18–30]

26.   T   The contract price in an installment sale is generally the total amount the seller will collect from the purchaser other than interest. [Computing the Gain for the Period, p. 18–19]

27.   F   They can elect a fiscal year if certain tests are met. [Partnerships and S Corporations, p. 18–4]

28.   T   The required tax payment system applies to fiscal year partnerships or S corporations. [Required Tax Payments, p. 18–5]

29.   T   The test is made in connection with a request to change to a natural business year. [IRS Requirements, p. 18–7]

30.   T   Interest on the deferred taxes is payable only for the portion of the taxes relating to the installment obligations in excess of $5 million. [Interest on Deferred Taxes, p. 18–25]

31.   F   The price has to be greater than $3,000. The price has to be greater than $3,000. [Imputed Interest, p. 18–21]

32.   T   The adjustment is often based on the historical relationship between inventory shrinkage and sales. [Inventory Shrinkage, p. 18–33]

Multiple Choice

1.   b   The application must be filed on or before the fifteenth day of the second calendar month following the close of the short period that results from the change in accounting period. [Changes in Accounting Period, p. 18–7]

2.   a $24,000 × (12/3) = $96,000 [Taxable Periods of Less Than One Year, p. 18–8)

3.   c   Imputed interest would be charged if the selling price were more than $3,000. [Imputed Interest, p. 18–21]

4.   a   Under the Lower of Cost or Market rule, if the offering price on the goods is not reduced, the goods must be valued at cost, thus, there is no write-off. [Lower of Cost or Market, p. 18–32]

5.   a   Under the completed contract method, no revenue from the contract is recognized until the contract is completed and accepted. [Completed Contract Method, p. 18–28]

6.   d $100,000 – 45,000 = $55,000 realized. Because the wife sold the stock four months later, the entire $55,000 realized gain must be recognized by the husband. [Related-Party Sales of Nondepreciable Property, p. 18–22]

7.   c   [($100,000 – $40,000) / $100,000] × $20,000 = $12,000[Computing the Gain for the Period, p. 18–19]

8.   a   [($100,000 – 40,000) / $100,000] × $16,000 = $9,600 [Computing the Gain for the Period, p. 18–19]

9.   d $155,000 selling price – $30,000 mortgage assumed + $10,000 excess of mortgage over basis = $135,000 contract price [Computing the Gain for the Period, p. 18–19]

10.   d   [$135,000/$135,000] × $35,000 = $35,000 [Computing the Gain for the Period, p. 18–19]

11.   b   [$135,000/$135,000] × $10,000 = $10,000 [Computing the Gain for the Period, p. 18–19]

12.   c   [$315,000/$450,000] × $500,000 = $350,000[Percentage of Completion Method, p. 18–29]

13.   a   In general, the partnership tax year must be the same as the tax year of the majority interest partners. [Partnerships and S Corporations, p. 18–4]

14.   b   ($40,000 − 34,000) / 3 years = $2,000 ordinary income [The LIFO Election, p. 18–35]

15.   c   (2/12) × $132,000 = $22,000 [Personal Service Corporations, p. 18–6]

16.   b   The year-end must be the same as the majority interest partners. [Partnerships and S Corporations, p. 18–4]

17.   c   The tort is deductible in the year paid. [All Events and Economic Performance Tests for Deductions, p. 18–13]

18.   b   Recurring payments within 8.5 months meet the economic performance test. [All Events and Economic Performance Tests for Deductions, p. 18–13]

19.   a $8,000 + $12,000 + $4,000 + $1,000 = $25,000 [Lower of Cost or Market, p. 18–32]

20.   d   Approval to change is not needed. [The LIFO Election, p. 18–35]

21.   b   ($4,000,000 / $10,000,000) × ($12,000,000 − $10,000,000) = $800,000 [Percentage of Completion Method, p. 18–29]

22.   c   In this case, payment is the means of satisfying economic performance. [All Events and Economic Performance Tests for Deductions, p. 18–13]

23.   d   Generally, if the contract does not charge at least the Federal rate, interest will be imputed at the Federal rate. [Imputed Interest, p. 18–21]

24.   a   The rate used in sales of land between family members is the lesser of the Federal rate or 6 percent. [Imputed Interest, p. 18–21]

25.   e   If the land is sold to a family member and then resold within two years, the gain is taxable to the family member. $210,000 − $70,000 = $140,000 [Related-Party Sales of Nondepreciable Property, p. 18–22]

Problems

1. $\$96,000 \times (2/12) \times 40.6\% = \$6,496$ [Required Tax Payments, p. 18–5]

2.   a.

Gross sales price		$120,000
Selling expenses		–($ 6,800)
Adjusted basis:		
Original cost	$80,000	
Capital improvements	$14,500	
Depreciation	–($ 5,300)	
		–($ 89,200)
Net Profit		$ 24,000

    b.   Gross profit percentage: $24,000/$120,000 = 20 percent. Taxable gain:

Amount received in year 7:	
Down payment	$20,000
12/1/year 7 payment	$10,000
Total received	$30,000
Gross profit %	×20%
Taxable gain	$ 6,000

    [Installment Method, p. 18–18]

CHAPTER 19

Deferred Compensation

CHAPTER HIGHLIGHTS

This chapter covers various deferred compensation plans that are available to employees and self-employed taxpayers. Deferred compensation means that an employee receives compensation after the services are performed. Contributions to such plans and income on the contributions are generally not taxed to employees until the funds are actually received. Such favorable tax treatment is meant to encourage deferred compensation plans that supplement the Social Security system.

KEY TERMS

Qualified Plan	Nonqualified Plans	SIMPLE Plans
Keogh Plan	Restricted Property Plan	Stock Options
IRAs	Section 401(k) Plans	Top Heavy Plans

OUTLINE

I. **QUALIFIED PENSION, PROFIT SHARING, AND STOCK BONUS PLANS**
   A. Types of Plans. The tax law provides substantial benefits for retirement plans that meet certain qualifications. Three types of plans qualify under the law: (1) pension, (2) profit sharing, and (3) stock bonus.

   A pension plan is a deferred compensation arrangement that provides for systematic payments of retirement benefits to employees who meet the requirements set forth in the plan. There are two basic types of pension plans: defined benefit plans and defined contribution plans.

   A profit-sharing plan is an arrangement established and maintained by an employer to provide for employee participation in the company's profits, either current or accumulated.

   A stock bonus plan is a plan established and maintained by an employer to provide contributions of the employer's stock to the plan. There is no requirement that contributions be dependent on profits.
   B. Qualification Requirements. To be "qualified," a plan must meet the following requirements:
      1) Exclusive benefit requirement
      2) Nondiscriminatory rules
      3) Participation and coverage requirements
      4) Vesting requirements
      5) Distribution requirements

   The plan must not discriminate in favor of employees who are highly compensated. A plan is not considered discriminatory if contributions and benefits uniformly relate to compensation.

   At a minimum, the plan must provide that all employees in the covered group who are 21 years of age are eligible to participate after completing one year of service. Furthermore, the plan must cover a reasonable percentage of the company's employees.

   The plan must meet certain vesting requirements for both the employer and employee contributions. The employee must, from the date of contribution, have a nonforfeitable right to the accrued benefits from his own contributions. Benefits from employer contributions must be nonforfeitable according to one of two minimum vesting schedules.

   Uniform minimum distribution rules exist for all qualified plans, IRAs, unfunded deferred compensation plans of state and local governments and tax-exempt employers, and tax-sheltered custodial accounts and annuities. Distributions must begin by April 1st of the calendar year following the calendar year in which the participant attains the age of 70½ or retires. A five percent owner or a traditional IRA owner must begin distributions no later than April 1st of the year following the year the owner reaches age 70½. This rule does not apply to Roth IRAs.

   Early distributions are subject to an additional 10 percent penalty tax.
   C. Tax Consequences to the Employee and Employer. The primary tax benefit of a qualified plan to the employee is that the employer's contributions to the plan are not subject to income taxation until such amounts are made available or distributed to the employee. In addition, earnings on the contributions are not taxable until withdrawn.

   Employee contributions have been previously subject to taxation. Therefore, part of the payments from the plan is excluded from the employee's income under the annuity rules of Section 72.

   An employee who receives a lump-sum distribution from a qualified plan is subject to various special rules on the distribution. See text for rules.
   D. Limitations on Contributions to and Benefits from Qualified Plans. Under a defined contribution plan, the annual addition to an employee's account cannot exceed the smaller of $30,000 or 25 percent of the employee's compensation. There are higher limits for defined benefit plans, see text.

E.   Section 401(k) Plans. A Section 401(k) plan allows participants to elect either to receive up to an annual limit in cash or to have a contribution made on their behalf to a profit sharing or stock bonus plan. The plan may also be a salary reduction agreement. Any pretax amount elected as a contribution is not includible in the employee's gross income and is 100 percent vested. The employer's contributions and earnings on the contributions are tax deferred.

F.   Employers with 100 or fewer employees who do not have a qualified retirement plan may establish a SIMPLE plan for employees. The plan can be a 401(k) plan or an IRA. Employees can make elective contributions of up to an annual maximum. Employers generally are required to match up to 3 percent of the employee's compensation.

II.   RETIREMENT PLANS FOR SELF-EMPLOYED INDIVIDUALS

Self-employed individuals and their employees are allowed to receive qualified retirement benefits under H.R. 10 (Keogh) plans.

A.   Coverage Requirements. Contributions and benefits of a self-employed individual are subject to the general percentage, ratio, and average benefits tests applied to other qualified plans.

B.   Contribution Limitations. The maximum annual contribution that may be made to a defined contribution Keogh plan is the smaller of $40,000 or 25 percent of earned income. Earned income is reduced by the Keogh contribution that means that the contribution is limited to 20 percent of income before the contribution.

III.   INDIVIDUAL RETIREMENT ACCOUNTS (IRAs)

A.   General Rules. All taxpayers may have an individual retirement account. For 2002–2004 tax years, the maximum contribution is the smaller of $3,000 ($6,000 for a spousal account) or 100 percent of compensation. If the taxpayer is covered by another qualified retirement plan, the deduction is phased out 20 cents on the dollar until it is no longer available. See text for phase-out range.

A taxpayer may make a contribution to an IRA any time before the original due date (April 15th) of his or her tax return and still claim the amount as a deduction for the year.

B.   Roth IRAs. Contributions to a Roth IRA are not deductible, however, the earnings and withdrawals after age 59½ are tax-free (if held for over five years). If the Roth IRA does not meet these tests, the part of the distribution that is in excess of a return of capital will be taxable. The maximum annual contribution to a Roth IRA is phased out starting at $95,000 for single taxpayers and $150,000 for married couples filing jointly.

C.   Coverdell Education Savings Accounts (CESA). The maximum that can be contributed to a CESA is $2,000 per year for each beneficiary. The contributions are not deductible. The maximum annual contribution to a CESA is phased-out starting at $95,000 for single taxpayers and $150,000 for married couples filing jointly. The CESA exclusion is not available in any year which the beneficiary claims the HOPE Credit or the Lifetime Learning Credit.

CESA distributions to pay for qualified higher education expenses are tax-free. Qualified education expenses are: tuition, fees, books, supplies, and related equipment. Room and board qualifies if the student is at least a half-time student. Any excess distributions are taxable.

Distributions from noneducation IRAs for qualified education expenses are not subject to the 10 percent penalty on early withdrawals.

D.   Simplified employee pension (SEPs) plans are available to employers as an alternative to regular qualified plans. The employer may contribute to an IRA covering an employee the lesser of 25 percent of the employee's earned income or $40,000.

E.   Penalty Taxes for Excess Contributions. There is a cumulative nondeductible 6 percent excise penalty tax imposed on the smaller of any excess contributions or the market value of the plan assets determined at the close of the tax year.

F.   Taxation of Benefits. A participant has a zero basis in his or her deductible contributions to an IRA, and once retirement payments are received, they are included in ordinary income. Payments made to a participant before age 59½ are subject to a nondeductible 10 percent penalty tax on such actual or constructive payments. Penalty-free withdrawals prior to age 59½ are allowed for certain medical, educational, and first-time home buyer expenses.

IV. NONQUALIFIED DEFERRED COMPENSATION PLANS

A.   Underlying Rationale for Tax Treatment. Nonqualified deferred compensation plans allow individuals to defer income taxes on income payments until they are possibly in a lower tax bracket. Unlike qualified plans, most deferred compensation plans do not have to meet the discrimination, funding, coverage, and other requirements.

B.   Tax Treatment to the Employer and Employee. In an unfunded NQDC plan, the employee relies upon the company's promise to make the compensation payment in the future. In this case, the employee is taxed when the compensation is paid or made available and the employer is allowed a deduction when the employee recognizes income.

Golden Parachutes. Certain excessive severance payments to employees may be penalized. The tax law denies a deduction to an employer who makes a cash payment to an employee that satisfies both the following conditions:

1)   the payment is contingent on a change of ownership of a corporation through a stock or assets acquisition, and

2)   the aggregate present value of the payment equals or exceeds three times the employee's average annual compensation (for the past five years).

Golden parachute payments rules do not apply to payments made to qualified pension, profit sharing, stock bonus, annuity, or SEP plans.

Publicly-Held Companies' Compensation Limitation. For purposes of the regular and alternative income tax, the deductible compensation for the top five executives of publicly-traded companies is limited to $1 million for each executive. There are several exceptions to this limitation. See text for details.

V. RESTRICTED PROPERTY PLANS

A.   General Provisions. A restricted property plan is an arrangement whereby an employer transfers property to an employee at no cost or at a bargain price. The fair market value of the transferred property is included in gross income of the employee the earlier of when the property is no longer subject to substantial risk of forfeiture or when the employee has the right to transfer property free of the substantial risk of forfeiture.

B.   Substantial Risk of Forfeiture. A substantial risk of forfeiture exists if a person's rights to full enjoyment of such property are conditioned on the future performance, or refraining from the performance, of substantial services by the employee. An employee may elect within 30 days after the receipt of restricted property, to recognize immediately, as ordinary income the excess of fair market value over the amount paid for the property. Any future appreciation is considered capital gain instead of ordinary income.

C.   Employer Deductions. An employer is allowed a tax deduction for restricted property for the same amount and at the same time that the employee is required to include the compensation in income.

VI. STOCK OPTIONS

A.   In General. A stock option gives an individual the right to purchase a stated number of shares of stock from a corporation at a certain price within a specified period.

B.   Incentive Stock Options. Incentive stock options (ISO) are designed to help corporations attract management. To qualify for incentive stock option treatment the option holder must be an employee of the corporation from the date the option is granted until three months before the date of exercise. Under this plan there are no tax consequences when an option is granted or exercised. Once the option is exercised and the stock is sold, any gain is long-term capital gain to the employee provided the employee holds the stock for a certain period.

The excess of the fair market value of the stock at the date of exercise over the option price is a tax preference item for the alternative minimum tax.

C.   Nonqualified Stock Options. The fair market value of nonqualified stock options must be included in the employee's income at the date the stock options are granted.

If the fair market value is not ascertainable, then the difference between the fair market value of the stock at the exercise date and the option price is ordinary income in the year of exercise.

The corporation will receive a deduction at the same time and in the same amount as the income recognized by the employee.

TEST FOR SELF-EVALUATION—CHAPTER 19

True or False

Indicate which of the following statements is true or false by circling the correct answer.

T F 1. The three basic types of qualified plans are pension plans, profit-sharing plans, and stock bonus plans.

T F 2. Profit-sharing plans maintain separate accounts for each participant in the plan.

T F 3. A stock bonus plan is a deferred compensation arrangement established to provide contributions to the plan of stock other than the employer's stock.

T F 4. The two types of qualified pension plans are defined contribution plans and defined benefit plans.

T F 5. A defined contribution plan provides a formula that defines the benefits employees are to receive.

T F 6. In a defined benefit plan, benefits are based on years of service and average compensation.

T F 7. The cost and reporting requirements are less burdensome for a defined contribution pension plan.

T F 8. The contributions or benefits of a qualified plan may discriminate in favor of employees who are officers, stockholders, or highly compensated.

T F 9. In all qualified plans, employer contributions must vest immediately.

T F 10. Employer contributions to qualified plans are not subject to taxation until such amounts are made available or distributed to the employees.

T F 11. It is possible for a taxpayer to be covered by a qualified retirement plan and have a Keogh plan to which contributions are made in the current year.

T F 12. All lump-sum distributions qualify for the special ten-year averaging rule.

T F 13. The maximum contribution to a defined contribution plan is the smaller of the annual indexed limit amount or 100 percent of the employee's compensation.

T F 14. For defined benefit plans, the annual maximum contribution is normally higher than for combined contribution plans.

T F 15. The maximum deduction permitted each year for contributions to profit sharing and stock bonus plans is 25 percent of the compensation paid or accrued with respect to the participants in the plan.

T F 16. All employees of a company must be covered under its Keogh plan in order for the plan to be qualified.

T F 17. All individual taxpayers with earned income can qualify for an individual retirement account, to which contributions may or may not be deductible.

T F 18. The maximum deductible IRA contribution for an unmarried taxpayer with AGI of $34,000 or less is $3,000, regardless of how many accounts the taxpayer has.

T F 19. Employee benefits under a qualified plan must vest under one of two alternative schedules.

T   F   20.   Unless special circumstances apply, the earliest age to withdraw funds without penalty from a deductible IRA is 592 years old.

T   F   21.   All IRA contributions of an individual are deductible.

T   F   22.   An employer with 225 employees can establish a SIMPLE plan for those employees as long as the employer matches any employee contributions to the plan to a maximum of 3 percent.

T   F   23.   Bea, a single taxpayer, receives $35,000 in alimony in the current year, her only income. She may contribute $3,000 to an IRA.

T   F   24.   The maximum annual contribution to a Roth IRA is phased-out at $95,000 for single taxpayers and at $150,000 for married couples filing jointly.

T   F   25.   Distributions from noneducation IRAs for qualified education expenses are not subject to the 10 percent penalty on early withdrawals.

T   F   26.   For tax years from 2002 to 2005, a taxpayers who is 50 years can make an additional $500 per year "catch-up" contribution to an IRA.

T   F   27.   For 2002, the maximum contribution to a Coverdell Education Saving Account (CESA) is $2,000 per year for all beneficiaries.

Multiple Choice

Choose the best answer for each of the following questions.

_____   1.   The qualified pension plan of Grossmont Corporation calls for both the employer and employee to contribute 6 percent of the employee's compensation to the plan. This plan is a:

a.   Defined benefit plan
b.   Defined contribution plan
c.   Profit-sharing plan
d.   Stock bonus plan

_____   2.   Dee has completed six years of service with her employer. Her pension plan uses "graded vesting," and does not include a Section 401(m) arrangement. What is Dee's nonforfeitable percentage?

a.   10%
b.   40%
c.   60%
d.   80%

_____   3.   Dee has completed six years of service with her employer. If the plan vests under "cliff vesting," what percentage of the employer's contributions must be vested?

a.   100%
b.   55%
c.   50%
d.   45%

_____ 4.   Karen, receives a $500,000 payment under a golden parachute agreement entered into last year. Karen's statutory base amount is $360,000. What amount of this payment is not deductible to the corporation under Section 280G?

        a. $–0–
        b. $120,000
        c. $360,000
        d. $140,000

_____ 5.   Sue is single and self-employed. During the current year, her adjusted gross income was $14,000, including interest of $12,500 and salary of $1,500. The maximum amount that could be contributed to an IRA and deducted by Sue is:

        a. $–0–
        b. $1,500
        c. $2,000
        d. $2,100

_____ 6.   Sue is single and self-employed. During the current year, her adjusted gross income was $14,000, all from salary. The maximum amount that could be contributed to an IRA and deducted by Sue is:

        a. $–0–
        b. $1,500
        c. $1,200
        d. $2,000

_____ 7.   I. Shade, C.P.A., is self-employed and has established a *defined contribution* Keogh (H.R. 10) plan. The plan states that he will contribute the maximum percentage of earned income to the plan. Shade has no employees. His self-employment income before any Keogh deduction for 2002 is $240,000. Shade's deduction for this plan is:

        a. $–0–
        b. $48,000
        c. $48,000, not to exceed the annual limitation
        d. $60,000

_____ 8.   Currently, the basic required minimum coverage for a qualified plan for all employees is:

        a.   25-years-old and three years of service
        b.   21-years-old and one year of service
        c.   18-years-old and three years of service
        d.   21-years-old and three years of service

_____ 9.   Tim was employed by Purple Corporation at a salary of $110,000. Purple Corporation contributes to a retirement plan for Tim that allows extra voluntary Section 401(k) contributions. What is the maximum additional amount that Tim may contribute to this plan?

        a.   15% × $110,000
        b.   20% × $110,000
        c.   The 401(k) plan annual limit
        d.   The regular IRA annual limit

_____ 10.   Pink Corporation and Tom (a cash basis employee) enter into an employment agreement that provides for an annual salary of $140,000. Of this amount, $120,000 is to be paid currently and $20,000 is to be paid in 10 installments on Tom's retirement. How much would be taxable to Tom in the current year?

a. $–0–
b. $100,000
c. $120,000
d. $140,000

_____ 11. In the current year, Toni is granted a nonqualified stock option to purchase 200 shares of stock from his employer at $9 per share. On the date the options are issued, the stock was selling on the New York Stock Exchange for $14 per share. For the current year, Toni should report:

a. $1,000 long-term capital gain
b. $1,000 ordinary income
c. $1,800 ordinary income
d. $1,800 long-term capital gain

_____ 12. On March 1, x0, Ted is granted a nonqualified stock option for 100 shares of common stock at $12 per share. On that date, there is no readily ascertainable fair market value for the stock. Ted exercised the option on May 1, x1, when the stock is selling for $20 per share. The stock is sold for $30 in x2. For x1, Ted should recognize:

a. No gain or loss
b. $800 ordinary income
c. $800 long-term capital gain
d. $1,200 ordinary income

_____ 13. Tina is a sole proprietor with six employees. She has offered her employees a SEP IRA, which all six have elected to participate in. William, an employee, has a salary of $18,000 for the current year. What is the maximum contribution to William's SEP-IRA?

a. $–0–
b. $2,000
c. $2,700
d. $4,500

_____ 14. On March 1, x0, Tess is given a nonqualified option on 100 shares of her employer's stock. The option price and FMV are $75 per share on the date the option is granted. Tess exercises the option on April 1, x0 when the price of the stock is $125 per share. She sells the stock on October 15, x2 for $200 per share. What is Tess's reported gain in x2?

a. $–0–
b. $12,500 long-term capital gain
c. $12,500 ordinary income
d. $5,000 long-term capital gain

_____ 15. Trudy has $15,000 in a deductible IRA and $5,000 in a nondeductible IRA. In the current year, Trudy withdraws $1,000 from the nondeductible IRA. What portion of the withdrawal is included in Trudy's income?

a. $–0–
b. $250
c. $750
d. $1,000

_____ 16. In the current year, Nancy is over 70½ years old. As of December 31 of last year, her IRA account had a balance in it of $157,300. Her life expectancy multiple is 14.3 and she has taken out a total of $22,000 from the IRA in prior years. Her required minimum distribution from this IRA is:

    a. $–0–
    b. $11,000
    c. $9,441
    d. $135,300

_____ 17. Gene has compensation (and AGI) for 2000 of $98,000 and Gene was an active participant in a qualified plan. What is the maximum amount that he may deduct for contributions to his regular IRA?

    a. $–0–
    b. $800
    c. $1,400
    d. $2,000

_____ 18. Zoe is a new employee in a qualified retirement plan. Zoe would be considered a highly compensated employee if:

    a.   she owns 6.0 percent of the stock of the company.
    b.   she is an officer or member of the top-paid group in the company and her salary is $75,000.
    c.   she is an officer in the company and her salary is $60,000.
    d.   she is a union steward and her salary is $52,000.

_____ 19. In order to be considered a "qualified" plan, a retirement plan must meet all these requirements except:

    a.   Certain vesting rules
    b.   Nondiscrimination rules
    c.   Exclusive benefit requirement
    d.   The _res judicata_ requirement

_____ 20. In which type of qualified plan does an employer's contribution to the employee's plan have to vest immediately?

    a.   SIMPLE plan
    b.   Defined benefit plan
    c.   Profit-sharing plan
    d.   Defined contribution plan

_____ 21. The compensation paid by Bass Corporation a plan participant of a profit-sharing plan in 2002 was $112,000. During 2002, Bass Corporation contributed $40,000 to the plan. What is Bass Corporation's deductible amount for 2002?

    a. $–0–
    b. $12,000
    c. $28,000
    d. $40,000

_____ 22. Same as question 21. What is Bass Corporation's contribution carryover (if any) from 2002 to 2003?

    a. $–0–
    b. $12,000
    c. $28,000
    d. $40,000

_____ 23.   Jim is married to Jennifer. Jim's salary is $75,000 and Jennifer is not employed outside the home. If Jim is covered by pension plan at work, what is the maximum amount Jim and Jennifer can contribute to an IRA?

     a.   Jim $3,000 and Jennifer $3,000
     b.   Jim $3,000 and Jennifer $–0–
     c.   Jim $–0– and Jennifer $3,000

_____ 24.   Bea has AGI of $103,000 in 2002. What the maximum amount she can contribute to a Roth IRA if she is a single taxpayer?

     a. $–0–
     b. $1,400
     c. $1,6000
     d. $3,000

_____ 25.   John establishes a Roth IRA at age 45 and contributes to it in various annual amounts for 20 years. The account is worth $100,000, consisting of $40,000 nondeductible contributions and $60,000 of accumulated earnings. If John (at age 65) withdraws $50,000, how much is taxable to him?

     a. $–0–
     b. $10,000
     c. $50,000
     d. $60,000

_____ 26.   John establishes a Roth IRA at age 35 and contributes to it in various annual amounts for 20 years. The account is worth $100,000, consisting of $40,000 nondeductible contributions and $60,000 of accumulated earnings. If John (at age 55) withdraws $50,000, how much is taxable to him?

     a. $–0–
     b. $10,000
     c. $50,000
     d. $60,000

_____ 27.   The maximum annual contribution to Coverdell Educational Savings Account (CSEA) for each beneficiary is?

     a. $500
     b. $1,000
     c. $1,500
     d. $2,000

_____ 28.   Ann receives a $3,000 distribution from her CSEA. She uses $2,000 to pay for qualified education expenses. On the date of the distribution her account balance is $8,000, of which $6,000 is her contributions. How much of the $3,000 distribution is a distribution of earnings (before any exclusion)?

     a. $–0–
     b. $750
     c. $2,000
     d. $2,250

_____ 29.   Ann receives a $3,000 distribution from her CSEA. She uses $2,000 to pay for qualified education expenses. On the date of the distribution her account balance is $8,000, of which $6,000 is her contributions. What is the taxable amount after the exclusion?

     a. $–0–
     b. $250
     c. $500
     d. $750

_____ 30.   Karen, age 55, has salary of $100,000 and maintains a regular IRA. If she qualifies for an IRA deduction (i.e., she is not covered by a qualified plan), what is the maximum deductible amount she can contribute for 2002?

     a. $–0–
     b. $3,000
     c. $3,500
     d. $6,000

SOLUTIONS TO CHAPTER 19 QUESTIONS

True or False

1. T   Pension plans, profit-sharing plans, and stock bonus plans are the three basic types of qualified plans. [Types of Plans, p. 19–3]

2. T   The plan must provide a definite, predetermined formula for allocating the contributions made to the trustee among the participants. [Profit Sharing Plans, p. 19–5]

3. F   A stock bonus plan uses the employer's stock. [Stock Bonus Plans, p. 19–6]

4. T   A defined benefit plan includes a formula that defines the benefits employees are to receive; a defined contribution plan defines the amount the employer is required to contribute. [Pension Plans, p. 19–4]

5. F   A defined contribution plan does not define benefits. [Pension Plans, p. 19–4]

6. T   A defined benefit plan is based on the years of service and average compensation. [Pension Plans, p. 19–4]

7. T   Defined contribution plan reporting requirements are less burdensome. [Concept Summary 19–1, p. 19–6]

8. F   Plans cannot discriminate. [Nondiscrimination Requirements, p. 19–7]

9. F   Vesting of employer contributions may occur over a period of time as prescribed by law. [Vesting Requirements, p. 19–9]

10. T   The employer contribution is, however, deductible immediately for purposes of the employer's income taxes. [In General, p. 19–11]

11. T   A taxpayer may be covered by a qualified retirement plan and also have a Keogh plan to which contributions are made in the current year. [Retirement Plans for Self-Employed Individuals, p. 19–19]

12. F   Ten-year averaging has been replaced with a 5-year forward averaging rule, to which certain limitations apply. [Lump-Sum Distributions from Qualified Plans, p. 19–12]

13. T   The $30,000 amount is to be indexed in future years. [Defined Contribution Plans, p. 19–15]

14. T   Defined benefit plans have higher annual maximum contributions. [Defined Benefit Plans, p. 19–15]

15. T   The maximum deduction for contributions to profit sharing and stock bonus plans is 15 percent of compensation paid or accrued to the participants in the plan. [Profit Sharing and Stock Bonus Plan Limitations, p. 19–16]

16. F   Employee coverage must follow the corporate coverage rules. [Coverage Requirements, p. 19–19]

17. T   If the taxpayer is an active participant in another qualified plan, the traditional IRA deduction limitation is phased out proportionately between certain adjusted gross income ranges. [General Rules, p. 19–20]

18. T   The actual deduction is limited to 100% of compensation. [General Rules, p. 19–20]

19. T   Under either alternative, the employee acquires nonforfeitable rights. [Vesting Requirements, p. 19–9]

20. T   Penalty-free withdrawals may be made to pay for medical expenses and certain other expenditures. [Taxation of Benefits, p. 19–26]

21.   F   There are AGI limitations for taxpayers covered under other qualified plan(s). [General Rules, p. 19–20]

22.   F   The maximum number of employees is 100. [SIMPLE Plans, p. 19–18]

23.   T   Alimony is considered to be earned income for purposes of IRA contributions. [Spousal IRA, p. 19–24]

24.   T   The phase-out ranges for Roth IRA contributions begin at $95,000 for single taxpayers and at $150,000 for married taxpayers filing jointly. [Roth IRAs, p. 19–21]

25.   T   Distributions from noneducation IRAs for qualified education expenses are not subject to the 10 percent penalty on early withdrawals. [Roth IRAs, p. 19–21]

26.   False   For tax years from 2002 to 2005, an additional $500 per year "catch-up" contribution is allowed. [IRA General Rules, p. 19–20]

27.   False   The annual CESA contribution limit is per beneficiaries, not for all beneficiaries. [Coverdell Education Savings Accounts, p. 19–22]

Multiple Choice

1.   b   A defined contribution pension plan defines the amount the employer is required to contribute. [Pension Plans, p. 19–4]

2.   d   See table in text. [Participation and Coverage Requirements, p. 19–7]

3.   a   After 5 years the benefits are 100 percent vested. [Vesting Requirements, p. 19–9]

4.   d $500,000 – $360,000 = $140,000 [Golden Parachute Arrangements, p. 19–30]

5.   b   Lesser of $2,000 or $1,500 [General Rules, p. 19–20]

6.   d   Lesser of $2,000 or $14,000 [General Rules, p. 19–20]

7.   c   20% × $240,000 = $48,000, however the maximum is $40,000. [Contribution Limitations, p. 19–19]

8.   b   A year of service is generally defined as the completion of 1,000 hours of service within a measuring period of 12 consecutive months. [Participation and Coverage Requirements, p. 19–7]

9.   c   The annual 401(k) plan limit. [General Rules, p. 19–17]

10.   c   Since $20,000 will not be paid until retirement, that amount is not considered to be income constructively received, but instead is deferred income. [Underlying Rationale for Tax Treatment, p. 19–29]

11.   b   ($14 – $9) × $200 = $1,000 [Nonqualified Stock Options, p. 19–37]

12.   b   ($20 – $12) × $100 = $800 [Nonqualified Stock Options, p. 19–37]

13.   d $18,000 × 25% = $4,500 [Simplified Employee Pension Plans, p. 19–23]

14.   b   ($200 – $75) × $100 = $12,500 LTCG [Nonqualified Stock Options, p. 19–37]

15.   c   ($15,000/$20,000) × $1,000 = $750 [Taxation of Benefits, p. 19–26]

16.   b $157,300/14.3 = $11,000 [Distribution Requirements, p. 19–10]

17.   a   Zero is deductible since the income is over the maximum phase-out amount. [General Rules, p. 19–20]

18.   a   Owning 5 percent or more of the company would establish an employee as being highly compensated. [Participation and Coverage Requirements, p. 19–7]

19. d In addition to answers a, b, and c, a qualified plan must meet vesting requirements and distribution requirements. [Qualification Requirements, p. 19–7]

20. a The employer's contribution must vest immediately for SIMPLE plans. [SIMPLE Plans, p. 19–18]

21. c $112,000 × 25% = $28,000 for 2002. [Profit Sharing and Stock Bonus Plan Limitations, p. 19–16]

22. b $40,000 – $28,000 = $12,000 into 2003. [Profit Sharing and Stock Bonus Plan Limitations, p. 19–16]

23. c Jennifer can contribute to an IRA if their AGI is less than $150,000. [General Rules, p. 19–20]

24. b $1,400 = $3,000 – [$3,000 × ($8,000/$15,000)] (2002) [Roth IRAs, p. 19–21]

25. a Since John is over 59½, there is no taxable income. [Roth IRAs, p. 19–21]

26. b $50,000 – $40,000 = $10,000 [Roth IRAs, p. 19–21]

27. d The maximum annual contribution is $2,000 [CESA, p. 19–22]

28. b $750 = $3,000 × .25 [($8,000 – $6,000)/$8,000] [CESA, p. 19–22]

29. b $250 = $750 × .333 [($3,000 – $2,000)/$3,000] [CESA, p. 19–22]

30. c $3,500 = $3,000 regular + $500 (catch-up). [IRA General Rules, p. 19–20]

CHAPTER 20

Corporations and Partnerships

CHAPTER HIGHLIGHTS

This chapter provides a brief overview of the tax provisions applicable to the formation and operation of corporations, S corporations, and partnerships, as well as the tax consequences of corporate liquidations.

KEY TERMS

Associations	Corporate Formation	S Corporation
Check-the-Box	Earnings & Profits	Partnerships
Corporate Tax Rates	Corporate Liquidation	

OUTLINE

I.   **WHAT IS A CORPORATION?**
    A.   Compliance with State Law. Although important, compliance with state law is not the only requirement to qualify for corporate tax status. The degree of business activity at the corporate level is the key consideration for corporate tax status.
    B.   Entity Classification Prior to 1997. Under the association approach, it is possible for an organization to be taxed as a corporation although it is not a legal corporation under state law. If an association has more corporate than noncorporate characteristics, then it will be taxed as a corporation. The corporate characteristics are:
       1)   Associates
       2)   Objective to carry on a business and divide the gains they're from
       3)   Continuity of life
       4)   Centralized management
       5)   Limited liability
       6)   Free transferability of interests

       According to the Regulations, if an organization has the first two characteristics and three of the last four, it is an association (corporation) for tax purposes.
    C.   Entity Classification after 1996. Under the IRS's "check-the-box" Regulations, unincorporated entities can elect to be taxed either as a partnership or as a corporation regardless of their corporate or noncorporate characteristics. Limited liability companies (LLCs) are treated as incorporated under state law, and they can elect to be taxed as a corporation or a partnership.

II. **INCOME TAX CONSIDERATIONS**
    A.   General Tax Consequences of Different Forms of Business Entities. A business may be conducted as a sole proprietorship, partnership, or corporation. Sole proprietorships and partnerships are not separate taxable entities; so all transactions are reported on the tax returns of the owners or partners. On the other hand, corporations (other than S corporations) are recognized under the tax law as separate taxpaying entities. S corporations are treated in a manner similar to partnerships.
    B.   Individuals and Corporations Compared—An Overview. Individual and corporate tax rules vary in several situations. These situations include:
       1)   Capital gains and losses
       2)   Carryback and carryover provisions
       3)   Charitable contribution limitations
       4)   Net operating losses
       5)   Special deductions for corporations
    C.   Specific Provisions Compared. Net capital gains of corporate taxpayers are included in ordinary income. Capital losses of corporations are deductible only against capital gains. Corporate capital losses carry back three years and forward five years. All capital loss carrybacks or carryovers become short-term capital losses.

       Corporations selling depreciable realty may have ordinary income in addition to that under Section 1250. Under Section 291, the additional ordinary income element is 20 percent of the excess Section 1245 recapture potential over the Section 1250 recapture.

       Corporate charitable contributions are limited to 10 percent of taxable income, computed without regard to the charitable contribution deduction, net operating loss carryback or capital loss carryback, and the dividends received deduction. Excess contributions are carried over to the succeeding five years.

       The net operating loss deduction for a corporation is usually equal to taxable income including any dividends received deduction. The NOL is carried back two years and forward twenty years. An election may be made to forgo the carryback period.

D. Deductions Available Only to Corporations. A corporate taxpayer is allowed a deduction for dividends received from other corporations. The amount of the deduction depends on the amount of stock owned in the dividend paying corporation. If the ownership percentage is less than 20 percent, then the deduction is 70 percent; if the ownership percentage is 20 percent or more and less than 80 percent, then the deduction is 80 percent; and if the ownership percentage is 80 percent or more, then the deduction is 100 percent. The deduction is limited to the appropriate percentage of taxable income computed without regard to any net operating loss deduction; the dividends received deduction, and any capital loss carryback. However, there is no taxable income limit if a net operating loss results from the dividends received deduction.

Corporations are entitled to amortize organizational expenses over a period of 60 months or more. Organizational expenses include legal and accounting services incident to organization, expenses of temporary directors, expenses of organizational meetings, and fees paid to the state of incorporation.

E. Determination of Corporate Tax Liability. The current corporate tax rates are as follows:

Taxable Income	Rate
0 – $50,000	15%
$50,001 – $75,000	25%
$75,001 – $100,000	34%
$100,001 – $335,000	39%
$335,001 – $10,000,000	34%
$10,000,001 – $15,000,000	35%
$15,000,001 – $18,333,333	38%
Over $18,333,333	35%

Qualified personal service corporations (PSCs) are taxed at a flat 35 percent rate on all taxable income. They do not get any benefit from the graduated rate schedule.

Corporations are subject to an alternative minimum tax similar to individual taxpayers. See Chapter 12.

F. Corporate Filing Requirements. Generally, corporations file tax returns on Form 1120, however, certain small corporations may file the corporate short Form 1120A. S corporations use Form 1120S. The corporate income tax return must be filed by the fifteenth day of the third month following the close of the tax year. Corporations must file a tax return even when they do not have taxable income. Estimated payments must be made quarterly if the tax liability is expected to be $500 or more.

G. Reconciliation of Corporate Taxable Income and Accounting Income. Corporate taxpayers must reconcile taxable income to financial statement income since these amounts are rarely the same. The reconciliation is done on Schedule M–1 of Form 1120.

III. **FORMING THE CORPORATION**

A. Capital Contributions. The receipt of money or property in exchange for capital stock or as a capital contribution is not income to the corporation. Contributions by individuals other than shareholders are not income to the corporation and a corporation has a zero basis in such contributions.

Debt financing is often more advantageous to a corporation than equity financing since interest payments are deductible and dividend payments are not. In certain instances, such as when a corporation issues debt with features similar to capital stock, the IRS may contend that the debt is really a form of stock and disallow the interest deduction.

B. Transfers to Controlled Corporations. If property is exchanged for stock in a corporation and the shareholders are in "control" of the corporation after the transfer, pursuant to Section 351, gain on the transfer is not recognized. Gain or loss is postponed by adjusting the basis of the stock and property. The basis of the stock received by the shareholder in a Section 351 transaction is equal to the basis of the property transferred plus any gain recognized by the shareholder, less the fair market value of any boot received by the shareholder. The basis of property received by the corporation is equal to the basis in the hands of the transferor plus any gain recognized to the transferor shareholder. Realized gain is recognized to the extent that the shareholder receives boot.

IV. OPERATING THE CORPORATION

A. Dividend Distributions. Corporate distributions of cash or property to shareholders are dividends to the extent the corporation has accumulated or current earnings and profits (E&P). Any distribution in excess of E&P is a nontaxable return of capital and reduces the basis of the stock held by the shareholder. If there is a distribution in excess of E&P and in excess of the shareholder's stock basis, the excess amount is treated as a capital gain (assuming the stock is a capital asset). While E&P is similar to retained earnings, numerous differences may arise in its calculation. For example, nontaxable stock dividends do not affect E&P.

Distributions of property are valued at fair market value. The shareholder's basis in the property received is also the fair market value. The corporation must recognize gain on the distribution of appreciated property to the shareholder.

In closely-held corporations, the IRS may contend that certain economic flows to a shareholder are constructive dividends. Therefore, the corporation and shareholder may lose certain tax benefits. Constructive dividends include:
1) Unreasonable compensation
2) Excessive rent paid to shareholders
3) Interest on certain debt to shareholders
4) Advances to shareholders
5) Interest-free or below-market loans
6) Certain shareholder use of corporate property
7) Absorption of personal expenses by the corporation
8) Bargain purchase of corporate property by shareholders

B. Stock Redemptions. Redemptions of stock in a corporation are treated as dividends under Section 301 unless the redemption can qualify as a sale or exchange under Section 302 or Section 303.

V. LIQUIDATING THE CORPORATION

A. General Rule of Section 331 and Exceptions. Under Section 331, shareholders recognize gain or loss (usually capital) in a corporate liquidation.

B. Exception to the General Rule. If the liquidating corporation is a subsidiary, then under Section 332, no gain or loss is recognized by the parent corporation on the liquidation.

C. Basis Determination. The shareholder's basis in property received in a liquidation is usually its fair market value. The basis of property received from a subsidiary under Section 332 is the basis of the property to the subsidiary, unless the basis rules of Section 338 apply. In such a case, the basis of the property to the parent is the parent's basis in the subsidiary's stock.

D. Effect of the Liquidation on the Corporation. Under the general rule of Section 336, the liquidating corporation recognizes any gain or loss, except in certain parent-subsidiary situations.

VI. THE S ELECTION

A. Justification for the Election. The S corporation election allows qualified small corporations to elect not to pay the corporate income tax and to pass the income through to shareholders. To qualify, a corporation must have the following characteristics:
1) Be a domestic corporation
2) Not be a member of an affiliated group
3) Have 75 or fewer shareholders
4) Have as its shareholders only individuals, estates, and certain trusts
5) Not have a nonresident alien shareholder
6) Have only one class of stock outstanding

B. Operational Rules. The S corporation is a tax-reporting entity, not a taxpaying entity. Taxable income and losses are reported by the shareholders.

Certain items pass through to the shareholders of an S corporation "as is." Examples of items that are passed from the S corporation to its shareholders without changing identity are:
1) Tax-exempt income
2) Capital gains and losses
3) Section 1231 gains and losses
4) Charitable contributions
5) Foreign tax credits
6) Depletion
7) Nonbusiness income and losses under Section 212
8) Intangible drilling costs
9) Investment interest and expenses under Section 163(d)
10) Certain portfolio income
11) Passive gains, losses, and credits under Section 469
12) Tax preference items and alternative minimum tax adjustments

Taxable income of the S corporation is equal to the net of all items that are not passed through "as is" to the shareholders. The dividends received deduction and net operating loss deductions are not allowed to the S corporation.

Taxable income and separately stated items are passed through to the shareholders as of the last day of the S corporation's tax year, allocated on a per share and per day of stock ownership basis.

The shareholder's basis in the S corporation's stock will be increased or decreased by the pass through of income or loss (including the separately stated items). Distributions will decrease the basis of the stock. Losses in excess of the basis are applied against the basis of loans that the shareholders may have made to the corporation, and any remaining loss is carried forward until there is basis against which to deduct the loss.

VII. **PARTNERSHIPS**
A. Nature of Partnership Taxation. Partnerships are not separate taxable entities. Instead partnership income is passed through to the partners. A partnership tax return is an information return only. It provides the necessary information to determine a partner's income and expenses.
B. Partnership Formation. Under Section 721 no gain or loss is recognized to a partnership or any of its partners on the transfer of property to a partnership in exchange for a capital interest in the partnership. If the partner receives money, an interest for services, or transfers property with a liability more than basis, gain may be recognized on the transfer.

The partner's basis in his or her partnership interest is the sum of money contributed plus the adjusted basis of other property transferred. A partner's basis is determined without regard to any amount on the partnership books, such as the capital or equity account. The partner's basis will be increased or decreased by gains, losses, contributions, withdrawals, and changes in partnership liabilities.

The basis of property contributed to a partnership by a partner is equal to the adjusted basis of the property to the partner.
C. Partnership Operation. Reporting partnership income requires that certain transactions be segregated and reported separately. Such items as charitable contributions, capital gains and losses, dividends, etc., must be allocated separately to the partners. Otherwise the taxable income of a partnership is calculated like that of an individual without the following deductions: 1) exemptions, 2) deduction for foreign taxes paid, 3) net operating losses, and 4) itemized deductions.

Partnership losses pass through to partners and are deductible to the extent of the partner's basis in the partnership interest at the end of the tax year. Losses in excess of the basis carry forward and can be used against future income in a manner similar to S corporation losses.

A partner engaging in a transaction with a partnership is regarded as a nonpartner. If the partner's direct or indirect interest is more than 50 percent, or the transaction is between two partnerships in which the same persons own more than 50 percent, losses from the sale or exchange of property will be disallowed.

Payments made by a partnership to one of its partners for services rendered or for the use of capital, to the extent they are determined without regard to the partnership income, are called guaranteed payments. Such payments are generally deductible by the partnership and must be reported as income by the partner.

TEST FOR SELF-EVALUATION—CHAPTER 20

True or False

Indicate which of the following statements is true or false by circling the correct answer.

T   F   1.   All legal corporations will be taxed as corporations for Federal tax purposes.

T   F   2.   It is possible for an organization that is not a legal corporation under state law to be taxed as a corporation for Federal tax purposes.

T   F   3.   Sole proprietorships and partnerships are not separate taxable entities.

T   F   4.   A regular corporation is recognized as a taxable entity.

T   F   5.   A partner engaging in a transaction with his partnership is generally regarded as a nonpartner or as an outsider. However, a loss on a sale or exchange between a partnership and a 60 percent partner would be disallowed.

T   F   6.   Net capital losses of a corporation are deductible against ordinary income.

T   F   7.   When carried back or forward, a corporate long-term capital loss becomes a short-term capital loss.

T   F   8.   Corporate charitable contributions are limited to 10 percent of taxable income computed without regard to the charitable contribution deduction, NOL carrybacks or capital loss carrybacks, and the dividends received deduction.

T   F   9.   A net operating loss deduction is carried back three years and forward five years.

T   F   10.   The dividends received deduction is always equal to 80 percent of dividends received.

T   F   11.   The purpose of the dividends received deduction is to prevent triple taxation.

T   F   12.   In 2002, a corporation with taxable income of $25,000,000 would be taxed at a 35 percent tax rate on all of its taxable income.

T   F   13.   Qualified organizational expenditures under Section 248 may be written off over 50 months or more.

T   F   14.   Expenses incident to the printing and sale of stock certificates will not qualify as Section 248 expenses.

T   F   15.   Each partner must include in income his or her share of partnership income and any guaranteed payments from the partnership whose tax year ends with or within the partner's tax year.

T   F   16.   A corporate tax return is due on the fifteenth day of the third month following the close of the tax year.

T   F   17.   The purpose of Schedule M–1 of Form 1120 is to reconcile retained earnings at the end of the year to the retained earnings at the beginning of the tax year.

T   F   18.   The receipt of money or property in exchange for stock produces recognized gain to the recipient corporation.

T   F   19.   If a corporation has excessive debt in its capital structure and a substantial portion of the debt is held by shareholders, the corporation may have thin capitalization problems.

T   F   20. Control, for purposes of nonrecognition of gain or loss under Section 351, means stock ownership of at least 80 percent of the total combined voting power of all classes of stock entitled to vote and at least 80 percent of the total number of shares of all other classes of stock.

T   F   21. Gain will never be recognized on a Section 351 transfer to a controlled corporation.

T   F   22. The term "earnings and profits" is defined in the Code.

T   F   23. Earnings and profits and retained earnings will always be the same amount.

T   F   24. Partnership losses reduce a partner's basis in his partnership interest, but not below zero and any excess is lost to the partner.

T   F   25. Since a partnership is not a taxable entity, it does not have to file any type of tax return.

T   F   26. A corporation with gross sales of $625,000 can file a Form 1120A (corporate short form) since its gross receipts are less than $1,000,000.

T   F   27. In 2002, Burra Corporation has taxable income of $60,000. Burra's corporate income tax before credits is $10,000.

T   F   28. Judy is a 40 percent partner is Salmon Partnership. During 2002, Salmon has income of $90,000 and Judy receives cash distributions of $31,000 from the partnership. Judy's taxable income from the partnership is $31,000.

T   F   29. Marlin Corporation (a profitable closely-held corporation) owns stock in Ford Motor Corporation. The Ford stock paid Marlin dividends of $12,000 during 2002. Marlin Corporation's dividend received deduction is $9,600 for 2002.

T   F   30. Sam transfers property with a basis of $25,000 and a fair market value of $20,000 to a new partnership for a 10 percent interest in the partnership. Sam's basis in the partnership interest is $25,000.

T   F   31. Under the proposed "check-the-box" Regulations, an unincorporated business entity can elect to be taxed as a corporation or partnership.

Multiple Choice

Choose the best answer for each of the following questions.

_____ 1. Amber Corporation's taxable income for 2002 was $120,000, all from regular operations. Amber's tax liability before credits would be:

    a. $57,600
    b. $44,100
    c. $30,050
    d. $26,400

_____ 2. Which of the following items do not pass through separately from an S corporation to its shareholders?

    a.   Long-term capital gains
    b.   Tax-exempt interest
    c.   Wages of employees
    d.   Short-term capital gains

_____ 3.   Which of the following could not be a shareholder in an S corporation?

     a.   Nonresident alien
     b.   Individual
     c.   Certain trusts
     d.   A shareholder's spouse

_____ 4.   In 2002, Beige Corporation had gross income of $80,000, including $50,000 of dividends received from domestic corporations of which it owned less than 20 percent of the stock. Beige had business expenses of $33,000. What is the 2002 dividends received deduction?

     a. $–0–
     b. $35,000
     c. $50,000
     d. $32,900

_____ 5.   In 2002, Blue Corporation had a net long-term capital loss. If this loss is carried over to Blue's 2002 income tax return, it will be treated as a(n):

     a.   Ordinary loss
     b.   Section 1231 loss
     c.   Long-term capital loss
     d.   Short-term capital loss

_____ 6.   Gray Corporation is a closely-held corporation. Its sole shareholder is Philo Gray. The corporation currently pays Philo a salary of $600,000 per year. A reasonable salary for a person in Philo's position would be $200,000 per year. During an IRS audit, the government will probably contend that there is a constructive dividend of:

     a. $–0–
     b. $200,000
     c. $400,000
     d. $600,000

_____ 7.   Black Corporation had taxable income of $100,000 before considering charitable contributions. If during the year the corporation gave $12,000 in cash to a qualified charitable organization, how much of the $12,000 contribution may the company deduct for the current year?

     a. $–0–
     b. $12,000
     c. $10,000
     d. $9,500

_____ 8.   Sharon contributes property with a basis of $15,000 and a fair market value of $18,000 to a partnership in exchange for a 25 percent interest therein. Her basis in the partnership interest is:

     a. $–0–
     b. $15,000
     c. $18,000
     d. $33,000

_____ 9.   Sharon contributes property with a basis of $15,000 and a fair market value of $18,000 to a partnership in exchange for a 25 percent interest therein. What is the basis of the property to the partnership if Sharon recognized no gain on the transfer of the property to the partnership?

     a. $–0–
     b. $15,000
     c. $18,000
     d. $33,000

_____ 10. Brown Corporation, a calendar year S corporation, has taxable income for 2002 of $25,000. If there is one shareholder and she receives a cash distribution from Brown of $40,000 on July 1, 2002, how much ordinary income should she report on her 2002 individual income tax return, assuming her basis is sufficient to cover any dividend?

    a. $100,000
    b. $60,000
    c. $25,000
    d. $40,000

_____ 11. White Corporation, an accrual basis calendar year taxpayer, was formed and became operational on July 1, 2002. The following expenses were incurred during its first year ofoperation: (1) $600 (expenses of organizational meetings), $300 (fee for state charter), and $300 (expenses for sale of stock). What is White Corporation's maximum organization expense deduction under Section 248 for 2002?

    a. $180
    b. $240
    c. $90
    d. $120

_____ 12. Red and White form Red & White Corporation. Red contributes cash of $50,000 and White contributes property with a basis of $20,000 and a fair market value of $50,000. If Red and White own all of the stock in Red & White Corporation immediately after the transfer, what is White's recognized gain on the transfer?

    a. $–0–
    b. $30,000
    c. $20,000
    d. $50,000

_____ 13. Red and White form Red & White Corporation. Red contributes cash of $50,000 and White contributes property with a basis of $20,000 and a fair market value of $50,000. If Red and White own all of the stock in Red & White Corporation immediately after the transfer, what is White's basis in the stock he receives from White Corporation?

    a. $–0–
    b. $30,000
    c. $50,000
    d. $20,000

_____ 14. Green Corporation has E&P of $25,000. In the current year, the corporation makes a $60,000 distribution to its only shareholder. The shareholder's basis in his Green stock is $20,000. From this distribution, the shareholder would have a capital gain of:

    a. $–0–
    b. $15,000
    c. $25,000
    d. $20,000

_____ 15. Diamond Corporation's only asset is raw land with an adjusted basis of $80,000 and a fair market value (net of tax on liquidation) of $135,000. Tony, an individual, owns all of the stock (basis of $90,000) in Diamond. The corporation distributes the land to Tony in complete liquidation. How much gain or loss should Tony report?

    a. $10,000 loss
    b. $45,000 gain
    c. $55,000 gain
    d. $10,000 gain

_____ 16.   Green Medical Group is a qualified personal service corporation. For 2002, the company has
            taxable income of $42,000. What is the tax liability for the corporation?

            a. $6,300
            b. $10,500
            c. $14,700
            d. $16,400

_____ 17.   Quincy owns a 60 percent interest in the capital and profits of the QRS Partnership. On October
            15, 2002, Quincy sells property to the partnership for its fair market value of $100,000. The property
            has a basis to Q of $120,000. On December 20, 2002, QRS sells the property to an outsider for
            $115,000. What is Quincy's recognized gain or loss in 2002 as a result of the sale of the property
            to the partnership?

            a. $–0–
            b.   ($20,000)
            c. $5,000
            d.   ($12,000)

_____ 18.   Drew contributes land (basis of $100,000 and fair market value of $150,000) to a partnership for
            a 40 percent interest in the partnership. The land is subject to a mortgage of $80,000, which is
            assumed by the partnership. What is Drew's basis in her partnership interest?

            a. $–0–
            b. $100,000
            c. $52,000
            d. $48,000

_____ 19.   A partnership is allowed which of the following deductions at the partnership level?

            a.   Section 162 trade or business expenses
            b.   Section 170 charitable contributions
            c.   Section 172 net operating losses from prior years
            d.   Section 212 production of income expenses

_____ 20.   Chad is a 40 percent shareholder in an S corporation. On January 1, 2002, his basis in the S
            corporation stock is $25,000. During 2002, Chad loans the corporation $5,000. For 2002, the corpora-
            tion has an operating loss of $90,000. What amount of loss may Chad deduct in 2002?

            a. $–0–
            b. $25,000
            c. $30,000
            d. $36,000

_____ 21.   A regular (C) corporation has a deficit in accumulated earnings and profits of $20,000 at the
            beginning of the current year. Current earnings and profits are $7,000. During the year, the
            corporation distributes $10,000 to its shareholders. How much of the distribution is taxable as a
            dividend to the shareholders?

            a. $–0–
            b. $3,000
            c. $10,000
            d. $7,000

_____ 22. In the current year, Yellow, Inc. (a retail furniture store) donates unsold furniture to the Goodwill Army (a qualified charity for the care of the needy). The furniture is inventory and has a basis to B of $20,000 and a fair market value of $26,000. What is Yellow's charitable contribution deduction for this gift?

a. $–0–
b. $20,000
c. $23,000
d. $26,000

_____ 23. A regular corporation with taxable income of $11,000,000 is taxed at a corporate tax rate of which of the following?

a. 34%
b. 35%
c. 38%
d. 39%

Problem

1. Violet Corporation reported taxable income, before special items, of $600,000. Selected information available from the corporate records is as follows:

Federal income tax expense	$204,000
Book depreciation	140,000
Tax depreciation	85,000
Life insurance proceeds on death of an officer	100,000

What is Violet's net income per books?

Net income per books	_____
Adjustments:	_____
	_____
	_____
	_____
Taxable income	_____

SOLUTIONS TO CHAPTER 20 QUESTIONS

True or False

1.   F   Some corporations may not be recognized as separate entities for tax purposes. [Compliance with State Law, p. 20–3]

2.   T   Tax law defines a corporation as including "Associations, joint stock companies, and insurance companies." [Entity Classification Prior to 997, p. 20–3]

3.   T   Sole proprietorships are not separate tax entities and partnerships, while separate entities, are not subject to income tax. [General Tax Consequences of Different Forms of Business Entities, p. 20–4]

4.   T   Income is taxed to the corporation as earned. [General Tax Consequences of Different Forms of Business Entities, p. 20–4]

5.   T   Losses are disallowed if the partner's interest is more than 50 percent. [Transactions Between Partner and Partnership, p. 20–33]

6.   F   Corporate capital losses can only offset capital gains. [Capital Gains and Losses, p. 20–6]

7.   T   For *noncorporate* taxpayers, however, carryovers of short-term capital losses retain their identity. [Capital Gains and Losses, p. 20–6]

8.   T   Any contributions in excess of the 10 percent limitation are carried forward to the five succeeding tax years. [Charitable Contributions, p. 20–8]

9.   F   NOLs are carried back two years and forward 20 years. [Net Operating Losses, p. 20–9]

10.   F   The dividends received deduction is equal to either 70 percent, 80 percent, or 100 percent of dividends received and may be subject to limitations based on taxable income. [Dividends Received Deduction, p. 20–10]

11.   T   Since the dividends received deduction may be less than 100 percent, the law provides only partial relief. [Dividends Received Deduction, p. 20–10]

12.   T   The 35 percent rate applies. [Income Tax Rates, p. 20–12]

13.   F   Section 248 expenses may be written off over 60 months or more. [Deduction of Organizational Expenditures, p. 20–11]

14.   T   These expenditures are generally added to the capital account and are not subject to amortization. [Deduction of Organizational Expenditures, p. 20–11]

15.   T   Guaranteed payments are included in partner income from the partnership tax year ending with or within the partner tax year. [Transactions between Partner and Partnership, p. 20–33]

16.   T   Corporations can receive an automatic extension of six months for filing the corporate return by filing Form 7004 by the due date of the return. [Corporate Filing Requirements, p. 20–13]

17.   F   Schedule M–1 reconciles financial net income to taxable income. [Reconciliation of Corporate Taxable Income and Accounting Income, p. 20–14]

18.   F   A corporation does not recognize a gain on the receipt of money or property in exchange for its stock. [Capital Contributions, p. 20–15]

19.   T   In such cases, the IRS may contend the debt is really an equity interest and will deny the shareholders the tax advantages of debt financing. [Thin Capitalization, p. 20–15]

20.   T   Control for purposes of nonrecognition of gain or loss under Section 351 means stock ownership of at least 80 percent of the total combined voting power and 80 percent of the total number of shares of all other classes of stock. [Transfers to Controlled Corporations, p. 20–16]

21.   F   Realized gain is recognized to the extent of boot received. [Basis Considerations and Computation of Gain, p. 20–16]

22.   F   E&P is not defined in the Code. [Concept of Earnings and Profit, p. 20–20]

23.   F   The calculation is not the same. [Concept of Earnings and Profit, p. 20–20]

24.   F   The excess losses carry forward for each partner. [Limitation on Partner's Share of Losses, p. 20–32]

25.   F   Partnerships file an information return, the Form 1065. [Nature of Partnership Taxation, p. 20–29]

26.   F   Gross sales have to be under $500,000. [Corporate Filing Requirements, p. 20–13]

27.   T   (15% × $50,000) + (25% × 10,000) = $10,000. [Income Tax Rates, p. 20–12]

28.   F   Her income is 40% × $90,000 = $36,000. [Measuring and Reporting Partnership Income, p. 20–32]

29.   F   70% × 12,000 = $8,400. (Assuming Marlin owns less than 20% of Ford). [Dividends Received Deduction, p. 20–10]

30.   T   The basis carries over to the partnership interest. [Basis of a Partnership Interest, p. 20–30]

31.   T   Entities with more than one owner can elect to be classified as either a partnership or a corporation. [Entity Classification after 1996, p. 20–4]

Multiple Choice

1.   c   15%($50,000) + 25%($25,000) + 34%($25,000) + 39%($20,000) = $30,050. [Income Tax Rates, p. 20–12]

2.   c   Wages of employees do not pass through separately from an S corporation to its shareholders. [Separately Stated Items, p. 20–27]

3.   a   Nonresident aliens may not be shareholders in an S corporation. [Justification for the Election, p. 20–25]

4.   d   70% × $50,000 = $35,000 general rule; 70% × $47,000 = $32,900 limitation. [Dividends Received Deduction, p. 20–10]

5.   d   Corporate loss carryovers are treated as short-term. [Capital Gains and Losses, p. 20–6]

6.   c $600,000 less $200,000. [Constructive Dividends, p. 20–21]

7.   c   10% × $100,000 = $10,000 maximum. [Charitable Contributions, p. 20–8]

8.   b   The basis is equal to the basis of the property contributed. [Basis of a Partnership Interest, p. 20–30]

9.   b   The basis to the partnership is equal to the basis of the property contributed. [Partnership's Basis in Contributed Property, p. 20–31]

10.   c   The income to the shareholder is the reportable income of the S corporation. [Separately Stated Items, p. 20–27]

11.   c   [($600 + 300)/60 months] × 6 months = $90. [Deduction of Organization Expenditures, p. 20–11]

12.   a   No gain is required to be recognized. [Transfers to Controlled Corporations, p. 20–16]

13.   d   The basis of the stock to White is the same as the basis of the property contributed. [Transfers to Controlled Corporations, p. 20–16]

14.   b $60,000 (distribution) − $25,000 (dividend) − $20,000 (return of capital) = $15,000 (capital gain) [Dividend Distributions, p. 20–19]

15.   b $135,000 − $90,000 = $45,000. [General Rule of Section 331, p. 20–23]

16.   c   35% × $42,000 = $14,700. [Income Tax Rates, p. 20–12]

17.   a   Q is a related party; therefore the loss is not recognized. [Transactions between Partner and Partnership, p. 20–33]

18.   c $100,000 − ($80,000 × 60%) = $52,000. [Basis of a Partnership Interest p. 20–30]

19.   a   [Measuring and Reporting Partnership Income, p. 20–31]

20.   c   40% × $90,000 = $36,000; however, the loss is limited to the basis in the S corporation stock plus the loan of $5,000, $30,000. [Basis Determination, p. 20–28]

21.   d   The distribution is taxable to the extent of current E&P. [Concept of Earnings and Profits, p. 20–20]

22.   c $20,000 + 50%($26,000 − $20,000) = $23,000. [Charitable Contributions, p. 20–8]

23.   b   The corporation will be taxed at 35 percent. [Income Tax Rates, p. 20–12]

Problem

1.

Net income per books	$441,000
Federal income tax	$204,000
Depreciation ($140,000 − $85,000)	$ 55,000
Life insurance proceeds	−($100,000)
Taxable income	$600,000

[Reconciliation of Corporate Taxable Income and Accounting Income, p. 20–14]